The Kovacs Guide to Electronic Library Collection Development

ESSENTIAL CORE SUBJECT
COLLECTIONS, SELECTION
CRITERIA, AND GUIDELINES

Second Edition

DIANE K. KOVACS

Neal-Schuman Publishers, Inc.

New York   **London**

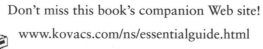

Don't miss this book's companion Web site!
www.kovacs.com/ns/essentialguide.html
Login name: colldev
Password: kovacs09

Published by Neal-Schuman Publishers, Inc.
100 William St., Suite 2004
New York, NY 10038

Printed and bound in the United States of America.

The paper used in this publication meets the minimum requirements of American National Standard for Information Sciences-Permanence of Paper for Printed Library Materials, ANSI Z39.48-1992.

Library of Congress Cataloging-in-Publication Data

Kovacs, Diane K. (Diane Kaye), 1962–
    The Kovacs guide to electronic library collection development : essential core subject collections, selection criteria, and guidelines / Diane K. Kovacs. — 2nd ed.
        p. cm.
    Includes bibliographical references and index.
    ISBN 978-1-55570-664-7 (alk. paper)
    1. Digital libraries—Collection development—United States. I. Title. II. Title: Guide to electronic library collection development.

ZA4080.5.K685 2009
025.2'84—dc22

                                                                        2009027772

TABLE OF CONTENTS

PART I:
GENERAL COLLECTION PLANNING
RECOMMENDATIONS

PART II:
RECOMMENDED PLANNING, EVALUATION, AND SELECTION CRITERIA: CORE COLLECTIONS AND COLLECTION TOOLS FOR MAJOR SUBJECT AREAS

LIST OF E-LIBRARY SUCCESS STORIES

PART I.
GENERAL COLLECTION PLANNING RECOMMENDATIONS

PART II.
RECOMMENDED PLANNING, EVALUATION, AND SELECTION CRITERIA: CORE COLLECTIONS AND COLLECTION TOOLS FOR MAJOR SUBJECT AREAS

LIST OF TABLES AND FIGURES

Part I
Tables and Figures

1. General Collection Development Principles for E-Resources

2. BRINGING IT ALL TOGETHER: SOME GENERAL CONSIDERATIONS FOR BUILDING, ORGANIZING, MANAGING, AND MAINTAINING E-LIBRARIES

3. E-RESOURCE LICENSING BASICS: GETTING WHAT YOU NEED FOR WHAT YOU ARE WILLING TO PAY

PART II
TABLES AND FIGURES

4. READY-REFERENCE AND CORE GOVERNMENT DOCUMENTS E-RESOURCES

5. JOBS AND EMPLOYMENT, CONSUMER INFORMATION, AND GENEALOGY E-RESOURCES

9. BIOLOGICAL SCIENCES E-RESOURCES

10. ENGINEERING, COMPUTER SCIENCES, MATHEMATICS, AND RELATED E-RESOURCES

11. PHYSICAL AND EARTH SCIENCES (ASTRONOMY, CHEMISTRY, GEOLOGY, METEOROLOGY, PHYSICS, ETC.) E-RESOURCES

12. SOCIAL SCIENCES (ANTHROPOLOGY, POLITICAL SCIENCE, PSYCHOLOGY, SOCIOLOGY, ETC.) E-RESOURCES

13. EDUCATION AND HOMEWORK E-RESOURCES

14. ARTS AND HUMANITIES (FINE ARTS, LANGUAGES, LITERATURE, PHILOSOPHY, HISTORY, ETC.) E-RESOURCES

FOREWORD

Frankly, if you're reading this foreword I'm astonished, because the meat of this book is certainly in the content Diane has amassed and created and put at your fingertips in one convenient place. Since I get to write this foreword, though, let me say a few things about the tome before you:

1. I consider it a major service to the library profession, since librarians engaged in e-collection development are eager (anxious? desperate?) for the information and wisdom it contains.
2. Not only is it a service to the profession, but it's an accessible, and readable, book.
3. There are sections here every librarian in the twenty-first century should read, not just e-collections librarians (the parts on content management systems and licensing, to name just two).
4. The material here is authoritative and informed, coming from an expert source.

In an economy when resources for e-collections become rare and dear, this book can save you money, effort, time, and budget heartache. I strongly suspect that this is a labor of love. I know that it is a cornerstone publication in e-resources collecting literature, and I therefore recommend it for every library that subscribes to more than one e-resource (once an e-reviewer, always an e-reviewer).

Cheryl LaGuardia
Research Librarian
Center for Jewish Studies
Center for Middle Eastern Studies,
   East Asian Languages, and Civilizations
The Freshman Seminar Program
Near Eastern Languages and Civilizations
Widener Library
Research Services
Harvard University
Cambridge, Massachusetts

INTRODUCTORY REMARKS

In 2005, Online Computer Library Center conducted a survey of over 3,000 individuals and learned (to their apparent dismay) that most people think of books when they think of libraries. Though the survey respondents felt libraries are an excellent source of quality information, they were largely unaware of libraries' electronic resources. A year later, a survey of faculty in higher education found that scholars are increasingly dependent on electronic information, less dependent on libraries as a gateway, but increasingly reliant on libraries' budgets to purchase the information they count on.

Times are changing, libraries are changing, but perceptions of libraries haven't yet caught up. People tend to think of print culture and digital culture as distinct entities. Traditionalists, "people of the book," grow anxious about the restlessness of digital natives. They fret about the devaluation of printed texts and the risk of being left behind. Others are delighted by new technologies and can't wait for the new to triumph over the old. Even librarians continue to make distinctions between real and virtual libraries, while in fact virtually every library is really both. The scientist accessing an article from her office through Google Scholar may not realize the library provided it or may forget that the alert she receives to keep up with new research is generated by a library database, but she'd notice if this access disappeared. On the other hand, an English professor who bemoans the fact that kids today spend all of their time in their dorm rooms playing games and pirating music has likely not visited the physical library lately. Ours is full of students, and they like books, "real" books, as they call them. I recently asked a class if they would like to download books from Amazon or Google to their cell phones. They looked at me as if I'd gone mad. "Who would want to read a book on a cell phone?" one finally asked.

For decades now we've conceptualized the shifts in our information environment as if we're crossing a frontier; once we've sorted out our visas and finally cleared customs, we'll be netizens living in a fully digital world. Yet in fact we live, and will continue to live for a long, long time, in a borderland with its own distinctive culture. Scholars of postcolonial societies recognize that these borderlands are not evolving from one to another and don't require residents to declare citizenship in only one. They are hybrid cultures that are fluid, constantly under negotiation, and enriched by their multiple heritages. So, too, is today's library and today's library user.

Though libraries have accepted that information is information regardless of format and that we need to serve our communities inside and beyond the walls of the library, our ability to figure out how to manage the digital parts of our collections is still evolving. How do we adapt our collection development policies to deal with electronic resources? What acquisitions processes do we need to deal with new formats? How do we help our patrons recognize authority in a read/write culture? How do we reconceptualize our activism on behalf of equitable access, patron privacy, fair use, and intellectual freedom given the new realities of licenses, DRM, pay-per-view, and business models that capture personal search behavior and turn it into a revenue-producing commodity?

Librarians, more than any other group, keep their finger on the pulse of changes in the information industries. This book will help librarians in any kind of library find the good stuff, match it to local needs, make it accessible, and develop processes to fold high-quality electronic resources into their traditional workflows. With examples taken from a variety of libraries around the world, in a format that is itself hybrid (the book is accompanied by a Web site that will be updated with new information), this resource will be a useful Baedecker's Guide to our rich and fluid information borderland.

Or, to cite another guidebook, don't panic.

Barbara Fister
Academic Librarian and Professor
Folke Bernadotte Memorial Library
Gustavus Adolphus College
St. Peter, Minnesota

REFERENCES

Housewright, Ron, and Roger Schonfeld. 2008. "Ithaka's 2006 Studies of Key Stakeholders in the Digital Transformation in Higher Education." Available: www.ithaka.org/research/Ithakas%202006%20 Studies%20of%20Key%20Stakeholders%20in%20the%20Digital%20Transformation%20in%20H igher%20Education.pdf.

Online Computer Library Center. 2005. "Perceptions of Libraries and Information Resources." Available: www.oclc.org/reports/2005perceptions.htm.

PREFACE

In practical terms, library services must be offered where and when our library users will use them. If library services are not present at the point in time and space where our library users and potential library users are seeking information, they will turn elsewhere for information mediation services. (Kovacs and Robinson, 2004)

SCOPE AND PURPOSE

Defining the mission of our libraries, defining what our purpose is and role in societal and technical contexts, is ongoing. Over the centuries we've redefined our roles, our physical structures, and even our reasons for existing. We promote and enhance education, support and enable information literacy, and try to deploy our services where the people we wish to serve are looking for information support. Balancing the value of the physical location and archiving of print and microform materials with the enhanced access of electronic resources (e-resources) and a library presence in Web 2.0 occupies us nearly a decade into this new century. Balance and growth, budget and quality, change and preservation are themes that have emerged in the past few years as e-library collections have matured in the context of the technologies we use. Are we book repositories or information service centers? Which should we focus on: information architecture or our physical buildings? Can we do both? Should we?

As did the first edition, this second edition of *The Kovacs Guide to Electronic Library Collection Development: Essential Core Subject Collections, Selection Criteria, and Guidelines* explores strategies, tools, and concepts for electronic library (e-library) collection planning. It explores how to build, expand, improve, and maintain an e-library collection.

Creating an e-library is an ambitious project for any library, because the process attempts to re-create the library collection and library services in virtual space. In its simplest form, an e-library is a collection of e-resources—e-resources from a variety of sources, including freely available Web sites and fee-based Web-accessible databases. Essentially, an e-library is a Web-published collection of e-resources. The e-library concept encompasses both the digital library and the virtual library. An e-library may include a digital library collection—a collection of electronic texts, images, multimedia files, etc., scanned, copied or transcribed from print or holographic primary documents or artifacts—and may include documents that were published originally in electronic format—born digital—or published in multiple formats. It may also offer library services, such as reference, the library catalog, circulation, and other document delivery services through the library Web site.

E-libraries manifest as Web pages published on a Web server, through content management systems (CMS), electronic resource management systems (ERMS), or the library catalog (ILS), and combinations of those options. Most e-libraries are accessible to users through Web browsers connected to the public Web, but some are accessible only through private company or organizational Intranets.

This second edition of *The Kovacs Guide to Electronic Library Collection Development: Essential Core Subject Collections, Selection Criteria, and Guidelines* again uses e-library case studies—success stories—to illustrate the diversity of e-libraries and provide practical information about how real life e-libraries are planned, created, managed, and grown. Learning from peer libraries who have developed strategies for collecting e-resources and constructing e-libraries is a recurring theme throughout this book.

The specific e-resources that are selected and how they are organized and made accessible will be unique for each library, but we can learn from sharing experiences. This second edition expands on and updates all of the core strategies, essential tools, and concepts introduced in the first edition. It also addresses the shifting environment in which e-libraries are created and managed today. Major changes include: integration of the library catalog including the cataloging of e-resources; integration of library services, such as virtual reference (real-time as well as e-mail or forms-based reference services), and document delivery; greater variety and scope of Web accessible fee-based databases, including full-text resource aggregators; and greater variety and scope of electronic journals (e-journals) and electronic books (e-books). The virtual reference topic discussed in Chapter 2 of the first edition, was developed into a completely new book, *The Virtual Reference Handbook: Interview and Information Delivery Techniques for the Chat and E-Mail Environment* (Neal Schuman, 2007). In the present text, virtual reference is discussed only as it relates to its impact on e-library collection decisions.

The Kovacs Guide to Electronic Library Collection Development: Essential Core Subject Collections, Selection Criteria, and Guidelines, Second Edition, is designed for any librarian who wants to develop, expand, or improve an e-library. The author has shaped *The Kovacs Guide* as a one-step resource that serves three distinct functions of electronic collection policies: to guide collection planning; to steer collection management; and to identify subject collection, criteria, and core e-resources.

The first function provides librarians with a collection-planning guide specifically written for collecting, evaluating, and selecting e-resources. A collection development plan is even more essential for high-quality e-library collection development than it is for building a collection of print or other formats. Every collection plan must consider library users' information needs and information-seeking behaviors (and expectations), and establish other library-appropriate selection criteria.

Collection management guidance, the second function of *The Kovacs Guide*, addresses issues including integration of the e-library collection and the library catalog, library services integration, e-resource management choices, and database licensing issues. It attempts to answer several essential e-library collection management questions: How much will it cost? How will it be paid for? Who will have access? How will access be managed/limited/monitored? How will the information be archived or otherwise safeguarded for the future? How will the e-library be made accessible, usable, and searchable?

The third function, as a collection development tool, is purely practical. What available resources support good e-library collection evaluation, selection, and collection (acquisition)? Which e-resources are core or essential in any given subject area?

ORGANIZATION

The Kovacs Guide to Electronic Library Collection Development, Second Edition, is arranged in two parts. Part I, "General Collection Planning Recommendations," explores all of the wide-ranging concerns of e-libraries. Part II details recommended planning, evaluation, and selection criteria; core collections; and collection tools for major subject areas to create or improve an e-library collection.

In Part I, Chapter 1, "General Collection Development Principles for E-Resources," reviews the e-library collection development literature and then presents a framework within which librarians can create a flexible working collection plan for creating and maintaining e-libraries. It explores the questions that must be answered to create a usable e-library collection plan. Part I, Chapter 1 recommends specific strategies for collecting, evaluating, and selecting e-resources, including a checklist/interview for preliminary planning and organization as well as a checklist/interview for creating a good e-library collection development plan individualized for each library's needs.

Part I, Chapter 2, "Bringing It All Together: Some General Considerations for Building, Organizing, Managing, and Maintaining E-Libraries," reviews the most critical e-library collection management and maintenance issues. The use of collection analysis (aka assessment or evaluation) tools to grow and maintain high-quality e-library collections is discussed. Collection management options (CMS, ERMS, etc.), including the creation of MARC records for e-resources and other forms of e-resource cataloging, are described.

Part I, Chapter 3, "E-Resources Licensing Basics," describes some of the various arrangements made and provides guidance on issues involved in licensing or purchasing Web-accessible databases.

In Part II, "Recommended Planning, Evaluation, and Selection Criteria: Core Collections and Collection Tools for Major Subject Areas," eleven chapters are each devoted to the collection development process and core e-resources collections for specific subject areas. These subject areas embrace the following broad subject areas: ready-reference, government documents, genealogy, jobs and employment, business, legal information, medical information, biological sciences, engineering, chemistry, physics, astronomy, mathematics, earth sciences, social sciences, education, the arts, and the humanities. Each chapter identifies subject-specific selection, evaluation, and organization criteria and recommends collection development tools within the subject area of focus. A core Web reference collection for each subject area is published on the companion Web site at www.kovacs.com/ns/essentialguide.html. The core collection development tools described in each area have been expanded to include e-docs (federal, state, and international) tools, and Web 2.0 related services such as peer-to-peer reviewing, and more.

E-Library Success Stories in each chapter illustrate the diversity and creativity of e-library builders and provide specific examples of e-libraries. Thomas Dowlings' LibWeb (http://lists.webjunction.org/libweb/) includes nearly 8,000 library Web sites worldwide and is updated daily. Michael Sauers' World Wide Web Library Directory (http://travelinlibrarian.info/libdir/) lists nearly 9,000 library Web sites in 130 countries. The LibDex site (www.libdex.com/) lists more than 18,000 library home pages, OPACS, and other library-related Web sites. These case study libraries represent different types of libraries, including public, academic, and special libraries, as well as library organizations. The coverage of the stories is international, but mainly limited to English language sites or those with an English language description.

The sites and e-resources discussed in each chapter, as well as the core reference e-resources for each subject, are maintained on the companion Web site at www.kovacs.com/ns/essentialguide .html. This password-protected site is exclusively for readers of *The Kovacs Guide to Electronic*

Library Collection Development, Second Edition. The login name and password are: colldev kovacs09. Readers are encouraged to bookmark the companion Web site. It will be updated frequently as the sites identified in these print pages move or expire and new, or even better, sites become available. Readers are also encouraged to send feedback on the sites chosen for inclusion in the core collection and suggestions for expanding it to diane@kovacs.com.

Librarians who create and maintain e-libraries are applying the best principles of traditional library collection development to e-resources. *The Kovacs Guide to Electronic Library Collection Development: Essential Core Subject Collections, Selection Criteria, and Guidelines*, Second Edition, serves as a resource for clarifying how the collection development process translates to the Web environment, as a guide for planning collection management, as a guide for developing selection criteria for specific subject areas, and as a collection of carefully selected resources for starting or expanding an e-library collection.

REFERENCE AND WEB SITES CITED

Kovacs, Diane K. (2007) *The Virtual Reference Handbook: Interview and Information Delivery Techniques for the Chat and E-Mail Environments*. New York: Neal-Schuman Publishers, published concurrently in the United Kingdom by Facet Publishers (2007).

Kovacs Diane K., and Robinson, Kara L. 2004. *The Kovacs Guide to Electronic Library Collection Development: Essential Core Subject Collections, Selection Criteria, and Guidelines*. New York: Neal-Schuman.

LibDex site. Available: www.libdex.com/.

LibWeb. Available: http://lists.webjunction.org/libweb/.

World Wide Web Library Directory. Available: http://travelinlibrarian.info/libdir/.

ACKNOWLEDGMENTS

This book is dedicated in memory of my mom, Jean Ann Engelbrecht, 1944–2008.

Thank you to my husband Michael J. Kovacs and to my good friend and sometime co-author Kara L. Robinson for making sure this book got written this year. Thank you to all of my excellent colleagues who shared their e-library building stories, their publications, their wisdom, and their support.

PART

I

GENERAL COLLECTION PLANNING RECOMMENDATIONS

1

GENERAL COLLECTION DEVELOPMENT PRINCIPLES FOR E-RESOURCES

Collection development plans and policies are written to guide the selection, acquisition, de-selection, and preservation processes of a library—in theory with regard to all formats. Collection plans synchronize the library's collection activity with the mission of the library and its parent institution and relate this activity to the needs of identified clientele such as undergraduate students and faculty researchers. . . . Collection plans guide the identification of priorities for selection, explain reasons for exclusion, establish directions to plan and direct development and change, and assist in the establishment of priorities of staff and budget for collection support activities. Collection plans are both internal documents and public relations tools; they are a means to communicate with partners in collection development outside the library and may be used to negotiate for funds within the parent institution. When accreditation agencies visit, collection plans help provide answers about support for programs. Detailed plans can assist libraries to make the best use of funds through cooperation in selection with other institutions. (Myall and Anderson, 2007: 237–238)

INTRODUCTION

Building an e-library demonstrates to our library users and our communities and organizations that we are committed to fulfilling their information needs. It also projects our willingness to change and progress as the technological infrastructure of our international communities and global economy shifts between the paper-based transmission and storage of information to the computer-based transmission and storage of information (no, we do not expect to see a "paperless" library any time soon). This willingness to progress and change is critical to the survival of libraries and the library profession as a modern entity. Maintaining high standards of selectivity and information quality and adhering to an underlying philosophy of education and service have made librarians an essential profession in the United States and around the world. Bringing this professionalism to the Web, we will certainly be welcomed as citizens—netizens—in the international Web community.

Two obvious technology factors have made it imperative for libraries to build e-resource collections for their current and potential library users: the ubiquity of personal computers and personal information and communication devices, aka mobile devices (iPods, Black-berries, PDAs, etc.), and the publication of major quantities of information on and through the Web.

> Because the products of our expressions are stored in digital form, people have created an array of editing and reuse tools that support repeated revision and massive sharing. Technical advances in representing digital information have also been made, but at present, much work remains to be done. High-resolution displays for visually manifested information and practical use in all shapes and sizes, from wall-size displays to tiny screens on cell phones and children's toys such as the Leapster. Portable headphones make music and conversation ubiquitous. All these advances represent base technological developments that support cyberspace, or cyber infrastructure. From the broad information field perspective, these enabling technologies make search engines, content-sharing services (e.g., del.icio.us and Flickr), and social environments like MySpace and Face-book possible. From a library and cultural memory perspective, digital libraries are based on integrated environments that assume that these enabling technological advances are persistently accessible. (Marchionini, 2008: 169)

In the twenty-first century, being an effective librarian in any type of library (public, academic, or special) requires expansion of the range of resources provided for library users through the library. Libraries must collect e-resources and make those resources accessible off site, outside of the physical library building. Steven Sowards' classic article clarifies why effective librarians should, do, and will create e-library reference collections:

- Selection: Users who can rely on reference Web sites save significant time by avoiding inefficient, inconclusive Web surfing.
- Endorsement: Librarians implicitly vouch for the quality of the linked sources: their relevance for solving a given problem, their consistent availability, and the accuracy and currency of their content.
- Organization: A well-designed site allows users to move rapidly and accurately among a large number of Web sites, finding a high proportion of relevant resources.
- Cooperation: These sites allow experienced librarians to share their knowledge of the Web with one another and with users, at all times of the day and irrespective of distance. (Sowards, 1998: 3)

Other benefits of establishing an e-library presence include:

- enhancing existing services for core user groups;
- providing new services to core user groups;
- attracting new library users; and
- providing new (or better) services to library users who are reluctant (or find it difficult) to come into the physical library.

E-libraries extend the librarian's role as information intermediary to the Web. E-libraries should be designed to promote the library's overall service mission to their community of library users. Libraries and librarians are adapting to the information needs and responding to the information-seeking behaviors of their users. In part, librarians adapt to these needs and behaviors by building e-resource collections, or e-libraries for short.

We must also respond to changes in how current and potential library users seek information. In the twenty-first century, information is portable. Information comes to the user through Web browsers on personal computers, cell phones, Blackberries, iPods, PDAs, and other portable information and communications devices.

On the Shifted Librarian blog (accessed January 14, 2009, at http://theshiftedlibrarian .com/stories/2002/01/19/whatIsAShiftedLibrarian.html), Jenny Levine, describes this process as "information shifting":

> To my mind, the biggest difference is that they expect information to come to them, whether it's via the Web, email, cell phone, online chat, whatever. And given the tip of the iceberg of technology we're seeing, it's going to have a big impact on how they expect to receive library services, which means librarians have to start adjusting now. I call that adjustment "shifting" because I think you have to start meeting these kids' information needs in their world, not yours. The library has to become more portable or "shifted".... Therefore, a "shifted librarian" is someone who is working to make libraries more portable. We're experimenting with new methods, even if we find out they don't work as well as we thought they would. Sometimes, we're waiting for our colleagues, our bosses, and even the kids to catch up, but we're still out there trying. And please don't think I don't love books and print, because I do. No amount of technology will ever replace them, and libraries will always be a haven for books. It's the extras that I'm concentrating on, especially as we try to serve our remote library users.

The pattern of our professional activities has clarified as our tools have changed. We identify, collect, evaluate, and organize information resources in order to facilitate our library users' searches for information. Our roles as librarians have been refined and focused on providing library users with the information they need, when they need it, where they need it, organized for logical access. Whether we are called reference librarians, collection development librarians, bibliographers, catalogers, or e-resource librarians, our jobs are increasingly centered on the information needs of current and potential library users.

Lewis (2007) has written a wise and sensible description of the changes libraries need to make to adapt to an information and publishing environment that takes place primarily through computer-mediated communications and has proposed equally wise and sensible strategies for adapting to the changing environment:

> As Google so powerfully proves every day, authority control and classification are no longer the only, or the best, answers. Academic libraries must find and articulate their roles in the current and future information ecology. If we cannot or will not do this, our campuses will invest in other priorities and the library will slowly, but surely, atrophy and become a little used museum of the book.... While librarians were moving with caution, users were not. (Lewis, 2007: 2, 5)

Lewis suggests two strategies. First, libraries need to embed their e-resources and print resources into publicly accessible search tools and databases such as Google (including Google Books and Google Scholar) and Open WorldCat. Second, librarians need to be present where research assistance is most needed; for example, a communication option or a link to a research guide or tutorial embedded in a learning management system at the point at which a course assignment requires research.

In the report "Changing Roles of Academic and Research Libraries," the Association of College and Research Libraries (ACRL) Roundtable on Technology and Change in Academic Libraries details these essential actions:

> There are three essential actions libraries must take to achieve the necessary transformation and remain vital forces on campus in the years ahead: First, libraries must evolve from institutions perceived primarily as the domain of the book to institutions that users clearly perceive as providing pathways to high-quality information in a variety of media and information sources.... Second, the culture of libraries and their staff must proceed beyond a mindset primarily of ownership and control to one that seeks to provide service and guidance in more useful ways, helping users find and use information that may be available through a range of providers, including libraries themselves, in electronic format.... Third, libraries must assert their evolving roles in more active ways, both in the context of their institutions and in the increasingly competitive markets for information dissemination and retrieval. Libraries must descend from what many have regarded as an increasingly isolated perch of presumed privilege and enter the contentious race to advance in the market for information services—what one participant in our roundtable termed "taking it to the streets." (Association of College and Research Libraries, 2006)

Many libraries choose to integrate the selection and acquisition of e-resources into the routine collection development responsibilities of all librarians. Other libraries choose to create e-resource librarian positions specifically for electronic resource support. In any case, these new responsibilities require technical, business and financial training, communications skills, and experience.

All librarians need to be comfortable navigating the Web through Web browsers. Some will need to be comfortable editing XHTML and CSS and/or working with content management systems (CMS) or electronic resource management systems (ERMS). Other more technical skills may be required for some responsibilities depending on the library and whether or not the library has information technology (IT) support available.

Librarians must also reach consensus about, and receive training in, specific selection criteria for e-resources and ensuring that those e-resources are accessible by library users. At this writing, Web browsers installed on typical personal computers are the dominant access interfaces. Some e-libraries are beginning to be designed to support access through mobile devices as well.

Librarians effectively develop their collections of e-resources based on the same basic collection policies articulated by libraries for print and other formats in which information resources are collected by their libraries. Most libraries have devoted considerable time in developing collections of materials that best serve their communities of library users. This work can be recycled in planning for an e-resources collection, although there are obviously unique criteria to be considered.

Selection is a process of comparing individual resources against criteria defined in a library's collection development policy, evaluating the quality, determining the relevancy of the resource to the information needs of your library users, and deciding whether the library can afford to provide access to a given print or e-resource. While library users may access many e-resources free of direct costs, other e-resources are fee-based and require some kind of subscription or licensing arrangement. One function of libraries has been to acquire costly sources and make them available to members of the community who cannot afford to pay for them personally. Continuing to make this information accessible is a role libraries can fill well.

Most fee-based databases are Web accessible. Web-accessible versions of reference sources and serials previously available only in print (or older electronic media) are among potential selection choices. E-books and e-serials access may be just as expensive as acquiring print versions and are often more expensive, especially if the cost of personnel to manage and maintain them is included. Some may still require that the print version be acquired in order to gain access to the electronic version. Many limitations exist as to the accessibility of current versions and archived access as well as limitations due to copyright issues and definitions of allowed users.

Even so-called free e-resources will require expenditure of staff time for identification, selection, evaluation, cataloging, link maintenance, and training. Sometimes apparently freely available e-resources may actually cost the library more overall than fee-based e-resources that also integrate technical and other kinds of support into the cost of access to the product.

The proliferation of Internet access around the world, especially access to and through the Web, has led to increased access to many types of information resources that were previously difficult or expensive to obtain. Current news and information is quickly delivered through the Web. Information sources, such as newspapers, newsletters, journals, books, dissertations, specialized bibliographic or full-text databases, statistical datasets, and even television and radio transcripts as well as actual video and audio transmissions, are accessible through the Web. Much content is even published directly to the Web instead of, or in advance of, print, television, or radio versions. Maps, photographs, and other graphic images are accessible through the Web individually and in digitized collections. Resources in a variety of media formats, once only available locally in libraries or agencies, are now accessible globally: information from local and national governments, nongovernmental organizations, industry trade organizations, community or campus specific information, and the list goes on. Library catalogs are among the most valuable resources accessible by the Web.

Google Books, Open Worldcat, and Jon Udell's LibraryLookup bookmarklet (http://weblog .infoworld.com/udell/stories/2002/12/11/librarylookup.html) take creative advantage of Web data-base standards to make it possible for users to search library catalogs in addition to searching online booksellers. Library users searching online booksellers that adhere to Web database standards can look up whether their local library owns a copy of the book they are thinking of buying. The Web also makes possible the sharing of resources among libraries so that the expenses of maintaining individual library catalogs, licensing databases, and creating digital library collections can be shared. Some have argued that the accessibility of information through the Web obviates the need for libraries or librarians (try searching Google for the phrase "no need for librarians"). We can argue convincingly to the contrary. The sheer volume and diversity of information made available through the Web creates a need for librarian intermediaries who will evaluate, organize, and simplify access for information library users. The Web makes a significant quantity of information available to users. Web search tools are easy to use and can be accessed or downloaded for free. The real problem for our users is not in finding information on the Web but finding information on the Web that is appropriate for their information need, of high quality, reliable, and authoritative. Through the efforts of librarians, our e-libraries can be collections of the most appropriate, the highest quality, and the most reliable and authoritative information resources for our library users.

The Web is both the shelves and the "books." The technical Web is an information storage and organization mechanism. The social (cultural, educational, business, etc.) Web is also a source or supplier of information.

The question for librarians is not whether the library is present in physical space or in Web—or virtual—space but that libraries are service organizations that fulfill the information needs of their current and potential users in both physical and virtual spaces. Libraries are not merely their collections of books and other information objects. The important word is library, whether we call it the virtual, digital, or e-library.

Ignoring the physical, technological underpinnings for now, we assert that the library is, at root, a collection of information selected for use of, and made useable for, a particular community. That community may be large or small, physically proximate or not, present or future, homogeneous or not, but it is essential that it be identified and at least partially understood. That is, proverbially like politics, all collections are local. (Keller et al., 2003)

DEFINITIONS AND WORD CHOICES: AN E-LIBRARY VOCABULARY

The e-library vocabulary is still evolving. Much word and phrase choice is based on consensus understanding or local usage. The e-library vocabulary situation is analogous to that of the car as it developed over time. At times, what in American English we now refer to as a "car" was called "auto" or "automobile" and was historically named a "horseless carriage." Some refer to a car by its make or model; for example, the author refers to her family cars as "the Focus" and "the Subaru." In that same vein, some librarians refer to their library's Web collections and/or Web-accessible services as an e-library, a virtual library, or a digital library or simply as "the library Web site." Many other words and phrases are used interchangeably that ultimately refer to the e-library or some individual piece of the e-library.

In an ongoing attempt to use the consensus vocabulary that will be the most meaningful to the most librarians, surveys were sent to library-related discussion lists and blogs, asking librarians to share the words and phrases they used to describe e-library concepts. The surveys were run on SurveyMonkey, and the survey link was sent out in May 2008 and again in August 2008. The discussion lists and blogs on the distribution list are listed in Table 1.1, and the survey is reproduced in Table 1.2. Librarians were also asked to choose the terms they use to refer to the people who use their libraries and whether their e-library used a CMS or ERMS. The answers to the previous questions will be reported in the next chapter. The survey results show a lower consensus on these concept terms than those of previous surveys. In the 2008 survey, 534 usable surveys were returned. The majority of respondents, 55 percent, were from academic libraries. 20 percent of respondents were from public libraries, 10 percent from primary or secondary school libraries, and 16 percent from special or other types of libraries. Percentages have been rounded to the nearest decimal. Table 1.3 reports the detailed breakdown of respondents by library type.

Although the majority of respondents indicate that they refer to the users of their libraries as patrons, 41 percent, or students, 34 percent, as reported in Table 1.4, in this edition we will

---

Table 1.1. Discussion Lists and Blogs Distribution for Library Vocabulary and Collection Development Tools Surveys

- LISNews and LISNewsWire Blogs: lisnews-owner@lishost.net
- ResourceShelf Blog: gary.price@resourceshelf.com
- acqnet-l@lists.ibiblio.org
- BUSLIB-L@LISTS.NAU.EDU
- CAPHIS@hslc.org
- COLLDV-L@usc.edu
- collib-l@ala.org
- dig_ref@LISTSERV.SYR.EDU

- eldnet-l@u.washington.edu
- ERIL-L@LISTSERV .BINGHAMTON.EDU
- genealib@mailman.acomp .usf.edu
- GOVDOC-L@lists.psu.edu
- law-lib@ucdavis.edu
- lawlibref@lists.washlaw.edu
- Libref-L@listserv.kent.edu
- LIS-LINK@jiscmail.ac.uk

- LIS-SCITECH@jiscmail.ac.uk
- livereference@yahoogroups.com
- LM_NET@LISTSERV.SYR.EDU
- MEDLIB-L@LIST.UVM.EDU
- Medref-L@listserv.kent.edu
- mla-cds@colldev.mlanet.org
- publib@webjunction.org
- SERIALST@LIST.UVM.EDU
- sts-l@ala.org
- web4lib@webjunction.org

Table 1.2. Library Vocabulary Survey Questions

1. Which library type best describes the library you work in/for/with?

2. Which word do you use most frequently to refer to the people who use your library?
   - Client
   - Patron
   - User
   - Customer
   - Student/Faculty
   - Other (please specify)

3. Which phrase means to you "a collection of electronic documents scanned or transcribed from print or holographic primary documents or artifacts and may include documents that were published originally in electronic format or published in dual format"
   - Electronic library (e-library)
   - Digital library
   - Virtual library
   - Other phrase used to identify the definition above.

4. Which phrase means to you "a Web-published collection of Web-accessible information resources." A(n) _____ may include a "digital library" collection or "virtual library" services."
   - Electronic library (e-library)
   - Digital library
   - Virtual library
   - Other phrase used to identify the definition above.

5. Which phrase means to you "_____ refers to the offering of library services through the Web."
   - Electronic library (e-library)
   - Digital library
   - Virtual library
   - Other phrase used to identify the definition above.

6. Does your library use a Content Management System (CMS) or Electronic Resource Management System (ERMS)?
   - Yes or No

7. If you chose yes in the question above, that your library does use a CMS (ERMS) to manage its e-library, what is the name of your system?

8. Additional comments or ideas:

(Please include your name and e-mail address if you would like feedback, otherwise this survey form is completely anonymous.)

use *library users* as our preferred term as it is more congruent with the concept of computer or electronic resource users than is the dignified but old fashioned concept of patron.

Digital library, electronic library (or e-library), and virtual library are used as virtually interchangeable terms as indicated by the survey results. *E-library* will continue to be the preferred term in this edition. But, it is possible we may be using the phrase *digital library* as the global concept term in future editions.

Table 1.5 shows that while 61 percent of librarians responding would use the phrase *digital library* to refer to "a collection of electronic documents scanned or transcribed from print or holographic primary documents or artifacts and may include documents that were published originally in electronic format or published in dual format," 25 percent would call that description an electronic library, and 5 percent would say virtual library.

As reported in Table 1.6, 35 percent of librarians who responded to the survey chose the phrase electronic library or e-library to describe "a Web-published collection of Web-accessible information resources. An ___ may include a 'digital library' collection or 'virtual library' services." 29 percent chose the phrase *digital library* and 24 percent chose *virtual library*. An additional 11.5 percent of respondents offered alternatives, such as "e-resources," "Web sites/Web pages," or "databases." Librarians use these phrases interchangeably as well.

Table 1.7 shows that 55 percent of librarians responding to the survey concur that a virtual library "...refers to the offering of library services through the Web," although 21 percent would use the phrase electronic library and 10 percent would use digital library.

Table 1.3. Which library type best describes the library you work in/for/with? Responses from Library Vocabulary Survey

Answer Options	Response Frequency	Response Count
Academic Library (with Graduate Programs)	40.4%	216
Academic Library (4 year)	9.4%	50
Academic Library (2 year)	4.9%	26
Elementary/Grade School Library (Primary School)	4.3%	23
High School Library	4.1%	22
Middle School Library	1.3%	7
Public (Large Urban)	5.1%	27
Public (Smaller Urban)	5.1%	27
Public (Suburban)	5.6%	30
Public (Rural or Small town)	3.6%	19
Special Library (Business)	3.2%	17
Special (Hospital)	2.2%	12
Special Library (Research Organization)	2.4%	13
Other type of Library	8.4%	45
	Answered question	534

Table 1.4. Which word do you use most frequently to refer to the people who use your library?

Answer Options	Response Frequency	Response Count
Client	2.8%	15
Patron	40.8%	222
User	13.4%	73
Customer	6.3%	34
Student/Faculty	34.0%	185
Other	2.8%	15
	Answered question	544

Table 1.5. Which phrase means to you "a collection of electronic documents scanned or transcribed from print or holographic primary documents or artifacts and may include documents that were published originally in electronic format or published in dual format"?

Answer Options	Response Frequency	Response Count
Electronic Library (E-Library)	25.0%	131
Digital Library	61.4%	321
Virtual Library	5.0%	26
Other Phrase Used to Identify the Definition Above.	8.6%	45
	Answered question	523

Table 1.6. Which phrase means to you "a Web-published collection of Web-accessible information resources"? A(n) _____ may include a "digital library" collection or "virtual library" services.

Answer Options	Response Frequency	Response Count
Electronic Library (E-Library)	35.2%	180
Digital Library	29.4%	150
Virtual Library	23.9%	122
Other Phrase Used to Identify the Definition Above.	11.5%	59
	Answered question	511

Table 1.7. Which phrase means to you "_____ refers to the offering of library services through the Web"?

Answer Options	Response Frequency	Response Count
Electronic Library (E-Library)	20.9%	102
Digital Library	10.4%	51
Virtual Library	55.0%	269
Other Phrase Used to Identify the Definition Above.	13.7%	67
	Answered question	489

In referring to reference or other library services that are offered through the Web, we'll use the phrase *virtual reference* or *virtual library* services although many libraries use the phrase *digital reference* instead.

Digital libraries is used in this text, specifically to refer to "a collection of electronic documents scanned or transcribed from print or holographic primary documents or artifacts and may include documents that were published originally in electronic format—born digital—or published in dual format." The term *e-resources* refers to any information product or service that is published through or on the Web.

Librarians may understand and use vocabulary quite differently from library users. Librarians' vocabulary choices may be confusing for many current and potential library users. John Kupersmith (2003) has published "Library Terms That Users Understand" (www.jkup.net/terms.html), based on compiling survey results and usability studies regarding terminology used on library Web sites. His intention is to provide usability data as well as "best practices" on which terms are most effective: "most users can understand them well enough to make productive choices" as labels for library resources and services. It may make sense to us to refer to online databases, but the library user may find "Search E-journals" or "Research by Subject" more understandable. John Kupersmith's analyses will help e-library builders make word choices and descriptions that better communicate information types and research functions for their current and potential library users. Our goal is to integrate library collections and services with the Web at the point of contact with our library users. We must shift to meet the information needs and information-seeking behavior of our library users regardless of what terms we used among ourselves to describe the shifting of the library to the Web.

K–12 students, librarians, or libraries are the terms used for primary and secondary educational level or school. K–12 refers to kindergarten through the 12th grade in the U.S. educational system. Primary being K–5 or 8, and secondary being 6 or 9–12 depending on local organization. Postsecondary is used to denote university and college level of education. Academic—university and college—libraries support users at the postsecondary educational levels.

THE E-LIBRARY COLLECTION DEVELOPMENT LITERATURE

E-library collection development began during the last two decades of the twentieth century. Many e-library collection development challenges have yet to be "solved." These challenges are heavily influenced by technology changes that seem to occur every other week. E-library collection development factors in the current decade of the twenty-first century have evolved from those that we fronted in the last decade of the twentieth century and continue to evolve as we learn and adapt.

Dunham and Davis (2008), Phillips and Williams (2004), Miller (2000), Thornton (2000), Coutts (1998), Norman (1997), and Fedunok (1997) have all thoroughly reviewed the literature relating to collection development of e-resources in general and Web resources in particular. Rather than duplicate the literature reviews provided by these authors, this section highlights specific articles that discuss key issues and themes for each time period.

TWENTIETH CENTURY

In 1994 and 1995, when the Internet first became accessible to the general public, Demas and colleagues (1995) and Piontek and Garlock (1995) were some of the first librarians to discuss practical guidelines for collection development of Internet resources as opposed to the mainly theoretical discussions of previous publications. The main themes discussed in articles published in the last half decade of the twentieth century included the following.

Collection development planning for e-resources is desirable. Collection of Internet resources can and should use the same collection criteria as those used for other resource formats (Demas et al., 1995; Johnson, 1997; Fedunok, 1997; Walters et al., 1998).

Building bridges between e-resources and print resources and finding commonalities between the old way of doing collection management and the necessary changes were frequently discussed. Demas and colleagues (1995) and Norman (1997) discussed establishing the "Taxonomy of Internet Resources." The taxonomy is adapted later in the "Developing an E-Library Collection Plan" section of this chapter.

Procedures for acquiring and processing Internet and other sources of e-resources (Norman, 1997) were of great interest in this early stage. Rioux's (1997) metaphor for e-library collection development as "hunting and gathering in cyberspace" is an amusing way to think about the process of free Web resource collection. Walters and colleagues (1998) identified three core selection criteria that apply to all information resources: content, coherence, and functionality.

The role of librarians in mediating access to e-resources for library users through building e-libraries continues to be of interest. Who will work in the library of the future? What will they be doing? Will there be a library in the future? (Fedunok, 1997; Guarino, 1998; Tennant, 1998; Rioux, 1997; Morville and Wickhorst, 1996).

Library resource sharing and the potential for collaboration given the distributed nature of e-resources were addressed in all previously cited articles. Everyone was writing about what could be done in terms of sharing collection development, growing library consortia, and interlibrary cooperation in building e-libraries.

TWENTY-FIRST CENTURY

> Collection development and management literature of the past seven years reveals distinct trends among issues, philosophy, and practice. Issues confronting collection development librarians prior to 1997, such as allocation formulas, dual roles for subject librarians, and access versus ownership, diminished in importance as more complex and critical challenges emerged from the vast expansion of information technology. New concerns—changes in scholarly communications and publishing, building digital collections, consortial collaboration, and quantitative assessment—have eclipsed previous topics, moving well beyond some of the traditional aspects of collection development practice. (Phillips and Williams, 2004: 273)

As interlibrary cooperation increased and more and more libraries found their users requesting e-resource access or bypassing the library in order to go directly to Web resources, the themes discussed in articles in the first half decade of the twenty-first century altered accordingly. These themes included the following.

Collection of e-resources requires a collection development policy, selection criteria, and planning for organization and maintenance especially in the context of interlibrary cooperation. The role of librarians in collecting e-resources and an ongoing discussion of the changes and current challenges in practical collection development and selection remains a central theme in this century (Ameen and Haider, 2007; Cassell, 2007; Connor and Wood, 2007; Genco and Kuzyk, 2007; Hoffman and Wood, 2007; Rotich and Munge, 2007; Fenner, 2006, Kovacs and Robinson, 2004; Casserly, 2002; Holleman, 2000; Intner, 2001; Baldwin, 2001; Blake and Surprenant, 2000; Kovacs and Elkordy, 2000; Latham, 2002; Duranceau and Hepfer, 2002; Lord and Ragon,

2001; Pitschmann, 2001; Sweetland, 2000). Note that most of the articles cited below also discuss collection development policy at some point or level.

"Clearly written guidelines not only help us with selecting materials, but also serve as a guide to effectively promoting these resources to library users . . . an effective policy should include how your library plans to handle the licensing, technical support, and group purchasing of e-resources" (Lord and Ragon, 2001: 42). Discussion of the process for creating and sustaining successful interlibrary cooperation and commitment to cooperation between libraries for resources sharing continue. Key aspects include patience, planning skills, organization, administration, and strong committed leadership of library consortia as well as cooperative collection development and the knowledge and skills required to make it work (Jeng, 2008; Cousins et al., 2008; Rossi, 2008; Ameen and Haider, 2007; Cassell, 2007; Clement, 2007; Johnson, 2007; Johnson and Luther, 2007; Rotich and Munge, 2007; Hirshon, 2006; Tonta, 2001; Lord and Ragon, 2001; Ekmekcioglu and Nicholson, 2001).

E-resource collection management has been a major theme in the most recent articles. E-resource management issues include the growth of e-resources as the primary method of publication, changes in scholarly communication mechanisms, the building of digital collections, the need for collection evaluation and assessment, managing licensing and access details, the need for clear guidelines for weeding e-resources, and planning for archiving and storage of both e-resources and obsolete or lower use print resources (Borin and Yi, 2008; Dillon, 2008; Henry et al., 2008; Sutton and Jacoby, 2008; Yu and Breivold, 2008; Cassell, 2007; Hunter, 2007; Jacobs, 2007; Lewis, 2007; McCracken, 2007; Schmidt et al., 2007; Schonfeld, 2007; Su, 2007; Wrubel, 2007; Ameen, 2006; Calhoun, 2006; Skaggs, 2006; Uddin and Janecek, 2006; Xie, 2006; Hiott and Beasley. 2005; Wood, 2005; Gregory, 2000).

Kay Ann Cassell's "Interviews with Collection Development Coordinators" (2007) highlighted some details that librarians are concerned with:

- the balance of print and e-resources to be acquired;
- how to market the library's resources to its users;
- budget strategies—redevelop allocation formula based on prioritizing various academic departments in terms of library service needs;
- working with committees to do e-resource selection;
- using conspectus for evaluation of collection;
- multiple campuses = e-resources by preference; and
- cataloging individual e-resource titles, individual articles, etc. so that they are searchable in the catalog by subject and can be linked directly from the catalog to the content.

Justifying the creation of e-libraries in order to support library users has emerged as an underlying theme (Dillon, 2008; Graham, 2008; Marchionini, 2008; Sutton and Jacoby, 2008; Lewis, 2007; McCracken, 2007; Pomerantz and Marchionini, 2007; Rotich and Munge, 2007; Wrubel, 2007; Morris and Larson, 2006; Uddin and Janecek, 2006; Agee, 2005; Hiott and Beasley, 2005; Liu, 2005; Wood, 2005; Keller et al., 2003; Lougee, 2002; Jascó, 2001; Quinn, 2001). The main idea is that e-libraries should be designed with enhanced service to library users clearly in mind, going beyond the collection as a collection of information objects and encouraging the idea that the user is the central focus of library services including the collection development process.

Collection of e-resources requires negotiation of financial and contractual relationships for access including archiving (Baldwin, 2001; Blake and Surprenant, 2000). Professional development, training needs, and competencies needed for librarians and subject specialists in collection development of e-resources and related technical training were addressed in the first years (Lord and Ragon, 2001; Pitschmann, 2001; Sweetland, 2000) and have continued to be analyzed (Cassell, 2007; Myall and Anderson, 2007). Librarians require training in e-resources collection development and reference skills in library schools as well as through continuing and professional education. More recently, the key issues in librarian training and competencies revolve around collection management skills, including licensing negotiations and financial knowledge. The quote that opens this chapter is from an excellent qualitative study done by Carolynne Myall and Sue Anderson (2007). They asked collection development and e-resources librarians to share their insights into the librarian competencies, professional development, and specific issues that must be integrated into the collection planning process in order to bring our professional skills to bear on the challenge of collecting and managing e-resources. A summary of their detailed findings indicate a consensus that librarians will need to bring flexibility, critical thinking, commitment to lifelong learning, strong communication and negotiation skills, and willingness to change to the job. Some of the specific professional competencies needed for modern library collection managers they identified include:

- ability to think critically and independently;
- leadership and teamwork skills;
- ability to work with other librarians, teaching faculty, and consortia;
- ability to analyze and select databases with curricular and user needs at the center of the process;
- good outreach and communications skills;
- flexibility and willingness to adapt quickly to change;
- confidence, curiosity, and persistence;
- ability to be proactive with a willingness to take risks;
- commitment to continuous learning;
- ability to develop a *comfort level with the unknown*;
- knowledge of budget management;
- ability to gather and analyze expenditure data;
- knowledge of licensing issues, contract negotiation, and legal terms; and
- knowledge of publishing and the vendor landscape. (Myall and Anderson, 2007: 245–247)

PRELIMINARY PLANNING

The first step is, of course, to decide if and why you want to build an e-library. Before beginning to plan for an e-library collection, there are some preliminary questions and issues to address. Planning ahead and mapping out the personnel, technology, and funding resources you have available will simplify the process. For the most part the preliminary planning questions relate to the time and commitment of personnel to the task of e-library construction as well as to basic technology and funding status, access, and availability. Other than general considerations and discussion in the e-library success stories, the specific software and hardware used for e-libraries is outside the scope of this book. *D-Lib Magazine* (www.dlib.org), as well as some of the other publications mentioned in the references, cover e-library technical issues in more depth. The discussion list Web4lib@sunsite.berkeley.edu-with archives available at http://sunsite.berkeley.edu/

Web4Lib/archive.html serves as the primary in-depth, Web-accessible e-library technical information source for many librarians.

The most important preliminary planning questions follow:

1. Is there a library consortia or similar organization in place that may provide some resources or support to the e-library project?
2. Is an Internet-connected computer running Web server software already available through your organization? Where? How do you access it? Who do you need to coordinate with to establish your e-library on the server?
3. What computer hardware and software are available for use in building the e-library? Will computer hardware and Web server or other e-library software (e.g., CMS or ERMS or Integrated Library System [ILS]) need to be purchased or otherwise acquired? What will it cost? How will it be funded?
4. Are people available who have the technical skills and subject area knowledge to produce and maintain an e-library by collecting, evaluating, and selecting resources and incorporating them into a Web site?
5. How many people/who will be available to plan, collect, evaluate, and select e-resources, and then to manage and maintain the e-library?
6. How much time do you estimate that responsible individuals will be able to commit to planning, collecting, evaluating, and selecting e-resources?
7. How much time do you estimate that responsible individuals will be able to commit to constructing, managing, and maintaining the e-library?
8. What kinds of training will responsible individuals need in order to create, manage, and maintain the e-library?

Is there a library consortia or similar organization in place that may provide some resources or support to the e-library project?

Libraries may already belong to or be able to join a library consortia or other similar organization that may be able to provide some personnel, technology, or funding support. The subsequent preliminary planning questions need to be answered in terms of the resources that can be supplied through a given library or by consortial organizations they may belong to, join, or create. Many library consortia share personnel, technology, and funding resources among their members in various ways and at different levels. These interlibrary collaborations are the essential context of e-library collection development and related virtual library services.

Is an Internet-connected computer running Web server software already available through your organization? Where? How do you access it? Who do you need to coordinate with to establish your e-library on the server?

Just ask. If your organization has a systems or IT (information technology) department, ask them. If your organization is affiliated with a library system, consortia, or other regional organization, you might ask them about using any Web server, CMS, ERMS, or ILS that they may maintain. All of the libraries in our e-library success story case studies had organizational or consortial access to essential hardware and software. Many e-library projects have been developed without the need for additional support or funding because the library already has access to appropriate hardware and software through the institution that they serve or through an organization in which they participate. The San Bernardino County Library's e-library, for example, is hosted on the San Bernardino County government's Web server. Other examples include BUBL, which is hosted by the Centre for Digital Library Research at Strathclyde University. Other libraries may have to make arrangements with commercial Internet service providers (ISPs) to host their e-library. Some may decide to purchase, install, and maintain their own computer hardware, network services, and server software.

WHAT COMPUTER HARDWARE AND SOFTWARE ARE AVAILABLE FOR USE IN BUILDING AN E-LIBRARY? WILL COMPUTER HARDWARE AND WEB SERVER OR OTHER E-LIBRARY SOFTWARE (E.G., CMS OR ERMS OR ILS) NEED TO BE PURCHASED OR OTHERWISE ACQUIRED? WHAT WILL IT COST? HOW WILL IT BE FUNDED?

If you determine that your library will need to purchase computers, an Internet connection, server software, or other related hardware and software, you'll need to investigate costs and funding. Many states are providing grant money to schools and public libraries for Internet projects. A U.S. federal agency, the Institute of Museum and Library Services (IMLS) also makes grants for a variety of library services, including electronic library projects, available through state libraries. Several types of grants are available, but the Library Services and Technology Act (LSTA) funding is the best known. The IMLS publishes a list of the chief officers at each state library with contact information at www.imls.gov/grants/library/gsla_cos.htm. At the Community of Science site (www.cos.com), a person can search for other library grant funding agency sites and companies that provide funding to support school and library Internet projects and other projects. The American Library Association Public Program Office (www.ala.org/Content/Navigation Menu/Our_ Association/Offices/Public_Programs_Office/Grants_and_Events/PPO_Grants_and_ Events.htm) regularly announces library grants opportunities. If you have at least a basic Internet connection you can use Web search tools to search for other sources of grants and funding information. A good strategy is to look at other e-libraries and learn what kinds of funding and support they have.

ARE PEOPLE AVAILABLE WHO HAVE THE TECHNICAL SKILLS AND SUBJECT AREA KNOWLEDGE TO PRODUCE AND MAINTAIN AN E-LIBRARY BY COLLECTING, EVALUATING, AND SELECTING RESOURCES AND INCORPORATING THEM INTO A WEB SITE?

The people who collect, evaluate, select, and organize the links will require basic and advanced Web searching and resource evaluation skills (see the "Web Information Evaluation Guidelines" section of this chapter). Knowledge of simple HTML elements and the URL format will be helpful for them as well. Those who create the Web pages will need to know how to author Web pages with HTML or an HTML editor, or they may need to be trained on how to input link information into a Web accessible database. Several previously cited authors have pointed out that the collection of Internet resources will be more efficient if the individuals chosen to collect resources in particular subject areas have some background in those subjects. Subject expertise will prove its value when appropriate e-resources are evaluated and selected for inclusion in the e-library. Depending on your choice, or the availability of a computer platform, the Web server, CMS, ERMS, or ILS software may require qualified computer professionals who are able to administer the computer system, Web server, and database software. In some cases you'll want a computer professional or other trained individual who is able to write scripts and programs in languages such as javascript, Java, PHP, Python, Perl, etc. Database programmers may also be necessary. Programmers will not be needed for simple HTML/XHTML and cascading style sheet (CSS) based Web sites. However, if your e-library make use of databases or will offer certain other types of interactivity, you will need a trained individual with at least basic programming skills and knowledge of database query languages.

HOW MANY PEOPLE/WHO WILL BE AVAILABLE TO PLAN, COLLECT, EVALUATE, AND SELECT E-RESOURCES, AND THEN TO MANAGE AND MAINTAIN THE E-LIBRARY? HOW MUCH TIME DO YOU ESTIMATE THAT RESPONSIBLE INDIVIDUALS WILL BE ABLE TO COMMIT TO PLANNING, COLLECTING, EVALUATING, AND SELECTING E-RESOURCES? HOW MUCH TIME DO YOU ESTIMATE THAT RESPONSIBLE INDIVIDUALS WILL BE ABLE TO COMMIT TO CONSTRUCTING AND MAINTAINING THE E-LIBRARY?

Constructing and maintaining e-libraries is very time consuming. Are personnel available who can spend time planning, implementing, and maintaining the e-library? Will you seek volunteers or students to assist in its construction and maintenance? Will you do all the work yourself? Will individuals be able to use paid "on-the-job" time or will they need to complete the work on unpaid personal time? Will you need to hire additional staff to support the e-library? Obviously, the more comprehensive you intend your e-library collection to be, the more time it will require.

How many people will be available to plan, collect, evaluate, and select e-resources and then to manage and maintain the e-library? The number of people needed to work on the e-library will depend on the scope of the e-library and the requirements for managing different forms of licensed e-resources. One person working with IT support can manage most small or very focused projects. One health sciences librarian maintains the Baptist Health e-library with support from the IT department of the Baptist Health system. Larger comprehensive projects, such as BUBL, require the participation of many subject librarians and technical support personnel.

WHAT KINDS OF TRAINING WILL RESPONSIBLE INDIVIDUALS NEED IN ORDER TO CREATE, MANAGE, AND MAINTAIN THE E-LIBRARY?

The answer to this question will vary depending on the staff you have available and the technical infrastructure of your e-library. However, any staff member who works on the e-library will benefit from solid training in four basic areas:

1. Knowledge of e-resource collection development tools and strategies
2. Detailed understanding of selection criteria and evaluation of information
3. Basic technology skills: Web browsing, search tools, applets for bookmarking and bibliography maintenance, and e-mail
4. Knowledge of one or more subject discipline's pattern of publication and user information-seeking behavior

Additional technical training may be appropriate for some staff members, depending on the kinds of IT support the e-library will require. Many librarians have found it necessary to learn to write or edit PHP, javascript, or database queries in the absence of other affordable IT support.

DEVELOPING AN E-LIBRARY COLLECTION DEVELOPMENT PLAN

Collection development (also known as collection management, materials management, or information resources management) involves the identification, selection, acquisition, and evaluation of library resources (e.g., print materials, audiovisual materials, and electronic resources) for a community of users. While it is the goal of collection development to meet the information needs of everyone in a user community, this is not ever entirely realized due to financial constraints, the diversity of user information needs, and the vast amount of available information.... Collection development is at the heart of what libraries do. It is in being able to meet the needs of individuals with the "right stuff" that we fulfill our missions. (*Collection Development Training for Arizona Public Libraries*. Accessed January 18, 2009 at www.lib.az.us/cdt/collman.aspx)

For nearly a decade the e-book *Collection Development Training for Arizona Public Libraries* (www.lib.az.us/cdt) has been updated and maintained on the Web. This e-book covers the collection development of all forms of information collected by libraries. It is a model for flexibility and user-focused library collection development.

A librarian without a collection development plan is like an airplane without a flight plan or jumping without a parachute or, as Peggy Johnson (2004, 2009) has been saying all along, "Libraries without collection development policies are like businesses without business plans" (72). A collection development plan is essential in guiding the selection of e-resources that will be included in the e-library. Without a clear collection development plan, collection development, management, and maintenance are needlessly more difficult. Collection management and maintenance are discussed in Part II, Chapter 5.

Several authors cited in the literature review provide some very fine overviews of good collection development planning. At its heart, an e-library collection development plan must rely on common sense and be user centered, not information object or container—for example, the book—centered choices and skills. A working collection development plan should provide a clear framework with flexibility in mind. A user-centered design is easier to keep flexible than is container centered collection design. User-centered design looks for the information needs of the user in whatever information objects they might be available. Information container centered planning looks at the management of the collection of the objects or containers that hold the information rather than looking to its development as a high quality source of information for users. The weeding section of any collection development plan, especially, must address obsolescence in advance—it will happen. E-resources will change forms, access locations or protocols, or simply go away. Print and other nonelectronic resources will need to be considered for storage or discard as and if they are used less or not at all.

If you have thoughtfully made your decisions in the collection development planning stage, building an e-library can be a routine part of overall library collection development. This checklist for drafting a user-centered collection development plan is a synthesis of the author's experience in building e-libraries and in learning from the experiences of other e-library builders:

1. What purpose will your e-library collection serve? For whom are you collecting e-resources?
2. What subject areas will you collect? What subtopics within those subject areas?
3. What types of e-resources will you collect?
4. What formats will you collect? Text (e-books, e-serials)? Multimedia (podcasts, video, etc.)?
5. How will you organize your e-resources? Will you use a CMS (or ERMS or ILS)? Will you catalog e-resources?
6. Will you plan to provide virtual reference services through your e-library? Asynchronous (e.g., e-mail) or synchronous (e.g., chat)? What other library services would you like to provide through your e-library? Why?
7. Will your e-library support distance learners? How? Who?

What purpose will your e-library collection serve? For whom are you collecting e-resources?

These questions are closely related. The purpose any library collection serves is contingent on the information needs of the communities of library users for which it is collected. The subject areas that will be included are defined by the purpose the library will serve for the intended community of library users. Selection criteria such as educational or reading level, professional, research, or recreational function or e-resources are formed from knowledge of the appropriateness for any given group of information users. Every library will have its own unique answer to these questions. There are no "right answers" or "best practices" in the details of the answers, but these are the right questions, and it is the best practice to ask them and find answers to them from your library's users.

Are your library's users members of the general public? Health care consumers? Children doing homework? In what subjects? Hobbyists? What hobbies? What ages and educational levels do the library users who will be using your e-library represent? Are you serving businesses? If so, what kinds of businesses? What kinds and levels of research will library users be doing? What subjects? Are they legal, medical, business, technical, or scientific professionals, teachers, graduate students, faculty, or undergraduates? Will your library users use the e-library for current awareness or recreation? The library user population characteristics will define the scope of your e-library subject coverage, establish the complexity level of resources collected, and outline the areas of information that will be collected. How will an e-library collection benefit your library users?

What subject areas will you collect? What subtopics within those subject areas?

In what subject areas do your library users need information? Nursing? Medicine? Business? Legal issues? Literature? Computer science? Reader's advisory? Recreational information? Music? Engineering? Geology? Zoology? Academic libraries tend to have an easier time identifying and prioritizing subject areas as they can use their organizations program and course listings as a guide. K–12 libraries have a similar structure to work within. Special libraries are guided by the nature of their parent organization's business, research, mission, etc. Public libraries have a major challenge to define the needs of the "general public," but they can be guided by experience, past circulation and reference statistics, and querying their users for their interests. Existing print collection development plans, if one exists, are an efficient way to begin. The University of Canterbury, Goddard College, University of Windsor, and many of the other e-library case studies in this book used their existing library collection development plans as the basis for e-library collection planning rather than developing completely new plans just for e-resource collection. Reviewing circulation and reference statistics as well as current database-use data can also inform the choice of subject areas and depth of subject that the e-library will include. If your e-library will serve distance learners, it will be desirable to know what programs and courses the e-library will be supporting.

What types of e-resources will you collect?

Some types of e-resource adapted to the digital environment and using Demas and colleagues' (1995) classic taxonomy as a foundation are the following:

- Directories (phone books, association, business, and organization directories)
- Dictionaries (English as well as international language translation dictionaries)

- Abstracts, indexes, and table of contents services (including those with full text of the journals and magazines indexed)
- Encyclopedias and almanacs
- Full-text and/or multimedia databases/digital libraries (collections of e-books, e-serials, recordings, videos, podcasts, images etc.)
- News and news services (current awareness) sources
- Key primary documents (company filings, laws, regulations, research data/reports, and statistical sources, etc.)
- Search engines
- Meta sites (e-resources that provide two or more of the other reference tool types in a single product/Web site)
- E-mail distributed discussions (such as, Listserv, Majordomo, or Listproc)
- Blogs, social networking tools, and other Web forums

The shapes that information takes when published on the Web is roughly analogous to the shapes it takes when published in print and some multimedia. The differences really have to do with the ways in which information and communication are patterned or shaped on the Web. Michael Sauers (2009) describes three aspects of how information and communication are patterned on Web 2.0: convergence, remixability, and participation.

"Convergence" describes the ways in which print (ink and paper and electronic), audio, video, and other sources of information although distributed on the Web have been brought together on the Web. Multiple forms of information have been made accessible via technical mechanisms including RSS (Really Simple Syndication), central databases such as Google (Books, Scholar, etc.) and Amazon.com's book search, and are globally searchable. This gives us a kind of central knowledgebase from which we can take advantage of the "remixability" of the data. We can pull the information from the converged sources and organize it into usable forms; for example, e-libraries, knowledgebases, research guides, etc. "Participation," professional and recreational, of humans through Web 2.0 communications tools then lets us share that content, that organized knowledge, with our colleagues and library users.

Will your e-library focus on e-resources that are free (or, rather, without direct cost to your library) or will the collection include fee-based resources that your library must pay for, negotiate licenses for, or participate in a cooperative arrangement to gain access? Freely available Web e-resources are not always the best resources, but when smaller or isolated libraries can mediate Web access to their library users they can often provide access to information they might not have been able to afford in the past. For example, every library regardless of size and location can have access to the full text of their own or any other U.S. state's law code or statutes, the full-text of the U.S. Revised Code, numerous international legal codes, as well as many other full-text legal information documents through the Legal Information Institute (www.law.cornell .edu). Even libraries that can't afford to purchase the large multivolume print set and updates or to purchase LexisNexis or Westlaw access can provide their library users with access to this information. LexisNexis and Westlaw are excellent Web-accessible legal and business research tools; however, they provide more content and searching power than many libraries need, and they are very expensive. Every library can now provide their library users with a searchable full-text and image database of patents and trademarks courtesy of the U.S. Patent and Trademark Office (www.uspto.gov) and the European Patent Office (www.epo.org). No longer is it necessary for everyone to pay for commercial patent database access or to purchase and maintain an expensive microform collection of patents. Granted, the USPTO patent and trademark databases do not allow the complex reporting and searching options that many special and academic libraries will need (commercial patent databases do provide the searching and reporting power required), but for everyone else the free patent search Web sites are invaluable.

WHAT FORMATS WILL YOU COLLECT? TEXT (E-BOOKS, E-SERIALS)? MULTIMEDIA (PODCASTS, VIDEO, ETC.)?

E-libraries can incorporate resources in many different formats. The main factor is whether library users will find them and whether they will want to use them. Audio files, podcasts in particular, are a popular course of information and learning among many scholars, music and medical students for example. Video may be a central format for e-libraries serving educators or who support a program in the performing arts or film-making.

HOW WILL YOU ORGANIZE YOUR E-RESOURCES? WILL YOU USE A CMS (OR ERMS OR ILS)? WILL YOU CATALOG E-RESOURCES?

E-resource organization is partially a matter of style and the persona of the organization. The simplest and probably the most accessible information structure for library user access is simple broad-subject organization, categorized by resource types and alphabetized under each subject and subtopic umbrella heading. Or, a library might want to have an organization based on their library divisions, departments, or branches; for example, periodicals department, special collections, medical library, or a particular branch library. There are many choices for organizing e-libraries, including Library of Congress, Dewey, unique taxonomies, as well as using the Dublin Core elements and MARC cataloging. BUBL uses the Dewey Decimal Classification (DDC) system. In *Information Architecture for the World Wide Web, Rosenfeld and Morville* (2006) describe the importance of rigorous adherence to international standards, the need to design with the users clearly in mind, and the specific criteria for usability and accessibility. This book is strongly recommended for anyone planning for the organization of an e-library collection. Using a CMS, depending on which product is chosen, can allow for multiple organizational and display options.

WILL YOU PLAN TO PROVIDE VIRTUAL REFERENCE SERVICES THROUGH YOUR E-LIBRARY? ASYNCHRONOUS (E.G., E-MAIL OR SYNCHRONOUS)? WHAT OTHER LIBRARY SERVICES WOULD YOU LIKE TO PROVIDE THROUGH YOUR E-LIBRARY? WHY?

It will be helpful to consider what services you will offer and to consider issues such as staffing, scope of service, costs of service, document delivery options, and other issues particular to your library and the library users you will serve. Once your collection plan is ready, collecting the resources to support the virtual reference service should be routine.

WILL YOUR E-LIBRARY SUPPORT DISTANCE LEARNERS? HOW? WHO?

Will the distance learners be professionals doing continuing education or getting an additional degree, undergraduates doing some on campus and some distance learning, or homeschooled children in the general population? What subject areas or professions are being served? What grade levels of homeschooled students will be served? Will the distance learners be local but outside of the physical library, or will they be in distant locations (e.g., another state or country)? Will the e-library need to include tutorials or instructions for using different resources? Will the e-library provide reference services or document delivery to distance learners? How? Both the Bainbridge Graduate Institute E-library Project and the Cambridge College Online Library e-library success stories detail how both of these libraries were developed entirely to support distance learners. Other libraries will also need to serve both distance and in-person users; for example, the Goddard College Library.

IDENTIFYING AND COLLECTING E-RESOURCES: USING THE WEB FOR COLLECTION DEVELOPMENT

The process of identifying and collecting e-resources is similar to that of identifying and collecting print resources. In collecting free Web resources, one difference is that the acquisitions process usually requires no financial or contractual exchanges. Licensing of fee-based e-resources is discussed in Part I, Chapter 3. This section discusses the various tools on and off the Web that you can use to identify, evaluate, and select e-resources. Core subject specific e-resource collection tools are included at the end of each chapter in Part II as appropriate. In general, you might use several types of collection tools.

Libraries collect reviews of books, multimedia, and e-resources in order to help both the librarians and the library users to make choices about specific information sources. Reader's advisory and print collection development tools are two sides of the same coin. Reader's advisory tools are the resources we use to help us recommend books to our library users that they may want to read for educational, recreational, or other reasons. Gerry McKiernan (2002) suggests that in addition to using the Web for Readers Advisory in the sense of bringing books and readers and readers and books together, that we also provide library database advisory services. He also lists a number of great readers advisory and database advisory services available on the Web.

Some collection development e-resources are designed specifically for the selection of reading matter and may be useful for both library users and library staff providing readers advisory services. For example, you might create a category called What Books to Read, which is then suborganized by nonfiction, fiction, fiction genres, and children's resources.

Print collection development tools are the resources we use to decide which books to acquire and include in the library collection to serve our library users educational, recreation, and other information needs. These same tools can be used for the collection of books, videos, and other locally held materials for our libraries. These types of information are especially useful for library staff making recommendations to library users or selecting print materials for acquisitions. Rabine and Brown (2000) recommend that a special collection development Web page or area be added to the library's e-library for the particular use of library staff. They also describe the kinds of tools that will be useful and recommend several specific sites. Nisonger (1997), Bybee and colleagues (1999), Rabine and Brown (2000), Schneider (1999), and Shook (2000) have written some of the most interesting of the classic articles about the use of the Web as a collection development tool. In more recent literature it is just "assumed" that the Web is a central tool for collection development. Nisonger (1997) was one of the first to write about the use of the Internet for support of collection development activities of all sorts. He identifies and describes in detail the relationship between the Web and collection management in libraries on three levels:

1. use of the Web to perform traditional functions for traditional materials (for example, using the Web to help select books and serials or evaluate the collection);
2. the application of traditional collection development functions to the Web (evaluation and selection of e-resources); and

3. the impact the Web's existence will have on traditional functions and materials (selecting fewer print resources because they can be accessed through the Web).

Nisonger and others envisioned the Web as one tool to use among other collection tools. They identified key Web sites, discussion lists (also called listservs), and e-mail. One of the most important benefits they describe is the use of the Web to work more efficiently by being able to see or ask about the collection policies and procedures of other libraries. The use of e-mail and other communications tools on the Web to learn about and communicate with vendors is another major asset. ACQWEB (www.acqweb.org/acqs.html) is the best and most complete collection development resource site.

Approximately every other year, the author has run surveys asking librarians to share which collection development tools they consider to be core or essential to their work. In May and August 2008, the survey was once again distributed. Past, present, and future surveys and results are posted at www.kovacs.com/misc.html.

The Collection Development Tools section at the end of this chapter and also on the companion Web Site (www.kovacs.com/ns/essentialguide.html) has been constructed for the past decade using these survey results as the main source of collection development tools. These collection development tools are selected for librarians to use as they build e-library collections. The discussion lists and blogs where the survey links were posted are listed in Table 1.1 earlier in this chapter. The collection development tools survey is reproduced in Table 1.8.

Print collection development tools are still well used. Table 1.9 lists the top five print collection development tools identified in the 2008 survey. The free Web sites that librarians reported as core or essential for collection development are numerous and reported in Table 1.10.

Table 1.8. Core Collection Development Tools Survey Questions

Collection Development Core Tools Survey: What books, journals, Web sites, etc. do you use to assist in making collection development decisions for both e-resources and print resources?

1. Which library type best describes the library you work in/for/with?
2. In which subject area(s) do you have collection development duties/responsibilities/role? (Check all that apply.)
3. What are the essential print titles (collection development related reference books) that you can't work without? (Please type the titles only—list up to three.)
4. What are the essential three free (not government published) Web-accessible collection development related Web sites that you can't work without? (Please type complete URL/Web address; e.g., amazon.com or barnesandnoble.com.)
5. What are the essential three (.gov) government published (state, federal, local, international) free Web-accessible collection development related tools that you can't work without? (Please type complete URL/Web address e.g., loc.gov.)
6. What are the essential three fee-based Web-accessible collection development related databases that you can't work without (Please type the simple title; e.g., Choice, BooksinPrint.com, etc.).
7. Does your library maintain a Web page or site to support collection development? If so please share the URL/Web address (e.g., http://lib.utsa.edu/Services/Collection_Development/cdtools .html).
8. Additional comments or ideas:

(Please include your name and e-mail address if you would like feedback, otherwise this survey form is completely anonymous.)

E-docs sites that support collection development have been cited from the earliest surveys. The top five e-docs used for collection development are listed in Table 1.11. The top five fee-based collection development e-resources are reported in Table 1.12.

Table 1.9. Top Five Print Resources Used as Collection Development Tools Identified in Survey

1. *Library Journal*
2. *ARBA: American Reference Books Annual*
3. *Booklist Reference Books Bulletin*
4. *Choice, Legal Information Buyer's Guide & Reference Manual, Ulrich's Periodicals Directory*
5. *Books in Print, Magazines for Libraries, School Library Journal*, other professional journals and publisher's catalogs.

Note: "None" and "Do not use print collection development tools" were the most frequent responses overall.

Table 1.10. Top Five Free Web Sites Used as Collection Development Tools Identified in Survey

1. Amazon.com: www.amazon.com
2. WorldCat: www.worldcat.org
3. Barnes & Noble: www.barnesandnoble.com
4. Google (Books, Scholar, etc.): www.google.com
5. Baker & Taylor: http://btol.com

Note: These sites got two votes each: AbeBooks (www.abebooks.com), Alibris (www.alibris.com), ALA (www.ala.org), and PBS (www.pbs.org).

Table 1.11. Top Five Government Documents Web Sites Used as Collection Development Tools Identified in Survey

1. Library of Congress: www.loc.gov (including Thomas and the LOC Catalog)
2. GPO Access: www.gpoaccess.gov/
3. Catalog of U. S. Government Publications: http://catalog.gpo.gov
4. FDLP desktop: www.fdlp.gov/
5. NLM LocatorPlus: http://locatorplus.gov/

Table 1.12. Top Five Fee-based Web Sites Used as Collection Development Tools Identified in Survey

1. Choice Reviews Online: www.cro2.org
2. Booksinprint.com: www.booksinprint.com/bip (including Global Books In Print)
3. Yankee Book Peddler: www.ybp.co/ (including YBP GOBI)
4. OCLC: www.oclc.org (various areas)
5. UlrichsWeb: www.ulrichsweb.com/ulrichsweb

Note: These sites got three votes each: EBSCOHost Electronic Journals Service (http://ejournals.ebsco.com), *Library Journal* (www.libraryjournal.com), RCLWeb Resources for College Libraries (www.rclweb.net), Doody's Core Titles (www.doody.com/dct). These sites got two vote each: Baker & Taylor's Title Source III (http://academiclibrary.btol.com), Novelist (www.ebscohost.com/novelist), *School Library Journal* (www.schoollibraryjournal.com).

WEB SITES THAT REVIEW AND EVALUATE E-RESOURCES: PEER E-LIBRARIES, SUBJECT COLLECTIONS/GUIDES, OR META SITES

The best place to look first for appropriate e-resources to collect is in other highly selective peer e-libraries, subject collections, guides, or meta sites. This strategy is analogous to searching other libraries' catalogs, searching OCLC Worldcat (www.oclc.org/worldcat), or using subject bibliographies to identify print or e-resources that other similar libraries with similar library user communities have selected.

A number of reliable peer e-libraries, subject collections, guides, and meta sites are included in the Collection Development Tools section. An annotated list of collection management and maintenance tools are appended to Part I, Chapter 3. Additional specific subject collection development tools are included with each chapter in Part II.

DISCUSSION LISTS (LISTSERV, ETC.), FORUMS/GROUPS, E-SERIALS, AND/OR BLOGS THAT POST OR PUBLISH REVIEWS AND EVALUATIONS OF E-RESOURCES

A second successful identification and selection strategy is to have each person responsible for collecting e-resources in a particular subject area subscribe to the core discussion lists and monitor the blogs related to that subject area. This strategy is analogous to asking colleagues in your library or subject specialists (e.g., faculty, researchers, physicians) through conversation in person, telephone, or postal mail for their opinions of library materials. Discussion lists and blogs are easy to find. Choosing which discussion lists and blogs will be most appropriate for a given subject can be difficult. Specific discussion lists (aka listservs) will be recommended in subsequent chapters.

COLLDV-L is a particularly active and useful discussion list for both print and e-resource collection development issues. Many discussion lists that focus on specific genres, authors, or even specific books can be identified using these tools. For example, the authors moderate DorothyL, a discussion list for people who read and write mystery books and related topics. Many librarians subscribe to DorothyL for reader's advisory purposes because readers post book reviews and authors and publishers post new book announcements.

Other discussion lists may be located by searching CataList: the official catalog of LISTSERV® lists (www.lsoft.com/lists/listref.html), FreeLists (www.freelists.org), Google Groups (http://groups .google.com) or Yahoo Groups (http://groups.yahoo.co).

Web logs, more commonly called blogs, are a good source of library-related news and print and e-resource reviews. Hundreds of library and information science related blogs are published and can be located using tools such as LibDex Library Weblogs (www.libdex.com/weblogs .html) and the Open Directory Project Library and Information Science Weblogs (www.dmoz .org/Reference/Libraries/Library_and_Information_Science/Weblogs) directories. Some examples include Gary Price's ResourceShelf (www.resourceshelf.com), Peter Scott's Library Blog (http:// xrefer.blogspot.com), John Hubbard's Library Link of the Day (www.tk421.net/ librarylink), and LIS-News, published by Blake Carver (www.lisnews.com) are four blogs that will be useful for anyone collecting e-resources. All of these blogs can be accessed using RSS feeds. LISFEEDS (www.lisfeeds.com) lists library and information science related podcasts, mp3s, and videos and provides complete access information as well as instructions for setting up your own RSS feeds. Webreference on RSS (www.webreference.com/authoring/languages/ xml/rss) also provides instructions on setting up RSS feeds. Tara Calishain's ResearchBuzz (www.researchbuzz.com) publishes sites with RSS feeds useful for researchers. LII's "New This Week" is also available through an RSS feed (http://lii.org/pub/htdocs/subscribe.htm).

E-serials that publish book reviews, written by librarians or other readers are also published on the Web. Most major and many smaller bookstore and publisher Web sites include book reviews as well. Many print journals and newsletters are now publishing electronic versions on the Web. These are discussed below. There are thousands of e-serials that publish reviews of e-resources. E-serials are those published only on the Web or distributed through e-mail. NewJour distributes e-mail announcements of new e-journals and newsletters to subscribers. The NewJour project archives (http://library.georgetown.edu/newjour) are a searchable directory of online journals and newsletters based on the NewJour distributions. Other collections of e-journals can be searched in JSTOR: The Scholarly Journal Archive (www.jstor.org) or the Directory of Open Access Journals (DOAJ) from the Budapest Open Archive Initiative (www.doaj.org). The SPARC Institutional Member Repositories (www.arl.org/sparc) are also good source of e-journals and other e-texts. The OPCIT (The Open Citation Project Reference Linking and Citation Analysis for Open Archives; http://opcit.eprints.org/explorearchives.shtml) site provides links to other e-journal and e-text archives.

One particularly useful e-newsletter is the Scout Report (http://scout.wisc.edu), which has been published continuously since 1994. The Internet Scout Project team collects and reviews e-resources and publishes the reviews in a weekly e-newsletter that is distributed through e-mail as well as published on their Web site. *D-Lib Magazine* (www.dlib.org) features a collection of e-resources each issue. Another good example is the Internet Tourbus e-newsletter published by Patrick Douglas Crispen and Bob Rankin. The Internet Tourbus is a "virtual tour of the best of the Internet, delivered by e-mail" (www.internettourbus.com).

PRINT BOOKS AND JOURNALS THAT REVIEW E-RESOURCES

All library and information science related journals as well as many other journals in other subject areas are now carrying regular columns or special issues that review a variety of relevant e-resources. Many of these print journals are archiving their e-resource reviews and other selected portions of the parent publication for free access on the Web or are available full-text online through fee-based e-journal subscriptions. Additional titles are included where appropriate in each of the subject chapters in Part II.

In the library profession, *Choice: Current Reviews for Academic Libraries* has been a standard collection development tool for all materials. *Choice* publishes Web resource reviews for resources in many general and specific subject areas. The reviews from previous years are archived on their Web site (www.ala.org/ala/mgrps/divs/acrl/publications/choice/index.cfm). *Booklist* (www.ala.org/ala/aboutala/hqops/publishing/booklist_publications/booklist/booklist.cfm) also publishes a "Reference on the Web" review section in each issue and archives the previous year's reviewed sites. The journals *College and Research Libraries News*, *American Libraries*, *Library Journal*, and others have also been publishing articles that evaluate and describe e-resources. One of the most useful and interesting is the "Internet Librarian" column in *American Libraries*. The column features discussions of different valuable, controversial, or otherwise interesting aspects of librarians' interactions with the Internet. The "Internet Librarian" columns and other articles from *American Libraries* are published on the Web site (www.ala.org/ala/alonline/index.cfm). *College and Research Libraries News* (www.ala.org/ala/mgrps/divs/acrl/publications/crlnews/collegeresearch.cfm) publishes Web resource reviews as well. Each issue features reviews of e-resources in some subject area. *Library Journal* (www.libraryjournal.com) also publishes reviews of both e-resources and print products.

WEB INFORMATION EVALUATION GUIDELINES

"The form of the materials is less critical than the quality of the ideas represented in those materials, and librarians and other stakeholders will continue to invest considerable effort in assessing the value of the materials they include in their libraries. In physical libraries, these efforts fall almost totally to librarians to select and acquire materials" (Pomerantz and Marchionini, 2007: 514).

We all use the same basic criteria for evaluating information every day. In evaluating information published on or through the Web it will be helpful to make those basic criteria explicit and to apply them consistently and rigorously. The real key is to know how to find the information that we need in order successfully to evaluate Web information. We may also need to teach our library users about Web information evaluation. In fact our role vis-à-vis Web information should be one of identifying, evaluating, and endorsing high quality sites. This section will discuss basic evaluative criteria, but more importantly it will discuss the specific places to look for the information that enable successful evaluation of a Web resource based on that evaluative criteria.

Quality of information on the Web varies precisely because anyone can publish or communicate information on the Web. In general, use the same criteria used to judge information from print or other media as well as the criteria we use to judge interpersonal communications. We must also consider some additional factors in evaluating Web information:

- Nature: awareness of the nature of Web information—stuff and good stuff on the Web.
- Problems: awareness and understanding of basic problems with information obtained from the Web.
- Source determination: how to acquire the information needed to determine the source of information obtained from the Web.

NATURE: AWARENESS OF THE NATURE OF WEB INFORMATION—STUFF AND GOOD STUFF ON THE WEB

In order to apply evaluation criteria to Web information, it is necessary to understand the nature, scope, and potential scope of information that can be found through the Web and including e-mail. A useful concept in explaining and teaching the nature of Web information is the concept of "stuff" and "good stuff." Most information on the Web is just "stuff"—irrelevant and sometimes unreliable. "Good stuff" is any of the information on the Web that is relevant to the information needs of a user and meets basic quality-of-information standards.

In general, "stuff" on the Web is found wherever people are expressing their opinions, ideas, and tastes, and providing their personal information. People just talking about recreational or personal matters using discussion lists, Web forums, social networking sites, chat, blogs, etc. make up a great deal of the "stuff" on the Web. It is important to keep in mind that a great deal of information on the Web is actually the transcripts or archives generated from these conversations. A noncomprehensive description of stuff on the Web includes the following:

- Personal Web sites that may offer valuable educational or research information, or recreation, entertainment, or one person's opinions
- Commercial sites that are just ads or that offer valuable information such as product support, directory services, tutorials, or other customer support services
- Government-generated information of all sorts—educational and research, recreation and entertainment, propaganda and misinformation—internationally, regionally, and locally

- Educational information from universities, colleges, schools, museums, and other organizations with educational missions
- Discussion lists, forums, social networking sites, chats, and blogs with educational, research, or professional intent or with recreational, entertainment, or opinion intent

Good Stuff on the Web

The reality is that one person's "stuff" might be another person's "good stuff." Personal or commercial Web sites may offer quality useful content. Discussion lists, Web forums, social networking sites, chats, and blogs may also supply high quality information either in ongoing conversation or in their archives on the Web. Web information types have their analogies in print and other media: a program on television can be something like *Entertainment Tonight*, or *The News Hour* with Jim Lehrer; a newspaper might be the *New York Times* or the *National Enquirer*; a talk radio program hosts might be Rachel Maddow, Diane Rehm, or Rush Limbaugh. Personal Web sites might contain only information about the opinions and personal life of an individual, or they might contain valuable educational, research, artistic, or recreation information. These can be valuable or useful for someone who is interested and needs the information they provide. For example, some excellent quilting, gardening, and history sites are published on personal Web sites by quilters, gardeners, and historians. Some of the best music, books, and movie reviews can also be found on personal Web sites. Commercial sites may simply be advertisements with no useful content, or they may provide access to product catalogs, technical support information, or e-commerce. Organizational pages may provide information for recreational, research, or educational interests that is useful or interesting for one user but not for another. Government Web sites generally provide information that is as good and sometimes better than governmental information provided in any other format. However, government Web pages may not include complete information or may restrict access to certain kinds of information.

The Web information "stuff" and "good stuff" concepts are useful as a loose model for clarifying the problem of classifying Web information. These concepts cannot help directly in solving the problems of evaluating e-resources as sources of information. This is because one person's "good stuff" might be another person's "stuff" or even another person's "bad stuff." Those assessing Web content simply cannot evaluate information based solely on the type of Web site or the domain address of the information provider. Librarians must explore other factors before they can render evaluative judgments.

We have discussed "stuff" and "good stuff," but as we all know, there is also "bad stuff" on the Web. "Bad stuff" is anything that you, your library users, or your community consider criminal, evil, or otherwise unacceptable. For example, for many people, racist, sexist, hate speech, violent antigovernment, historical revisionist, or pornography sites are "bad stuff." For some sociology, political science, criminal justice, or psychology researchers—especially where libraries, as opposed to private individuals, are concerned—these sites might be useful as sources for sociological, political, legal, psychological, or economic research.

PROBLEMS: AWARENESS AND UNDERSTANDING OF BASIC PROBLEMS WITH INFORMATION OBTAINED FROM THE WEB

Some basic problems with information obtained from the Web, or just about anywhere else for that matter, are listed here in order of their observed frequency on the Web:

- Typos
- Factual errors (accidental or deliberate)
- Opinion stated as fact
- Out-of-date information
- Bias
- Deliberate fraud

Typos

The information provided on the Web comes from many sources. Typos are one of the most prevalent problems because anyone can publish and often no editors or publishing agencies review the information. The two most likely causes of typos are inaccurate typing because of the informality of the medium and ignorance of the language. English tends to be the "lingua franca" of the Web, but many varieties or dialects of English exist. Some typos may in fact be spelling variants rather than errors, e.g., color or colour (Ballard and Gunther, 2003). "Typographical Errors in Library Databases" (http://faculty.quinnipiac.edu/libraries/tballard/typoscomplete.html) publish the results of their ongoing analysis of the typos that occur in library catalogs, Web sites, and other library related sources.

Factual Errors (Accidental or Deliberate)

These usually happen because people simply are not checking or sometimes are just recalling information from confused memories. During a search workshop taught by the author in 1993, the only answer we could find on the Internet to the question "What was the year of the first Thanksgiving?" was 1676. According to the Information Please: Online Dictionary, Internet Encyclopedia, and Almanac Reference (www.infoplease.com), the actual year of the first Thanksgiving is either 1621, 1789, or 1863 depending on whether you mean the first celebration or the year that it was declared a holiday by George Washington or Abraham Lincoln. The answer we found in 1993—at a site that no longer exists—was supplied by a sixth grader at a suburban Chicago school. This example is not meant to imply that sixth graders are always a source of inaccurate information. A sixth grader might publish accurate information if he or she acquires the facts from an authoritative source (teacher, reference book, or e-resource).

Opinion Stated as Fact

Web users can easily post their opinions on the Web. They may or may not present them as opinions. They may present them as facts. Evaluating the facts must take in the manner or style in which they are presented, the person expressing the opinion, the context, and the authority and credibility of the person expressing the opinion as fact. This problem is unhappily prevalent. Do you question the veracity of something just because of who published it, how the person said it, and where the person said it? Where the Web is concerned, yes, you must question the veracity of information based on who said it and how and where they said it. You have to ask, "Did the person/doctor/engineer/sixth grader have training, education, experience, or do research that gives him or her the authority to provide the opinion?" A related issue is the fact that the actual live person who publishes information on the Web can create an online identity that looks good but has no connection to the reality of the person's real life. This means that checking offline sources to verify authority and credibility of sensitive content (e.g., medical, legal, and some business and technical information) is essential. Can the person expressing the opinion as fact provide documentation/proof that what he or she says is accurate? What type of information is provided online to make these determinations? In the next section we'll discuss strategies for answering these questions about Web information. We do the same kinds of evaluation when we work with print and other media. Many editors and peer reviewers in some cases verify the author of a book, chapter, or article, their sources, research data, training, and background before accepting his or her work for publication. This editorial process does not always succeed but it is important. Libraries often rely on a publisher's reputation in making collection decisions. During the acquisitions process, librarians rationalize that if a particular publisher with a good reputation and known editorial process accepted and published a book, chapter, or journal, then it is very likely to be of good quality.

Web information evaluation is more difficult because it requires more primary research by librarians and users if it is to be done well. One unique factor is that much information on the Web is actually in the context of an ongoing conversation. Discussion lists, Web forums, social networking sites, chat, and blogs may be text based, but they are really more akin to speech than to publications. The difference between speech and published information is primarily formality of the language. A three-judge panel that heard the initial arguments in *ACLU v. Reno* (521 U. S. 844; 117 S. Ct. 2329; 1997) found that "tens of thousands of users are engaging in conversations on a huge range of subjects." Twelve years after that ruling it is more credible to say tens or even hundreds of millions of users. But it is no exaggeration to conclude that the content on the Web is as diverse as human thought. Some transcripts of this worldwide conversation are literate and/or authoritative, and others are not.

Out-of-Date Information

Considering how easy it can be to update Web pages and other Web information sources, the amount of out-of-date information online is surprising. But people don't always have the time or ability to update information or to take it offline when it is obsolete. Another problem is that the information may not be time stamped or dated. This happened recently when a very old news story about airline bankruptcy came up on a newsfeed without a date. Another example is student or teacher project Web sites that remain online long after the project is finished and the student graduates or the teacher moves on to other courses. Since so much information is in discussion list archives and Web forums, it is important to check the dates of the individual postings in such archives as well as on any other Web resource that might be included in your e-library collection.

Bias

Bias is a bigger problem with all sources of information than many people realize. Every publication medium has the potential to provide slanted information to influence how people think about something. An illustrative example is the "Dihydrogen Monoxide Research Division" (www.dhmo.org). The DHMO.org site uses hyperbole, negative statistics, and words that are meant to scare and alarm people; for example, dangers, alerts, truth, cancer, DHMO kills children. None of the information or facts are false. The bias used in presenting the information gives a skewed sense of the meaning of the information. Only when the user pauses to consider the elemental identity of dihydrogen monoxide does it become clear that this site is intended to illustrate the problems of bias. This site also illustrates the need for selection of resources that take into account educational attainment, reading level, and information needs. The reader needs to have at least some basic chemistry education. "Di-" (two-) hydrogen atoms, H_2, plus mono- (one-) oxygen atom, O, makes $H2O$. The DHMO.org site is all about water. Election campaign information is biased, almost by definition. For that matter, so is all advertising information. Probably every piece of information reflects bias of some kind due to the subjectivity of people doing the writing.

The degree, type of, intentionality, and reason for bias must be considered in evaluating information sources.

Deliberate Fraud

Deliberate fraud is a growing problem given the social nature of the Web. Medical, financial, and other consumer frauds are common. The best defense is to be skeptical of any claim that is too good to be true or is presented as a miracle. Know where to check to see if an offer or claim really is too good to be true. Advertising claims made on Web sites can be checked and frauds and other problems may be reported using the FTC: Bureau of Consumer Protection site (www .ftc.gov/bcp/index.shtml), on which the Federal Trade Commission reports ongoing Web and offline fraud investigations and warnings, or the Quackwatch Web site (www.quackwatch.com) for consumer health frauds. International and interstate business or financial frauds may a be verified by reviewing the U.S. Secret Service Advisories (www.secretservice .gov/advisories.shtml) of business and consumer scams, frauds, and related crimes, as well as terrorist threats being investigated by the U.S. Treasury law enforcement divisions. Other valuable sources of information are Quatloos! Cyber-Museum of Scams and Frauds (www.quatloos.com), Scamorama (www .scamorama.com), and Scambusters (www.scambusters.org).

SOURCE DETERMINATION: HOW TO ACQUIRE THE INFORMATION NEEDED TO DETERMINE THE SOURCE OF INFORMATION OBTAINED FROM THE WEB

Evaluation criteria for Web information can be reduced to five key concepts:

1. Purpose for the publication of the information
2. Authority and credibility of the information source
3. Accuracy of the information
4. Security of the information: Is the site liable to be hacked and information altered? Does the site request library users to submit personal or financial information? Privacy of the library user when using the information
5. Timeliness of the information in terms of whether it is intended to be current or historical information and the needs of the library user

It is useful to remember the mnemonic PAST: purpose and privacy, authority and accuracy, source and security, and timeliness.

These criteria can be verified if we can find information to answer the following five questions. In the following discussion these questions and strategies are clustered together because the strategies for finding the answers to the questions are similar or the same.

1. Who provided the information?
2. What is the purpose for which the information is being provided?
3. What is their editorial process or reputation of the editor, publisher, or information provider if any?
4. Do they have the authority or expertise to provide information on a given topic?
5. Is the information provided intended as current information or for historical purposes? Does currency affect the quality of the information? When was the last update of the information?

Reading carefully through a Web site should be sufficient to locate identifying information about the information provider and their authority as well as about the purpose for which the information is provided, their editorial process (if any), and whether or not it is meant to be current information or provided for historical purposes.

If you cannot, at least, find out who provided the information, then you cannot use it in a library, teaching, or research environment. Most librarians have been trained to cite a source when we answer a question. For example, earlier in this chapter we said, "According to the Information Please: Online Dictionary, Internet Encyclopedia, and Almanac Reference (www.infoplease.com), the actual year of the first Thanksgiving is either 1621, 1789, or 1863 depending on whether you mean the first celebration or the year that it was declared a holiday by George Washington or Abraham Lincoln." To find this answer, we first read through Web pages associated with the site. In this case we clicked on the "About" link at the bottom of the page and found that the publisher of this Web site is the same company that publishes the classic print *Information Please Almanac*. They have a fifty plus year history behind them. Furthermore, they provided contact information so we can telephone or e-mail to talk to a person. This is a best-case example.

Some Web sites do not provide such easy access to the information provider's identification information. To find the answers to these questions, the first thing you need to do is read carefully through the Web site. Most usable Web sites will provide an "About," "Who we are," or contact information in some manner. You may need to read through two or more pages, but it is necessary to read thoroughly and carefully through the site.

Recall the DHMO.org site we discussed earlier? Careful reading of the homepage shows that at the very bottom just above the copyright statement that identifies the person responsible for the site is a notice: "Note: content veracity not implied."

Use your Web browser options to look at the page or document info or the page or document source and look for possible author identification and/or publication date in <meta> tag fields. For example, if you look at the "Page Source" for www.kovacs.com, you will see: <meta name="Author" content="Diane K. Kovacs">.

If you still cannot find contact information on the Web page, or in the page source, and if the content is valuable enough (or you have reason to believe that contact information was left off inadvertently), then try looking up the Web site domain in a WHOIS server (accessed February 8, 2009, at http://en.wikipedia.org/wiki/WHOIS). WHOIS servers supply basic contact information for the owner(s) of a given domain name. Although some domain name owners elect to hide their identity, it is possible to find out at least that fact.

Once you have an identified information provider, the next step is to read through the Web site again to find out the education, experience, research background, or other qualifications the person claims in order to establish the authority and credibility of the information provider. If the authority information is not on the Web site and if the information is critical, e-mail the person or organization identified as responsible and ask them to answer the questions about their authority and credibility. There should be an e-mail address, Web form, or other contact information on a well-designed Web page. Lack of contact information may also indicate that no one is willing to take responsibility for the content of the Web page. If you have reason to believe that the attribution information was left out inadvertently and the information is valuable, here are some other strategies.

If you are a subject expert, use your own judgment or ask a subject expert to review the information. Find reviews of any given site by qualified reviewers or use selective subject directory/e-library collections to identify any additional information that other librarians have located.

When you are participating in or reading the archives of discussion lists, Web forums, social networking sites, etc., ask the writer to qualify himself or herself. There is nothing wrong with asking. There is nothing wrong with doing a search offline or in commercial databases to verify or validate the authority of an information provider. You can search either print reference or e-resources to see if he or she published anything else in print or other media, or you can search to verify that he or she is a licensed medical professional, engineer, member of a state bar association, or otherwise professionally qualified.

Verifying the security and privacy of Web information security and privacy are important features of accessing the Internet, because in essence there is no privacy on the Internet. If a Web site is not asking for personal or financial information, then the library user's security and privacy are of an issue. However, the fact that hackers can attack a Web site and alter its content directly impacts the user's ability to verify the information found there and to protect his or her own user information.

If security of personal or financial information is important, then use your Web browser functions to verify security of a Web page. You can set most browsers to warn you when you are entering or leaving a secure page. Secure Web servers ensure that only the intended recipient of your information can receive and use it. This is analogous to your calling an 800 number and ordering from a catalog. Putting your information into a form on an insecure Web page is analogous to giving out your credit card information over a cell phone or to someone who called you and solicited the information from you. Never include your credit card information or other personal financial information in an e-mail message. The one exception is if you are using some form of encryption on your e-mail.

Computer crackers have altered the information stored on a number of important Web sites, including the CIA Web site. Crackers can break into most standard Web servers unless great care is taken to configure and maintain server security. True information security requires excellent server security and a reliable certification and authentication system between the suppliers of the information and the Web server. This helps to ensure that only individuals authorized by the information provider may add or change information on the Web site. If privacy of information-seeking behavior is an important factor for you or your library users, then the Web might not be a good choice for you. There is no privacy on the Web.

Google your own name to see all of the Web published documents, discussion lists, etc. that your name appears in. Even when you transmit e-mail, your message passes through many servers and may be intercepted either accidentally or purposely. E-mail is easily printed or forwarded to others. When you connect to a Web page you can be counted and your movements through the site tracked. The Electronic Privacy Center (http://epic.org) provides a collection of tools (http://epic.org/privacy/tools.html) to test the privacy or lack thereof provided by your particular connection to the Internet. The collection also includes software tools to help ensure your privacy online. The best strategy to ensure privacy is to use an Internet-connected computer available to the public at a library or Internet cafe. Then the only thing Web site owners can discover about you is where you connected from and that someone there is interested in their site. However, library users should be aware that certain actions, such as visiting certain types of Web site or sending e-mail or other messaging that seems to threaten a prominent individual or national security, might trigger law enforcement action to track them.

Another issue related to security and privacy is the use of "cookies" by Web sites to record your activities and to store information like logins and passwords for your personal connections to their site. A "cookie" is described on Wikipedia (accessed February 8, 2009, at http://en .wikipedia.org/wiki/HTTP_cookie) in the following terms: "'HTTP cookies,' more commonly referred to as Web cookies, tracking cookies or just cookies, are parcels of text sent by a server to a Web client (usually a browser) and then sent back unchanged by the client each time it accesses that server. HTTP cookies are used for authenticating, session tracking (state maintenance), and maintaining specific information about users, such as site preferences or the contents of their electronic shopping carts."

Cookies are the Web equivalent of the "frequent shopper card." In exchange for marketing information and a certain loss of privacy, the library user may receive benefits, such as free and simple access to a site. However, use of browser cookies on public Internet computers may be problematic. If cookie-based registrations or logins are used at public Internet computers there is a danger that the next library user using that terminal will be able to access the private information of other library users.

Evaluation of reader's advisory and print collection development information is a simpler matter. The main criteria will be to identify who is writing the reviews and whether his or her credentials as a reviewer are acceptable in the context of the kinds of materials being reviewed. For example, a sixth grader may be a qualified reviewer of the books of Madeline L'Engle or J. K. Rowling.

E-Resource Selection Criteria

After analyzing e-resources selection criteria and collection development policies from many libraries, Pitschmann (2001) outlined the following selection criteria that apply to all sources of information but especially to e-resources selection:

- context: origin or provenance, content, relationship with other resources (e.g., aggregates);
- content: validity (authorship, authority, credibility), accuracy, authority, uniqueness, completeness, coverage, currency, and audience;
- accessibility (form/use): composition and organization, navigational features, adherence to standards, user support, terms and conditions of access, system integrity (stability and accessibility of the hosting system); and
- process or technical: information integrity (security, maintenance), site integrity (stability of the site over time).

Selection criteria for any kind of information resource are derived from the answers arrived at during the collection planning process. The most critical question is always: does the content and scope of information on the Web site meet an information need of the library's community of library users? If the collection plan has defined the intention and scope of the e-library, then use those factors to make initial Web resource selections.

E-resources have some unique selection criteria not shared with print or other physical formats. The key e-resource selection criteria are the following:

- Access and design
- Archiving
- Costs, licensing, and user access control

Access and Design

Access and design criteria for e-resources involve establishing user accessibility in terms of intellectual, physical, and technological access. The design of an e-resource is integral to access but also applies to the content scope and depth. The access and design questions that must be asked and answered (as well as is possible in terms of your e-library's users) are many:

1. Does the resource meet some information need of the e-library's intended library users?
2. Does the resource provide the information at a level and language suitable to the age, educational background, and subject interests of the e-library's intended library users?
3. Does the resource provide information in a document delivery or technology format that you want to include in your e-library?
4. Is the content unique, or is it readily available elsewhere?
5. Has copyright been respected?
6. Is the language accessible to the majority of your e-library users? Are headings clear and descriptive, or do they use jargon unknown to the average user? Is text well written with acceptable grammar and spelling?
7. If there is advertising, what is its relevance and proportion to the rest of the site?
8. Are there reviews of the e-resource? How many other sites link to this one?
9. Is a Web resource stable and consistent over time? Is it usually possible to reach the site, or is it overloaded? Is it stable, or has the URL changed frequently? Is the URL stated in the text of the Web page? Does the resource display in the Web browser within a reasonable amount of time over the expected mode of access?
10. Is the site open to everyone, or do parts require membership and/or fees? If there is a charge, what are the terms? Are any rules for use stated up front? Are the scope and limits clearly stated? Is the title informative?
11. Does the content fit the stated scope? Does the content meet the standards for accuracy, authority, timeliness, security, and privacy tested for during the evaluation process?
12. Is the site easily navigable with your Web browser? Do essential instructions appear before links and interactive portions? Do all of the parts work? Is using the site intuitive, or are parts likely to be misunderstood? Can you find your way around and easily locate a particular page from any other page? Is it obvious when you move to a new site, or does an outside link appear internal? Is the structure stable, or do features disappear between visits?
13. Is the site easily usable with your Web browser? Is the textual content of the individual Web pages concise, or do you have to scroll? Does it look and feel friendly? Are backgrounds or other visual elements distracting or cluttered?
14. If the site makes heavy use of multimedia or requires downloading of additional software, how will this affect any of your e-library users with older browsers, slower connections, or who are behind firewalls, or using filtering software, etc.?
15. Does the resource allow for access by disabled individuals who may need to use text-to-voice software or other enabling tools?
16. Is the site written in standard HTML/XHTML, or have proprietary extensions been used? Does it use standard multimedia formats? Must you download additional software to use it?

WAVE (http://wave.webaim.org) is a tool that allows you to submit the URL of a Web page and evaluates its physical and technical accessibility. Analysis is based on documentation from browser vendors when available. E-resources vary in accessibility.

ARCHIVING

Not every electronic version of an information product is superior to the print version. This is especially true if back files of an index or database are not available or not archived on the Web. Will the information provider provide "back issues" or archives of the resource? Will you need to make arrangements to store such information locally if needed? Will licensing agreements cover archiving options? This is especially important in the case of e-serials or current information that will become valuable historical information over time or ongoing scientific research information. The information may be archived in print publications, microform, on electronic storage media, or simply kept available on the Web for an indeterminate period as long as researchers are assured that it will be archived and available in the future. Obviously, researchers may prefer that it be archived in some format that is easily accessible. It is possible for libraries to negotiate licensing that includes the agreement that they may locally archive resources or make arrangements for archiving in a project such as the LOCKSS (Lots of Copies Keep Stuff Safe) project based at the Stanford University Libraries (www.lockss.org/lockss/Home). The free Web may be more ephemeral. The Internet Archive Project (www.archive.org), created by Brewster Kahle, attempts to archive free Web sites. For example, they have the American Library Association (ALA) site (www.ala.org) archived back to 1996 and has archived a different ALA site (http://ala8.ala.org) back to 1999.

COSTS, LICENSING, AND USER ACCESS CONTROL

Many e-resources are fee-based with various options for licensing. The library will need to give consideration not only to the cost of access to the e-resource but also to any licensing arrangements or user access control that must be exercised. For instance, will the resource be accessible only by users from within the library's domain, authorized IP addresses only, or can any library user from any location access the resource by using a login and password or library card number? Does the library have the necessary computer and systems resources to provide access to the resource given the terms of the license agreement? How will user authentication be achieved? Can the database be networked or be used with a locally developed end-user interface? What is the total cost of implementation? A librarian can almost always justify fee-based licensed access to an e-resource that meets other core selection criteria, if funding is available, by clarifying that any given e-resource can be accessible to a very large number of users both in the physical library and at remote locations through the e-library.

E-LIBRARY SUCCESS STORY

FLOWER MOUND PUBLIC LIBRARY
Flower Mound, Texas, United States
www.fmlibrary.net
Contact: Viccy Kemp, viccykemp@gmail.com

A. Collection Planning (e.g., goal setting and identification of users, technology/personnel choices)

The Flower Mound Public Library Web site was created only recently when the town of Flower Mound hired a Web master. The e-library collection has the simple goal of providing access to information for and promoting library services to the citizens of Flower Mound, Texas, and the surrounding towns in Denton County. "We are a public library with no desire to provide academic

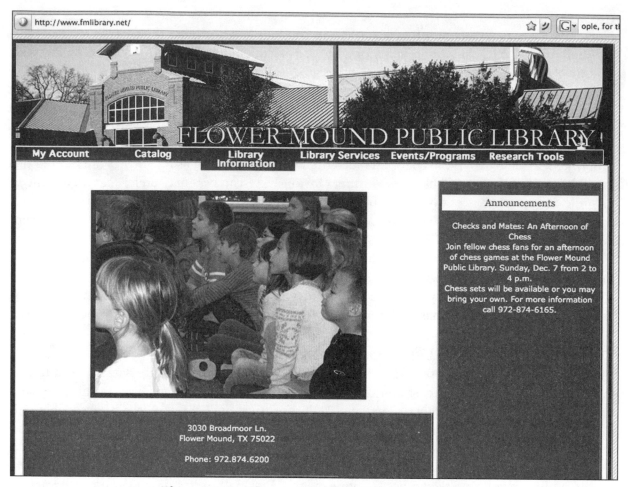

Figure 1.1. Flower Mound Public Library

or subject specializations for our users." A collection development policy is being written as user needs and library strengths and weaknesses are identified.

B. Collection Strategies (e.g., selection criteria, identification of resources, licensing, and related user information needs)

In building the e-library the most important criteria is cost of both resources and personnel. "Cost is our primary concern. The current budget for material acquisition is $100,000.00. The amount is not sufficient to allow the library to buy as many items as we need to serve our population."

Licensing agreements negotiated by the library allows remote access to one library card holder at a time. The e-library provides access to Reference USA (www.referenceusa.com), EbscoHost for Public Libraries (www.ebscohost.com/thisMarket.php?marketID=6), Facts On File (http://factsonfile.info basepublishing.com/newsservices.asp), Gale Virtual Reference Library (http://infotrac.galegroup.com), Magill's Medical Guide from Salem Health (http://health.salem press.com/?cookieSet=1), Morningstar Investment Research Center (www.morningstar.com), and NoveList (www.ebscohost.com/thisTopic.php?marketID=6&topicID=16). "The Library pays for access to the above databases from a Standing Order budget line, which is $61,000.00 this year. The State provides access to the Texshare databases (http://dev.texshare.edu/texshare/pl/) and the Library is assessed a fee for that access based on population and library usage."

E-books are provided through a contract with NetLibrary paid for by the town of Flower Mound. "The account must be set up within the library, but once that is done, the customer can access NetLibrary from home. No archiving or guarantees of access are made at this time. Usage Statistics are generated though a report from NetLibrary every month."

Although the library does not yet offer virtual reference sources, they do have a very well used interlibrary loan service. "Last year the Flower Mound Public Library conducted 1,243 ILL transactions."

C. Collection Organization (e.g., content management systems, Web server choices, personnel responsibilities, etc.)

Library staff provide content for the e-library site and select resources to be included in the collection based on user needs. The town's Webmaster posts the staff provided material and maintains the Web site. "Various staff members provide content. I write a monthly book review; other staff members write children's book reviews which are posted for an electronic newsletter that Town blasts to citizens once a month. This newsletter contains Library specific items such as programs scheduled through the month (Mother Goose Times; Storytimes; Anime club meetings, etc.)."

Collection responsibilities are still evolving. At this time there is no formal mechanism or process for suggestion new resources to be added. Library staff identify new e-resources as well as print materials and other media formats using professional journals such as *Library Journal*, *Booklist, Publishers Weekly, Brodart* (BIBZ.com), etc.

D. Collection Maintenance (e.g., link checking, ongoing weeding, and growth of the e-library collection)

The town's Webmaster does all of the site maintenance and any link checking that is done. The library is open to feedback from users and actively solicits suggestions for new services and resources. "All suggestions are considered. Cost and usage is a major deciding point. For example, FMPL will probably end its subscription to *Morningstar* based on that fact it is only used about eight times a month."

E-books are cataloged by the Flower Mound Public Library cataloger using batches of records sent from OCLC. No other resources are cataloged at this time. Future plans are limited by lack of staff and money, but ideally the e-library will grow in both collection and library services to serve the citizens of Denton County, Texas.

SOME FINAL THOUGHTS

Identification, evaluation, and selection of e-resources have become routine. Instead of being concerned with if we should do so we are more concerned with how we will do so most efficiently and effectively to serve the information needs of our libraries' users. Further discussion of e-resource selection criteria, especially access and design and archiving are discussed in the next two chapters. The management and maintenance aspects of e-resource selection are covered in more depth in Part I, Chapter 2. Licensing aspects of e-resources are discussed in Part I, Chapter 3.

REFERENCES AND WEB SITES CITED

Agee, Jim. 2005. "Collection Evaluation: A Foundation for Collection Development." *Collection Building* 24, no. 3: 92–95.

Ameen, Kanwal. 2006. "Collection Management Policy (CMP): A Framework to Achieve Library Goals." Available: http://eprints.rclis.org/6810/ (accessed December 31, 2008).

Ameen, Kanwal, and S. J. Haider. 2007. "Evolving Paradigm and Challenges of Collection Management (CM) in University Libraries of Pakistan." *Collection Building* 26, no. 2: 54–58.

Association of College and Research Libraries. 2006. "Changing Roles of Academic and Research Libraries." Roundtable on Technology and Change in Academic Libraries, November 2–3, 2006, Chicago, IL. Available: www.ala.org/ala/mgrps/divs/acrl/issues/future/changingroles.cfm (accessed January 7, 2009).

Baldwin, Virginia A. 2001. "Collection Development in the New Millenium: Evaluating, Selecting, Annotating, Organizing for Ease of Access, Reevaluating, and Updating E-Resources." In *Electronic Collection Management* (pp. 67–96), edited by S. D. McGinnis. Binghamton, NY: The Haworth Press. Available: http://digitalcommons.unl.edu/libraryscience/52/ (accessed January 14, 2009).

Ballard, T., and T. Gunther. 2003. "Typographical Errors in Library Databases." Available: http://faculty.quinnipiac.edu/libraries/tballard/typoscomplete.html (accessed January 14, 2009).

Blake, Virgil L. P., and Thomas T. Surprenant. 2000. "Navigating the Parallel Universe: Education for Collection Management in the Electronic Age." *Library Trends* 48, no. 4 (Spring): 891–922.

Borin, Jacqueline, and Hua Yi. 2008. "Indicators for Collection Evaluation: A New Dimensional Framework." *Collection Building* 27, no. 4: 136–143.

Bybee, Howard C., Patricia A. Frade, Shannon L. Hoffman, Robert S. Means, and Pao-Shan Wu. 1999. "Working the Web: WWW Strategies for Collection Development and Technical Services." *Technical Services Quarterly* 16 no. 4: 45–61.

Calhoun, Karen. 2006. "The Changing Nature of the Catalog and Its Integration with Other Discovery Tools." Prepared for the Library of Congress. Available: www.loc.gov/catdir/calhoun-report-final.pdf.

Cassell, Kay Ann. 2007. "Interviews with Collection Development Coordinators." *Collection Building* 26, no. 3: 91–93.

Casserly, Mary F. 2002. "Developing a Concept of Collection for the Digital Age." *portal: Libraries and the Academy* 2, no. 4: 577–587.

Clement, Susanne. 2007. "Skills for Effective Participation in Consortia: Preparing for Collaborating and Collaboration." *Collection Management* 32, no. 1/2: 191–204.

Connor, Elizabeth, and M. Sandra Wood, eds. 2007. *Electronic Resources in Medical Libraries: Issues and Solutions*. Binghamton, NY: The Haworth Press (published simultaneously as *Journal of Electronic Resources in Medical Libraries* 4, no. 1/2).

Cousins, J., S. Chambers, and E. van der Meulen. 2008. "Uncovering Cultural Heritage Through Collaboration." *International Journal of Digital Libraries* 9: 125–138. Available: http://portal.acm.org/citation.cfm?id=1473126 (accessed January 7, 2009).

Coutts, Margaret M. 1998. "Collecting for the Researcher in an Electronic Environment." *Library Review* 47, no. 5/6: 282–289.

Demas, Samuel G., P. McDonald, and G. Lawrence. 1995. "The Internet and Collection Development: Mainstreaming Selection of Internet Resources." *Library Resources and Technical Services* 39, no. 3: 275–290.

Dillon, Dennis. 2008. "A World Infinite and Accessible: Digital Ubiquity, the Adaptable Library, and the End of Information." *Journal of Library Administration* 48, no. 1: 69–83.

Dunham, Barbara S., and Trisha L. Davis. 2008. "Literature of Acquisitions in Review, 1996–2003." *Library Resources & Technical Services* 52, no 4: 238–253.

Duranceau, Ellen, and Cindy Hepfer. 2002. "Staffing for Electronic Resource Management." *Serials Review* 28, no. 4 (Winter): 316–320. Available: http://dspace.mit.edu/handle/1721.1/31207 (accessed January 14, 2009).

Ekmekcioglu, Cuna, and Dennis Nicholson. 2001. *An Evaluation of the Current Approach to Collaborative Collection Management in SCURL Libraries and Alternatives to Conspectus: Report and Recommendations on Collection Strength Measurement Methodologies for Use in SCURL Libraries. Final*

Report of the RSLP SCONE project Annexe A.2. Available: http://scone.strath.ac.uk/FinalReport/ SCONEFPNXA1.pdf (accessed January 7, 2009).

Fedunok, Suzanne. 1997. "Hammurabi and the Electronic Age: Documenting Electronic Collection Decisions." *RQ* 36, no. 1: 86–90.

Fenner, Audrey, ed. 2006. *Integrating Print and Digital Resources in Library Collection.* Binghamton, NY: The Haworth Press.

Genco, Barbara, and Raya Kuzyk. 2007. "20 Maxims for Collection Building." *Library Journal* 132, no. 15: 32–35.

Graham, Wayne. 2008. "Reaching Users Through Facebook: A Guide to Implementing Facebook Athenaeum." *The Code4Lib Journal* 5. Available: http://journal.code4lib.org/articles/490.

Gregory, Vicki L. 2000. *Selecting and Managing E-Resources.* New York: Neal-Schuman.

Guarino, Patricia H. 1998. "Making the Internet a Part of the Library's Collection." In *Public Library Collection Development in the Information Age*, edited by Annabel K. Stephens. Binghamton, NY: The Haworth Press.

Henry, Elizabeth, Rachel Longstaff, and Doris Van Kampen. 2008. "Collection Analysis Outcomes in an Academic Library." *Collection Building* 27, no. 3: 113–117.

Hiott, Judith, and Carla Beasley. 2005. "Electronic Collection Management: Completing the Cycle—Experiences at Two Libraries." *Acquisitions Librarian* 17, no. 33/34: 159–178.

Hirshon, Arnold. 2006. "Believing Six Impossible Things Before Breakfast: Electronic Resource Collection Management in a Consortial Environment." In *eLearning and Digital Publishing* (pp. 151–171), edited by Hsianghoo Steve Ching, Paul W. T. Poon, and Carmel McNaught. Available: www.scribd.com/doc/2151577/eLearning-and-Digital-Publishing.

Hoffman, Frank W., and Richard J. Wood. 2007. *Library Collection Development Policies: School Libraries and Learning Resource Centers.* Lanham, MD: Scarecrow Press.

Holleman, Curt. 2000. "E-Resources: Are Basic Criteria for the Selection of Materials Changing?" *Library Trends* 48, no. 4 (Spring): 694–711.

Hunter, Karen. 2007. "The End of Print Journals: (In)Frequently Asked Questions." *Journal of Library Administration* 46, no. 2: 119–132.

Intner, Sheila. 2001. "Impact of the Internet on Collection Development: Where Are We Now? Where Are We Headed? An Informal Study." *Library Collection, Acquisitions, and Technical Services* 25: 307–322.

Jacobs, Mark, ed. 2007. *Electronic Resources Librarianship and Management of Digital Information: Emerging Professional Roles.* Binghamton, NY: The Haworth Press.

Jascó, Péter. 2001. "Promoting the Library by Using Technology." *Computers in Libraries* 21, no. 8 (September): 58–61.

Jeng, Judy. 2008. "Evaluation of the New Jersey Digital Highway." *Information Technology and Libraries* (December): 17–24.

Johnson, Doug. 2007. "Managing the Intangible: Digital Resources in School Libraries." *Library Media Connection* (August/December): 46–49.

Johnson, Peggy. 1997. "Collection Development Policies and Electronic Information Resources." In *Collection Management for the 21st Century*, edited by G. E. Gorman and Ruth H. Miller. Westport, CT: Greenwood Press.

Johnson, Peggy. 2004. *Fundamentals of Collection Development & Management.* Chicago: American Library Association.

Johnson, Peggy. 2009. *Fundamentals of Collection Development and Management*, 2nd edition. Chicago: American Library Association.

Johnson, Richard K., and Judy Luther. 2007. "The E-only Tipping Point for Journals: What's Ahead in the Print-to-Electronic Transition Zone." Association of Research Libraries. Available: www.arl.org/bm~doc/Electronic_Transition.pdf (accessed January 7, 2009).

Keller, Michael A., Victoria A. Reich, and Andrew C. Herkovic. 2003. "What Is a Library Anymore, Anyway?" *First Monday* 8, no. 5. Available: http://firstmonday.org/htbin/cgiwrap/bin/ojs/index.php/fm/article/view/1053/973 (accessed February 8, 2009).

Kovacs, Diane K., and Angela Elkordy. 2000. "Collection Development in Cyberspace: Building an Electronic Library Collection" *Library Hi-Tech* 18, no. 4: 335–359.

Kovacs, Diane K., and Kara L. Robinson. 2004. *The Kovacs Guide to Electronic Library Collection Development: Essential Core Subject Collections, Selection Criteria, and Guidelines.* New York: Neal-Schuman.

Kupersmith, J. 2003. "Library Terms that Users Understand." Available: www.jkup.net/terms.html (accessed January 14, 2009).

Latham, Joyce. 2002. "To Link, or Not to Link." *School Library Journal* 48, no. 5 (Spring): 20–23.

Lewis, David W. 2007. "A Strategy for Academic Libraries in the First Quarter of the 21st Century." IDeA: IUPUI Digital Archive, University Library Faculty Research Collection. Available: https://idea.iupui.edu:8443/dspace/bitstream/1805/953/1/DWLewis_Strategy.pdf (accessed January 16, 2009).

Liu, Ziming. 2005. "Print vs. Electronic Resources: A Study of User Perceptions, Preferences, and Use." *Information Processing and Management* 42: 583–592.

Lord, Jonathan, and Bart Ragon. 2001. "Working Together to Develop Electronic Collections." *Computers in Libraries* 21, no. 5 (May): 40–45.

Lougee, Wendy Pradt. 2002. *Diffuse Libraries: Emergent Roles for the Research Library in the Digital Age.* Washington, DC: Council on Library and Information Resources. Available: www.clir.org/pubs/reports/pub108/contents.html (accessed January 7, 2009).

Marchionini, Gary. 2008. "Human–Information Interaction Research and Development." Library & Information Science Research 30: 165–174.

McCracken, Elaine. 2007. "Description of and Access to Electronic Resources (ER): Transitioning into the Digital Age." *Collection Management* 32, no. 3/4: 259–275.

McKiernan, Gerry. 2002. "Library Database Advisors—Innovative Augmented Digital Services." *Library Hi Tech News* 19 no. 4: 51.

Miller, Ruth H. 2000. "E-Resources and Academic Libraries, 1980–2000: A Historical Perspective." *Library Trends* 48, no. 4 (Spring): 645–671.

Morris, Kathleen, and Betsy Larson. 2006. "Revolution or Revelation? Acquisitions for the Digital Library." *The Acquisitions Librarian* 35/36: 97–105.

Morville, Peter S., and Susan J. Wickhorst. 1996. "Building Subject-specific Guides to Internet Resources." *Internet Research: Electronic Networking Applications and Policy* 6, no. 4: 27–32.

Myall, Carolynne, and Sue Anderson. 2007. "Can This Orthodoxy Be Saved? Enhancing the Usefulness of Collection Plans in the Digital Environment." *Collection Management* 32, no. 3/4: 235–258.

Nisonger, Thomas E. 1997. "The Internet and Collection Management in Academic Libraries: Opportunities and Challenges." In *Collection Management for the 21st Century* (pp. 29–57), edited by G. E. Gorman and R. H. Miller. Westport, CT: Greenwood Press.

Norman, O. Gene. 1997. "The Impact of Electronic Information Sources on Collection Development: A Survey of Current Practice." *Library Hi Tech* 15, no. 1–2: 123–132.

Phillips, Linda L., and Sara R. Williams. 2004. "Collection Development Embraces the Digital Age." *Library Resources & Technical Services* 48, no. 4 (October): 273–299. Available: www.accessmylibrary.com/coms2/summary_0286-14597547_ITM (accessed January 18, 2009).

Piontek, Sherry, and Kristen L. Garlock. 1995. "Creating a World Wide Web Resource Collection." *Collection Building* 1, no. 1: 12–18.

Pitschmann, Louis A. 2001. *Building Sustainable Collections of Free Third-party E-Resources.* Washington, DC: Digital Library Federation, Council on Library and Information Resources. Available: http://books.google.com/books?id=xf3ALkRlOr8C&printsec=frontcover&dq=Building+Sustainable+Collections+of+Free+Third-Party#PPP7,M1 (accessed January 14, 2009).

Pomerantz, Jeffrey, and Gary Marchionini. 2007. "The Digital Library as Place." *Journal of Documentation* 63, no. 4: 505–533.

Quinn, Aimee C. 2001. "Collection Development in the Electronic Library: The Future Isn't What It Used to Be." *DttP: Documents to the People* 29, no. 3: 11–12.

Rabine, Julie L., and Linda A. Brown. 1999. "The Selection Connection: Creating an Internal Web Page for Collection Development." *LRTS* (August): 44–49.

Rioux, Margaret A. 1997. "Hunting and Gathering in Cyberspace: Finding and Selecting E-resources for the Library's Virtual Collection." In *Pioneering New Serials Frontiers: From Petroglyphs to Cyberserials*, edited by Christine Christiansen and Cecelia Leathem. Binghamton, NY: The Haworth Press.

Rosenfeld, Louis, and Peter S. Morville. 2006. *Information Architecture for the World Wide Web*, 3rd edition. Sebastapol, CA: O'Reilly and Associates.

Rossi, Martha. 2008. "The Power of Partnership—Cooperative Online Resource Purchasing Programs." *Library Media Connection* (April/May): 58–60.

Rotich, Daniel C., and Evans M. Munge. 2007. "An Overview of Electronic Information Resources Sharing Initiatives in Kenyan Universities." *South African Journal of Library and Information Science* 73, no. 1: 64–74.

Sauers, Michael. 2009. *Searching 2.0*. New York: Neal-Schuman.

Schmidt, Karen, Wendy Allen Shelburne, and David Steven Vess. 2007. "Approaches to Selection, Access, and Collection Development in the Web World: A Case Study with Fugitive Literature." *Library Resources & Technical Services* 52, no. 3: 184–191.

Schneider, Karen. 1999. "Internet Librarian: Let Your Fingers Do the Collection Development—Online." *American Libraries* May: 100.

Schonfeld, Roger C. 2007. "Getting from Here to There, Safely: Library Strategic Planning for the Transition Away from Print Journals." *The Serials Librarian* 52, no. 1/2: 183–189.

Shook, G. 2000. "Web Acquisitions and Collection Development." *The Christian Librarian* (April): 52–53.

Skaggs, Bethany Latham. 2006. "Assessing an Integrated Government Documents Collection." *Collection Building* 25, no. 1: 14–18.

Sowards, Steven W. 1998. "A Typology for Ready Reference Websites in Libraries." *First Monday* 3, no. 5. Available: http://firstmonday.org/htbin/cgiwrap/bin/ojs/index.php/fm/article/view/594/515 (accessed January 14, 2009).

Su, Di, ed. 2007. *Collection Development Issues in the Online Environment*. Binghamton, NY: The Haworth Press.

Sutton, Allison M., and JoAnn Jacoby. 2008. "A Comparative Study of Book and Journal Use in Four Social Science Disciplines." *Behavioral & Social Sciences Librarian* 27, no 1: 1–33.

Sweetland, James H. 2000. "Reviewing the World Wide Web—Theory versus Reality." *Library Trends* 48, no. 4 (Spring): 748–768.

Tennant, Roy. 1998. "The Art and Science of Digital Bibliography." *Library Journal* 123, no. 17: 28–29.

Thornton, Glenda A. 2000. "Impact of E-Resources on Collection Development, the Roles of Librarians, and Library Consortia." *Library Trends* 48, no. 4 (Spring): 842–856.

Tonta, Yasar. 2001. "Collection Development of Electronic Information Resources in Turkish University Libraries." *Library Collection, Acquisitions, and Technical Services* 25: 291–298.

Uddin, Mohammad Nasir, and Paul Janecek. 2006. "The Implementation of Faceted Classification in Web Site Searching and Browsing." *Online Information Review* 31, no. 2: 218–233.

Walters, William H., Samuel G. Demas, L. Stewart, and Jennifer Weintraub. 1998. "Guidelines for Collecting Aggregations of E-resources." *Information Technology and Libraries* 17, no. 3 (September): 157–161.

Wood, Kelly. 2005. "Academic Libraries and the Print vs. Electronic Serials Debate." Paper for LIBR 520 Collection Management, University of British Columbia School of Library, Archival and Information Studies. Available: www.slais.ubc.ca/COURSES/libr559f/04-05-st1/portfolios/K_Woods/Files/serials paper.pdf (accessed January 7, 2009).

Wrubel, Laura S. 2007. "Improving Access to Electronic Resources (ER) Through Usability Testing." *Collection Management* 32, no. 1/2: 225–234.

Xie, Hong (Iris). 2006. "Evaluation of Digital Libraries: Criteria and Problems from Users' Perspectives." *Library & Information Science Research* 28: 433–452.

Yu, Holly, and Scott Breivold, eds. 2008. *Electronic Resource Management in Libraries: Research and Practice.* Hershey, PA: Information Sciences Press.

WEB SITES CITED

ACLU vs. Reno Supreme Court Decision. Available: http://caselaw.lp.findlaw.com/cgi-bin/getcase.pl?court=us&navby=case&vol=521&invol=844 (accessed January 16, 2009).

ACQWEB. Available: www.acqweb.org/acqs.html (accessed January 14, 2009).

American Libraries. Available: www.ala.org/ala/alonline/index.cfm (accessed January 14, 2009).

Booklist. Available: www.ala.org/ala/aboutala/hqops/publishing/booklist_publications/booklist/booklist.cfm (accessed January 16, 2009).

CataList: the official catalog of LISTSERV® lists. Available: www.lsoft.com/lists/listref.html (accessed February 8, 2009).

Choice: Current Reviews for Academic Libraries. Available: www.ala.org/ala/mgrps/divs/acrl/publications/choice/index.cfm (accessed January 16, 2009).

Collection Development Training for Arizona Public Libraries. Available: www.lib.az.us/cdt (accessed January 16, 2009).

College and Research Libraries News. Available: www.ala.org/ala/mgrps/divs/acrl/publications/crlnews/collegeresearch.cfm (accessed January 14, 2009).

DihydrogenMonoxide Research Division DHMO.org created by Tom Way. Available: www.dhmo.org (accessed January 14, 2009).

Directory of Open Access Journals (DOAJ). Available: www.doaj.org (accessed January 20, 2009).

D-Lib Magazine. Available: www.dlib.org (accessed February 8, 2009).

Electronic Privacy Information Center. Available: http://epic.org (accessed January 16, 2009).

Encyclopedia Britannica. Available: www.britannica.com (accessed January 14, 2009).

European Patent Office. Available: www.epo.org (accessed January 16, 2009).

FreeLists. Available: www.freelists.org (accessed February 8, 2009).

FTC: Bureau of Consumer Protection site. Available: www.ftc.gov/bcp/index.shtml (accessed January 14, 2009).

Google. Available: www.google.com (accessed January 14, 2009).

Google Groups. Available: http://groups.google.com (accessed February 8, 2009).

Information Please Almanac. Available: www.infoplease.com (accessed January 14, 2009).

Institute of Museum and Library Services (IMLS). Available: www.imls.gov (accessed January 2009).

The Internet Archive Project. Available: www.archive.org (accessed January 14, 2009).

The Internet Tourbus. Available: www.internettourbus.com (accessed January 14, 2009).

Jon Udell LibraryLookup. Available: http://weblog.infoworld.com/udell/stories/2002/12/11/librarylookup.html (accessed January 16, 2009).

JSTOR. Available: www.jstor.org (accessed January 20, 2009).

Legal Information Institute. Available: www.law.cornell.edu (accessed January 16, 2009).

LexisNexis/LexisNexis Academic. Available: http://academic.lexisnexis.com/online-services/academic-overview.aspx (accessed January 7, 2009).

LibDex Library Weblogs. Available: www.libdex.com/weblogs.html (accessed January 7, 2009).

Librarian's Internet Index. "New This Week." Available: http://lii.org/pub/htdocs/subscribe.htm (accessed February 8, 2009).

Library Journal. Available: www.libraryjournal.com (accessed January 14, 2009).

LISFEEDS. Available: www.lisfeeds.com (accessed February 8, 2009).

LOCKSS Program. Available: www.lockss.org/lockss/Home (accessed January 7, 2009).

NewJour. Available: http://library.georgetown.edu/newjour (accessed January 20, 2009).

Open Directory Project Library and Information Science Weblogs. Available: www.dmoz.org/Reference/Libraries/Library_and_Information_Science/Weblogs (accessed January 29, 2009).

Open Worldcat/OCLC Worldcat. Available: www.oclc.org/worldcat (accessed January 14, 2009).

Quackwatch. Available: www.quackwatch.com (accessed January 14, 2009).

Quatloos! Cyber-Museum of Scams and Frauds. Available: www.quatloos.com (accessed January 16, 2009).

ResearchBuzz. Available: www.researchbuzz.com (accessed February 8, 2009).

Scambusters. Available: www.scambusters.org (accessed January 16, 2009).

Scamorama. Available: www.scamorama.com (accessed January 16, 2009).

The Scout Report. Available: http://scout.wisc.edu/Reports/ScoutReport/Current (accessed February 8, 2009).

SPARC Institutional Member Repositories. Available: www.arl.org/sparc (accessed January 20, 2009).

U. S. Patent and Trademark Office. Available: www.uspto.gov (accessed January 16, 2009).

U. S. Secret Service Advisories. Available: www.secretservice.gov/advisories.shtml.

Wayback Machine. Available: www.waybackmachine.org.

Web4lib archives. Available: http://lists.webjunction.org/web4lib.

Webreference on RSS. Available: www.webreference.com/authoring/languages/xml/rss.

Westlaw/Westlaw Campus. Available: http://campus.westlaw.com (accessed January 7, 2009).

Who Am I? Available: www.mall-net.com/cgibin/whoami.cgi?src=webcons.

Yahoo Groups. Available: http://groups.yahoo.com/ (accessed February 8, 2009).

COLLECTION DEVELOPMENT TOOLS
(USEFUL FOR READER'S ADVISORY)

META SITES

ACQLink
http://link.bubl.ac.uk/acqlink
> UK based Web site that supports acquisition and collection development library activities.

ACQWEB
www.acqweb.org
> Web site and discussion for acquisitions and collection development librarians. Note that this site is moving to Ibiblio.org, but as of December 30, 2008 it has not yet permanently relocated.

AllReaders.com Home Page
www.allreaders.com
> Reader's advisory tool recommends books by plot, theme, character, and other options.

Amazon.com
www.amazon.com
> Online bookstore that has searchable database of over 2.5 million books in and out of print. Reviews from professional review sources as well as reviews by readers.

Beaucoup
www.beaucoup.com
> Over 2,500 search sites, including topics of parallel/Meta, Reviewed/What's New, Music, Science, Health, Employment, etc.

Booklist
www.ala.org/ala/aboutala/hqops/publishing/booklist_publications/booklist/booklist.cfm
> This is the "digital counterpart of the American Library Association's *BookList* magazine." It reviews thousands of the latest books (adult, children, reference), electronic reference tools, and audiovisual materials.

Booktv.org
www.booktv.org
> A great site for interviews with authors, summaries of books, and information on the publishing industry. "Each weekend, Book TV on C-SPAN2 will feature 48 hours of nonfiction books from 8am Saturday to 8am Monday. This Web site will enhance information on those books, provide an opportunity to watch or listen to programs you might have missed, and provide additional information not available on the cable network."

BUBL/5:15
http://bubl.ac.uk
> Highly selective, relevant, librarian-evaluated resources in all academic subject areas.

Choice: Current Reviews for Academic Libraries
www.ala.org/ala/mgrps/divs/acrl/publications/choice/index.cfm

Collection Development Training for Arizona Public Libraries
www.lib.az.us/cdt/
> Web-based collection development training published by the Arizona Department of Library, Archives, and Public Records.

College and Research Libraries News Internet Resources
www.ala.org/ala/mgrps/divs/acrl/publications/crlnews/internetresources.cfm

Archives and index to articles regarding Internet Resources from 1998 to present. The Internet Resources wiki allows for updating of these articles http://wikis.ala.org/acrl/index.php/Internet_resources_wiki.

C&RL News Internet Reviews

www.ala.org/ala/mgrps/divs/acrl/publications/crlnews/internetreviews.cfm

Archives and index to Internet Review columns from 1994 to present.

David Magier's Library World Bookmarks

www.columbia.edu/~magier/libworld.html

Categorized (outline format) links to all kinds of sites related to libraries and librarians.

Digital Librarian

www.digital-librarian.com

Selected "best of the Web" resources maintained by Margaret Vail Anderson, a librarian in Cortland, New York.

DOAJ: The Directory of Open Access Journals (from the Budapest Open Archive Initiative)

www.doaj.org

More than 10 percent of all journals published are included in the DOAJ at this time.

Gelman Library Research Guides

www.gwu.edu/gelman/guides/index.html

This resource has annotated lists of important information sources (including subject-oriented Web pages) in specific subject areas.

Glossary—Abebooks

http://dogbert.abebooks.com/docs/HelpCentral/Glossary/buyerIndex.shtml

This comprehensive list of book-related terms relating to book sizes, book condition, common abbreviations, and a general glossary is included as well.

Glossary of Bibliographic Information by Language

http://staff.library.mun.ca/staff/toolbox/lang/biblang.htm

Terms are divided by language and do not appear in alphabetical order, but with the use of your browsers "find in page" feature this should be easy to use.

Gutenberg Project

www.gutenberg.org

Since 1971, Michael Hart has coordinated volunteers who are transcribing the text of public domain books into electronic format. Nearly 7,000 e-books are available free through the Project Gutenberg Web sites.

HERO: Library Resources

www.hero.ac.uk

Resources reviewed by librarians at colleges and universities in the UK. HERO: Higher Education and Research Opportunities in the UK.

INFOMINE: Scholarly Internet Resource Collections

http://infomine.ucr.edu/

"INFOMINE contains over 14,000 links. Substantive databases, electronic journals, guides to the Internet for most disciplines, textbooks and conference proceedings are among the many types of resources."

InFoPeople Project

www.infopeople.org

What started as a project to provide public access in the library has evolved into training opportunities for information specialists as well as online guides and links to information technology. The project "improves the quality of information access to the people of California by upgrading the skills, resources and tools available through libraries."

Internet Scout Project

http://scout.wisc.edu

> Annotated links to the different activities of the Internet Scout project, including the Scout Report (and its archive), toolkits, and blog.

Intute

www.intute.ac.uk

> Intute is a multisubject e-library maintained by a consortium of United Kingdom university and academic organization Library partners (www.intute.ac.uk/about.html) who carefully select and evaluate all the health and life sciences e-resources that are open source or otherwise freely available on the Web. Pieces of it were previously known as BIOME, OMNI, BIORES, and other smaller databases. Although hosted in the UK, the scope of these collections is international. The scope of the collection includes arts and humanities, health and life sciences, science engineering and technology, social sciences, and related fields. The collection is searchable and browseable.

Intute: Virtual Training Suite

www.vts.intute.ac.uk

> Collection of Internet research tutorials for multiple academic subject areas.

Librarians' Internet Index

http://lii.org

> Evaluated, annotated, and searchable collection of Internet resources (academic and popular) organized by subject. *LII News* e-newsletter announces newly added sites and other news about LII.

National Library of Australia: Find

www.nla.gov.au/find

> Selective collection of evaluated Web resources that are easy to browse and search. Also contains subject lists of e-mail discussion groups, online newspapers by country, and reference materials.

Neat New Stuff We Found This Week

http://marylaine.com/neatnew.html

> Listing of links of various choice sites with a comment about each. Most sites listed are informational, but few may considered "just for fun."

NewJour Archives

http://library.georgetown.edu/newjour

> NewJour is a directory of e-serials that are published on the Internet either through e-mail or on the Web. NewJour has been compiling e-serials since 1993. The NewJour mailing list announces new e-serials as they are made available. Ann Shumelda Okerson, Associate University Librarian, Yale University, and James J. O'Donnell, Provost, Georgetown University developed the NewJour project.

North Carolina State University Library—Electronic Resources by Subject

www.lib.ncsu.edu/subjects

> Listing and links to research, reference, database, and journals.

Overbooked

www.overbooked.org

> Reader's advisory tool specializes in literary and genre fiction information. Includes author Web pages and annotated lists of nonfiction, fiction, and mystery book reviews.

Pinakes: A Subject Launchpad, Heriot-Watt University, Edinburgh, United Kingdom

www.hw.ac.uk/libWWW/irn/pinakes/pinakes.html

Prepub Alert

www.libraryjournal.com/community/Book+Reviews/47112.html?layout=sectionsMain&verticalid=151&industry=PrePub%20Alert

Lists publishing information and provides a synopsis for upcoming fiction and nonfiction in the months ahead.

PubList

www.PubList.com

Undergoing technical improvements at this time. Site is still searchable for free in-depth information relating to 150,000 periodicals worldwide.

The Reader's Robot: A Reader's Advisory Service

www.tnrdlib.bc.ca/rr.html

Visually attractive collection of genre fiction and nonfiction book reviews. Search on by a concept called "appeal." Select a genre, then a mood, style, plot theme, etc.

Reference Reviews Europe Online

http://rre.casalini.it/rreo.htm

Fee-based with some free content collection of reviews of reference books published in Europe.

WebExhibits

http://webexhibits.org

Novel collections of art, culture, and science Web sites. Hundreds of exhibits. Sponsored by the U. S. Department of Education, National Gallery of Art, Brandeis University, and others.

Webrary: Search MatchBook

www.webrary.org/rs/matchbooksearch.html

Morton Grove Public Library reader's advisory tool to match the reader with the books they will find interesting.

whichbook.net

www.whichbook.net/sounded/index.html

Choose books by mood and style, etc.

Wired for Books

http://wiredforbooks.org

Ohio University sponsored site that publishes book reviews and RealAudio readings.

World Wide Web Virtual Library

http://vlib.org

Individuals maintain the separate collections of this library at separate locations. Contact person listed at each site. Oldest catalog on the Web. High quality, annotated collection of searchable Internet resources arranged by subject. The entire central database may be downloaded for use by other e-library collectors.

DIGITAL LIBRARIES DIRECTORIES OR COLLECTIONS OF DIGITAL LIBRARIES (DIGITAL LIBRARIES OF E-BOOKS, E-SERIALS, IMAGES, RECORDINGS, AND OTHER ARTIFACTS)

Association of African Universities, Database of African Theses and Dissertations

www.aau.org/datad/database/login.php

Brewster Kahle builds a free digital library | Video on TED.com

www.ted.com/index.php/talks/brewster_kahle_builds_a_free_digital_library.html

California Digital Library

www.cdlib.org

An integrated Web gateway to digital collections, services, and tools.

Claremont College Digital Library

http://ccdl.libraries.claremont.edu/collections.php

Council on Library and Information Resources (CLIR) Reports

www.clir.org/pubs/reports/reports.html

Reports on all aspects of digital and e-libraries collections, management, planning, and building.

DMC: OhioLINK Digital Media Center

http://dmc.ohiolink.edu

E-LIS

http://eprints.rclis.org

> International open repository of E-Prints in Library and Information Science.

Escholarship Editions, California Digital Library

www.escholarship.org/editions

> "The eScholarship Editions collection includes almost 2,000 books from academic presses on a range of topics, including art, science, history, music, religion, and fiction...over 500 of the titles are available to the public. Print versions of many of the electronic books can be purchased directly from the publishers."

Escholarship Repository, California Digital Library

http://repositories.cdlib.org/escholarship

> Open source repository of scholarly articles, reports, books submitted by University of California units.

Europeana

http://europeana.eu/portal

> The European digital library opened to overwhelming interest. Crashed. Should be back online in October 2009.

Google Book Search

http://books.google.com

> Full-text book databases with multiple issues regarding copyright and publishers lawsuits in the works. The current settlement is complex. (Posted on COLLIB-L: In the google books code to insert a search box onto your page-which you can get at https://services.google.com/inquiry/books_email? hl=en-add <input name="as_brr" type="hidden" value="1" /> to the end of the form code before the form closes. This sets the default to full-text view only, although patrons are able to change it back as soon as the results show up.)

Google Scholar (Citation Index)

http://scholar.google.com

> Index/search tool for scholarly articles across disciplines. Some articles are archived in open-access databases and others are citations only with links to the publisher's sites.

IMLS Digital Content Gateway

http://imlsdcc.grainger.uiuc.edu

Internet Archive Project

www.archive.org/index.php

Internet Archive and Open Content Alliance Project

www.opencontentalliance.org

> Purpose is to scan and/or archive as many open-access texts as possible and archive them. Some overlap with the Gutenberg project, but this project collects current and future texts as well as retrospective content.

JSTOR: The Scholarly Journal Archive

www.jstor.org

> Archives of open access initiative journals specifically focused on scholarly journals. Fee-based with some free access.

Librarian's E-Library

www.google.com/coop/cse?cx=015271347771663724636%3Acmwvisovdsg

NetLibrary (OCLC)
www.oclc.org/netlibrary/default.htm

Odeo
http://odeo.com/
Search free mp3s, audio, television files, etc.

Open Library (Open Library)
http://openlibrary.org
> Creating a Web page, catalog record using multiple classification options, for every book published. Links from book pages to Gutenburg project, Internet Archives, Worldcat, and to bookstores. This project is a partnership with the Internet Archive Project (www.archive.org/index.php) and uses the Open Archives Initiative protocols (www.openarchives.org).

Open-access Text Archive
www.archive.org/details/texts

OpenDOAR
www.opendoar.org
> OpenDOAR is an authoritative directory of academic open access repositories. Each OpenDOAR repository has been visited by project staff to check the information that is recorded here. This in-depth approach does not rely on automated analysis and gives a quality-controlled list of repositories.

Project MUSE
http://muse.jhu.edu/about/muse/index.html
> Searchable archives of scholarly journals. Fee-based with some free access.

SPARC Institutional Member Repositories
www.arl.org/sparc/
> Scholarly journals archiving projects.

E-SERIALS, BLOGS, DISCUSSION LISTS, AND DIRECTORIES OF E-SERIALS, BLOGS, AND DISCUSSION LISTS, ETC.

ACQNET
http://lists.ibiblio.org/mailman/listinfo/acqnet-l
> Discussion list for acquisitions and collection development librarians.

ALCTSDEU
http://lists.ala.org/sympa/info/alctsdeu
> ALCTS Duplicates Exchange Union

American Library Association Mailing List Service
http://lists.ala.org/sympa/lists
> ALA mailing lists along with subscription options and archives where available.

BACKSERV
http://lists.swetsblackwell.com/mailman/listinfo/backserv
> Focuses entirely on the informal exchange of serial back issues and books among libraries.

CataList: the official catalog of LISTSERV Lists
www.lsoft.com/lists/listref.html
> Nearly 100,000 public discussion lists run on the LISTSERV software all over the world.

The Charleston Review
www.charlestonco.com
> Critical reviews of Web Products for Information Professionals. Articles, reports, reviews, and much more on this site.

Choice: Current Reviews for Academic Libraries
www.ala.org/ala/mgrps/divs/acrl/publications/choice/index.cfm
> "Timely," "Concise," "Authoritative," and "easy-to-use" reviews by experts of books and electronic media.

COLLDV-L
http://serials.infomotions.com/colldv-l
> Moderated: discussion for library collection development officers, bibliographers, and selectors plus others involved with library collection development, including interested publishers and vendors.

Collections 2.0 Content and Community the Future of Library Collections Blog
http://collections2point0.wordpress.com

CONSDIST
http://cool-palimpsest.stanford.edu/byform/mailing-lists/cdl
> Discussion list of collection and preservation of library, archives, and museum materials.

Current Cites
http://lists.webjunction.org/currentcites

D-Lib Magazine
www.dlib.org/dlib.html

DOROTHYL
www.dorothyl.com
> Discussion of mystery literature—good reader's advisory discussions. Begun in 1991.

FreeLists
www.freelists.org
> Free mailing list host site with directory of hosted lists.

Friends: Social Networking Sites for Engaged Library Services
http://onlinesocialnetworks.blogspot.com

Google Groups
http://groups.google.com
> Archives of many Usenet news feeds as well as current mailing lists and other similar resources.

Internet Resources Newsletter
www.hw.ac.uk/libWWW/irn/irn.html
> "A free newsletter for academics, students, engineers, scientists & social scientists." Published by Heriot-Watt University Library.

The Internet Tourbus
www.tourbus.com
> "TOURBUS is a free e-mail newsletter published twice a week, and read by about 100,000 people in 130 countries around the globe" that provides "in-depth reviews of the most useful, fun and interesting sites on the Net." Archived.

LibDex
www.libdex.com
> Directory of libraries with a Web presence.

LibDex: Library Weblogs
www.libdex.com/weblogs.html
> Index of blogs relating to librarianship and information specialists.

Librarians' Internet Index "New This Week"
http://lii.org/pub/htdocs/subscribe.htm
> E-newsletter and RSS feed for announcing newly added e-resources.

Library Journal
www.libraryjournal.com/community/Book+Reviews/47112.html
"LJ combines news, features, and commentary with analyses of public policy, technology, and management developments. In addition, some 7,500 evaluative reviews written by librarians help readers make their purchasing decisions: reviews of everything from books, audio and video, CD-ROMs, websites, and magazines."

LibWeb
http://lists.webjunction.org/libweb
Directory of libraries with a Web presence.

LISFEEDS
www.lisfeeds.com
Collection of library and information science related podcasts, mp3s, videos and other related multimedia.

Net-Gold
http://groups.yahoo.com/group/net-gold
Discussion/distribution list maintained by David Dillard, Temple University jwne@temple.edu. Additional archives and subscription options: http://groups.yahoo.com/group/net-gold, http://listserv .temple.edu/archives/net-gold.html, http://groups.google.com/group/net-gold?hl=en, http://net-gold .jiglu.com.

Open Directory Project Library and Information Science Weblogs
www.dmoz.org/Reference/Libraries/Library_and_Information_Science/Weblogs
Directory of library and information science blogs.

ResearchBuzz
www.researchbuzz.com
"News about search engines, databases, and other information collections."

Scholarly Electronic Publishing Bibliography
www.digital-scholarship.org/sepb/sepb.html

Shelf Awareness: Daily Enlightenment for the Book Trade
www.shelf-awareness.com/index.html
E-newsletter for libraries, bookstores, etc., regarding reviews, awards, selling/buying trends, etc.

Special Libraries Association Discussion Lists
www.sla.org/content/community/lists/divisionlists5979.cfm
Discussions for all types of special libraries.

WebWatch
www.libraryjournal.com/community/Book+Reviews/47112.html
Monthly online review of the best Web sites dealing with monthly (usually social or information issues) subject.

World Wide Web Library Directory
http://travelinlibrarian.info/libdir
Directory of libraries with a Web presence.

Yahoo Groups
http://groups.yahoo.com
Yahoo Groups new incorporates the discussion lists hosted by several smaller services, for example egroups.com. Search for the discussions in which you are interested.

2

BRINGING IT ALL TOGETHER: SOME GENERAL CONSIDERATIONS FOR BUILDING, ORGANIZING, MANAGING, AND MAINTAINING E-LIBRARIES

A library is more than a pile of books. A library adds value to information resources by organizing them and making them available. Additionally, a library serves distinct sets of shareholders: communities of frequent, casual, and potential users. Unlike museums, it is seldom the materials in libraries that attract people but rather the ideas carried by the materials, the conceptual structures that support access and the community of stakeholders who use the library. Because books and other physical information resources and people occupy physical space, libraries have evolved complexes of buildings, rooms, and mobile spaces in which books and other materials and people come together. These spaces are manifestations of the library as place. Place, however, is more than physical space....Places are defined by functions and communities....These fundamental characteristics of libraries—systematic access to information resources, the ideas represented by those resources, and sets of human stakeholders—also extend to digital libraries. (Pomerantz and Marchionini, 2007: 505–506)

INTRODUCTION

The quote that opens this chapter is from an article by Pomerantz and Marchionini (2007) in which they describe the concept of the library as a place—whether that place is physical or virtual. Both library places store and organize information. Both library places are managed and maintained by people (librarians, administrators, etc.) for people (library users and communities). Both library places select information to store and organize to support access by users. "We believe that libraries are fundamentally spatial, but that the definition of space must be broadened: the most critical element of this space may not be that it is either physical or virtual, but that it is intellectual" (Pomerantz and Marchionini, 2007: 528).

Building an e-library is an ongoing process. Identifying, evaluating, selecting, and collecting e-resources are just the beginning. Once the e-resources are collected they must be organized, managed, and maintained. This process will eventually include "weeding" and will always include "shelf-reading"—that is, link checking and site verification in the Web context. This chapter provides information and background for organizing, managing, and maintaining your e-library collection.

BUILDING AND ORGANIZING THE E-LIBRARY

The simplest e-library construction is a Web page with links and annotations. The creation of a Web page with links and annotations for collected e-resources is relatively simple. All that is required is a basic knowledge of HTML/XHTML and a text editor or wysiwyg (what you see is what you get) HTML editor. HTML editors all require knowledge of HTML/XHTML to a greater or lesser degree in order to be used effectively, which is not to say that you couldn't cobble something together with them even if you knew nothing of HTML, XHTML, or cascading style sheets (CSS). The author uses Dreamweaver with BBEDIT to work on the companion Web site but is in the process of converting the site to use the Drupal CMS (content management system). See the Web Developer's Virtual Library (http://wdvl.internet.com/Reviews/HTML) for reviews of free and fee-based HTML editing software.

You may also choose to make your e-library available on the public Web or via an internal intranet (intraorganizational TCP/IP [transmission-control protocol/Internet protocol] network). The Baptist Health e-library case study in Part II, Chapter 8, describes their e-library collection as available only on the parent company's intranet and only to those with logins and passwords on that intranet.

INFORMATION ARCHITECTURE

Organizing information is how we begin to form knowledge. Knowledge is essentially information organized and connected in meaningful patterns. Information architecture is organizing, labeling, and enabling search and navigation systems, and "[t]he art and science of shaping information products and experiences to support usability and findability" (Rosenfeld and Morville, 2006: 4).

Usability and findability are the goal of organization, labeling, search, and navigation systems. Usability requires understanding of the information seeking needs and behavior of the intended users. A well thought out and carefully crafted e-library information architecture should make the e-library resources usable and findable by its users.

Organizing a simple Web page or collection of pages (Web site) is limited to the simpler kinds of flat organization such as subject, subtopic, resource type, and alphabetical organization. Labeling and annotation are the aspects that enable searching and also the users' ability to browse the page(s) to locate the e-resources they will want to access.

Organizing an e-library, just as in organizing a physical library, also means defining areas or space where users can socialize or study or interact with one another. Social networking tools can easily be integrated into simple Web sites and tailored to the individual needs of libraries and users. This has the further effect of projecting a welcoming presence from the library to the users in the e-library. Something as simple as adding a link to a form or e-mail address to allow users to interact with library staff is viewed by users as a positive. A library social networking presence can also be linked to and from the e-library; for example, through Facebook (Graham, 2009; Mitchell, 2006). The library becomes part of the Web community through its e-library.

As discussed in the previous chapter, there are many choices for organizing e-libraries, including traditional Dewey and Library of Congress, Dublin Core Metadata (discussed more fully in the "Cataloging E-Resources" section), taxonomies, folksonomies, tagging, and more. In the physical library, classifications systems organize the storage and retrieval of the information containers stored there. Web site classification systems define the virtual library space itself. Information architecture is an exercise in classification. The classification scheme is derived from the information content and then also describes the space and the navigation structures for users of that information.

In a fascinating example, Uddin and Janecek (2006) developed a faceted classification system using Ranganathan's criteria to create a taxonomy and thesaurus. This classification was implemented to define the information architecture of the e-resource collection. They implemented their taxonomy using a CMS. The classification scheme, thesaurus, or facets are stored in a knowledgebase in the relational database component of their CMS. The content and an index to the content are were also stored in the relational database. The user interface component of their CMS enabled searching and navigation as well as search retrieval display options by making use of the content, index, and classification schemes mediated by the user's decisions. They based their taxonomy on Ranganathan but they began with an analysis of the user's information needs and the information content, subject, scope, and depth. They derived four categories of knowledge required for planning a taxonomy and then building the e-library:

1. Purpose—why the document/information will be used;
2. Topic—"aboutness" of the document/information object, subject addressed;
3. People—person concerned/described by the document; and
4. Area—space or places of the document. (Uddin and Janecek, 2006: 226)

To make use of these user mediated and content specific complex information architectures the e-library must be created using Web relational database tools such as content management systems (CMS) or some form of integrated library system (ILS). ILSs are essentially library catalog software that integrates e-resources management options with other library catalog functions. An ILS is usually a CMS and an ERMS with a library catalog. Our catalogs have been our content management systems when our content was primarily print books and journals.

CONTENT MANAGEMENT SYSTEMS

Content management systems (CMS) are Web platforms used to manage and publish information content: "A CMS can provide organised workflow, cataloguing and metadata tools and can separate the content from its presentation layout and design by a template builder. Thus, it is important in reducing the workload of managing a large web site, such as the tedium in creating, moving, deleting and organising the contents by many members" (Uddin and Janecek, 2006: 223).

Generally speaking, CMS software is used to organize e-resources for display, searching, and retrieval. A related kind of software electronic resource management systems (ERMS), are primarily for managing and maintaining e-resources collections; that is, for tracking subscriptions, license details, archival status, acquisitions details, and costs. An ERMS may serve as a CMS and vice-versa. In this chapter, CMS are discussed under the topics of organization and information architecture and ERMS are discussed under the topics of management and maintenance.

From the time of publication of *Building Electronic Library Collections* in 2000 to the first edition of this text in 2004 and now, it seems less likely to find the same person(s) identifying, selecting, evaluating, and collection e-resources also managing and maintaining the software and hardware through which the e-library is made accessible. This book emphasizes collection development of the e-library rather than the selection of software and hardware on which to make the e-library available. For the most part, databases and hardware are managed and maintained if not specifically selected by IT staff, hopefully in partnership with the library. That said, to work in partnership with IT staff, and to manage content within a given system, it is helpful to have some basic knowledge of the current technology. In some cases librarians will need to learn enough to be able to choose, implement, manage, and maintain e-library related software with minimal or no IT support. Grace Lillevig, eBranch Librarian, Harris County Public Library, and her colleagues chose, implemented, and now manage and maintain the Drupal CMS as their e-library system (personal communication, February 10, 2009, www.hcpl.net/drupal). In another example, the Health InfoNet of Alabama e-library (success story in Part II, Chapter 4), is managed and maintained by the IT staff at the National Institutes of Health (NIH). Librarians manage content and work in partnership with the IT staff to ensure usable and accessible information architecture.

Given the wealth and diversity of e-resources available for incorporation into e-libraries, many libraries are using a Web-accessible database or a CMS to organize e-library collections. CMS also incorporate search and navigation options and may make the e-resources more accessible. This section reviews source for learning more about CMS and the technical terminology that you will encounter. This review is for individuals with no Web server administration experience and is as basic as I can make it.

Five Things We Really Need to Know about Content Management Systems

1. Content management systems are relational database based e-resource and Web site management tools. Not all relational databases are CMS, but all CMS have a relational database component.
2. CMS can be structured like blogs, storefronts, catalogs, wikis, and combinations of these concepts. The listed forms are usually fairly simple to install and plug information into using defaults.
3. Standard XHTML and external CSS underlie the programming and structure of most high quality/usable CMS. You must understand/be able to create with Web standards to choose and use CMS well to design the sites managed. Terminology related to CMS will be reviewed in this chapter.
4. CMS can be commercial (e.g., Collage, Ektron, etc.) or "open source" (Drupal, Evergreen, etc.) software. Neither form is inexpensive. Open source, although usually free of direct costs, can be more expensive to implement than commercial alternatives given required technical and programming support, high speed high end network and computer storage, and long term maintenance requirements. Commercial CMS may not include that required support in the base costs. Verify carefully the actual costs of either choice in the context of your organizations needs and existing support.
5. Open source and commercial CMS are easy to locate. CMS Watch on the Web Content Management Channel (www.cmswatch.com/CMS/Vendors/?printable=1) maintains a list of current CMS vendors both commercial and open source with reviews of each and links to full-text articles topics related to CMS choices.

Other good sources of CMS information are the CMS Review Listing (www.cms review.com/CMSListing.html) and OSS4LIB the open source software and libraries blog (http://oss4lib.org). Other open source options can be found in Source Forge (http://sourceforge.net/). Search for "Content Management System" or "CMS" to see a long list of open source CMS options.

Many great CMS options are open source, but require a fairly high level of technical skills to install, set up, and maintain. Commercial options may offer technical support. BUBL and INFOMINE both utilize CMS software that was custom programmed within their own organizations. Some of the best open source CMS options are from these kinds of sources. See Open-Source Initiative at http://en.wikipedia.org/wiki/Open_Source_Initiative.

In the Library Vocabulary surveys sent to librarians in May and in August 2008, librarians were asked if their libraries used either a CMS or an ERMS, and if so, which software did they use? Table 1.1 in the previous chapter lists the discussion lists and blogs where the survey was posted. Table 1.2 in the previous chapter reproduces the survey questions. Past, present, and future surveys and results are posted at www.kovacs.com/misc.html. Table 2.1 contains the interesting result that relatively few of the respondent's libraries were using either types of software.

ERMS software used most frequently by respondents are listed in Table 2.2. Many people reported that they knew their library used some form of ERMS but did not know what it was. A good number of respondents report using ERMS tools that are built into or offered as an additional service of their ILS.

Of those who reported using a CMS to organize their e-library collections there was great variety in the choices and an equal number using open source software as were using commercial software. Table 2.3 reports the most frequently mentioned CMS software in the survey.

Table 2.1. Does your library use a Content Management System (CMS) or Electronic Resource Management System (ERMS)?

Answer Options	Response Frequency	Response Count
Yes	31.2%	159
No	68.8%	350
	Answered question	509

Table 2.2. ERMS Software Mentioned Most Frequently by Respondents in Library Vocabulary Survey in Order of Frequency

1. Serials Solutions 360 Resource Manager: www.serialsolutions.net/index.html
2. Innovative Interfaces (III) ERM: www.iii.com/products/electronic_resource.shtml
3. ExLibris Verde (ERMS): www.exlibrisgroup.com/category/VerdeOverview
4. Follett Destiny: www.follettsoftware.com/sub/destiny_solutions

Table 2.3. CMS Software Mentioned by Respondents in Library Vocabulary Survey in Order of Frequency

1. ContentDM: www.contentdm.com
2. DSpace: www.dspace.org
3. Drupal: http://drupal.org
4. Cascade Server (CMS): www.hannonhill.com/products/cascade-server/index.html
5. EBSCO's A-to-Z: www2.ebsco.com/en-us/ProductsServices/atoz/Pages/index.aspx
6. Vignette: www.vignette.com
7. DigiTool: www.exlibrisgroup.com/category/DigiToolOverview
8. Estrada CMS: www.estradacms.com/513
9. Joomla: www.joomla.org
10. PLONE CMS: http://plone.org
11. Sakai: http://sakaiproject.org/portal
12. Ektron: www.ektron.com/index.aspx

Example CMS on Library Web Sites

These sites were chosen because they were recommended by colleagues participating in one of the e-library collection development courses taught by the author:

- Alliance Library System Virtual Library Second Life Info Island Project's written collection development plan is available on a site using the Drupal CMS (http://infoisland.org/drupal/collections).
- Georgia Library Public Information Network for Electronic Services (PINES) developed Evergreen (http://gapines.org/opac/en-US/skin/default/xml/index.xml). Evergreen is an ILS. Open source software, documentation, and lists of other libraries using Evergreen is available at www.evergreen-ils.org.
- University of Nebraska at Kearney is using Ektron (http://rosi.unk.edu, www .unk.edu/website/ektron/index.php?id=2191 or www.ektron.com).
- University of Minnesota Libraries developed LibData (http://courses.lib.umn .edu). The open source code is available from http://libdata.sourceforge.net).
- St. Cloud State University is using LibData (http://research.stcloudstate.edu).
- Ithaca College Library developed SubjectsPlus (www.ithaca.edu/library or www.ithacalibrary.com/subsplus).
- University of Michigan Graduate Library developed Research Guide (www.lib .umich.edu/grad/guide). The open source code is available from http://research guide.sourceforge.net.
- University of Notre Dame is using myLibrary personalized library portal software under development by Eric Lease Morgan and colleagues (http://dewey.library.nd .edu/ mylibrary). Development site can be found at http://mylibrary.library.nd.edu.
- LibraryThing for Libraries (www.librarything.com/forlibraries) is another option.

E-LIBRARY COLLECTION MANAGEMENT AND MAINTENANCE

"The biggest drawbacks with e-resources are cost, the fact they are all on different interfaces, they are difficult to keep track of after you get them (true for books, but worse for e-resources, particularly when you get them through a consortial arrangement) and the fact that you cannot search across them in one search" (Kara L. Robinson, Reference and Instruction Librarian, Kent State University, personal communication, February 10, 2009).

In this section, we use the phrase "e-library collection maintenance and management" to refer to management and maintenance of the collection of e-resources that make up the e-library. Although this may rely on server, hardware, database management, and maintenance, this section is more interested in the information content and objects that are being managed and maintained with that technology foundation.

E-library or rather E-resource collection management and maintenance is the part of collection development that includes user needs assessment or information seeking behavior studies, evaluation or assessment of the e-library collection, archiving and preservation, cooperative collection development, and policy development in the context of budgeting for and licensing e-resources. E-resource collection management policies both inform and emerge from the collection development policy.

User needs assessment (including information seeking behavior studies) establishes the subject(s) scope and depth of the information to be collected and the information delivery mechanisms that are most accessible and usable as the first step in collection development. The user needs assessment process continues in the process of growing and maintaining the e-library. The evaluation or assessment of the e-library collection in terms of subject coverage and scope and quality of content in the context of usability is necessary for managing growth and maintenance in the context of budgeting. How that evaluation or assessment is performed may be the most critical aspect. Do you compare the collection to other collections or to a list of titles that "should" be in a certain type of collection? Do you assess the collection's usefulness, accessibility, and usability for the intended users? Or do you try to accomplish both?

Budgeting is the process of detailing available personnel and time as well as money. If an e-library were a garden, then the person detailing the budget would be the head gardener. The time, effort, and money that the gardener(s) is able to put into the garden are critical to the success of the garden in the same way that time, effort, and money put into an e-library are critical to ensure its success.

Archiving and preservation in the e-library is similar in intention to that of the physical library, except that the archiving and preservation take place in virtual or digital space. Knowledge and understanding of the technologies required and their limitations is essential. Storing a digital object is a different technical challenge than storing a physical object.

Myall and Anderson (2007) suggest that a written collection management policy section be included in the collection development plan for each library. They suggest that librarians "Abandon the pursuit of perfection and comprehensiveness that has dogged many library collection projects" (251–253) and acknowledge the subjective nature of collection development and assessment to ensure workable collection management plans based firmly in the realities of budgeting.

There are some obvious questions that must be asked and answered in managing e-library collections that don't necessarily apply to print or other physical formats:

1. How do we select or collect e-resources appropriate for library user needs and balance and prioritize within a budget? What is meant by the concept "select" or the concept "collect"?
2. How do we evaluate or assess the e-library? In terms of the titles collected? Subject coverage? User satisfaction? What specifically—what object or container or content—is selected or collected?

3. What is the difference between access and ownership in terms of managing e-resources? How do we apply inventory control to e-resources?
4. How do we balance print and e-resources to best serve current and future library users?
5. What does it mean to archive and preserve e-resources?
6. What does it mean to weed or deselect e-resources?

The following sections address some of the tools and strategies that libraries can use for e-resource management and maintenance in general. Cooperative collection development, and licensing e-resources will be discussed in Part I, Chapter 3.

EVALUATING OR ASSESSING THE E-LIBRARY COLLECTION

Collection analysis or assessments are performed to supply information to clarify the e-library's goals in the context of its mission and budget, justify budgeting priorities, and inform ongoing management and maintenance of the e-library.

> Without collection evaluations that provide a clear assessment of available resources, future collection management budgeting, format consideration, selection, or de-selection may be inefficient and at risk. Librarians in large or small libraries can employ the collection evaluation methods in this article to gain meaningful information about their own holdings. Wise collection building is dependent on a foundation of current resource assessment. (Agee, 2005: 95)

In "Collection Evaluation: A Foundation for Collection Development," Jim Agee (2005) discusses several approaches to evaluating or assessing any library collection. Given the more virtual and more user centered nature of e-libraries, the user-centered evaluation and the assessment of specific subject scope and depth are likely to be the most functional.

Borin and Yi (2008) reviewed a large number of both user centered and collection centered evaluations and assessment studies in order to get a sense of which methods were the most effective at gathering data to address e-library collection management questions and then to build a model and develop some guidelines for e-library assessment. Their study identifies several factors that assessment and evaluation can and should address that will be useful in informing ongoing e-library collection management and maintenance. A summary of these:

1. Use ratios to help balance hybrid collections e.g., ratios of print to e-resources, books to journals, e-books to books, etc.
2. Balance user centered and collection centered evaluation guidelines.
3. General capacity of the collection, including its age and size and whether it is meeting the needs of intended users.
4. Use subject specific standards for those areas of a collection instead of looking at entire collection at once.
5. Look at the scholarly publishing environment(s) for specific subject areas and compare the e-library collection to the output from those forms.
6. Evaluate collection usage. How do users use the collection? What interest is there among users in using the collection? Evaluate user accesses such as viewing, printing, downloading, etc.
7. User studies including focus groups, surveys, etc. looking at user actual activities and/or thoughts and opinions while using or not using the e-library collection.

8. Environmental factors including the goals and purposes of the organization or community served by the e-library. What is taught? What is the budget? What new programs and growth are planned? How does the organization or community compare with other similar organizations or communities?

9. Comparisons with other similar e-libraries and especially those in consortial relationships.

Answering the questions described in the previous section will require at least minimal user needs studies, some basic collection content assessment, and a clear description of the library's goals and budgeting.

User needs assessment in our e-library context can be reduced to two simple questions:

1. Who is using the e-library and what are they using it for?
2. Who do we want to use the library and what would they want to use the e-library for?

Question number one can be answered easily, if not comprehensively, by a simple Web form or link to a librarian's e-mail address on the e-library Web site that encourages users to evaluate and comment on the e-library Web site contents and organization. All of the e-library success stories in this edition make use of these simple but reliable feedback mechanisms to inform ongoing maintenance of the e-library and for consideration for e-library management choices.

This kind of feedback will allow you to make informed decisions about how well your e-library is serving your library users. However, straight "mailto" links may attract spammers who use spiders to troll through Web pages looking for e-mail addresses to steal. Web forms and some fairly good javascript e-mail link security scripts may prevent this kind of problem.

User needs and collection assessments, in the most practical sense, are conducted by librarians as part of their daily routine in working as intermediaries between their users and their collections:

> User services are enhanced by good collection development and management skills. In many large academic libraries, the subject specialist selects materials for a specific discipline or disciplines. These librarians are also providers of user services: reference, instruction, and service as the liaison to an assigned department, school, or college. Developing library collections that are relevant to academic programs and ongoing research enhances the ability of subject specialists to provide effective instruction, reference, and information delivery services to their constituencies. A general expectation is that the subject specialist will become familiar with the ongoing, long-term research projects and the information-seeking behavior of faculty and graduate students. (Sutton and Jacoby, 2009: 3–4)

Although there has been an attempt in the past to evaluate collections on some perceived objective or ideal collection, in reality the evaluation of the collection and the assessment of user needs are inextricably interrelated. The most in-depth user study must be performed in the context of a clear awareness of the scope and depth of the collection in which the user study is based. The only meaningful collection evaluation must be conducted in the context of whether it meets a particular group of users' information needs.

The more in-depth forms of both kinds of evaluation and assessment will cost more in terms of time, personnel, and potentially money to conduct. These in-depth evaluation and assessments can provide tangible data that can be used for justifying expenditures, marketing, seeking additional funding and support, and many other activities.

In their small-scale but targeted user study, conducted with social sciences faculty in the context of the e-library and physical library at the University of Illinois, Sutton and Jacoby (2008) gathered a great deal of useful collection management and maintenance data that will be used to grow and improve both the e-library and physical library's collections. Along with details of specific print and e-resource preferences and whether the library provided those the faculty needed and used, they found that some faculty reported that they did not need the library because they could just use databases on the Web. The interesting detail was that many of the specified Web databases were actually licensed through the library but appeared to be freely available through the organizational Web site. Users did not realize that the library was paying for them. Another problem was vocabulary. What the librarians meant by the concept of database was not necessarily what the faculty surveyed thought of as a database. Most found the library valuable. Most took advantage of document delivery options offered through the library. The local data relevant to the users within the context of the specific collection was very informative.

Large scale global user studies can also be useful in establishing base data for prioritizing expenditures or building or deselecting some areas of the collection. Xie (2006) asked users to identify their own criteria for evaluating an e-library (called digital library in their article). The results indicate that usability and collection quality were paramount. Usability was affected by both system performance and support offered by library personnel in accessing the collection. Users reported that being asked their opinion in and of itself made them more likely to give a positive evaluation.

"It is vital to assess the current state of a collection so that this information can be used in future planning processes. In this way, libraries can determine how best to allocate resources in order to select materials that meet user needs. This is a major component of competent collection management" (Skaggs, 2006: 14).

Collection assessment in its most basic form is simply outlining the collection in terms of comparisons to peer—or ideal—library collections. The intention is straightforward. The question asked is do we have all the print or e-resources that we ought of have if we are a library like that other library or the library we aspire to be? The challenge is to find objective factors to use in making comparisons between collections. Do you use e-resource title lists or bibliographies? Do you use e-resource title lists and bibliographies created as ideal collections or those generated by reports from peer e-libraries' collection data? How deep does the comparison run? Do you compare lists of e-journal or e-book titles or the titles of the vendor databases? How is quality judged in terms of the e-resource lists and bibliographies? Are any user studies applied in gauging the quality of the e-resources or is some "objective" idea of scholarly value applied? In what measures might both be important? Some basic steps for planning an e-library collection assessment follow:

1. Review the e-library collection development policy (or that section of the overall library collection development policy) to clarify the goals and purposes of the collection. If no e-library collection development policy is available then create one.
2. Locate e-resource title lists and e-library collection descriptions. Choose those that would be most appropriate in comparing your e-library collection with. Which lists or descriptions most closely resemble the ideal e-library in terms of the goals and purposes of the collection?
3. Look for conspectus guides and/or software to use in describing the depth, levels, and accessibility of the items in the collection.

4. Identify your e-library's internal e-resource titles and the defined access for each e-resource.
5. Identify any access or usage data relevant to your e-resource titles.
6. Identify your e-library's expenditures data. What is the cost of each e-resource title, including supporting personnel and technological aspects.

In one published e-library collection assessment example, Stephens and colleagues (2009) assessed and evaluated the Safari e-books collection for currency, usage, and availability of recent publications. Their intent was to evaluate its usefulness for users looking for the most current technical reference e-books. Their study found the collection to be as current as users required.

In *Assessment of Collections in a Consortial Environment: Experiences from Ohio*, OhioLink libraries report their individual collection assessments in the context of the consortial environment (Lupone, 2009). As a source of collection data from other libraries the OCLC's WorldCat Collection Analysis (WCA) tool is good. In several studies making use of the WCA or comparing it to other methods of assessment, librarians reported that they thought it was a good tool for learning to do collection analysis. The WCA provided valuable insight into collection strengths and weaknesses. Beals (2006) used a simple analysis tool on humanities collections—the brief test—and the RLG conspectus test that has been integrated into the OCLC's WCA and found both worked well (Henry et al., 2009; Beals and Gilmour, 2007; Beals, 2006).

Schonfeld (2007) recommends that libraries conduct a strategic format review in light of their uniqueness such as user expectations, organizational structure, and consortial planning.

Gary Shirk (2007) discusses how we can visually map data from our library collections in order to "see" how to make changes and improvements:

> Like a topological display of the world, information about our collections or collecting practices visualized in its entirety may provide useful insights about how the collection compares to other collections, how it is developing overtime, unintended gaps in the collection, strengths and weaknesses in the support of interdisciplinary studies, the extent to which collection contributes to the whole of the consortia in which you participate, the scatter of material needed for one discipline across the full subject scope of the library, and so on. The value is that relationships hidden from view just 35 feet up become crystal clear at 35,000 feet above. (Shirk, 2007: 106)

BALANCING PRINT AND ELECTRONIC RESOURCES

> In the pre–World Wide Web environment, library collections consisted exclusively of items that could be counted, labeled, housed, and tracked. Materials that were difficult to inventory, such as realia, pamphlets, and brochures, were slow to be incorporated into our collections, only marginally included as unprocessed items, or deemed to be out of collection scope. Particularly important materials in problematic formats were sometimes re-formatted or relegated to the special collections stacks where they could be given the required attention and oversight.... Of course librarians acknowledge the increasing importance of, and reliance on, digital resources, but "a pragmatic view of the future of libraries" is one in which the collection is a hybrid, that is, a mix of analog and digital resources. (Casserly, 2002: 580–581)

As much as e-resources dominate the global information environment, there is still a place for print and other physical media in libraries—not just in our archives and special collections that archive and preserve the historical or the unique but the books and magazines that people read daily. The question that seems most relevant when discussing print versus e-resource is what do we do when/if the power goes out and we can't get on the computer? To what extent does our library need to support information needs when there is no electrical power to provide access to e-resources? The author has worked with librarians in countries where the power comes from solar batteries or from other intermittent suppliers and the library's computers are available only as long as those batteries or transmissions last. Remember how librarians in California coped during the rolling blackouts a few years ago? This very day in Ohio, the author could not get on the Web to upload this manuscript until power was restored.

Beyond the issue of energy infrastructure is also that of accessibility. For some reading on a computer screen is uncomfortable. E-book vendors have tried various readers and screens for reading with very limited success. Print on paper for extended reading will be a preference until technology can solve the problem of readability. The newest Kindle does not do this.

Another issue of balancing print and e-resources is funding. How do you make a choice, or prioritize which formats will be favored? Does your energy infrastructure have a reliability problem? Can your library afford to collect multiple formats of the same titles/information sources? Are multiple formats even available?

Lewis (2007) points out that libraries can benefit economically in converting from print based to e-resource based processing. There are savings to be had in not processing print and using those resources instead to process e-resources. Temporarily duplicate processing will happen, but there is much in processing workflows that is just routine and not essential. "If the library community can establish regional or national strategies for the storage and long-term preservation of print collections, then individual libraries can confidently retire, or discard, their legacy print collections, especially those that are available in digital formats, and ultimately move to repurpose high value campus space" (Lewis, 2007: 7).

The question of print versus e-resources and balancing them is not one easily answered. As with so many questions, each library will need to answer differently and based on the specific needs of their users and the environment in which library services are offered. The future holds lots of librarian retraining and lots of rethinking workflows, from cataloging to metadata creation.

ELECTRONIC RESOURCE MANAGEMENT SYSTEMS (ERMS)

Electronic resource management systems (ERMS) are used "...to keep track of a library's digital titles, subscription and vendor/publisher information, and link resolution with more accuracy and less duplication" (McCracken, 2007: 261). ERMS are systems designed to manage the details involved in the acquisitions of e-resources, including subscription and licensing details, usage, cost, and access tracking and data gathering. In general, an ERMS is used for record keeping and budgeting activities, while CMS are used for access and authority control. In some respects these functions can overlap. Several good stand-alone ERMS both commercial and open source are available and many ILS integrate some form of ERMS (Breeding, 2008; Fons and Jewell, 2007; Boss, 2006).

Fons and Jewell (2007) report the status of the Digital Library Federation's Electronic Resource Management Initiative (ERMI). ERMI was initiated to detail the functions that a good ERMS should have, including interoperability within ILS, data elements that an ERMS should be able to generate regarding the collection it is managing and specific items related to licensing agreements and interoperability with vendor acquisitions systems.

The COUNTER (Counting Online Usage of NeTworked Electronic Resources) (www.project counter.org) project also emerged from the original ERMI project to define specific data gathering, access and usage tracking, terminology, processing of usage data, standards for report layout, format, and delivery. An ERMS that is COUNTER compliant will generate the specified data and tracking in the formats defined by the standard. A vendor who is COUNTER compliant will supply data about a given e-resource in a format that can be used by a COUNTER compliant ERMS. The latter will be mentioned again in the next chapter. From the COUNTER project emerged the Standardized Usage Statistics Harvesting Initiative or SUSHI (www.niso.org/work rooms/sushi) protocol for harvesting usage data.

A good ERMS should be able to handle all levels of licensing data and be able to make comparisons between licensing details between two e-resources, and report collection management related data in a usable format. One of the most valuable standards to emerge from this initiative is the one involving link resolvers—from a CMS, ILS, library catalog, or other Web interface—connecting to or through an ERMS:

> In the case of the link resolver, patrons accessing licensed content should have a clear understanding of access rights and restrictions as well as relevant administrative data describing the nature and availability of the desired content. As ERM systems evolve, they should provide the local link resolver with the appropriate data, such as:
>
> - License terms of use
> - To provide patrons with detailed notification of permitted and restricted uses
> - Scope notes
> - Describing the nature and features available from the licensed resource
> - Technical requirements
> - Browser versions required and suggestions on secondary applications required for accessing content
> - Advisory notes
> - Warning of current or planned system outages
> - Announcing new features or content provided through the library's subscription
> - Promotion of the library's sponsorship of access to the content (Fons and Jewell, 2007: 164)

Given the results of some of the user studies reviewed, these features should help to minimize user confusion about which e-resources are freely available on the general Web and which are paid for by their library. These standards also are solid step in the direction of interoperable systems that are needed as library technology evolves. In many ways the concept of an ERMS replaces the inventory control function of the library catalog as well as being a relational database foundation for access and use of e-resources.

CATALOGING E-RESOURCES

In response to the major technological changes in the world around libraries, some librarians feel that we can simply update our catalogs and management systems. Others posit that the projects such as the Hathi Trust (www.hathitrust.org) or Google Books (http://books.google.com) plus OCLC's WorldCat (www.worldcat.org) could replace the local catalog—why do we need to continue to maintain local catalogs? Why not implement a central database with holdings information? In this section both points of view are reviewed.

Why Catalog E-Resources?

Libraries catalog books, videos, DVDs, maps, and a multitude of other information forms and artifacts in order to organize them so that the people who wish to read, consult, or view them can easily identify and retrieve these sources. E-resource cataloging studies have found that cataloging e-resource increases use and awareness of e-resources through the library (see, e.g., Skaggs 2006).

Adding or creating catalog records for e-resources in the library catalog accomplishes three important goals for libraries:

1. It establishes a uniform user interface for searching for Web sites, books, serials, and other e-resources that the library owns or provides access to.
2. It encourages the use of high quality e-resources.
3. It encourages standards for Web resource quality and interaccessibility.

Libraries who have a policy of cataloging e-resources, such as the OhioLINK Libraries (www.ohiolink.edu) and especially the Kent State University Libraries (www.library.kent.edu), do not attempt to catalog every Web site but rather choose carefully which e-resources to catalog. The key question is, will cataloging a given e-resource add to library users' access to the kinds of information they are looking for?

In general, e-resources to be cataloged are identified by a reference or technical services librarian or on occasion by students or faculty members. Some libraries have developed automatic cataloging of e-resources. Selecting librarians fill out a form and a perl script turns it into a basic catalog record (Harcourt et al., 2006).

The data entry field number 856 is used to add electronic access information; that is, the URL. When a library user retrieves a Web resource record, they may link directly to the site from the catalog, such as www.ohiolink.edu.

If a catalog record for the Web resource exists in OCLC, the decision may be made to download it to the catalog. If the e-resource will require original cataloging, catalogers look for the following criteria:

- Unique content—content that is clearly identifiable and can be adequately described through cataloging
- Metadata information or other clearly identifiable bibliographic information that can be extracted to create a catalog record
- Clearly and easily identified information provider or source
- Information analogous to publisher that includes detailed attribution and valid contact information
- Credible documentation that the e-resource content will be stable or continue for a foreseeable future
- Content up-to-date or otherwise clearly identified as historical, time-stamped
- Authoritative content based on authoritative and credible information provider or source—content verifiable as factual, research-supported, or otherwise possessing scholarly value
- Appropriate education level
- Accessibility—the e-resource is easily navigated and follows the basic guidelines for accessibility
- Commercial aspect is minimal or otherwise does not affect the value of the content

What Does Cataloging Mean?

In this exciting, sometimes chaotic, Googleized environment where patrons demand instant access and prefer simple keyword searches, often at the expense of precision and accuracy, what can librarians offer researchers? What can they do differently? How can they contribute, as in the past 200 years, to the organization of information? Librarians must stay abreast of current trends in information technology, management, organization, and description and educate themselves and their staff as new technologies and new initiatives in cataloging metadata develop. The international library and information community must continue to move in positive directions, build new systems that enhance library catalogs, and integrate multiple database functions. (McCracken, 2007: 274)

Elaine McCracken's (2007) article "Description of and Access to Electronic Resources (ER): Transitioning into the Digital Age" begins with a historical tribute to the catalog and its original goals and purposes and transitions to the current issues for libraries to deal with in changing the catalog to newer more interoperable database options.

Cataloging e-resources does not necessarily mean that libraries will keep trying to make the MARC record work in ways it was not designed to work. Librarians may use a variety of other flexible and powerful database tools to catalog e-resources. For example, Dennis Nicholson describes BUBL (e-library success story at the end of this chapter) as a catalog of Web links. The BUBL project developed BUBL Link 5:15, which is now the searchable catalog used to organize and access the resources collected on BUBL.

Developers are exploring many alternatives, including XML, as well as ways to make the MARC record work with Web resource metadata. In this section we will overview some of the issues related to cataloging e-resources with the MARC format as well as point to examples and resources of other metadata options.

Calhoun (2006) reviewed the literature on information seeking behavior of our users, including those using Google and other search engines and conducted some structured interviews. Her main findings and recommendations are that library catalogs as they currently exist are "long on problems and short on unique benefits for users" (9). Traditional cataloging is not cost-effectiveness and it does not integrate well into the global information infrastructure.

Calhoun proposed integrating catalogs with open Web discovery tools but uncovered obstacles to this idea mainly in the reluctance and resistance of library staff to implement the changes in workflow and bibliographic control that are necessary. Other obstacles are the money and cooperation needed for large-scale collaborations and copyright laws. We have seen some of these obstacles surmounted with varying results with Hathi Trust (www.hathitrust.org), Google Books (http://books.google.com), and WorldCat (www.worldcat.org).

A summary of recommendations for further study of the cost and user effectiveness of library catalogs includes the needs to define and prioritize the community(ies) to be served, including geographical locations, fields of study, number of users, whether they currently use the library catalogs or not, their current information-seeking behaviors, and what theses users need from the "catalog" or from the library to assist their research as well as to look at the options in terms of technologies. What does the library actually need to do to make their print and e-resources collections usable and accessible to their users?

Cataloging Electronic Resources: OCLC-MARC Coding Guidelines (www.oclc.org/support/documentation/worldcat/cataloging/electronicresources/default.htm) are the current AACR2 2002 based e-resource cataloging guidelines. Negotiations are in process to update these guidelines based on Resource Description and Access (RDA) guidelines (www.rdaonline.org).

RDA will be the new standard for resource description and access designed for the digital world. Built on the foundations established by AACR2 2002, RDA provides a comprehensive set of guidelines and instructions on resource description and access covering all types of content and media. RDA is intended to create a bridge between AACR2 2002 and real metadata, but some consider it too little change too slowly and it does not involve computer database and information architecture experts from other knowledge domains.

> While the goals of the progressive librarians building new interconnected library services are admirable, they need to be achieved in short order if libraries are to retain their users' loyalty. It does not seem to matter to most users that libraries currently are the only conduits for a wealth of published literature that is not available for open access on the public Internet. Users will engage with services that provide materials quickly and with the least effort.... The role of the cataloging rules in enabling or disabling these goals is not just a matter of insuring that library systems can accept metadata from non-library sources, and that library metadata can leak out into the public network environment. We must set the stage, with our standards and our use of technology, for library bibliographic services that serve today's users. These users are increasingly ones who have never known a world without computers, much less a world without the Internet. The new generation of users begins each information quest with a few typed keywords into an online query box. When seeking a book whose title they only partly remember, many of them turn to Amazon. There they not only get the bibliographic information that they sought but also find themselves in a reassuring online community that reviews, recommends, and encourages them to take part. (Coyle and Hillman, 2007)

Some History of E-Resource Cataloging

For the past decade, catalogers have been developing various strategies for cataloging Web and other e-resources. OCLC has provided leadership in the assessment of Internet resources for cataloging and the development of cataloging standards. They began a series of Internet resource cataloging experiments in 1992 based on the assumptions that the AACR2, 2nd edition, Chapter 9, Computer Files guidelines were adequate for creating cataloging records of Internet resources and that Internet resources provided sufficient data for creation of minimal-level cataloging records. In that pre-Web era, most Internet resources were downloaded as computer-readable files through FTP or Gopher or by logging in through a telnet session. The advent of the Web added layers of complexity and problems of data uniformity that had to be addressed if e-resources were to be cataloged in the MARC format. Nancy B. Olsen's (2003) pioneering work *Cataloging Internet Resources* was one of the first (1997) sources for descriptive cataloging of e-resources using the MARC format. The 2002 Anglo-American Cataloging Rules (AACR 2002) described a new paradigm for cataloging e-resources. AACR2 refers to e-resources as Integrating Resources and addresses them in much the same way as loose-leaf serials or monographs that have continuous updates and supplements (Maurer, 2003, personal communication). However, AACR2 2002 failed to address the role of metadata or other related issues in describing e-resources. In *Cataloging Nonprint and Internet Resources: A How-To-Do-It Manual for Librarians*, Mary Beth Weber (2002) addressed these issues and described the cataloging of e-resources in a thoughtful and understandable manner. She introduced the key relationships between MARC and metadata and how they impact the cataloging of e-resources. Dublin Core Metadata and cataloging e-resources catalogers are working with the Dublin Core Metadata Initiative (Dublin Core for short) (http://dublincore.org) to develop Web resource data elements that can be used in the creation of MARC or other types of catalog/database records.

The Dublin Core Metadata Element Set is a vocabulary of 15 properties for use in resource description or metadata elements that are determined by Web site builders/Web page creators and placed in the meta tags of the Web page or pages that are the entry point of a given Web site. Search engines can use these metadata tags (http://dublincore.org/documents/dces) as a uniform source of information to index Web sites as well as to establish standards that allow for interoperability between search tools, including library catalogs. Automated tools exist to aid in the creation of metadata and to aid in the conversion of metadata tags to MARC fields. The Library of Congress Network Development and MARC Standards Office has published a Cross-walk for mapping between the 15 Dublin Core data elements and the MARC21 bibliographic data elements (www.loc.gov/marc/dccross.html). OCLC CorC/Connexion OCLSs Cooperative Online Resource Catalog (CorC) began in 1999 as an attempt to combine high quality descriptive cataloging and the 15 elements of the Dublin Core Metadata in the MARC record. Hundreds of thousands of MARC records for e-resources were created by more than 500 libraries in 23 countries. The OCLC CorC service was integrated into the OCLC Connexion (www.oclc.org/connexion) service in July 2002. MARC is a library-specific format. Only libraries use this format. It is rigid and obsolete. In short, it is not industry standard in regard to current database technology.

What Can Libraries Do Now?

Some method of cataloging e-resources—whether using MARC or another form of metadata—will benefit libraries and their users. Sanford Berman (2000) makes the best case for cataloging all of a library's resources in all formats. His credo "Why Catalog?" should identify and make accessible a library's resources in all formats. That identification and access should be swift and painless. The language and structure of catalog entries should be familiar and comprehensible. And catalogers should recognize that they do what they do not to please bosses and not to mindlessly adhere to rules and protocols but to serve their information desk colleagues and the public. That is whom they are working for (Berman, 2000: 11).

Some catalogers work to adapt MARC to modern database standards through transitioning AACR2 2002 to RDA. Others recommend that MARC be abandoned in favor of industry-standard database technologies, such as XML (eXtensible Mark-up Language). Libraries exist to serve the present and future needs of a community of users. To do this well, they need to use the very best that technology has to offer. With the advent of the Web, XML, portable computing, and other technological advances, libraries can become flexible, responsive organizations that serve their users in exciting new ways. Or not. If libraries cling to outdated standards, they will find it increasingly difficult to serve their users as they expect and deserve.

XML is a markup language used to define electronic data records. XML is a markup language for documents containing structured information. Structured information contains both content (words, pictures, etc.) and some indication of what role that content plays (for example, content in a section heading has a different meaning from content in a footnote, which means something different than content in a figure caption or content in a database table, etc.). Almost all documents have some structure. The word *document* refers not only to traditional documents, like this one but also to myriad other XML data formats. These include vector graphics, e-commerce transactions, mathematical equations, object metadata, server APIs, and a thousand other kinds of structured information. The Library of Congress MARC in XML documentation defines XML standards for MARC (www.loc.gov/marc/marcxml.html). XMLMARC (http://xmlmarc.stanford.edu) software for converting MARC records to XML format was created by the Stanford University Libraries.

Currently, libraries have many technology choices open to them. The important issue remains our role as information intermediaries regardless of the technology choices we make. "As Google so powerfully proves every day, authority control and classification are no longer the only, or the best, answers. Academic libraries must find and articulate their roles in the current and future information ecology. If we cannot or will not do this, our campuses will invest in other priorities and the library will slowly, but surely, atrophy and become a little used museum of the book" (Lewis, 2007: 2).

ARCHIVING ELECTRONIC RESOURCES

> . . . we seek to explore a metaphoric conceptualization of the archive as a living eco-system, where information and its delivery systems are recognized as dynamic, highly changeable, and inhabited by humans. If we want to keep data alive, strategies involving all players in the ecosystem—publishers, librarians, archivists, information consumers, and authors—are vital. (Martin and Coleman, 2002: 1)

Archiving of e-resources—digital content—at this time involves making multiple copies and storing them in multiple locations. Constant backups and regular migrations when formats change are a persistent problem but routine. In fact, the state or e-resources archiving is very much analogous to that of early manuscript archiving and preservation. The medium on which the information is recorded and the mechanisms for recording in both cases decay or can otherwise be lost or destroyed. In the early times we were recording with berry juice on pounded bark, various inks on animal skins or papyrus, or carving in stone, inscribing on clay and other frangible media. Now we are recording in our imaginations with electrons on plastics. The transition phase between the oldest publishing media and the newest—print on pulp or rag paper—is in many ways much more durable in terms of archiving and preservation.

The physical preservation technologies will evolve and we will find more efficient ways to archive using the technologies. Projects such as the LOCKSS (lockss.stanford.edu) and the Internet Archives Archive-It program (www.archive-it.org) are a step forward. The cycle of hardware and software—document format software specifically—obsolescence is a major problem. Converting older e-resources to newer formats so they can continue to be usable is a challenge. Software vendors, digital archivists, and librarians are all working on standards for document format; for example, Adobe PDF format.

> In a digital world, libraries and universities can be publishers, scholars can build libraries on their Web sites, and vendors can be archivists. Traditional collection management values may soon reach a digital wall that challenges the definition of collection, along with assumptions about collection building. The digital environment demands new approaches to collecting for future generations. (Phillips and Williams, 2004: 283)

The question of who is responsible for archiving is less clear. Archiving policies among publishers and vendors of e-resources vary. Some will allow agreements permitting archiving by libraries and others resist. Who actually does the archiving and what information architectures and formats are used is also still a question. Some librarians have explored these issues and propose some good ideas for the future (Hunter, 2007; Johnson and Luther, 2007; Moghaddam, 2007; Schmidt et al., 2007). "If we want to end print, we must have bullet-proof digital archiving of electronic journals. We are making progress, but there are many, many issues still to be settled" (Hunter, 2007: 132).

Johnson and Luther (2007) discuss the options and examples for consortial archiving of e-journals and other content. Library consortia (such as OhioLink and the Ontario Council of University Libraries) have mounted some licensed e-journals on their own systems with publisher agreement. Via agreements with publishers, a few national libraries are taking on roles in digital preservation of journal articles (e.g., National Library of Medicine in the United States and Koninklijke Bibliotheek in The Netherlands). Many libraries rely on provisions of license agreements with publishers as their main assurance that an e-journal will be preserved over time. "As reflected in these examples, the anticipated technical complexity and expense of digital preservation have motivated libraries to pursue collective rather than unilateral approaches to the challenge" (Johnson and Luther, 2007: 10).

Another issue with archiving is where you set the boundaries of what should be archived (Kaczmarek, 2006). Archiving of digital cultural materials is a specific example (Mason, 2007). The library discussed by Mason is required to archive cultural materials— government documents, Web sites, etc.—regardless of format. At what point is "cultural materials" just junk? At what point is it valuable information for future generations? How can we know?

Digital Libraries

Many individual libraries are creating digital library projects or are planning to do so. Such projects are labor intensive and complex. In this section we discuss some of the basics as well as resources for learning more about the creation of digital collections that will be Web accessible. Creating digital collections may involved scanning, transcribing, retyping, photographing, or otherwise reproducing in electronic format full text, data, images, maps, and other artifacts held by a library, data creator/provider, or other archival organization. Those digitized documents and other artifacts must also be organized in a database of some kind so that they can be searched and retrieved by users. The Digital Library Federation (DLF) (www.diglib.org) and the DSpace Federation (www.dspace.org) are both consortia of academic and research libraries that share standards and best practices for creating and managing digital collections in the net-worked environment. DSpace is developing a digital repository system. DLF members assist one another in creating and managing digital collections. The DLF Web site publishes standards and links to publications, such as the IMLS report "A Framework of Guidance for Building Good Digital Collections" (2009) (www.imls.gov/pubs/forumframework.htm). DLF supports the Open Archives Initiative (OAI) (www.openarchives.org) and plans to develop Internet gateways through which users will access distributed digital library holdings as if they were part of a single uniform collection.

Some digital collections are preservation projects designed to ensure that fragile historical materials are available for future generations. Libraries participate in many local history projects and preservation projects. The American Memory Project (http://memory.loc.gov) digital collection created by the Library of Congress is one of the most comprehensive and best known of these kinds of projects. Many individual state library organizations have begun state level Memory Projects, such as the Ohio Memory Project (www.ohiomemory.org). The USGenWeb Digital Library (www.rootsweb.ancestry.com/~usgenweb) project is an example of individual volunteers cooperating in digitizing historical documents and sharing them through the Web. Many guides and documents on the Web and in print aim to share standards and practices, assist libraries in creating their own digital collections, or to discuss the database software, metadata encoding and transmission, or other technical issues.

E-LIBRARY SUCCESS STORY

BUBL INFORMATION SERVICE

Centre for Digital Library Research (CDLR), Strathclyde University
Glasgow, Scotland, United Kingdom
http://bubl.ac.uk
Contact: Dennis Nicholson, Director CDLR, d.m.nicholson@strath.ac.uk

A. Collection Planning (e.g., goal setting and identification of users, technology/personnel choices)

BUBL, originally named the BUlletin Board for Libraries, was one of the first and is still one of the best current information and Web resource collection tools for librarians. It was set up under Project Jupiter as a text only pre-Web, pre-gopher service, based at University of Glasgow. When funding for the original project ended in 1991, a group of librarians from the Universities of Strathclyde and Glasgow, coordinated at Strathclyde by Dennis Nicholson, voluntarily took on the task of turning BUBL into a service. "When the project closed, they were going to close BUBL down and I offered to take it over, started running it with others on a volunteer basis and eventually widened its scope with the help of many others over many years so that it became the service we have today."

In its embryonic experimental form, BUBL was a central place to post and share files extracted from mailing lists, job listings, and original news and discussion among librarians and library school students. By 1993, however, Gopher and Web servers with links to Internet resources of library and information science interest were in place and access to Internet resources beyond LIS was beginning to come on stream—the beginnings of the BUBL "Subject Tree" and (in time) the BUBL LINK (LIbraries of Networked Knowledge) service.

BUBL received funding from the Joint Information Systems Committee (JISC) in 1994 and 1995. In January 1995, JISC began funding BUBL as a UK national information service offering an all-subject-areas approach to free internet resources and a specialist service to LIS professionals. As the Web became the dominant Internet service, the focus for BUBL reviewers shifted increasingly to Web resources and an experimental catalogue, offering Web, gopher, and Z39.50 access to a searchable catalogue was developed (1994–1995). In 1996/1997 as part of the move from UKOLN to Strathclyde, Alan Dawson (now a senior researcher/programmer at CDLR), developed embryonic LINK demonstrator as the initial basis for BUBL Link 5:15, which is now the searchable catalog used to organize and access the resources collected on BUBL.

"Our aim is still to offer a directory of key quality resources in most subject areas. Up until recently our main focus was serving UK Higher and Further Education, although we always tried to be more inclusive than that. During 2008, however, we began actively working with (and getting some resource from) the Scottish Library and Information Council (SLIC). SLIC is the official representative body for libraries to the Scottish Government (Libraries are a devolved area). Accordingly, we are likely to move more officially to aiming to be more inclusive in terms of who we seek to serve, bringing Public Library users—and citizens generally—into the frame. This process is at an early stage, but is slowly picking up speed. We still have a focus on the academic aspects, however, particularly in Library and Information Science, where we are supporting the E-LIS (http://eprints.rclis.org/) open repository effort." A collection development plan was written and is revised as the needs of the users and the technology, social, and political environments evolve.

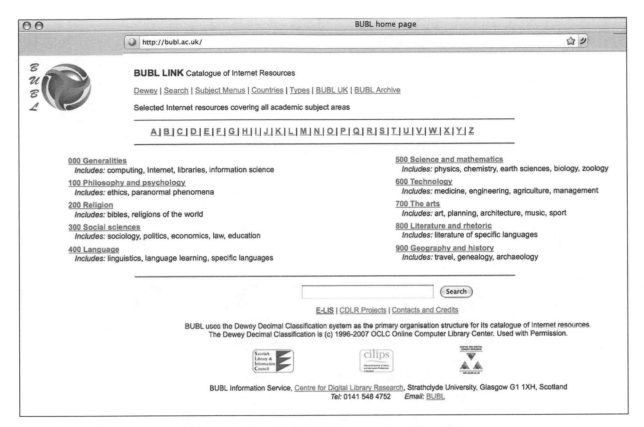

Figure 2.1. BUBL Information Service

B. Collection Strategies (e.g., selection criteria, identification of resources, licensing, and related user information needs)

BUBL is an essential e-library collection development tool for librarians. "However, it soon became apparent that much of the information being made available on BUBL was of direct interest to the wider academic community and was being widely used by non-librarians. Consequently, BUBL has broadened its approach, and whilst a specialist service is still provided to the UK's library and information science community, the service has for some time been aimed towards the UK higher education academic and research community more generally. BUBL caters for all levels of academia throughout the world and selectively covers all subject areas. As it becomes an integral part of the Scottish Cooperative Infrastructure, BUBL will aim to extend its audience beyond HE and FE into the public and school library sectors and to support general public access for lifelong learners and other users of the UK 'People's Network.'"

BUBL staff monitor mailing lists on which Web resources in various subject areas area announced. They also receive recommendations of new Web resources and search directly on the Web for new sites. They then link to the Web resource and review and evaluate it for inclusion in the BUBL catalog. On the BUBL site (http://bubl.ac.uk/admin) administrative details, articles, annual report, and the FAQ provide information about the scope and selection process (http://bubl.ac.uk/admin/faq.htm). BUBL staff collaborate to cover different subject areas. Duplication is prevented by making updates on a regular monthly basis and communication between the staff members.

All resources selected for BUBL must be freely available, good quality, known source, relevant subject matter and they must either enhance the existing collection or fill a gap. Freely available e-books are included in the BUBL collection. BUBL does not collect licensed or fee-based resources. BUBL has become an integral part of the CDLR at Strathclyde University and is now funded and maintained by the CDLR as part of its research activities and SLIC. Although it does not currently offer virtual reference services, these may be developed in the future as part of the Scottish Cooperative Infrastructure. Discussions regarding possible BUBL support for distance learning programs in Scotland are taking place.

"One thing we are considering is bringing social networking into the equation. In the distant past, we tried to run BUBL (the BUBL Subject Tree) with community support. The recent focus on social networking begins to make it more feasible to foster a support community. This is at an early stage but we are looking to get librarians, students, teachers, and others into the mix through a social networking site called BUBL Community." BUBL staff select, evaluate, and collect resources continuously. Links are updated each month and announced at http:// bubl.ac.uk/link/updates/current.html and through the Lis-Link discussion list (www.jiscmail .ac.uk/lists/lis-link.html).

BUBL does not provide access to fee-based Web accessible database directly and does not plan to do so in the future. The BUBL mission is to provide free and high quality Web resources. The CDLR has created digital collections, which will in time be available via a BUBL view on CDLR resources as well as via other user landscapes (see, for example, http://gdl.cdlr.strath.ac.uk).

C. Collection Organization (e.g., content management systems, Web server choices, personnel responsibilities, etc.)

BUBL runs on the Scottish Portals for Education, Information and Research (SPEIR) server. (http://speir.cdlr.strath.ac.uk). BUBL is built on Cold Fusion on an MS SQL server. The hardware, software, and technical support are funded through the SPEIR project. Collectors access it via an access interface to SQL Server. Staff who work on the BUBL site have degrees in library and information science and have training in the cataloging procedures specific to BUBL. Staff members do what they can to support BUBL as they have time and other work for CDLR allows.

"About 7 people are involved, some at SLIC, some at CDLR, but this gives a very false impression of the resourcing. The main work on updating and maintaining service content takes up about 3 person days a week at present. Others in the group are only called into play as and when (meetings, technical support). This level of resourcing is all that is currently feasible, but we'd hope to improve that as the collaboration with SLIC moves ahead and also as we attempt to build BUBL Community."

Various paid staff members are all responsible for adding records to the BUBL catalog. They add to existing records in the catalog, in the interest of having an additional set of eyes checking each record for grammar, style, Dewey Decimal Classification, and keywords. Collection strategies used by collectors include serendipitous discovery in the process of related research, monitoring professional journals, as well as specific searching for quality resources to include. Feedback from users assists in link checking and in making choices for resources to include as well as alerting collectors to resource needs.

D. Collection Maintenance (e.g., link checking, ongoing weeding, and growth of the e-library collection)

BUBL organization is continuously reviewed. Staff members discuss all changes and the person who makes a suggestion generally implements the change. BUBL coordinates maintenance and organization within the context of the "Scottish Information Environment." "We work with

SLIC, not just on BUBL, but other elements of the 'Scottish Information Environment.' This includes CAIRNS (http://cairns.lib.strath.ac.uk), a distributed Z39.50 database and also SCONE (http://scone.strath.ac.uk/service/index.cfm), a collections database. So, although there is no direct link from BUBL to these other elements at present, we expect to move to a situation where these are all elements of a single service (there are other parts of it as well; e.g., SLAINTE, www.slainte.org.uk)."

SOME FINAL THOUGHTS ON E-LIBRARY MAINTENANCE

E-library maintenance is the ongoing process of reviewing content and organization to update and growing the e-library. Some steps to consider routine in ongoing maintenance:

- Stay in touch with the Web server administrator regarding software updates and changes.
- Weed the E-library—regularly review and check links, etc.
- Provide a mechanism for e-library users to evaluate and comment on the e-library contents and organization; take their comments into consideration for maintenance activity.
- Review e-library information architecture and reorganize as necessary. Run usability studies.
- Review, update, and grow the contents of the e-library.
- Maintain clear communications between IT staff and the library.

When working in partnership with IT staff it is important to maintain communications regarding changes in the system or the needs of the users in regard to system access. When upgrading or installing software or hardware, IT staff may alter access to e-libraries by adding or deleting directories structures, changing input permission status for database access, and other related system changes. We saw some of these kinds of problems in the information architecture changes to the American Library Association Web site (www.ala.org) in spring 2003 and fall 2008 especially. Developing and maintaining good communications with Web server or CMS administrators helps to ensure that you are not taken by surprise and that you will have input into any major changes that are planned.

- Weed the e-library—regularly review and check links, etc.

This includes weeding or deselecting content that is out of date, not used or reorganizing it to make it more usable. Libraries use a variety of tools to decide what to weed from their e-library—Google Analytics (Spitzer and Brown, 2007), usage data from CMS, ILS, etc. Weeding refreshes and renews the e-library.

Maintenance of your e-library requires that someone regularly checks the links to make sure they are current and working. Software is available to assist you with this type of maintenance. Subscribe to the Web4lib listserv, or search the archives to find recommendations for link-checking software. The e-library case studies include details about what link-checking software is used if it is used. The Open Directory List of Link Management Tools (www.dmoz.org/Computers/Software/Internet/Site_Management/Link_Management) offers hundreds of choices. However tedious it may be, you must also check links manually. This allows you to review and verify that the Web site not only still links properly but that it still provides the same information that it did when you originally annotated and added it to your e-library collection. We recommend that you plan to check links manually as often as possible, because things really do change or go away. For example, A Web Hub for Developing Administrative Metadata for Electronic Resource Management (accessed January 12, 2009 at www.library.cornell.edu/elicensestudy/home.html) is not a dead link, but the site is no longer current. Visitors are notified that the site is no longer maintained. However you manage your links, check them frequently. Dead links mean frustration for e-library users and defeats the purposes of the e-library in providing good access to information.

- Provide a mechanism for e-library users to evaluate and comment on the e-library contents and organization; take their comments into consideration for maintenance activity.

This routine consideration will help with link checking and with ongoing review of information architecture and user and usability studies.

- Review e-library information architecture and reorganize as necessary. Run usability studies.

    There are a number of factors which can affect a library site's usability. The navigational structure must make sense to a user who has little experience with research or who approaches the research process in a different way than might a librarian. The user should be able to predict link destinations and how each section of the site is different from others. The language used on the site is closely related to the link structure. Do users understand the meaning of terms they read on database, e-journal, and e-resource Web sites? Do terms on the site used to describe concepts match user language, or are they library jargon? The ability of a site to be easily scanned and quickly understood also affects usability. Large blocks of text with well-intended instructions can undermine a site's usability as the elements users look for are obscured and navigation obstructed. The factors described above contribute to or detract from usability more than colors, images, fonts, or other graphic elements. While graphic design has a role in the creation of a visually pleasing Web page, engineers have found that it plays little role in a site's usability. (Wrubel, 2007: 227)

E-libraries grow and the needs of library users may change. It will be necessary to reorganize to accommodate both or either situation. It may be decided to reorganize the e-library with management/database software or to add search capabilities.

- Review, update, and grow the contents of the e-library.

E-library content should always be reviewed regularly. The only limitations to the growth of an e-library collection are disk space, the time and energy of the collectors, and the library's budget for fee-based e-resources. Maintaining the Web-accessible e-library will also include ongoing collection and incorporation of new resources. New and better review sources, as well as new and better e-resources, are made available literally every day.

This book's companion Web site will continue to annotate and include new, or newly discovered, or recommended e-library collection development tools as well as additions and corrections to the "core web" reference collections referred to in each chapter of Part II. You may also ask to be e-mailed when resources are added or updated.

REFERENCES AND WEB SITES CITED

"A Framework of Guidance for Building Good Digital Collections." Available: www.imls.gov/pubs/forumframework.htm (accessed January 7, 2009).

Agee, Jim. 2005. "Collection Evaluation: A Foundation for Collection Development." *Collection Building* 24, no. 3: 92–95.

Beals, Jennifer Benedetto. 2006 "Assessing Library Collections Using Brief Test Methodology" *Electronic Journal of Academic and Special Librarianship* 7, no. 3. Available: http://southernlibrarianship.icaap .org/content/v07n03/beals_j01.htm.

Beals, Jennifer Benedetto, and Ron Gilmour. 2007. "Assessing Collections Using Brief Tests and WorldCat Collection Analysis." *Collection Building* 26, no. 4: 135–136.

Berman, Sanford. 2000. "Berman's Bag: Why Catalog?" *Unabashed Librarian* 116: 11–12. Available: www.sanfordberman.org/biblinks/2000.htm (accessed January 12, 2009).

Borin, Jacqueline, and Hua Yi. 2008. "Indicators for Collection Evaluation: A New Dimensional Framework." *Collection Building* 27, no. 4: 136–143.

Boss, Richard W. 2006. "Digital Collection Management." *Public Library Association Tech Notes.* Available: www.ala.org/ala/mgrps/divs/pla/plapublications/platechnotes/digitalcollectionsmanagement2006 .doc (accessed January 7, 2009).

Breeding, Marshall. 2008. "Helping You Buy: Electronic Resource Management Systems." *Computers in Libraries* 28, no. 28: 6–17, 94–96. Available: www.librarytechnology.org/ltg-displaytext.pl?RC= 13437.

Calhoun, Karen. 2006. "The Changing Nature of the Catalog and Its Integration with Other Discovery Tools." Prepared for the Library of Congress. Available: www.loc.gov/catdir/calhoun-report-final.pdf.

Casserly, Mary F. 2002. "Developing a Concept of Collection for the Digital Age." *portal: Libraries and the Academy* 2, no. 4: 577–587.

Coyle, Karen, and Diane Hillman. 2007. "Resource Description and Access (RDA): Cataloging Rules for the 20th Century." *D-Lib Magazine* 13, no 1/2. Available: www.dlib.org/dlib/january07/coyle/ 01coyle.html.

Fons, Theodore A., and Timothy D. Jewell. 2007. "Envisioning the Future of ERM Systems." *The Serials Librarian* 52, no. 1/2: 151–166.

Graham, Wayne. 2009. "Reaching Users Through Facebook: A Guide to Implementing Facebook Athenaeum." *The Code4Lib Journal* 5. Available: http://journal.code4lib.org/articles/490.

Harcourt, Kate, Melanie Wacker, and Iris Wolley. 2006. "Automated Access Level Cataloging for Internet Resources at Columbia University Libraries." *Library Resources and Technical Services* 51, no. 3: 212–225.

Henry, Elizabeth, Rachel Longstaff, and Doris Van Kampen. 2009. "Collection Analysis Outcomes in an Academic Library." *Collection Building* 27, no. 3: 113–117.

Hunter, Karen. 2007. "The End of Print Journals: (In)Frequently Asked Questions." *Journal of Library Administration* 46, no. 2: 119–132.

Johnson, Richard K., and Judy Luther. 2007. "The E-only Tipping Point for Journals: What's Ahead in the Print-to-Electronic Transition Zone." Washington, DC: Association of Research Libraries. Available: www.arl.org/bm~doc/Electronic_Transition.pdf (accessed January 7, 2009).

Kaczmarek, Joanne. 2006. "The Complexities of Digital Resources: Collection Boundaries and Management Responsibilities." *Journal of Archival Organization* 4, no.1/2: 215–227.

Lewis, David W. 2007. "A Strategy for Academic Libraries in the First Quarter of the 21st Century." IDeA: IUPUI Digital Archive, University Library Faculty Research Collection. Available: https://idea.iupui.edu:8443/dspace/bitstream/1805/953/1/DWLewis_Strategy.pdf.

Lupone, George. 2009. *Assessment of Collections in a Consortial Environment: Experiences from Ohio.* New York: Routledge.

Martin, Julia, and David Coleman. 2002. "Change The Metaphor: The Archive As an Ecosystem." *The Journal of Electronic Publishing* 7, no. 3. Available: http://quod.lib.umich.edu/cgi/t/text/text-idx?c=jep;view=text;rgn=main;idno=3336451.0007.301 (accessed January 7, 2009).

Mason, Ingrid. 2007. "Virtual Preservation: How Has Digital Culture Influenced Our Ideas about Permanence? Changing Practice in a National Legal Deposit Library." *Library Trends* 56, no. 1: 198–215.

McCracken, Elaine. 2007. "Description of and Access to Electronic Resources (ER): Transitioning into the Digital Age." *Collection Management* 32, no. 3/4: 259–275.

Mitchell, Steve. 2006. "Machine Assistance in Collection Building: New Tools, Research, Issues, and Reflections." *Information Technology & Libraries* 25 (December): 190–216.

Moghaddam, Golnessa Galyani. 2007. "Archiving Challenges of Scholarly Electronic Journals: How do Publishers Manage Them?" *Serials Review* 33, no. 2: 81–90. Available: http://eprints.rclis.org/archive/00011175/01/Archiving_Challenges_of_Scholarly_Electronic_Journal_How_do_publishers_manage_them.pdf (accessed January 7, 2009).

Myall, Carolynne, and Sue Anderson. 2007. "Can This Orthodoxy Be Saved? Enhancing the Usefulness of Collection Plans in the Digital Environment." *Collection Management* 32, no. 3/4: 235–259.

Olsen, Nancy B. 2003. *Cataloging Internet Resources*, 2nd edition. Dublin, OH: OCLC Online Computer Library Center.

Phillips, Linda L., and Sara R. Williams. 2004. "Collection Development Embraces the Digital Age." *Library Resources & Technical Services* 48, no. 4 (October): 273–299. Available: www.accessmylibrary.com/coms2/summary_0286-14597547_ITM (accessed January 18, 2009).

Pomerantz, Jeffrey, and Gary Marchionini. 2007. "The Digital Library as Place." *Journal of Documentation* 63, no. 4: 505–533. Available: http://dlist.sir.arizona.edu/1987 (accessed January 7, 2009).

Rosenfeld, Louis, and Peter S. Morville. 2006. *Information Architecture for the World Wide Web*, 3rd edition. Sebastopol, CA; O'Reilly and Associates, Inc.

Schmidt, Karen, Wendy Allen Shelburne, and David Steven Vess. 2007. "Approaches to Selection, Access, and Collection Development in the Web World: A Case Study with Fugitive Literature." *Library Resources & Technical Services* 52, no. 3: 184–191.

Schonfeld, Roger C. 2007. "Getting from Here to There, Safely: Library Strategic Planning for the Transition Away from Print Journals." *The Serials Librarian* 52, no. 1/2: 183–189.

Shirk, Gary. 2007. "Toward a Topography of Library Collections." *Library Administration* 46, no. 1: 99–111.

Skaggs, Bethany Latham. 2006. "Assessing an Integrated Government Documents Collection." *Collection Building* 25, no. 1: 14–19.

Spitzer, Stephan, and Stephen Brown. 2007. "A Checkup with Open Source Software Revitalizes an Early Electronic Resource Portal." *Computers in Libraries* 27, no. 8: 10–15.

Stephens, Jane, Pauline Melgoza, and Gang (Gary) Wan. 2009. "Safari Books Online: Currency, Usage and Book Release Policies of an E-book Database." *Collection Building* 27, no. 1: 14–17.

Sutton, Allison M., and JoAnn Jacoby. 2009. "A Comparative Study of Book and Journal Use in Four Social Science Disciplines." *Behavioral & Social Sciences Librarian* 27, no. 1: 1–33.

Uddin, Mohammad Nasir, and Paul Janecek. 2006. "The Implementation of Faceted Classification in Web Site Searching and Browsing." *Online Information Review* 31, no. 2: 218–233.

Weber, Mary Beth. 2002. *Cataloging Nonprint and Internet Resources: A How-To-Do-It Manual for Librarians*. New York: Neal-Schuman.

Wrubel, Laura S. 2007. "Improving Access to Electronic Resources (ER) Through Usability Testing." *Collection Management* 32, no. 1/2: 225–234.

Xie, Hong (Iris). 2006. "Evaluation of Digital Libraries: Criteria and Problems from Users' Perspectives." *Library & Information Science Research* 28: 433–452.

WEB SITES CITED

The American Memory Project. Available: http://memory.loc.gov (accessed January 9, 2009).

Archive-It. Available: www.archive-it.org/ (accessed February 12, 2009).

Cataloging Electronic Resources: OCLC-MARC Coding Guidelines. Available: www.oclc.org/support/documentation/worldcat/cataloging/electronicresources/default.htm (accessed February 12, 2009).

CMS Review Listing. Available: www.cmsreview.com/CMSListing.html (accessed January 12, 2009).

CMS Watch (Web Content Management Channel). Available: www.cmswatch.com/CMS/Vendors/?printable=1 (accessed January 12, 2009).

COUNTER (Counting Online Usage of NeTworked Electronic Resources). Available: www.projectcounter.org (accessed January 9, 2009).

Digital Library Federation (DLF). Available: www.diglib.org (accessed January 9, 2009).

DSPACE. Available: www.dspace.org (accessed January 9, 2009).

Dublin Core Metadata Initiative. Available: http://dublincore.org (accessed February 12, 2009).

Dublin Core to MARC Crosswalk. Available: www.loc.gov/marc/dccross.html (accessed February 12, 2009).

Google. Available: www.google.com (accessed January 14, 2009).

Google Analytics. Available: www.google.com/analytics (accessed January 14, 2009).

Hathi Trust. Available: www.hathitrust.org (accessed January 14, 2009).

MARC in XML. Available: www.loc.gov/marc/marcxml.html (accessed February 12, 2009).

OCLC Connexion. Available: www.oclc.org/connexion (accessed February 12, 2009).

OCLC World Cat. Available: www.worldcat.org (accessed January 14, 2009).

Ohio Memory Project. Available: www.ohiomemory.org (accessed January 9, 2009).

Open Archives Initiative (OAI). Available: www.openarchives.org (accessed January 9, 2009).

Open Directory Project Link Management Tools list. Available: www.dmoz.org/Computers/Software/Internet/Site_Management/Link_Management/ (accessed January 12, 2009).

OSS4LIB. Available: http://oss4lib.org (accessed January 12, 2009).

RDA: Resource Description and Access. Available: www.rdaonline.org (accessed February 12, 2009).

Source Forge. Available: http://sourceforge.net (accessed January 12, 2009).

SUSHI (Standardized Usage Statistics Harvesting Initiative). Available: www.niso.org/workrooms/sushi (accessed January 9, 2009).

The USGenWeb. Available: www.rootsweb.ancestry.com/~usgenweb (accessed January 9, 2009).

Wikipedia. Available: http://wikipedia.org (accessed January 16, 2009).

XMLMARC. Available: http://xmlmarc.stanford.edu (accessed February 12, 2009).

CHAPTER

3

E-RESOURCE LICENSING BASICS: GETTING WHAT YOU NEED FOR WHAT YOU ARE WILLING TO PAY

Aside from planning for the future, libraries can undertake a number of practical measures now, such as inspecting license agreements carefully; making the most of opportunities to negotiate terms with publishers; participating in efforts to educate and lobby Congress on copyright issues as they relate to the information-sharing objective of libraries; reviewing collection development policies to ensure that they not only addresses the possibility of disappearing electronic resources, but also provide an appropriate contingency plan; and whenever feasible and legal, retaining or advocating for an archive of database contents or perpetual access. Furthermore, the library profession needs to understand the impact of legislation not only on libraries, but also on copyright holders. As long as legislation is imbalanced, addressing only one set of wrongs (e.g., infringement on behalf of the copyright holder or content provider), the struggle for equity will continue. Only through discussion and compromise can both users and copyright holders produce meaningful legislation. (Lee and Wu, 2007: 95)

INTRODUCTION

A majority of the core reference tools used in libraries are now published as e-resources. In fact, although print reference tools persist, many of the classic print reference tools are now available as e-resources. Commercial e-resource vendors want to make the best profit possible. Even otherwise free Web e-resources may require the library to agree to a license. In a complex legal environment, with constantly evolving technologies and increasing user demand it is a challenge for each library to make the best deal possible when negotiating e-resource licenses. As a result it is increasingly useful for libraries to form or join consortia. A very optimistic note is the NISO Shared E-Resource Understanding (SERU) released in February 2008 (www.niso.org/workrooms/seru). The SERU Working Group began in 2006 to develop guidelines for libraries and vendors to use to reduce the use of licensing agreements. This document clarifies a framework of good faith and shared understandings that when implemented reduces the number of licensing agreements libraries and consortia must manage and the amount of time such negotiations occupy.

The *American Heritage Dictionary of the English Language*, Fourth Edition, defines license as "official or legal permission to do or own a specified thing (accessed January 11, 2009, at http://dictionary.reference.com/browse/license). Generally, the term license is used to refer to the agreement requiring commitment of time and/or money on the part of a licensee to use or access a resource, and on the part of the licensor to provide defined access to a resource with specific content and format. Any agreement between the licensee and a resource supplier (licensor) is, under this definition, a license. This agreement could be something as simple as the free registration required by some sites, the click-through agreement required before using new software or accessing a Web site, or something as complex as the contract between a large consortium with multiple users and sites and a major database vendor.

Although each licensing negotiation between a vendor and a library (or other organization) is unique, there is much that we can learn and build on from our colleagues' experiences. In this environment, librarians who build e-library collections, even if they are not the individuals directly responsible for negotiating and signing the licenses, need to become familiar with licensure issues and terminology. Being able to identify the limitations and restrictions inherent in license agreements is essential in making selection decisions. Developing definitions for license terms, such as *authorized user*, helps greatly to clarify the needs of the library and the goals to be met by the electronic library. In this chapter, we provide a basic introduction to licensing concepts that impact how you will make selection decisions. This chapter does not attempt to teach all of the intricacies of licenses and their negotiation. The publications cited in the next section are all useful for those who will be part of a license negotiation. This chapter does not in any sense attempt to provide legal advice or guidance. It is strongly recommended that you consult with your organization's legal counsel or otherwise making use of legal counsel before signing any license agreement or contract.

RECENT LITERATURE ON LICENSING E-RESOURCES

The process of licensing of e-resources has become commonplace. Several books and articles provide both introductions and foundations for understanding the process. The majority of these publications are written for a librarian audience that needs in-depth information regarding licensing and consortial agreements. That said, all librarians who participate in e-resource selection or use e-resources for reference service will find the basics of professional interest.

Yale University Libraries and Council on Library and Information Resources cosponsored meta site LibLicense: Licensing Digital Information (www.library.yale.edu/~llicense/index.shtml) continues to be a central clearinghouse for the most current licensing related information for librarians. The LibLicense meta site and discussion list also promotes key practical knowledge and competencies as well as guidance on consortia building.

> Librarians who work with each other within a consortium must communicate effectively and efficiently, build trust among and between their institutions, adhere to agreements, and follow through on issues in a timely manner. As mentioned, libraries often belong to several different consortia at the same time—from state-mandated groups to those concerned with a single product to broad-based networks and peer-institutional organizations. The management of these diverse cooperative agreements can place a strain on librarians, library volunteers, and consortial staff. The paradox is that e-content has

made library collaborations easier and more complicated—they are, certainly, less tangible than traditional print-based sharing has been. Collaboration doesn't just happen—library professionals make it happen. The path to a successful collaboration will vary widely from library to library and from consortium to consortium....The key to the completion of a successful consortial deal, regardless of organizational structure, is a mutual trust that everyone involved will accomplish their assigned tasks. (Clement, 2007: 193–194)

Clement's study explores the qualifications and competencies that librarians have or need to acquire in order to function as collection development or acquisitions librarians. The competencies required for librarians working with licensed e-resources are somewhat different than those needed for traditional print acquisitions. There is much more to negotiation than just the legal details. There is a lot of on-the-job learning for collection development librarians working with licensing, but most especially with consortial agreements. The key is not whether to participate but how to participate most effectively. Librarians need financial skills, communications skills, and negotiation skills:

Some of the skill sets that the participants indicated are very important for successful consortial participation were:
- Evaluating databases (60%)
- Negotiation skills (57%)
- Attention to details (57%)
- Familiarity with licensing terms (52%)
- Communication skills (50%)
- Familiarity with copyright issues (43%) (Clement, 2007: 200)

Clement explores some ideas for specific courses and continuing and professional education that is needed for educating librarians working with e-resources. Genco clarifies the need for education and training for librarians:

The impact of technology has transformed libraries. What we're trying to teach in library school now is that the job requires skills of inquiry, investigation, and rethinking. Collection development, vendor relationships, ethics, stewardship of collections—all these things continue, but the environment is entirely changed and will keep changing indefinitely....Books are no longer just physical objects in codexform—they're audio, Braille, large print, paperback, and electronic. There are so many ways the same content can be repurposed or reformatted. Our focus in libraries for too long has been on managing the container holding the information, not on managing and presenting the content within. (Genco and Kuzyk, 2007: 15–16)

Licensing in Libraries: Practical and Ethical Aspects edited by Karen Rupp-Serrano (2005) contains a number of articles that address specific issues in implementing access to e-resources in libraries. Topics range from consortial licensing issues, verifying copyright protection, ensuring that public domain information remains in the public domain, and the real costs of access to how to explain licensing terms to users when access policies are in place.

Guide to Licensing and Acquiring Electronic Information (Bosch et al., 2005) is an ALCTS Acquisitions and Collection Management Guide. This publication details the format types, licensing possibilities, and detailed costing of acquiring access to e-resources. They detail the technical and personnel requirements for different licensing options as well as practical details in implementing access to specific formats. This text covers non-Web-accessible e-resources such as DVDs that might be licensed for local use.

Classic books such as *Licensing Digital Content* by Lesley Ellen Harris (2002) and *Selecting and Managing E-Resources* by Vicki L. Gregory (2000) continue to provide a solid foundation for those who will be participating in license negotiations, making e-resource selections, or making use of e-resources in delivering reference services to users.

In *Licensing Digital Content*, Harris starts at the very beginning of the licensing process: when the librarian is selecting e-resources for an e-library. The first chapter revolves around the key question that every librarian should ask when selecting a new resource: when and if to license a given e-resource. "Licensing comes into play when you want to use electronic or digital content such as a database or periodical, or when someone wants to use such content owned by your library" (Harris, 2002: 2).

In Chapter 2, Harris points out 12 common misconceptions in the licensing process that librarians should be aware of when making selection decisions. Chapter 4 is extremely valuable because it identifies and defines the key legal terms found in license agreements. In Chapter 7, Harris provides the equivalent of an FAQ for digital content licensing, including such common questions as, "What does third-party rights mean? and May a license prohibit interlibrary loans?" (Harris, 2002: 1045). An excellent glossary as well as a listing of additional resources to consult is provided.

In *Selecting and Managing E-Resources*, Gregory provides a full and complete discussion of key issues for libraries selecting and managing e-resources. Chapter 7 focuses entirely on the key issues of copyright and licensing agreements. This chapter makes an important distinction between purchased versus licensed content. This is a key issue when trying to determine the fair use rights of the library purchaser and regarding the library's long-term access to the material (Gregory, 2000: 69). When making selection decisions, whether an outright purchase or a license agreement would be of greater benefit to your institution is an essential question to answer. The list of best practice suggestions also provides a useful means of learning how other libraries are working through these issues. The parts of the chapter dealing with license negotiation, selecting a license negotiator and managing licenses are not essential reading since they delve into administrative processes that may not pertain to the selecting librarian, but they do provide insight into the licensing process as a whole.

Alford's (2002) classic article "Negotiating and Analyzing Electronic License Agreements" also contains valuable content for both selectors and negotiators. Alford focuses on the licensing of legal information, though much of the content applies to other e-resources as well. Librarians will find the negotiating points section useful for its identification and detailed analysis of topics that overlap the selection process. This section discusses issues such as price, users, access, types of use, and archiving. The article also discusses the licensing principles endorsed by various groups and reviews three different standard licenses.

Another classic, Metz (2000) discussed the transitions from the selection process to the licensing process. In larger institutions, the move from the decision to collect to negotiations and the making of final arrangements signals a transfer of responsibility from the chief collection development officer to the head of library acquisitions. In smaller institutions, these roles are often combined in one person (Metz, 2000: 718). Whether your role as a builder of electronic library collections also includes the negotiation of licensing agreements or not, this article will make you aware of the differences between how vendors define terms such as *authorized user* and how a particular library would. These issues can come into play during negotiations and can sometimes result in a library not being able to provide access to an e-resource that has been selected. Metz also discusses other areas of potential difficulty between vendor and library.

Metzinger Miller's (2003) article "Behind Every Great Virtual Library Stand Many Great Licenses" is a clear and detailed identification of the most important factors for e-library users can complicate license negotiations with vendors. Among the factors that a selector must consider are: reaching a particular population supporting distance education and sustaining online education, including both Web-based and Web-enhanced courses (Metzinger Miller, 2003). Metzinger Miller takes examples of typical clauses in license agreements and uses them to demonstrate the questions that a library must answer, both in selecting a resource and then negotiating for it. Of particular note for selectors are the samples that focus on authorized users and remote sites. Both are key concerns and should be helping to drive any selection decisions.

More recently, e-books licensing issues are frequent topics of discussion. Most articles mention that the license limitations that most e-book vendors have placed on access, printing, and downloading have made all e-books unpopular with many users (Cleto, 2008; Sottong, 2009; Connaway and Wicht, 2007; Hernon et al., 2007; Sandler et al., 2007; Rice, 2006). There are too many problems that won't go away. Sottong (2009) is typical in reporting usability results: "...when the patron gave up because of the difficulty of reading on the screen or the inability to print and copy" (45).

Connaway and Wicht reviewed the literature on e-books published between 2000 and 2007. They find that although initially enthusiastic, librarians have found e-books difficult to promote to users because of the problems. E-books that are strictly reference tools have been popular among medical, engineering, and computer sciences users who are primarily looking for short pieces of specific information rather than trying to actually read an entire book online.

One article voiced optimism that publishers and vendors would overcome the problems that make e-books unpopular and along with the increasingly e-resource oriented teaching and learning environment this will improve e-book usage (Sandler et al., 2007).

LICENSE ISSUES FOR SELECTING AND REFERENCE LIBRARIANS

Before selecting a given e-resource and negotiating a license agreement, clarify and codify an understanding of your library users and your library organization's information needs. First ask yourself how you will be using this particular content in your library. Librarians should be asking that question about every resource chosen for an e-library, but it serves a double purpose when it comes time to negotiate a license. The answer to this question permits libraries to make certain that groups of users (such as distance learning students) or types of use (electronic reserves for example) are not specifically excluded in the license agreement. After selecting a resource, make a list of all of the things that you and your library users might do with the e-resource. By doing so you can arm the negotiator with the right type of knowledge. Remember that you selected the resource to make it available to your users. The selecting librarians must help the negotiating librarians to determine which are the make or break issues. Creating a list makes it less likely you'll overlook rights and limits that are important to your users. For most libraries this list should include the following:

- Archiving
- Accessibility and usability for virtual reference service/distance learning students/e-reserves/interlibrary loan (ILL)

- Printing, downloading, e-mailing
- Examining licenses
- Click-through licenses

What happens to licensed digital content when the license is concluded? Does the library retain access or ownership in any way? What happens if the vendor goes out of business? Archiving of materials previously licensed tends to decrease the amount of fees available under a license agreement. Not surprisingly, this is an issue where there is usually considerable disagreement between the library and the licensor:

> Preservation and access in the digital environment. . . . A number of multi-library systems or consortia are collaboratively licensing online journals and retaining a single print subscription as an archival back-up. But as the focus has shifted from print to electronic publication, online editions are increasingly being accepted as the *de facto* "journals of record." As a consequence, librarians and publishers are searching for ways to protect their long-term interests in the online editions. There is growing interest in preserving electronic journals and, among librarians, in insuring their access persists over the long term. While publishers generally recognize the value of assuring that digital files will be available and usable over the life of their enterprise, libraries have a longer preservation horizon, reflecting their traditional mission and the need to maintain the backfile access rights they had in the print environment. They have been reluctant to accept publishers as credible stewards of preservation because of threats to publisher continuity or solvency in changing markets. Yet, because libraries are licensing online journals as a service rather than acquiring ownership of a physical artifact, preservation and long-term access solutions require collaboration by the publisher. Beyond the issue of how electronic files will be migrated or otherwise preserved over time (and how this will be financed), is the issue of whether subscribing libraries will have access to subscribed content if they no longer are paying an annual license fee. Although some publishers have viewed persistent access commitments as a liability or a forgone opportunity, there are a number of examples of agreements to address preservation needs: Some libraries are moving to e-only once journals have established digital preservation arrangements with Portico, an electronic archiving service supported by libraries and publishers. (Johnson and Luther, 2007)

Can the resource be used to provide reference assistance to users of virtual or digital reference services, who may not be physically present in the library? Are there restrictions that might prohibit registered students from accessing the resource from off campus? How can licenses be negotiated to ensure that virtual reference services and distance learners are able to access and use the e-resource? How important is it that the e-resource be accessible and usable for virtual reference services and/or distance learners? Can the content be placed on reserve in either its electronic or print versions? A related question would be whether the material might be used in course packs. Can the content from the e-resource be used to fill ILL requests?

A corollary to the accessibility and usability questions is: In what formats can the content be delivered for library user use? Is the e-resource of any use or value if the information is difficult to deliver to the intended users through their preferred information delivery options? It is likely that librarians may not be able to see in advance the license for a particular product. This is particularly true in the case of commercial resources where licenses are typically negotiated between the vendor and each individual institution. This has become less of an issue when library consortia are negotiating. When individualized negotiations were the norm, numerous publishers included a nondisclosure provision in their contracts, especially in contracts negotiated with larger institutions. They do this so that librarians at one institution would not be able to share the details of their deal with other librarians. This is a problem when vendors will not share licensing agreements in advance and make one library a better or worse deal than another.

Some e-resources will have click-through licenses that librarians should review immediately and prior to completion of the click-through. A click-through agreement requires users to affirmatively click on a button indicating their acceptance of the licensing agreement before they can install the software or view the information. If you select a resource that has a click-through agreement, be certain to take the time to know the provisions included with the license, as these are nonnegotiable. Once someone agrees, they are bound to the agreement as written. This is particularly necessary in libraries where Internet access is open. If a library user responds affirmatively to a click-through license and then abuses the conditions therein, it is possible that the library may be held partially responsible.

KEY LICENSE TERMS AND SECTIONS

> Librarians selecting e-resources will benefit from familiarity with some of the key terms that are standard in most licenses. Thinking of these legal terms in the context of your user population and needs is especially beneficial. Authorized users are the individuals permitted within the scope of the license to use the resource. By preference, librarians will want this definition to be as broad as possible to permit access to the largest number of library users; whereas a vendor will be seeking a narrower range of users to limit access or will negotiate higher fees for broader authorized user definitions. For an academic institution, users should at least include the current faculty, staff, and students of the university. Distance education students, temporary researchers, and library users walking into the library on campus should fall within the definition of users. (Alford, 2002: 636)

The key terms and sections in licensing agreements are:

- Definitions
- Fair use
- Rights granted
- Site
- Digital rights management (DRM)
- Concurrent users and COUNTER compliance

The definitions section is the most important in a licensing agreement, because it is where the agreed-to definitions of terms are spelled out. Though many selectors may not have a role in negotiating the terms of the license agreement, their input is still necessary to the process. Selecting and reference librarians must help identify the needs of the library's users as well as classifying those users. This process needs to begin long before any negotiations take place.

Libraries will want to make sure that a license does not restrict fair use rights. There should be no restrictions in the electronic license agreement that would be more restrictive than that provided under the copyright law for printed materials. In other words, if you select a resource, you want your library users to be able to use it without having to worrying about excessive restrictions (Lee and Wu, 2007).

The rights granted clause delineates which specific rights the library is granted as licensee. Printing and downloading are two of the rights that you should keep in mind when selecting. An e-resource that doesn't allow your users to print or download is probably not worth the effort to license. This is one major problem with many e-book vendors. They restrict printing and downloading to such a degree that most nonreference texts are unusable (Cleto, 2008; Sottong, 2009; Connaway and Wicht, 2007; Hernon et al., 2007; Rice, 2006).

In dealing with a license where use is tied to a particular site (called a site license), the definition of the term *site* is very important. Is it defined as a physical location, such as a single building or a campus, or is it defined as an IP (Internet protocol) address range or a geographical region; for example, residents or "authorized users" of a specific region (CBUC) or state (OPLIN)?

In the process of licensing e-books and some other e-content, there are other levels of complexity to consider. The major area is digital rights management (DRM) limitations to protect intellectual property rights. These often actually disable the ability of the user to make use of the information when they limit or prevent printing, downloading, or viewing more than a preset amount of content.

DRM issues are the key to usability or lack thereof. One apparent idea of vendors is that the e-book collection serves primarily as a shopping catalog. So libraries license access to e-books and this brings more print book sales to the vendor. DRM often places limits on the number of concurrent users or how many people can use it at the same time. If the e-resources is available only to one or two users at a time but the library wishes to make it available to several thousand students or members of the public, there is an essential conflict of interests. COUNTER compliance (www.projectcounter.org) or compliance with the industry standard for usage measurements is a related issue. Does the vendor comply with the standards for measuring usage? Are extra charges incurred for different levels of usage?

> There are three basic models of eBook licensing that seem to cover most vendors, with a few variations and one notable exception. The print model of eBook licensing treats the eBook the same as a print book present in the library. The book is offered for checkout, and once checked out, cannot be accessed by other users. The other dominant model follows the familiar "database subscription" model, and parallels subscriptions to such resources as InfoTrac OneFile, with an annual subscription fee and unlimited simultaneous access for users. The final model is the free or open access model, which encompasses all those eBook collections that are available for free on the Web. (Rice, 2006: 28)

Another e-book specific licensing issue is the availability of MARC records, because cataloging e-books makes them more usable and accessible. Does the license indicate ownership of the e-book content by the library or only access via a limited subscription? Does the license allow for changing or adding or deleting titles from the subscribed e-books?

OUTSIDE FACTORS AFFECTING E-RESOURCE LICENSES

Once your library has selected a given e-resource and negotiated a workable license with the vendor, the licensing process may have only just begun. Outside factors may change the content, format, or accessibility of the resource or change the legal status of the license after the fact. Librarians will want to be aware that this can happen and try to determine how such factors may affect the license or the e-resource content and usability. One example of an outside factor that changed the content and format of several e-resources—specifically full-text e-journal consolidators—was the court case *New York Times v. Tasini*. The case revolved around six freelance authors who sued the *New York Times* for licensing their articles to full-text vendors, such as LexisNexis, in violation of the authors' copyright. The court held that the authors were correct and as a result the articles in question were removed from a number of licensed resources. Fortunately, the effect of the Tasini decision is primarily retrospective. Most publisher author agreements now include specific details about the copyright of e-versions of the content (Lee and Wu, 2007).

Governmental actions, either through policy or legislation may also change the terms of licensing agreements especially in regard to content. It has happened several times in the past decade that certain government agencies in the United States (and some other countries as well) for various legitimate (e.g., data privacy) or suspect reasons have removed content from their Web sites. In many of those cases, no alternative source of that data is available, leaving an unfilled gap in many collections. Decisions to sell content that was previously available free of charge is another way in which the content, format, and accessibility of e-resources can change, thus requiring libraries that had been accessing Web content for free to license or otherwise pay for that content. The passage of legislation can have unexpected and problematic repercussions. Laws such as the Digital Millennium Copyright Act can transform a library's rights regarding information and to whom it may be delivered and in what form and whether it can be archived (Cleto, 2008; Sottong, 2008; Connaway and Wicht, 2007; Rice, 2006).

Other laws, such as the USA PATRIOT Act, can alter the relationship between libraries, e-resources, and their users. All of these factors may affect the legal status of the license. Another potential problem is UCITA, the Uniform Computer Information Transactions Act, which is a proposed law that if it is adopted more widely will be a major source of headaches for libraries and others. Librarians should be aware of how pervasive UCITA will be in their daily lives. Moreover, library administrators (and others) should be aware that there has been a steady push in the digital information industry to have contracts control their products rather than copyright law.

> UCITA provides vendors with a wide berth for dictating license terms that effectively override the doctrine of first sale, which permits a purchaser of a copyrighted work to resell, loan, or "otherwise dispose of possession of that copy." The doctrine of first sale is at the core of library circulation operations, and it countenances the addition of donated materials to library collections.... In short, UCITA, although well-intentioned, places few restrictions on providers, and consequently, the potential for abuse threatens the ability of libraries to provide information and services. Whenever possible in negotiating licenses, libraries should check to see if forum choice dictates a UCITA state. If so, libraries should attempt to change the terms to a more agreeable forum. (Lee and Wu, 2007: 90)

One of the problems of UCITA is that it would allow software publishers to change the terms of the contract after purchase. Even though UCITA has been adopted by only two states so far (Maryland and Virginia), it may affect some libraries current licenses. For example, many large software vendors and publishers are located in Virginia, and with UCITA enactment in Virginia, its effects may be felt in states that have not passed UCITA through licensing contract provisions specifying the law of Virginia as being applicable to the license in question. If these choices of law provisions become common and are ultimately upheld by the courts, many vendors and publishers could simply establish a presence in Virginia or Maryland (and any other state that adopts UCITA) in order to take advantage nationwide of the additional protections offered them by UCITA. The American Library Association, Washington Office, maintains an UCITA Updates Web site at www.ala.org/ala/aboutala/offices/wo/woissues/copyrightb/statelegislation/ucita/ucita.cfm.

E-LIBRARY SUCCESS STORY

BIBLIOTECA DIGITAL DE CATALUNYA (BDC)
Consorci de Biblioteques Universitàries de Catalunya (CBUC)
Barcelona, Spain
www.cbuc.es
Contact: Núria Comellas, Librarian-Projects Assistant, ncomellas@cbuc.es, and Lluís Anglada, Director, langlada@cbuc.es

A. Collection Planning (e.g., goal setting and identification of users, technology/personnel choices)

The Biblioteca Digital de Catalunya (BDC) (Catalan Digital Library) is a shared, central e-library collection the 15 public university library members of the Consorci de Biblioteques Universitàries de Catalunya (CBUC) (Consortium of Catalan University Libraries). CBUC was formed in 1996 with an agreement between the eight Catalan academic libraries and the National Library of Catalonia to build a union catalog. As the union catalog plan was implemented, CBUC studied and demonstrated the potential benefits of purchasing equipment and central database licensing negotiation for the member libraries. In 1998, CBUC received initial funding from the Catalan government to begin building the BDC.

The BDC is designed so that each member library can either access shared resources from the CBUC page or link directly from the member library Web site to any of the shared resources. It is not designed for library access but rather for the member libraries to incorporate shared resources into their individual e-library Web sites. The goals of the BDC project are: "to provide a core set of multidisciplinary e-resources (with some advantages in price and access conditions) to all of our consortium members, the Catalan university libraries. The result should be that any university student or faculty in any CBUC member library has the same amount of "basic" e-information to do their work/research. From the repositories side, the goal is to collect all the intellectual production from Catalan universities, along with the dissemination of open access publications in Catalan or published in Catalonia. The first design and licensing negotiations for commercial e-resources took place in 1997-8, and first deals started in January 1999 (Academic Press e-journals, Aranzadi [Spanish law database], Econlit+ERIC+Medline from Ovid, MathSciNet from AMS).... From 2000 onwards, BDC licensing program has expanded by adding several open access digital repositories built to collect CBUC members' publications like theses, working papers, OA journals, etc."

The direct users of the BDC are the Catalan university libraries and librarians, but ultimately their library users—faculty and students—are the main beneficiaries of the BDC. Those ultimate library users are not usually aware of the role played by the CBUC in maintaining the collaboration.

The CBUC members (including associated members) are:

Universitat de Barcelona (www.bib.ub.es/bub/bub.htm or http://www.ub.es)
Universitat Autònoma de Barcelona (www.bib.uab.es or www.uab.es)
Universitat Politècnica de Catalunya (http://bibliotecnica.upc.es or www.upc.es)
Universitat Pompeu Fabra (www.upf.es/bib/index.htm or www.upf.es)
Universitat de Girona (http://biblioteca.udg.es or http://www.udg.es)
Universitat de Lleida (www2.bib.udl.es or www.udl.es)
Universitat Rovira i Virgili (www.urv.es/biblioteca/marcos.htm or www.urv.es)

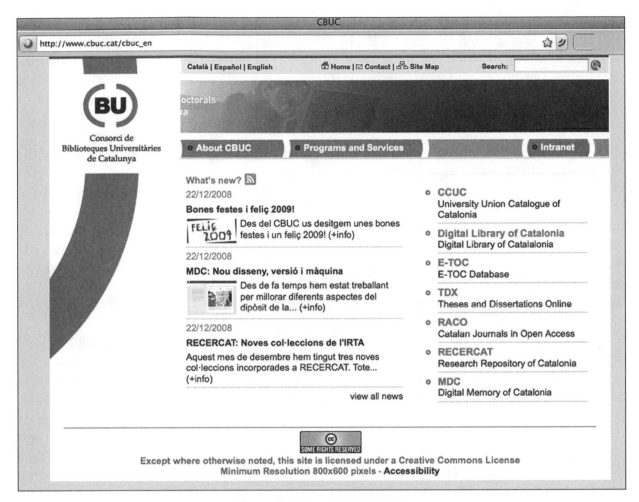

Figure 3.1. CBUC BDC

Universitat Oberta de Catalunya (http://xina.uoc.es/cat/inici.html or www.uoc.edu/
    web/cat/index.html)

Biblioteca de Catalunya (www.gencat.es/bc)

Universitat Jaume I (www.uji.es/CA/cd/ or http://www.uji.es)

Universitat de Vic (www.uvic.cat/biblioteca/ca/inici.html or www.uvic.cat)

Universitat d'Andorra (www.uda.ad/index.php?option=com_content&task=view&
    id=75&Itemid=163 or www.uda.ad)

Universitat de les Illes Balears (www.uib.es/servei/biblioteca or www.uib.es)

Universitat Ramon Llull (www.url.edu/cont/url/biblioteques.php or www.url.edu)

Universitat Internacional de Catalunya (www.uic.es/ca/biblioteca or www.uic.es)

Most of the licensed e-resources are available to remote authorized users at each member library, so any distance learners are supported. "One of our members (Universitat Oberta de Catalunya) is a distance learning university, therefore BDC is also open to its users (home-schoolers and faculty, mainly). Besides, most of our e-resources vendors allow the remote access from home (via authorized IP ranges) for any CBUC member."

The CBUC created a flexible collection plan that is designed to change and grow as the member libraries need, the technologies and e-resources change and grow. The current policy is online at www.cbuc.es/cbuc_en/programes_i_serveis/bdc/qu_s. "In the first years, we thought the main part of BDC licensing would be bibliographic databases, but soon we discovered that full text and specially e-journals were the backbone of the digital library. In the last 3 or 4 years the 'all for all' model (a 'must' for many years) seems to be coming to its end, and we already tried some opt-in deals to allow some CBUC members (maybe those with bigger budgets) to upgrade their e-collection with resources that might not be affordable or interesting for all but are for some members."

B. Collection Strategies (e.g., selection criteria, identification of resources, licensing, and related user information needs)

The overall goal of the BDC is to build a strong collection of critical scientific content from the most authoritative sources. The priority is to collect and make available the highest level scientific information for faculty and research library users. User studies (Borrego et al., 2007, Urbano et al. 2004) reveal a strong preference for full text rather than merely bibliographic databases. Some attention is being given to acquiring additional undergraduate level e-resources as well, including image databases. A recently completed and ongoing collection analysis reassures CBUC that they have been very successful in meeting their goal for the BDC core content.

"We provide fee-based access to thirty-something databases, many of them including full-text articles (Business Source Elite, Factiva, etc.). However, the main part of our licensing deals are on e-journals (more than 10,000 titles from the main academic publishers). A list of licensed resources is available at the left hand side of the web page http://www.cbuc.cat/cbuc_en/programes_i_serveis/bdc/acc_s_per_t_tols."

Member libraries pay the main costs for the licensed databases, e-books, and e-journals, with some costs being covered by the Catalonian government. Wherever possible, licensing agreements must include remote access for authorized users of each member library. Archiving arrangements are also made in the licenses and include arrangements such as: fee-based access to vendor's server to paid information in case of termination, etc. "We currently have 7 licenses for e-books at a consortium level: nearly 8,000 titles in total. The main part comes from Springer (including Lecture Notes in Computer Science), followed by netLibrary, Safari Tech Books Online, Oxford Reference Online (ORO), Gale Virtual Reference Library and Harrison's Online. Usage level is very important in reference and textbooks like Safari or ORO. Besides, over 900 Spanish law e-books are included in our subscription to a Spanish law database called VLEX. We're considering some more e-book packages to be subscribed/purchased in the future."

CBUC catalogs all e-resources into their union catalog (www.cbuc.cat/cbuc_en/programes_i_serveis/ccuc). "Individual CBUC libraries can copy the record in their local catalogs. In 2007, nearly 70% of all the volumes (not just electronic) were copied from external services or among CBUC members. We can track use of the records by the copy cataloguing statistics."

Digital library collections and scholarly repositories are ongoing projects with the CBUC consortia and for many of the individual member libraries. The BDC serves as a central access point for the individual library projects and other academic Web sites, digital libraries, and scholarly repository projects created by Catalan organizations.

"BDC can be a 'shop window' for many CBUC members' open access activities. There was a common interest early in 2000 to build cooperative repositories to gather, disseminate and preserve CBUC members' academic output. Nowadays we have 4 repositories: TDX (theses), Recercat (working papers), RACO (current Catalan full text journals) and MDC (Catalan ancient journals, photographs, maps, posters, ex-libris, etc.). There is another one in process for learning objects, to be called MDX. More information on the left frame of http://www.cbuc.cat/cbuc_en/programes_i_serveis."

Interlibrary loan and document delivery have been a part of CBUC's services among member libraries since 1997 and have been very successful. Future projects to create library user initiated interlibrary loan options are underway (www.cbuc.cat/cbuc_en/programes_i_serveis/pica). CBUC member libraries have begun to develop a consortium-wide virtual reference service using Questionpoint software. Member libraries have created a common policies document, and some member libraries have begun their virtual reference service. "The next stage will be to evaluate/improve the performance of the local services and also to move to a cooperative knowledge base of answers/questions."

C. Collection Organization (e.g., content management systems, Web server choices, personnel responsibilities, etc.)

The BDC currently consists of individual maintained Web pages with resource descriptions and access links to the licensed and other e-resources. They do not yet use an ERMS but are considering Millenium for e-resource management. The site uses SFXlink resolver to manage e-serials access and MetaLib software as a meta search tool. All maintenance is done directly by the CBUC staff members. The digital libraries and repositories within the BDC site are managed using several different CMS options and an a technology partner.

"Digitized e-resources (repositories) are managed using mainly open source software (DSpace, OJS, NDLTD) and also a commercial one (CONTENTdm). We have a technological partner (CESCA) to help us maintaining hardware/software. Each CBUC member library uploads its files from the repositories' administrative Web access; this work can be done from the library of from other departments such as the university press offices. CBUC librarians coordinate the projects, making use of periodic meetings with CBUC members' representatives to keep up-to-date information on new developments or common problems. Individual documents in the repositories are also catalogued in the union and local catalogs, and can be searched through CBUC's MetaLib."

Three full-time librarians, two part-time librarians, and one computer staff person support the CBUC BDC project. One and a half full-time equivalent librarians support licensing, and one and half full-time equivalent librarians support repositories. "The first person hired for BDC in 1997 immediately began working on consortial licensing of fee-based e-resources. Later on, this position incorporated the set-up and maintenance of repositories. In 2004 an existing CBUC librarian was designated to be responsible for repositories only. In 2005 an assistant librarian was incorporated to help the two BDC librarians. We also have two paid library school students who work part-time."

The CBUC Board of Directors along with working groups formed by member library librarians for specific areas make collection strategy decisions. "Collectors meet 3–4 times a year to evaluate new (and also already subscribed) information resources. Repositories are added to almost daily, each time a theses is submitted or a working paper is delivered at the university. Each CBUC member library is responsible for uploading files regularly, following CBUC guidelines."

Newly acquired BDC e-resources are catalogued in the union catalog and also activated in the CBUC SFX/MetaLib software. Individual CBUC member libraries are then responsible for adding the links through their own e-library Web pages. Collectors use a variety of collection development tools in making e-resource acquisition decisions. Professional library or subject area journals, reviews from professional colleagues in discussion lists, as well as other consortia e-library recommendations are all used in evaluating potential e-resources.

D. Collection Maintenance (e.g., link checking, ongoing weeding, and growth of the e-library collection)

Maintenance of fee-based e-resources is done monthly. "[W]e're using SFX link resolver, which has been a huge management improvement since we installed it a couple of years ago. The repository links are quite stable, although some of them are provided by third-parties. For instance, the Recercat repository is built on DSpace, and permanent links are provided by Handle.net. Checking is not done on a periodical basis, but very few links are lost."

User feedback is gathered continuously through meetings and formal surveys. "In our case "users" means member libraries. Our job as a consortium is to do what our libraries tell us to do, if the proposals fit in the BDC objectives (and if funds and resources are available)."

The BDC information architecture is reviewed at the beginning of each year to document the current status of each project and any new ideas to be developed. "Annual reviews are conducted by our consortium director (with the acquiescence of individual library directors) and presented to our consortium Government Board. Responsibilities for upgrades, etc., are then undertaken by the pertinent librarians in the CBUC."

Future plans for the BDC, improved cross-database searching, Web 2.0 functionalities for users, etc. are under development. "Regarding cross-database search tools we are currently using MetaLib, though we think we still have quite a long way to go before we got real advantages of it. We also just finished the implementation of a new ILS (Millennium) for our union catalog and local catalogs, which will allow us to implement some web 2.0 facilities (book covers, comments from users, etc.) and also interact better with databases and e-journals we have in the BDC."

CBUC has done several user and collection analysis studies on the BDC. They frequently collaborate with the University of Barcelona's Library School. Two of the most recently published (in English) are the following:

Borrego, Ángel, Lluís M. Anglada i de Ferrer, Maite Barrios, and Núria Comellas. 2007. "Use and Users of Electronic Journals at Catalan Universities: The Results of a Survey." *The Journal of Academic Librarianship* 33, no. 1 (January): 67–75. Preprint at http://hdl.handle.net/2072/3692.

Urbano, Cristóbal, Lluís M. Anglada i de Ferrer, Ángel Borrego, Carme Cantos, Antonio Cosculluela, and Núria Comellas. 2004. "The Use of Consortially Purchased Electronic Journals by the CBUC (2000–2003)." D-Lib Magazine 10, no. 6. Available: www.dlib.org/dlib/june04/anglada/06anglada.html.

"We also did an article about our open access (repositories) activities for a Spanish journal:

Actividades open access de los consorcios del SELL y del CBUC." 2005. *El profesional de la información* 14, núm. 4 (julio-agosto): 280–285. Available: www.elprofesional delainformacion.com/contenidos/2005/julio/280.pdf."

"In 2009, we're preparing new reports on ten years of usage (BDC is celebrating its 10th anniversary!) and users (we'd like to have 'real' feedback from individual users, to know what are their feelings and suggestions for a better collection in the future)."

Some Final Thoughts on E-Resource Licensing

User-centered collection analysis is central to inform licensing negotiations—cost, usability, accessibility, and archiving are all critical. The central challenges of building e-library collections have shifted from selecting and evaluating appropriate e-resources to negotiating and licensing to ensure access and usability. We are not only occupied with selecting and evaluating the best information resources for our users, we're also occupied with making sure that our users have access to usable e-resources. Cost is only one piece—though a major piece—of e-resource licensing. Keep in mind that a license will set the terms of your usage of the resource, which may include restricting use that might otherwise be considered "fair use" under copyright law. Maintaining public domain and fair use access under copyright laws and protecting our libraries and our users from the erosion of those rights requires a great deal of our attention. At the same time we respect the rights of intellectual property owners and creators to profit from their work reasonably. Be aware and know what your library or organization finds acceptable.

References and Web Sites Cited

Alford, Duncan E. 2002. "Negotiating and Analyzing Electronic License Agreements." *Law Library Journal* 94, no. 4: 6214. Available: www.aallnet.org/products/pub_llj_v94n04/2002-39.pdf (accessed January 9, 2009).

Bielefield, Arlene, and Lawrence Cheeseman. 1999. *Interpreting and Negotiating Licensing Agreements: A Guidebook for the Library, Research, and Teaching Professions.* New York: Neal-Schuman.

Bosch, Stephen, Patricia A. Promis, and Chris Sugnet, with Trisha Davis. 2005. *Guide to Licensing and Acquiring Electronic Information.* ALCTS Acquisitions Guides, no. 13; Collection Management and Development Guides, no. 13. Chicago: Association for Library Collections and Technical Services (ALCTS), American Library Association.

Clement, Susanne. 2007. "Skills for Effective Participation in Consortia: Preparing for Collaborating and Collaboration." *Collection Management* 32, no. 1/2: 191–204.

Cleto, Cynthia. 2008. "10 Steps to Implementing an eBook Collection: A Guide for Librarians." *Against the Grain* (February): 47–48.

Connaway, Lynn, and Heather L. Wicht. 2007. "What Happened to the E-Book Revolution?: The Gradual Integration of E-Books into Academic Libraries." *The Journal of Electronic Publishing* 10, no. 3. Available: http://hdl.handle.net/2027/spo.3336451.0010.302.

Genco, Barbara, and Raya Kuzyk. 2007. "20 Maxims for Collection Building." *Library Journal* 132, no. 15: 32–35.

Gregory, Vicki L. 2000. *Selecting and Managing E-Resources.* New York: Neal-Schuman.

Harris, Lesley Ellen. 2002. *Licensing Digital Content: A Practical Guide for Librarians.* Chicago: American Library Association.

Hernon, Peter, Rosita Hopper, Michael R. Leach, Laura L. Saunders, and Jane Zhang. 2007. "E-Book Use by Students: Undergraduates in Economics, Literature, and Nursing." *The Journal of Academic Librarianship* 33, no. 1: 3–13.

Johnson, Richard K., and Judy Luther. 2007. "The E-Only Tipping Point for Journals: What's Ahead in the Print-to-Electronic Transition Zone." Association of Research Libraries. Available: www.arl.org/bm~doc/Electronic_Transition.pdf (accessed January 7, 2009).

Lee, Leslie A., and Michelle M. Wu. 2007. "DMCA, CTEA, UCITA... Oh My! An Overview of Copyright Law and Its Impact on Library Acquisitions and Collection Development of Electronic Resources." In *Collection Development Issues in the Online Environment*, edited by Di Su. Binghamton, NY: The Haworth Press.

Metz, Paul. 2000. "Principles of Selection for E-Resources." *Library Trends* 48, no. 4: 71–129. Available: http://findarticles.com/p/articles/mi_m1387/is_4_48/ai_65806153 (accessed January 9, 2009).

Metzinger Miller, Kathryn. 2003. "Behind Every Great Virtual Library Stand Many Great Licenses." *Library Journal Net Connect* 128, no. 1: 20–22.

New York Times Co. v. Tasini, 533 U. S. 483; 121 S. Ct. 2381; 150 L. Ed. 2d 500; 2001 U. S. LEXIS 4667.

Rice, Scott. 2006. "Own or Rent? A Survey of eBook Licensing Models." *Against the Grain* 18, no. 3: 28–29.

Rupp-Serrano, Karen, ed. 2005. *Licensing in Libraries: Practical and Ethical Aspects*. Binghamton, NY: The Haworth Press. (Published simultaneously as *Journal of Library Administration* 42, no. 3/4).

Sandler, Mark, Kim Armstrong, and Bob Nardini. 2007. "Market Formation for E-Books: Diffusion, Confusion or Delusion." *The Journal of Electronic Publishing* 10, no. 3. Available: http://hdl.handle.net/2027/spo.3336451.0010.310 (accessed January 7, 2009).

Sottong, Stephen. 2009. "The Elusive E-Book: Are E-Books Finally Ready for Prime Time?" *American Libraries* 39, no. 5: 44–49.

WEB SITES CITED

COUNTER (Counting Online Usage of NeTworked Electronic Resources). Available: www.project counter.org (accessed January 9, 2009).

LibLicense: Licensing Digital Information. Available: www.library.yale.edu/~llicense/index.shtml (accessed January 9, 2009).

NISO (National Information Standards Organization) Shared E-Resource Understanding (SERU). Available: www.niso.org/workrooms/seru (accessed January 9, 2009).

OPLIN: Ohio Public Information Network. Available: www.oplin.lib.oh.us (accessed January 16, 2009).

UCITA Updates, American Library Association, Washington Office. Available: www.ala.org/ala/aboutala/offices/wo/woissues/copyrightb/statelegislation/ucita/ucita.cfm (accessed January 9, 2009).

Collection Management and Maintenance Tools

Archiving, Cataloging, Metadata, Assessment/Analysis, Licensing, and Miscellaneous Collection Maintenance Tools

Archive-It

www.archive-it.org

Internet Archive subscription program for archiving primary data from Web sites. "Allows institutions to build and preserve collections of born digital content. Through our user-friendly Web application, Archive-It partners can harvest, catalog, manage, and browse their archived collections. Collections are hosted at the Internet Archive data center and are accessible to the public with full-text search."

Beyond Bookmarks: Schemes for Organizing the Web

www.public.iastate.edu/~CYBERSTACKS/CTW.htm

Overview of different classification systems and how they might be used to organize Web resources.

CLOCKSS Program

www.clockss.org/clockss/Home

Will go live in 2009. "CLOCKSS (Controlled LOCKSS) is a joint venture between the world's leading scholarly publishers and research libraries whose mission is to build a sustainable, geographically distributed dark archive with which to ensure the long-term survival of Web-based scholarly publications for the benefit of the greater global research community."

Copyright Clearance Center

www.copyright.com

CCC assists libraries and individuals in obtaining permissions for use of copyrighted material and clarifying the process.

COUNTER (Counting Online Usage of NeTworked Electronic Resources)

www.projectcounter.org

"The use of online information resources is growing rapidly. It is widely agreed by producers and purchasers of information that the use of these resources should be measured in a more consistent way. Librarians want to understand better how the information they buy from a variety of sources is being used; publishers want to know how the information products they disseminate are being accessed. An essential requirement to meet these objectives is an agreed international set of standards and protocols governing the recording and exchange of online usage data. The COUNTER Codes of Practice provide these standards and protocols and are published in full on this website."

Creative Commons

http://creativecommons.org

"Creative Commons is a nonprofit corporation dedicated to making it easier for people to share and build upon the work of others, consistent with the rules of copyright. We provide free licenses and other legal tools to mark creative work with the freedom the creator wants it to carry, so others can share, remix, use commercially, or any combination thereof."

Digital Library Federation (DLF)

www.diglib.org

Multiple areas of support for digital library/e-library development—collections, archiving, licensing, database control, etc.

Digital Preservation: National Digital Information Infrastructure and Preservation Program (Library of Congress)

www.digitalpreservation.gov

DSPACE

www.dspace.org

"DSpace captures your data in any format—in text, video, audio, and data. It distributes it over the web. It indexes your work, so users can search and retrieve your items. It preserves your digital work over the long term. DSpace provides a way to manage your research materials and publications in a professionally maintained repository to give them greater visibility and accessibility over time."

Dublin Core Metadata Initiative

http://dublincore.org

"The Dublin Core Metadata Initiative is an open organization engaged in the development of interoperable online metadata standards that support a broad range of purposes and business models. DCMI's activities include work on architecture and modeling, discussions and collaborative work in DCMI Communities and DCMI Task Groups, annual conferences and workshops, standards liaison, and educational efforts to promote widespread acceptance of metadata standards and practices." See especially Diane Hillman, "Using Dublin Core," http://dublincore.org/documents/usageguide/elements.shtml (accessed December 31, 2008).

Dublin Core to MARC Crosswalk

www.loc.gov/marc/dccross.html

The Library of Congress Network Development and MARC Standards Office has published a Crosswalk for mapping between the fifteen Dublin Core data elements and the MARC21 bibliographic data elements.

Educause/Cornell Institute for Computer Policy and Law

www.educause.edu/icpl/863?time=1229891921

"...the Institute incorporates experts from a wide variety of fields, including chief information officers, judicial-system administrators, librarians, attorneys, policy advisors and many others. The Institute supports the professional development of information technology, policy and legal professionals within higher education to facilitate the creation and administration of effective information technology policies. It also monitors and analyzes changes in technology and law to assess the impact of those changes on academic information technology policy."

Golddust Project

www.hull.ac.uk/golddust

Usage data mining and user information matching experiment.

Hathi Trust

www.hathitrust.org

"HathiTrust was conceived as a collaboration of the thirteen universities of the Committee on Institutional Cooperation and the University of California system to establish a repository for these universities to archive and share their digitized collections. Partnership is open to all who share this grand vision."

International Federation of Library Associations: Licensing Principles

www.ifla.org/V/ebpb/copy.htm

Prepared by IFLA's Committee on Copyright and Other Legal Matters (CLM) 2001.

International Federation of Library Associations: Metadata Resources

www.ifla.org/II/metadata.htm

Digital Libraries: MetaData resources, articles, and discussions about many topics relating to metadata, such as meta search, meta gateway, meta server, meta repository, and metadata entry.

Internet Archive and Open Content Alliance Project

www.opencontentalliance.org

Purpose is to scan and/or archive as many open-access texts as possible and archive them. Some overlap with the Gutenberg project, but this project collects current and future texts as well as retrospective content.

Kupersmith, John, "Library Terms That Users Understand"
www.jkup.net/terms.html

>   Librarians' understanding and uses of vocabulary may be quite different from library patrons'. Librarian's vocabulary choices may be confusing for many current and potential patrons. John Kupersmith has published "Library Terms That Users Understand" (www.jkup.net/terms.html) based on user studies of terminology used on library Web sites. His intention is to provide usability data as well as "best practices" on which terms are most effective; "most users can understand them well enough to make productive choices" as labels for library resources and services. It may make sense to us to refer to online databases, but the patron may find "Search Electronic Journals" or "Research by Subject" more understandable.

LibLicense: Licensing Digital Information
www.library.yale.edu/~llicense/index.shtml

>   Yale University Libraries and Council on Library and Information Resources cosponsored meta site for sharing core practical skills, knowledge, and guidance for librarians negotiating licenses for e-resources.

License Agreements for Electronic Products and Services: Frequently Asked Questions
www.cendi.gov/publications/01-3lic_agree.html

>   Detailed overview of the guidelines that government agencies and libraries should use for negotiating licenses for e-resources and other products.

LOCKSS Program
www.lockss.org/lockss/Home

>   "LOCKSS (Lots of Copies Keep Stuff Safe), based at the Stanford University Libraries, is an international community initiative that provides libraries with digital preservation tools and support so that they can easily and inexpensively collect and preserve their own copies of authorized e-content. LOCKSS, in its tenth year, provides libraries with the open-source software and support to preserve today's web-published materials for tomorrow's readers while building their own collections and acquiring a copy of the assets they pay for, instead of simply leasing them."

MARC in XML
www.loc.gov/marc/marcxml.html

>   The Library of Congress MARC in XML documentation defines XML standards for MARC.

Metadata
www.ukoln.ac.uk/metadata

>   Reviews "current approaches to resource description and looks at future options for metadata in the wider context of resource discovery."

METS (Metadata Encoding and Transmission Standard)
www.loc.gov/standards/mets

>   "The METS schema is a standard for encoding descriptive, administrative, and structural metadata regarding objects within a digital library, expressed using the XML schema language of the World Wide Web Consortium. The standard is maintained in the Network Development and MARC Standards Office of the Library of Congress, and is being developed as an initiative of the Digital Library Federation."

MINERVA Project
www.minervaeurope.org

>   Especially good usability guidelines for testing digital library usability.

NISO (National Information Standards Organization) Shared E-Resource Understanding (SERU)
www.niso.org/workrooms/seru

>   The SERU Working Group began in 2006 to develop guidelines for libraries and vendors to use to reduce the use of licensing agreements. This document clarifies a framework of good faith and shared

understandings that when implemented reduces the number of licensing agreements libraries and consortia must manage and the amount of time such negotiations occupy.

OCLC Office of Research and Special Projects
www.oclc.org/research
Conference listings, research projects, and publications relating to resource management.

OPCIT (The Open Citation Project)
http://opcit.eprints.org
Reference linking and citation analysis for Open Archives.

Open Archives Initiative (OAI)
www.openarchives.org
Collection of protocols for interoperability and standards for open archives projects; for example, OAI-PMH (Open Archives Initiative Protocol for Metadata Harvesting).

Open Library (Open Library)
http://openlibrary.org
Creating a Web page catalog record using multiple classification options for every book published. Links from book pages to Gutenburg project, Internet Archives, Worldcat, and to bookstores. This project is a partnership with the Internet Archive Project (www.archive.org/index.php) and uses the Open Archives Initiative protocols (www.openarchives.org).

Open-access Text Archive
www.archive.org/details/texts

Portico
www.portico.org
"The scale and complexity of the infrastructure and operation necessary to preserve core electronic scholarly literature exceeds that which can be supported by any individual library or institutional budget. After extensive, iterative discussion in the library and publisher communities, the Portico electronic archiving service has been shaped in response to this need. Initial support for Portico is provided by The Andrew W. Mellon Foundation, Ithaka, the Library of Congress, and JSTOR. Portico offers a service which provides a permanent archive of electronic scholarly journals."

Public Library Association (PLA) TechNotes
www.ala.org/ala/mgrps/divs/pla/plapublications/platechnotes/index.cfm
Collection of reports, articles, and guides relating to e-library technology.

RDA: Resource Description and Access
www.rdaonline.org
RDA is the new standard for resource description and access designed for the digital world. Built on the foundations established by AACR2, RDA provides a comprehensive set of guidelines and instructions on resource description and access covering all types of content and media.

Science Commons
http://sciencecommons.org
Project to encourage the sharing of scientific data and publications in Web repositories.

SUSHI (Standardized Usage Statistics Harvesting Initiative)
www.niso.org/workrooms/sushi
Protocol for harvesting usage data.

UCITA Updates, American Library Association, Washington Office
www.ala.org/ala/aboutala/offices/wo/woissues/copyrightb/statelegislation/ucita/ucita.cfm
XMLMARC
http://xmlmarc.stanford.edu
Software for converting MARC records to XML format, created by the Stanford University Libraries.

CMS (Content Managment Systems), ERMS (Electronic Resource Management Systems), Meta Search (Federated Search), and Related Software Tools Vendors/Sources

CMS Watch (Web Content Management Channel)
www.cmswatch.com/CMS/Vendors/?printable=1

Includes a list of current CMS vendors both commercial and open source with reviews of each and links to full-text articles on the topic of CMS.

Deep Web Technologies
www.deepwebtech.com

Vendor of federated search software used in sites such as Science.gov (www.science.gov).

Drupal
http://drupal.org

Open source CMS. The Alliance Library System Virtual Library Second Life Info Island Project's written collection development plan is available on a site using the Drupal CMS (http://infoisland.org/drupal/collections).

Ektron CMS
www.ektron.com

University of Nebraska at Kearney using Ektron: http://rosi.unk.edu or www.unk.edu/website/ektron/index.php?id=2191.

Evergeen
www.evergreen-ils.org

Georgia Library Public Information Network for Electronic Services (PINES) developed Evergreen (http://gapines.org/opac/en-US/skin/default/xml/index.xml). Evergreen is an ILS. Open source software, documentation, and lists of other libraries using Evergreen is available.

FEDORA (Flexible Extensible Digital Object Repository Architecture)
www.fedora.info

Open source digital library/scholarly repository management software.

Google Analytics
www.google.com/analytics

Google's Web site usage and statistics utility. Free with some fee-based options. Can be implemented in any Web site.

Index Data
www.indexdata.dk

Vendor of open source and licensed proxy server and meta search tools.

iVia: Open Source Internet Portal and Virtual Library System
http://ivia.ucr.edu

The INFOMINE project developed and uses iVi.

LibData: Library Page Authoring Environment
http://libdata.sourceforge.net

Open source content management system developed by the University of Minnesota Libraries (http://courses.lib.umn.edu). St. Cloud State University is using LibData (http://research.stcloudstate.edu).

LibQUAL+(TM)
www.libqual.org

"LibQUAL+(TM) is a suite of services that libraries use to solicit, track, understand, and act upon users' opinions of service quality."

Library-specific CMS developed by Ithaca College Library
www.ithaca.edu/library

LibraryThing for Libraries
www.librarything.com/forlibraries
> Catalog your books online with Web 2.0 communications tools integrated.

The Mambo Foundation
http://mambo-foundation.org
> Open source content management system.

The Metasearch Infrastructure Project
www.cdlib.org/inside/projects/metasearch
> "The Metasearch Infrastructure Project is creating an infrastructure that campus libraries and CDL can use to tailor search portals for particular audiences and needs. Steve Toub is the project manager, please contact him if you have any questions or comments."

myLibrary
http://mylibrary.library.nd.edu
> Personalized library portal software under development by Eric Lease Morgan and colleagues. University of Notre Dame is using myLibrary (http://dewey.library.nd.edu/mylibrary).

OCLS, Scirus, ELSEVIER Serials Full-text Open URL Linking
http://libraryconnect.elsevier.com/lcn/0504/lcn050410.html#scirus

Overdrive
www.overdrive.com
> Multimedia download management service mainly for public libraries. Many free downloads available as well.

PLONE
http://plone.org
> Open source content management system also referred to as Collage.

Reason Content Management System: Simplified Collaborative Web Publishing
https://apps.carleton.edu/opensource/reason

Research Guide
http://researchguide.sourceforge.net
> University of Michigan Graduate Library developed CMS (www.lib.umich.edu/grad/guide).

Search Engine Watch
http://searchenginewatch.com
> Database of search engine facts, guides, and resources to various categories of search engines, such as kids search engines, specialty, meta search, etc.

Serials Solutions
www.serialssolutions.com
> Vendor of very popular e-journal and other e-resource management systems as well as the 360 Search federated search software.

Springshare LibGuides Library Facebook Application
http://support.springshare.com/?p=41

SubjectsPlus
www.ithacalibrary.com/subsplus

TDNet
www.tdnet.com
> Vendor of e-serials and e-book management systems.

Technical Processing Online Tools

http://tpot.ucsd.edu

> Library technical processing Web resources. Some restricted areas.

W3C Web Accessibility Initiative

www.w3.org/WAI/References

> "Highlights the work of organizations around the world in improving accessibility for people with disabilities."

WebDewey (OCLC, Latest Versions)

www.oclc.org/dewey/versions/webdewey

WebFeat

www.webfeat.org

> One of the first vendors to offer federated search software and e-resource management tools.

WebSite-Watcher

www.aignes.com

> Automatically check Web pages for updates and changes.

WordPress MU

http://mu.wordpress.org

> Open source blog software.

WorldCat Collection Analysis

www.oclc.org/collectionanalysis/about/default.htm

> Web-based service that provides analysis and comparison of library collections based on holdings information contained in the WorldCat database.

WorldCat Link Manager (OCLC, Resource Sharing and Delivery)

www.oclc.org/linkmanager/default.htm

WorldCat Selection (OCLC, Management Services and Systems)

www.oclc.org/selection

> Selection management service from OCLC in partnership with materials vendors.

ZOPE

www.zope.org

> Open source application server for developing CMS (intranets, portals, etc.).

Zotero

www.zotero.org

> Zotero "is a free, easy-to-use Firefox extension to help you collect, manage, and cite your research sources. It lives right where you do your work—in the web browser itself."

E-SERIALS, BLOGS, DISCUSSION LISTS, ETC.

ACQNET

http://lists.ibiblio.org/mailman/listinfo/acqnet-l

> Discussion list for acquisitions and collection development librarians.

American Libraries

www.ala.org/ala/alonline

> Visit the online version of the ALA's news publication. Besides providing all the news on libraries and librarians, articles about trends in spending and costs of publications appear here regularly.

Ariadne: The Web Version

www.ariadne.ac.uk

> This quarterly newsletter reports "on information service developments and information networking issues worldwide, keeping the busy practitioner abreast of current digital library initiatives."

COLLDV-L

http://serials.infomotions.com/colldv-l

 Moderated: discussion for library collection development officers, bibliographers, and selectors plus others involved with library collection development, including interested publishers and vendors.

Collections 2.0

http://collections2point0.wordpress.com

 Steve Harris's blog on the future of library collections.

Collections 2.0 Content and Community the Future of Library Collections Blog

http://collections2point0.wordpress.com

CONSDIST

http://cool-palimpsest.stanford.edu/byform/mailing-lists/cdl

 Discussion list of collection and preservation of library, archives and museum materials.

Copyright Laws Blog

www.copyrightlawscom.blogspot.com

 Lesley Ellen Harris shares copyright information and advice as well as courses online.

Council on Library and Information Resources (CLIR) Reports

www.clir.org/pubs/reports/reports.html

 Reports on all aspects of digital and e-libraries collections, management, planning, and building.

C&RL News (College & Research Libraries News)

www.ala.org/ala/mgrps/divs/acrl/publications/crljournal/collegeresearch.cfm

 Online version of magazine. Some articles available online.

Current Cites

http://lists.webjunction.org/currentcites

EContentMag.com

www.econtentmag.com/Issues/706-December-2008.htm

 Web magazine that publishes research and news about digital content.

Friends: Social Networking Sites for Engaged Library Services

http://onlinesocialnetworks.blogspot.com

Information Science Today Blog

http://infoscienceblog.blogspot.com

Information Wants to Be Free

http://meredith.wolfwater.com/wordpress/index.php

LIBLICENSE-L

www.library.yale.edu/~llicense/mailing-list.shtml

 This is a "moderated list for the discussion of issues related to the licensing of digital information by academic and research libraries. Increasingly, libraries are being inundated with information created in digital format and transmitted and accessed via computers. This list is designed to assist librarians and others concerned with the licensing of information in digital format in dealing with some of the unique challenges faced by this new medium. Information providers (creators, publishers, and vendors) who deal with libraries are welcomed as members of LIBLICENSE-L."

Librarians Matter

http://librariansmatter.com

 Blogger: Kathryn Greenhill.

Licensing Digital Content Blog

www.licensingdigitalcontent.blogspot.com

 Lesley Ellen Harris shares excellent licensing ideas and advice as well as courses online.

Public Library Association Tech Notes

www.ala.org/ala/mgrps/divs/pla/plapublications/platechnotes

Excellent short articles on all topics related to e-resources collection and management among other issues.

RezLibris

www.rezlibris.com

The magazine for librarians involved in virtual worlds such as Second Life (http://secondlife.com).

Scholarship 2.0 Blog on Scholarly publishing

http://feeds.feedburner.com/Scholarship20

SERIALST

http://list.uvm.edu/archives/serialst.html

Serials discussion list covers collection management of serials.

Special Libraries Association

www.sla.org

"...(SLA) is the international association representing the interests of thousands of information professionals in over seventy countries. Special librarians are information resource experts who collect, analyze, evaluate, package, and disseminate information to facilitate accurate decision-making in corporate, academic, and government settings. The Association offers a variety of programs and services designed to help its members serve their customers more effectively and succeed in an increasingly challenging environment of information management and technology." Special Libraries Association Discussion Lists (www.sla.org/content/community/lists/divisionlists5979.cfm).

Subject Index to Literature on Electronic Sources of Information

http://library2.usask.ca/~dworacze/SUBJIN_A.HTM

Web4Lib

http://lists.webjunction.org/web4lib

Directories, programs, tutorials, discussion topics, and links to digital library maintenance, tools, and updates.

PART

II

RECOMMENDED PLANNING, EVALUATION, AND SELECTION CRITERIA: CORE COLLECTIONS AND COLLECTION TOOLS FOR MAJOR SUBJECT AREAS

CHAPTER

4

READY-REFERENCE AND CORE GOVERNMENT DOCUMENTS E-RESOURCES

As the use of electronic reference sources becomes commonplace, virtual reference services are expanding in scope, modes, and popularity. Simultaneously, reference practices are evolving as well. One concept that may be challenged by these trends is the notion of the core reference collection. What are the sources that form this core collection, and what are its characteristics? Are similar sources used to answer users' questions in virtual and traditional reference? How do core collections of public and academic libraries differ? An analysis of 1,851 e-mail and chat reference transactions from public and academic libraries reveals that the notion of a core reference collection persists in the world of virtual reference services. In both types of libraries, responses to patrons showed a skewed bibliographic distribution; librarians used a small group of sources to answer most of the questions. Almost all sources used were electronic. Academic libraries tended to make greater use of fee-based sources, but public libraries more often used sources freely available on the Web. (Shachaf and Shaw, 2008: 291)

DEVELOPING A COLLECTION PLAN FOR READY-REFERENCE AND CORE GOVERNMENT DOCUMENTS E-RESOURCES (E-DOCS)

When you begin providing reference service in a new library, or after your reference collection has been reorganized in some way, and sometimes as a library user, what are the first things you look for? You look for the core ready-reference tools that you will need to assist library users or to answer your own research questions. In our imagination we can reach back from the desk or walk over to a particular section and pull out the reference books we will use most often. Similarly, we need to become familiar with the reference e-resources accessible from our reference desk or office computers or from remote locations when staffing a virtual reference service. Similarly, a core Web ready-reference collection will contain the resources that both librarians and library users will use most often and be organized in such a way that users and librarians can easily locate those resources. Ready-reference tools are those sources of information—print or e-resources—that will answer quickly and accurately most discrete fact, single concept, specific search, simple answer reference questions. Ready-reference and specific search queries presuppose specific answers and specific sources, which, with practice, the librarian can locate quickly.

In the classic *Introduction to Reference Work: Basic Information Services*, Eighth Edition, Volume 1, William A. Katz (2001) assumed that the ready-reference collections of most libraries would include e-resources. E-resources are an integral part of basic information services. Using a Web search engine, or a specific known e-resource, may not be the best source of ready-reference answers. For library users who are not physically in the library or for very up-to-date information it may be the first or only choice. Creating e-libraries with a good collection of high quality e-resources and making them available through the library Web site will increase the likelihood that library users will choose the best ready-reference sources. This is also a good strategy for promoting the value of the library as information source for library users. Some e-library builders even add information about equivalent print sources that are available in the library to their annotations for e-resources. When is it best to use a digital or a printed ready-reference source? Answer: Use the source where the best answers may be found quickly. Library functionality plays a positive role:

> In a world in which news arrives every second, only to be debunked in the next, where an article you read on the Web yesterday has turned into a reproachful "404 error" today, a world in which nothing seems certain or durable, the library is a safe place where you can always find answers. . . . But it is in that plural—answers—that things get complicated. You cannot find the answer, you will find many, many answers, and they do not agree with each other. Like a fractal image, every time you look a little closer, more complexity reveals itself. You cannot get to the bottom of it. All you find is more questions. And that is what is so subversive about libraries. They provide a seemingly orderly means of approaching that which resists fixity. And the experienced researcher would not have it any other way. (Fister, 2005: 101)

Core government documents (e-docs) are grouped in this chapter because, like ready-reference e-resources, e-docs are multisubject. Another rationale for this organization is that there are core e-docs finding tools and databases that will be useful for ready-reference research. In this chapter we will discuss the main e-docs used for ready-reference, and in subsequent chapters those e-docs that are core for specific subject areas will be covered as appropriate.

E-docs are published by many government agencies both in the United States and internationally. State, local, and regional government agencies also publish e-resources. In fact, the majority of U.S. federal agencies publish both required and supplemental information as e-docs. Much information and data that was previously unavailable or difficult to locate is now accessible.

Some history and background is useful to keep in mind when accessing U.S. Government produced e-docs. The Government Printing Office (GPO) (www.gpo.gov) was "established by Congress in 1813 to print and publish documents for the U.S. Congress, other branches of the U.S. Government, as well as the public." Currently the GPO uses the Web as the major printing and publishing mode. The Federal Depository Library Program (FDLP) was established by the U.S. Congress at the same time as the mechanism for distributing government information to libraries to ensure public access (www.access.gpo.gov/su_docs/fdlp/about.html). At this time, there are 1,250 depository libraries receiving print and e-docs from the GPO. Increasingly Web publication is the preferred method. In reality, given that the majority of e-docs are now produced in digital formats, any and every library can provide access to government published information in a manner similar to that intended by the FDLP. "Federal documents pose an interesting parallel to e-books. By 2005, 92% of all documents distributed to depository libraries were available in electronic form" (Lewis, 2007: 6).

WHAT PURPOSE WILL YOUR COLLECTIONS SERVE? FOR WHOM ARE YOU COLLECTING E-RESOURCES?

Ready-reference sources at the most basic level provide quick, simple, factual answers. Definitions of words; contact information for individuals, organizations, and companies; statistics from health, geography, politico-economic, business, and other areas of interest; and biographical information are all frequently requested ready-reference types of information. A Web ready-reference collection will need to include e-resources that can be used to quickly answer these questions with high quality answers. E-docs are generally high quality information, but may or may not be easily and quickly searched. Statistical sources are especially valuable and increasingly abundant. However, although there are a large number of high quality e-doc statistical sites, they may be a challenge to search quickly. Most require that PDF or other files be downloaded and read carefully to locate the desired statistical data.

In addition to the overall quality of the information provided by ready-reference e-resources, librarians need to pay some attention to the educational level of library users. Will your ready-reference e-resources serve elementary or secondary level students doing homework? Distance learners in a college program? Health care consumers looking for medical definitions? Will your library users be looking for current awareness information such as news, weather, sports, theater and movie, celebrity information, or similar kinds of information? Will your library users be looking for statistical information of various kinds? As always, each library will be guided by the needs of their library users in deciding what to collect for their ready-reference e-library.

WHAT TYPES OF E-RESOURCES WILL YOU COLLECT?

Ready-reference e-resources tend to resemble closely the print resources on which they are based, probably because the organization or information architecture has proven practical. There are essentially eight core ready-reference tool types:

- Directories (phone books, association, business, and organization directories)
- Dictionaries (English as well as international language translation dictionaries)
- Abstracts, indexes, and table of contents services (including those with full text of the journals and magazines indexed)
- Encyclopedias and almanacs
- Full-text and/or multimedia databases/digital libraries (collections of e-books, e-serials, recordings, videos, podcasts, images, etc.)
- News and news services (current awareness) sources
- Key primary documents (company filings, laws, regulations, research data/reports, and statistical sources, etc.)
- Search engines
- Meta sites (e-resources that provide two or more of the other reference tool types in a single product/Web site)
- Bibliographies/bibliographic databases

Directories are one of the most frequently required type of ready-reference tool. Every subject chapter in this book includes discussion of specific directories for that subject. The Web has enhanced the scope and currency of directory information as well as of access to more information. Gale Publishing, for example, has a Web site where authors, scholars, and organizational representatives can input their current information (www.gale-edit.com) for American Men and Women of Science, Biography Resource Center, Contemporary Authors and Something about the Author, Directory of American Scholars, Encyclopedia of Associations, etc. This is in contrast to the print-only days when such information was collected by postal mail and then had to be sorted and added to a print directory and thus be over a year old by the time it got to print. The Hoovers Online directory has similar current information for companies.

There are a few abstracting and indexing tools that are freely available on the Web. However, nearly all the standard indexes are fee-based Web accessible databases. For example, some solid high-use reference tools such as the *Consumer Index* (www.consumerreports.com) has partially free indexing, and the *Readers' Guide to Periodical Literature* (www.hwwilson.com) was one of the first to be published online. An important thing to consider when using these Web-accessible indexes is that the back files may not yet be in electronic form. One of a number of growing exceptions, the *Readers' Guide to Periodical Literature* is available from 1890–1982 in the databases searchable through the H. W. Wilson database collection.

Dictionaries are essential ready-reference tools. Searching Web dictionaries can be very convenient when no print dictionary is available. However, it is often faster to reach over and pull a print dictionary off the shelf. There are, however, extensive language and specific topic, technical area, and specialty dictionaries available on the Web that may be otherwise difficult to obtain in print. However, it is very important to be aware of identity of the publishers and the sources of the dictionary information published on the Web. Several sites with dictionaries amount to no more than some individual's glossary of terms or an open site for collecting personal definitions, so evaluate carefully. These can be useful sources for those researching popular culture or current slang; for example, the *Urban Dictionary* (www.urbandictionary.com).

Encyclopedias and almanacs are also frequently available on the Web. Many excellent titles are available, either for free or partially free. For example, the *Information Please Almanac* (www.infoplease.com) and *Encyclopedia Britannica* (www.britannica.com) both offer some basic information for free, though premium full-text access is only available for a subscription fee. Wikipedia (http://wikipedia.org) and Citizendium (http://en.citizendium.org) are both scholarly social intellectual networking experiments attempting to create—very successfully—an encyclopedia of everything. Keeping in mind the need to be aware of the sources, Wikipedia especially is an outstanding reference tool. It is not meant to be a research database but rather a place to begin researching to get the background information and some links and citations to begin with.

News and news services, including weather, entertainment, and sports information in a current and interactive form that has never been available in the past, is now available on the Web. For example, we can get transcripts as well as video of breaking news (e.g., Associated Press—www.ap.org, Reuters—www.reuters.com, BBC News—http://news.bbc.co.uk, or McClatchy—www.mcclatchydc.com), play-by-play sports (e.g., ESPN—http://espn.go.com or many team or sports organization created Web sites). Celebrities from Shakira (www.shakira.com) to the Cleveland Orchestra (www.clevelandorchestra.com) maintain Web sites with their current information. The weather information (www.weather.com, www.nws.noaa.gov, or www.wunderground.com, and others) was one of the first types of current awareness resource to be made available through the Web. Whenever we travel, we check the weather report for where were going by connecting to the weather reports on the Web. The Web is without peer in terms of its ability to deliver up-to-the-second news and popular culture information. Interview transcripts, videos, song lyrics, audio files, or photographs are readily available through the Web. News and popular culture are kinds of information for which there is a need in all types of libraries. Everyone from child to adult who uses a library may need or desire current awareness information. In a time when most people have their own computer and Internet access, most users are probably not calling the library or coming in to read the newspapers. A core collection of high quality current awareness resources might be an attractive tool from which library users can begin. A current awareness collection can be very broadly inclusive with listings of many news and news services online. Or it can be focused on current awareness in a narrower subject field, such as business, law, medicine, or science and technology.

Primary documents, including images, multimedia files, and text that is born digital or electronic copies of primary documents are available through the Web to an extent never possible with print-only publication and even with physical archives and special collections. Laws, regulations, court decisions, public company filings, statistical information, research reports, and a huge array of related documentation are available through the Web to everyone with an Internet connected computer. Digital libraries are developing to archive, manage, and preserve information that is born digital as well as conserving and recording other formats.

Full text of research reports, statistical data, laws, regulations, court decisions, public company filings, financial, and budget data, transcripts of government meetings, and more are published online by the governments of many countries, regions, and local governmental entities. Australian, Canadian, European Union, the United Kingdom and United States examples are used in this discussion because they all publish in English; however, many other countries also provide excellent government Web sites. The European Union site Europa (http://europa.eu) provides full-text government publications in all the languages of Europe.

Australia's central government Web site (www.australia.gov.au) is the best place to begin a search for central, regional, or local government published full-text information for that country. To find information provided by the central, provincial, and other government agencies in Canada begin at the Government of Canada (www.canada.gc.ca) meta site. In the United Kingdom the central government meta-site designed specifically for accessibility and usability for citizens is Directgov (www.direct.gov.uk) to locate government published information from all of levels of government.

In the United States begin with the citizen oriented USA.gov site (www.usa.gov) or the researcher and librarian oriented GPOAccess site (www.gpoaccess.gov). Google Uncle Sam (www.google.com/unclesam) is an even better way to cross search multiple U.S. government e-docs (Klein, 2008).

These examples are all central meta sites and link to most if not all of the Web publications of the agencies or other levels of government under the central government. For example, in the U.S. public company required filings—10K and other required reports—are filed and searchable full-text through the U.S. Securities and Exchange Commission Edgar database (http://sec.gov). The U.S. Bureau of the Census (www.census.gov) is the ultimate place to find population and economic statistical data. Both of these sites can be found using either of the central government meta sites. The Legal Information Institute (http://law.cornell.edu) and other international law reference tools are covered in Part II, Chapter 7.

Bibliographies and bibliographic databases have established a new and powerful existence on the Web. Sites such as Amazon.com, Barnes and Noble (www.barnesandnoble.com), Powell's Books (www.powells.com), and the Independent Online Book Sellers Association (www.ioba.org) not only sell books, but they also provide the opportunity for individuals to post reviews and bibliographies on a variety of themes. Many individual and organizational sites publish bibliographies of particular authors or genres. Two of the author's favorite bibliography sites are the L-Space Web (www.lspace.org), which features the works of Terry Pratchett (compiled by the L-Space Librarians), and George Simenon's Maigret (www.trussel.com/f_maig.htm), which exclusively features Simenon's works featuring Inspector Maigret (as compiled by Steve Trussell). Many similar kinds of bibliographic resource exist on the Web for both recreational reading and academic scholarship; for example, the Eudora Welty bibliography (www.olemiss.edu/depts/english/ms-writers/dir/welty_eudora/bib.html) and the Winston Churchill bibliography (www.winstonchurchill.org).

HOW WILL YOU ORGANIZE YOUR E-RESOURCES?

Some e-libraries organize by ready-reference source type. For the Internet Public Library (http://ipl.org) organizes by source type under the main category Reference. Other libraries organize by the topic area or kind of question answered. Cleveland Public Library (cpl.org) organizes under "Do Research" and then research category. The best way to organize is so that your library users and staff can find the information they need quickly and easily.

Google, Wikipedia, and other similar search tools are popular choices for users to find quick answers on the Web. Google and Wikipedia are not our enemies. We must co-opt them, incorporate them into what we do and do so effectively so that our users know that the library is a viable participant in the Web and a source of high quality answers.

> Alternative information sources may not be as extensive or as authoritative as those housed in or subscribed to by the library, but they are good enough and they fit easily and seamlessly into the lives that our students, and increasingly our faculty, live.... Both students and faculty will use the general Web search engines as their primary discovery tools. Library tools, resources, and expertise need to be where the users are. The simple truth is: if you can't get to the library from Google, you won't go there. Libraries need to use linking strategies to make this simple and easy. It should also be transparent. (Lewis, 2007: 10–11)

A carefully chosen and well organized ready-reference or e-docs collection will make the researchers task easier when they need to find the right or best answers. Having a very well organized collection online also means that search engines such as Google can index them so the chances of your library having a role in locating the best answers is increased. Barbara Genco and Raya Kuzyk also make the case for high quality collections of reference e-resources:

> Reference is dead; long live reference.... With the dramatic reduction in print reference materials and the number of ready-reference information questions we field—customers now instead going to the World Wide Web—we have to rethink traditional notions of reference as well as how to organize our collections and what kind of collections we should have. We should be using our reference skills both to create and develop content and to deliver it to our customers so that they can get authoritative information that is vetted and organized by librarians. I still think librarians do it best. Just look around: people with library degrees are no longer working exclusively in libraries. Tech companies consider job applicants with library degrees as real assets. That's because today's librarians are so adept at using technology, they have a remarkable kind of energy. (Genco and Kuzyk, 2007: 18)

IDENTIFYING, COLLECTING, AND SELECTING READY-REFERENCE AND CORE GOVERNMENT DOCUMENTS E-RESOURCES

The difficult part of identifying, collecting, and selecting Web ready-reference resources will be choosing from the plethora of resources and evaluating the quality of information each resource provides. Making use of the e-resources and print resources that review ready-reference and e-docs will simplify this process.

WEB SITES THAT REVIEW AND EVALUATE E-RESOURCES: PEER E-LIBRARIES, SUBJECT COLLECTIONS/GUIDES, OR META SITES

The Internet Public Library (http://ipl.org) is an excellent ready-reference Web resource collection tool, as is the Librarian's Internet Index (http://lii.org). Both sites provide high quality, carefully selected Web sites under the category of ready-reference. Most of the Web sites included in the core collection were found in one or more of the case study e-libraries under their Ready-Reference, Reference Desk, or Reference Collection headings.

Gary Price's ResourceShelf (www.resourceshelf.com) and John Hubbard's Library Link of the Day (www.tk421.net/librarylink) are published as RSS feeds but are also Web sites that review and evaluate ready-reference e-resources regularly and archive those reviews. In his long running column "Péter's Digital Reference Shelf" (www.gale.cengage.com/free_resources/reference/index.htm), Péter Jascó reviews reference Web sites and databases. His reviews are careful, thorough, and frequently critical. Jascó's reviews provide details that some other reviewers might skim over such as search tool functionality, archiving of backfiles, availability of source information, and more.

The following two sites organize central access to the majority of U.S. Federal information published on the Web. They do not link to all such information directly but rather link to specific agency, project, or related U.S. Federal sites. As we will see in subsequent chapters, it is often most efficient to know which agency or project site to begin with rather than to try to go through the central sites every time. But these two sites will be very useful when you or the patron is not certain exactly where to begin.

GPOAccess, which will become FDsys during 2009 (www.gpoaccess.gov), is a service of the U.S. GPO and is the official portal for U.S. federal e-docs. It is funded by the FDLP. USA.Gov/GobiernoUSA.Gov (was FirstGov) (www.usa.gov and www.usa.gov/gobiernousa) is designed to be more accessible for the general public. The attempt is made to organize and link to all related Web sites and not only to official publications. FirstGov actually began with a gift from the Federal Search Foundation, a nonprofit organization established by Eric Brewer (www.cs.berkeley.edu/~brewer) and went online in 2000. It is now federally funded.

DISCUSSION LISTS (LISTSERV, ETC.), FORUMS/GROUPS, E-SERIALS, AND/OR BLOGS THAT POST OR PUBLISH REVIEWS AND EVALUATIONS OF E-RESOURCES

Essentially any library reference related discussion list will at times discuss ready-reference e-resources. Monitoring your favorite discussion or browsing the archives will be fruitful. LIBREF-L, COLLIB-L, ERIL-L, and PUBLIB were very useful in the process of writing this book. GOVDOC-L (http://govdoc-l.org) is the central discussion list for government documents librarians and those interested in the management, acquisition, and reference use of government documents.

Interestingly, many of the Web sites and RSS feeds discussed in this and other chapters also have e-newsletter subscription options. For example, ResourceShelf invites subscription to a weekly reminder and highlights e-newsletter via e-mail each Thursday.

PRINT BOOKS AND JOURNALS THAT REVIEW E-RESOURCES

Every library related journal published in print has at some time reviewed or otherwise discussed ready-reference e-resources. All of the books and journals cited in Part I, Chapter 1, under this section heading include discussion of ready-reference resources. Many of the subject specific books, mentioned in other chapters, do address ready-reference sources. Because of the nature of e-resources few print books on this topic stay current beyond a couple of years.

EVALUATION GUIDELINES AND SELECTION CRITERIA: THE CORE WEB READY-REFERENCE AND CORE WEB GOVERNMENT DOCUMENTS COLLECTIONS

Any ready-reference e-resource is only as good as the information provider, news, or data sources. The best rule of thumb for evaluating ready-reference e-resources is to look for authors, publishers, organizational, or news organizations that you know and recognize for having a good reputation. Look for source attributions, contact information, and the mission or intention in providing the information. Be especially careful in evaluating current awareness sites. If the site declares that the information is provided for entertainment purposes only, its value as a source for facts is questionable. Some of these sites are pure gossip. Some sites are deliberately malicious. Others are merely biased, while still others are blatantly propaganda.

Follow the evaluation guidelines discussed in Part I, Chapter 1, in evaluating any ready-reference Web resource for inclusion in your e-library collection. Accepting the evaluation of a high quality collection from peer libraries sites is a reasonable strategy. Check the selection criteria of each e-library collection. You cannot always assume that if any given library has included a resource in their e-library collection that they have carefully evaluated it or in fact evaluated it with the same quality standards as you have determined for your own e-library collection, but it is a reasonable assumption.

In May and August 2008, librarians were surveyed to elicit their core or essential ready reference tools. These surveys were run using SurveyMonkey. Past, present, and future surveys and results are posted at www.kovacs.com/misc.html. The discussion lists and blogs where the survey link was posted are listed in Table 4.1. The survey is reproduced in Table 4.2. In those same months, librarians were surveyed about their core or essential e-docs reference tools. That survey is reproduced in Table 4.3.

Table 4.1. Discussion Lists and Blogs Distribution for Ready-Reference and Government Documents Reference Tools Surveys

LISNews and LISNewsWire Blogs:
  lisnews-owner@lishost.net
ResourceShelf Blog:
  gary.price@resourceshelf.com
acqnet-l@lists.ibiblio.org
BUSLIB-L@LISTS.NAU.EDU
CAPHIS@hslc.org
COLLDV-L@usc.edu
collib-l@ala.org
dig_ref@LISTSERV.SYR.EDU
eldnet-l@u.washington.edu
ERIL-L@LISTSERV.BINGHAMTON.EDU
genealib@mailman.acomp.usf.edu
GOVDOC-L@lists.psu.edu

law-lib@ucdavis.edu
lawlibref@lists.washlaw.edu
Libref-L@listserv.kent.edu
LIS-LINK@jiscmail.ac.uk
LIS-SCITECH@jiscmail.ac.uk
livereference@yahoogroups.com
LM_NET@LISTSERV.SYR.EDU
MEDLIB-L@LIST.UVM.EDU
Medref-L@listserv.kent.edu
mla-cds@colldev.mlanet.org
publib@webjunction.org
SERIALST@LIST.UVM.EDU
sts-l@ala.org
web4lib@webjunction.org

The core Web ready-reference and core government documents collections on the companion Web site (www.kovacs.com/ns/essentialguide.html) were initially created using the survey results from these surveys along with results from similar 2005 and 2006 surveys as core and model collections. This collection is intended for librarians to use as a source of e-resources they might

Table 4.2. Core Ready-Reference Tools Survey Questions

1. Which library type best describes the library you work in/for/with?
2. In which subject area(s) are you most likely to answer ready reference questions? (check all that apply)
3. What are the essential three print titles (reference books) that you can't work without in answering ready reference questions? (Please type the title only.)
4. What are the essential three free (not government published) Web-accessible databases that you can't work without in answering ready reference questions? (Please type complete URL/Web address; e.g., www.dictionary.com.)
5. What are the essential three (.gov) government published (state, federal, local, international) free Web-accessible databases that you can't work without in answering ready reference questions? (Please type complete URL/Web address; e.g., medlineplus.gov.)
6. What are the essential three fee-based Web-accessible databases that you can't work without in answering ready reference questions? (Please type the title only.)
7. Does your library maintain a Web page or site to support ready reference? If so, please share the URL/Web address (e.g., www.cpl.org/index.php?q=node/102).
8. Additional comments or ideas:

(Please include your name and e-mail address if you would like feedback, otherwise this survey form is completely anonymous.)

Table 4.3. Core Government Documents Reference Tools Survey Questions

1. Which library type best describes the library you work in/for/with?
2. In which subject area(s) are you most likely to answer reference questions by using government documents? (Check all that apply.)
3. What are the essential three print government documents that you can't work without in answering reference questions (e.g., laws, codes, statistics, etc.)? (Please type the title only.)
4. What are the essential three free Web-accessible government document databases that you can't work without in answering reference questions (e.g., laws, codes, statistics, etc.)? (Please type complete URL/Web address; e.g., www.uspto.gov.)
5. What are the essential three fee-based Web-accessible government document databases that you can't work without in answering reference questions (e.g., laws, codes, statistics, etc.)? (Please type complete URL/Web address; e.g., statusa.gov.)
6. What is a "typical" reference question that you might answer in your library using government documents?
7. Does your library maintain a Web page or site to support government documents reference? If so, please share the URL/Web address (e.g., http://www.cpl.org/index.php?q=node/102).
8. Additional comments or ideas:

(Please include your name and e-mail address if you would like feedback, otherwise this survey form is completely anonymous.)

select for their ready-reference or e-docs e-library collections. Fee-based e-resources are included when they offer free-trials or have some information available without requiring a fee.

Core print reference tools in both the ready-reference and e-docs categories were collected. Table 4.4 lists the top five print ready reference tools identified in the survey and Table 4.5 reproduces the results for the top five print e-docs reference tools. The free Web sites that librarians reported as core or essential to their work for ready-reference are given in Table 4.6. Government documents Web sites that librarians feel are core or essential to their ready-reference work are listed in Table 4.7. In this most recent survey, fee-based e-resources used for ready-reference were for the first time more numerous than free Web sites or even e-docs. The top five—by number of librarians mentioning that e-resource—core or essential fee-based ready reference e-resources are given in Table 4.8.

Government documents print reference tools are relatively unpopular. Several respondents mentioned that they do not use print e-docs at all. Table 4.5 lists those print e-docs reference titles that librarians report continuing to use. The top five most used free e-docs reference Web sites are listed in Table 4.9. It is no surprise that these titles overlap with the core print e-docs reference tools. Many librarians also report using commercial value-added or otherwise fee-based e-docs tools for reference. These fee-based sources are listed in Table 4.10.

Table 4.4. Top Five Print Ready-Reference Tools Identified in Survey

1. Styles guides (various APA, MLA, Chicago, etc.), *Statistical Abstract of the United States*
2. Dictionaries (English language, including *Merriam-Webster Collegiate; Oxford English*, 3rd New International
3. *World Book Encyclopedia, World Almanac and Book of Facts*, other almanac and encyclopedia (no titles given)
4. Local phone books
5. Medical dictionaries (including *Mosby's Medical, Nursing, and Health Professions; Dorland's Medical Dictionary of Syndromes*)

Note: These print reference tools got three votes each: *Bieber's Dictionary of Legal Abbreviations, Black's Law Dictionary, Encyclopedia Britannica, Physician's Desk Reference (PDR)*, and *Wards Business Directory of Public & Private Co.* These print reference tools got two votes each: *A to Zoo: A subject guide to picturebooks, The Bluebook, CRC Handbook of Chemistry and Physics, DSM IV, Gale Encyclopedia of Medicine, Mental Measurements Yearbook*, and *Value Line*.

Table 4.5. Top Five Print Government Documents Reference Tools Identified in Survey

1. *Statistical Abstract of the United States*
2. *United States Code/United States Code Annotated*
3. *Occupational Outlook Handbook, United States Government Manual*, state specific statutes, codes, and guides
4. *Code of Federal Regulations/Federal Register*
5. *United States Statutes at Large, CIA World Factbook*, Census Bureau Publications

Note: These print reference tools got two votes each: *Monthly Catalog of U.S. Government Publications, Budget of the United States Government*, and *United States Reports*.

Table 4.6. Top Five Free Web Ready-Reference Tools Identified in Survey

1. Google: www.google.com, and Google Scholar: http://scholar.google.com/
2. Wikipedia: http://en.wikipedia.org/wiki/Main_Page
3. Amazon.com: www.amazon.com
4. Librarians' Internet Index: www.lii.org, WorldCat: www.worldcat.org
5. The Internet Movie Database: www.imdb.com

Note: These sites got three votes each: Ask (www.ask.com), Bartleby.com (www.bartleby.com), Dictionary.com (www.dictionary.com), Mapquest (www.mapquest.com). These sites got two votes each: AnyWho (www.anywho.com/index.html), FindLaw (www.findlaw.com, Internet Archive (www.archive.org/index.php), Merriam-Webster (www.merriam-webster.com), Orbis Yale University Library Catalog (http://orbis.library.yale.edu/cgi-bin/Pwebrecon.cgi?DB=local&PAGE=First), Internet Public Library (www.ipl.org), Yahoo! (www.yahoo.com), Zimmerman's Research Guide (www.lexisnexis.com/infopro/Zimmerman).

Table 4.7. Top Five Government Documents Web Sites Used as Ready-Reference Tools Identified in Survey

1. MedlinePlus: www.medlineplus.gov or state, local, city government Web sites
2. THOMAS, Library of Congress: www.thomas.gov
3. U.S. Census Bureau/American Factfinder: www.census.gov, http://factfinder.census.gov/home/saff/main.html, www.usa.gov
4. Internal Revenue Service: www.irs.gov, GPO (Government Printing Office) Access: www.gpoaccess.gov
5. Bureau of Labor Statistics: www.bls.gov, PubMed: www.ncbi.nlm.nih.gov/pubmed, Center for Disease Control and Prevention: http://cdc.gov, National Institute of Standards and Technology/(NIST) Chemistry Webbook: www.nist.gov or http://webbook.nist.gov

Note: These sites got two votes each: CIA The World Factbook (www.cia.gov/library/publications/the-world-factbook/index.html), Code of Federal Regulations (www.gpoaccess.gov/cfr/index.html), ERIC (Education Resources Information Center; www.eric.ed.gov), Fedstats (www.fedstats.gov), Statistical Abstracts of the United States (www.census.gov/compendia/statab/), The United Nations (www.un.org).

Table 4.8. Top Five Fee-based Ready-Reference E-Resources Identified in Survey

1. Academic Search Complete/Academic Search Premier (EBSCO): www.ebscohost.com/thisTopic.php?marketID=1&topicID=633 or www.ebscohost.com/thisTopic.php?topicID=1&marketID=1, LexisNexis/LexisNexis Academic: http://academic.lexisnexis.com/online-services/academic-overview.aspx
2. OVID CINAHL/Medline/PsycINFO: www.ovid.com, Thomsen-Gail Reference Databases/Virtual Reference/Reference Center (was Infotrac): www.gale.cengage.com, Westlaw/Westlaw Campus: http://campus.westlaw.com
3. Reference USA: www.referenceusa.com
4. EBSCOhost: www.ebscohost.com, Literature Resource Center (Gale): www.gale.cengage.com, JSTOR: www.jstor.org
5. ABI/Inform (ProQuest): www.proquest.com/en-US/catalogs/databases/detail/abi_inform.shtml, Biography Resource Center (Gale): www.gale.cengage.com/BiographyRC

Note: These e-resources received three votes each: Credio Reference (http://corp.credoreference.com), Encyclopedia Britannica Online (www.britannica.com), Hein OnLine (agency case law, CFR, FR, presidential communications) (www.heinonline.org), UptoDate (www.uptodate.com/home/index.html), Worldcat (www.worldcat.org).

Table 4.9. Top Five Free Government Documents Reference Web Sites Identified in Survey

1. U.S. Census Bureau/American Factfinder: www.census.gov or http://factfinder.census.gov/home/saff/main.html
2. GPO Access: www.gpoaccess.gov/
3. THOMAS, Library of Congress: www.thomas.gov
4. Bureau of Labor Statistics: www.bls.gov
5. Catalog of U.S. Government Publications: http://catalog.gpo.gov/, USA.Gov: www.usa.gov

Note: These sites got three votes each: Code of Federal Regulations/Federal Register (www.gpoaccess.gov/cfr/index.html), Patent and Trademark Office (www.uspto.gov), Internal Revenue Service (IRS) (www.irs.gov). These sites got two votes each: American Memory Project (LOC) (http://memory.loc.gov/ammem/index.html), National Technical Information Services (NTIS) (www.ntis.gov).

Table 4.10. Top Five Fee-based Government Documents Reference E-Resources Identified in Survey

1. LexisNexis Congressional Universe: http://web.lexis-nexis.com/congcomp
2. Stat-USA: www.stat-usa.gov
3. LexisNexis/LexisNexis Academic: http://academic.lexisnexis.com/online-services/academic-overview.aspx, Westlaw/Westlaw Campus: http://campus.westlaw.com
4. CQExpress Electronic Library/CQResearcher (Congressional Quarterly): http://library.cqpress.com, LexisNexis Statistical: http://web.lexisnexis.com/statuniv, PACER: http://pacer.uspci.uscourts.gov
5. Hein OnLine (agency case law, CFR, FR, presidential communications): www.heinonline.org, Legaltrac (Infotrac/Gale): www.gale.cengage.com/servlet/ItemDetailServlet?region=9&imprint=000&titleCode=INFO31&type=4&id=172054, Lexis Nexis Serial Set: http://academic.lexisnexis.com/online-services/us-serial-set-digital-overview.aspx

E-LIBRARY SUCCESS STORY

NLM GO LOCAL PROJECT: HEALTH INFONET OF ALABAMA

Public and Medical Libraries of Alabama
Birmingham, Alabama, United States
www.healthinfonet.org
http://apps.nlm.nih.gov/medlineplus/local/alabama/homepage.cfm?areaid=3
Contacts: Catherine Hogan Smith, khogan@uab.edu, and Steven L. MacCall, PhD, smaccal@bama.ua.edu

A. Collection Planning (e.g., goal setting and identification of users, technology/personnel choices)

Health InfoNet of Alabama was created by University of Alabama, Lister Hill Library of the Health Sciences Librarian, Catherine Hogan Smith. It is a public library medical library partnership to provide consumer health information. She was inspired by the Connecticut Healthnet (http://library.uchc.edu/departm/hnet) services. The Health InfoNet of Alabama Web site is just the most visible and important of the resources and services provided by the project. "The InfoNet site is now a part of the National Library of Medicine's MedlinePlus 'Go Local' network

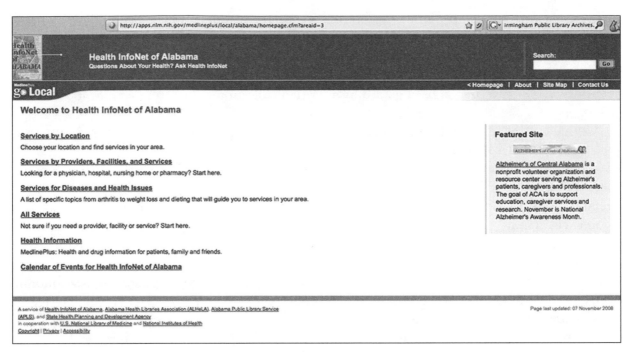

Figure 4.1. Health InfoNet of Alabama: NLM Go Local

of consumer health sites, which include a database of local health services specific to the area. The first pilot Go Local site was in North Carolina around 2002. I heard about their pilot at a meeting of the Regional Medical Library in Baltimore (Univ. of Maryland Baltimore) that winter and was very excited about the possibilities this program might portend for my own Health InfoNet of Alabama CHIS. In 2004, NLM put out a call for proposals from other localities/ states (some states, such as Texas, have more than one Go Local project) around the U.S. who wanted to participate in the program. With the expanded partnership and support of the Alabama Public Library Service, Alabama Health Libraries Association, State Health Planning and Development Agency, Network of Alabama Academic Libraries and the University of South Alabama Biomedical Library, in addition to the original partners of UAB Lister Hill Library and the Jefferson/Shelby County public libraries, I submitted our proposal in April of 2004, and Health InfoNet was accepted as the Alabama affiliate for the Go Local program. We were subsequently awarded some funding which allowed us to work with Steven MacCall at the Univ. of Alabama School of Library and Information Studies to hire a graduate student assistant part-time to work on the database. With his help, and others, we were able to go live in late 2005."

The purpose of Health InfoNet of Alabama is, as always, to provide "access to high quality consumer health information that is accurate, timely, unbiased and relevant to the citizens of Alabama. (From our mission statement.) We do this through our network of public and medical libraries in the state which work together to provide up-to-date, authoritative medical collections and trained staff throughout the state for ready access by consumers. The site itself, one of the important resources of this service, is focused on providing access to quality-filtered health information online for users, mainly through MedlinePlus, as well as a robust database of health services around the state."

Health InfoNet is designed for Alabama residents and is also used frequently by referring professionals including health care providers, social workers, teachers, etc. The primary user group is Alabama residents, but I've found that secondary groups include referring professionals such as health care providers, social workers, teachers, etc.

The project does not directly support any distance learning programs, but there are plans to provide training modules on the site for health care consumers and professionals within the next year or two. The project has been guided by a written collection policy from its inception.

B. Collection Strategies (e.g., selection criteria, identification of resources, licensing, and related user information needs)

Resources are chosen based on the information needs of health care consumer in Alabama specifically. Other criteria include recommendations by health care related organizations or agencies who provide services or support sites that they would like included in the Health InfoNet collection.

Feedback from users and from librarians guides selection of specific types of information that they wish to be added; for example, holistic medicine providers. Special emphasis is on free or low cost services and resources. "Since we are a relatively poor state with many socioeconomic obstacles to good health care, I try to stress the addition of health care services available free or on a sliding scale for those without insurance, as well as other relevant social services."

Listings may include health care practices as well as some health related commercial services. "Our collection guidelines and standards are currently under review due to questions that have come up without easy answers, such as when to omit certain services such as weight loss plans that may be questionable.... Records are not created for individual health care practitioners, only those with a 'named practice,' e.g., 'Lovell Pediatrics' instead of 'Janice Lovell, M.D.'"

The fee-based Web-accessible databases that are available to citizens of Alabama through the Alabama Virtual Library (www.virtual.lib.al.us) are included through Health Infonet: "There is a record for AVL in the database on our site and link from there to AVL, however NLM does not currently allow more prominent links to fee-based services online. Individual libraries in the network also have site licenses for consumer databases, such as UAB Lister Hill Library's subscription access to NORD and ConsumerLab. However in general those licenses do not allow for remote access by the general public, so users must come into the library to use them or request specific information through the Health InfoNet network of libraries (public and medical)."

There are currently no e-books provided through Health InfoNet although some individual libraries in the network may provide e-books to their users. The UAB Lister Hill Library and other libraries in the Health InfoNet network catalog their e-books and usage is tracked for accesses through their systems.

Although Health InfoNet does not originate any digitized collections, individual libraries within the Health InfoNet network of libraries do provide digitized collections, such as the UAB Historical Collections (www.uab.edu/historical) and the Birmingham Public Library Digital Collections (www.bplonline.org/resources/Digital_Project).

Health InfoNet does provide virtual reference service through an e-mail form at http://apps .nlm.nih.gov/medlineplus/local/alabama/contactus.cfm?areaid=3. There have been very few uses of this service yet.

C. Collection Organization (e.g., content management systems, Web server choices, personnel responsibilities, etc.)

Health Infonet is hosted on a National Library of Medicine site and uses Cold Fusion for database structures. All technical support is provided by NLM staff. Catherine Hogan Smith is responsible for coordinating the project with assistance from some paid staff, student interns, and some volunteers. Officially she is expected to spend 50 percent of her time on the Go Local project but of course this varies from week to week depending on project needs.

"There has been a mix of volunteer and paid 'staff' working on Go Local. A couple of fellow medical librarians in the state helped administer it, especially at the beginning. Besides these 'Local Administrator' roles, there are NLM-designated roles of 'selector' and 'reviewer' and it was decided at the beginning that while volunteer selectors—those who identify appropriate services and enter them into the database—do not necessarily need to be MLS librarians, the reviewers of the records, responsible for making sure the records adhere to local standards of acquisition and formatting, should be.... There are others who support this effort (from 20+ to less than 6 active at any one time), but I would say they generally spend 1% or less time on it (unfortunately) unless it is a student intern whose grade or stipend is contingent on their efforts, usually measured in hours spent working on the records. I do ask that anyone who volunteers agree to spend at least one hour per week on the records, but that doesn't work out sometimes, especially for people who have to fit this in among multiple responsibilities. (I should know about that!).

"Other than myself, the first person hired to work on the Go Local database was UA SLIS student Paul Mussleman, with grant funding and a partnership with Prof. Steven MacCall as his primary supervisor. He was hired in the fall of 2004 to help us get the database ready for launch in 2005. He received tuition support plus a small stipend to spend 20 hours per week adding records and validating those that were imported from the State Health Planning and Development Agency (state licensing agency) and from the old Health InfoNet Web site database of Jefferson/Shelby County health services. Another student hired, in summer 2007, was UAB medical student Conley Carr, who was paid to devote 10 hours per week to add new records and audit existing ones in the database."

All of the other student interns who have worked on this project have done so in exchange for a portion of their grade in a particular course. Although an MLS is not required for all supportive positions for the project everyone—public librarians, academic librarians, students, staff, and volunteers—must go through training on project policies, technologies, etc. Catherine Hogan Smith traveled all over Alabama to deliver personal training to ensure that everyone was known to her and understood the project goals.

"Some of this training was supported by the Alabama Public Library Service, some by the Alabama Health Libraries Association, and some by the NLM grant funding for the project. Much has been supported by the flagship library in this program, my own UAB Lister Hill Library."

Volunteers include both UAB library school students as well as library staff from the UAB Lister Hill Library and University of South Alabama Biomedical Library (with some of these in Mobile trained by my partners at USA). Some of the library staff have been able to integrate work on the Health InfoNet project into their regular paid library duties. "This past year, with the Lister Hill Library's print collections dwindling, the library administration decided that those staff who had been working primarily on processing of print materials (binding, checking in, shelving, etc.) should have some of their hours devoted to helping me with the Go Local database. This has helped somewhat, although their interest in the project varies according to the individual, naturally."

Grants and other sources of funding have been sought for and received that have allowed the project to recruit UAB faculty and students to dedicate time on the database. "It has also been extremely helpful when I am able to get funding or curriculum support (or both) from a partner, such as Steven MacCall at UA or a couple of the health education professors at UAB's school of education, who help me recruit dedicated students to work a substantial period of time on the database. This is when I really see some progress in upgrading the database. (There have even been one or two medical students who have done some work on the database, and there is also a movement to recruit some of the UAB sociology students to work on it, particularly those records for services targeting the homeless and uninsured, which are sometimes difficult to ferret out.)"

Sources for adding records include the "State Health Planning and Development Agency health service files (licensed health facilities), telephone books from around the state (also provided by SHPDA), word of mouth and contacts made at health fairs and exhibits, directories (e.g., the Alabama Referral Directory to community services and United Way), referrals from other resources (e.g., the UAB 1917 Clinic for HIV patients 'Community Resource Directory for Jefferson County'), Web searches, and, yes, serendipity."

D. Collection Maintenance (e.g., link checking, ongoing weeding, and growth of the e-library collection)

Not all services included in the Health InfoNet have Web sites. So some records are Web sites and others contain other forms of contact; for example, in-person schedules, addresses, phone numbers, etc. Each selector or reviewer is expected to spend at least an hour a week searching for appropriate new entries as well as reviewing and updating existing records. It is their responsibility to make sure that adequate contact information is available for each record. Guidelines for the format and content of each record are included at the end of this case study.

Link-checking software is run once per week and any problem links are referred to the administrators. "There is an NLM-developed program for automatically checking links every week. I receive a report of the number of broken links in my email, then I log on to check the links myself and correct them or delete the link as appropriate."

User feedback or suggestions for specific resources to be included is solicited through form on the MLA Go Local site at http://apps.nlm.nih.gov/medlineplus/local/alabama/contactus .cfm?areaid=3. "We are also participating in a project to intermittently survey users of the Go Local websites, through the use of pop-up surveys. Naturally, I take suggestions from users and service providers very seriously and do everything I can to satisfy their requests. I try to respond personally to each request within 24–72 hours of the request."

Review of the e-library takes place annually and an annual self-assessment report is produced for the project. The future of the project in terms of technologies used or added; for example, social networking or additional database search options will be decided by the NLM Go Local project. "As far as the Health InfoNet of Alabama project goes, our 'expansion' goal at this point is to cover as thoroughly as possible all areas of the state in terms of local health service records in the database."

Health InfoNet of Alabama
MedlinePlus Go Local Participation Initiative
Standards: Resource Selection and Indexing
Revised February 2008

Eligibility standards for inclusion in Health InfoNet of Alabama/Go Local database of health services:

> Service can be categorized within National Library of Medicine (NLM) Go Local Service
> Terms (see www.nlm.nih.gov/medlineplus/golocaldocs/Local_Term_Definitions.doc).
> Service should have a local presence within Alabama.

Add separate record for subordinate services of larger facilities (e.g., home health service of a hospital) only if there is some distinct identification of that service in a directory, Web page, or other authoritative source.

Records are not currently entered for individual health practitioners unless they have a named practice (e.g., Dr. Bob's Orthopedics).

Record formatting standards include:

In general, use the spelled out form of the name of the service in the "name of site" field as opposed to an abbreviated form (exception: when the name of the service is widely and/or officially known in its abbreviated form or as an acronym—for example, AARP—that version may be used).

Directory fields ("name of site, address 1 and address 2, city, and organization) should be in ALL CAPS.

Do not use any punctuation marks, such as periods or apostrophes, in the directory fields.

Address: use the U.S. Postal Service list of approved abbreviations for common address formats, such as ST for street and DR for drive. When in doubt, the indexer may verify the address abbreviations by using the USPS Zip Code Finder (www.usps.com/zip4).

Phone number: required for Alabama Go Local system records. Use the following format: (123) 456-7890. (This format also applies to any toll-free numbers. Do not add any descriptive letters or "toll-free" for the toll-free numbers.)

Description: the "description" field in Go Local records should be in regular case letters, beginning with a capital letter and ending with a period, even if it is not a complete sentence or even just a word or two.

REFERENCES AND WEB SITES CITED

Fister, Barbara. 2005. "Smoke and Mirrors: Finding Order in a Chaotic World." *Research Strategies* 20, no. 3: 99–107.

Garvin, Peggy. 2008. "The Government Domain: Wrapping Up 2008." LLRX.com. December. Available: www.llrx.com/columns/govdomain40.htm (accessed December 28, 2008).

Genco, Barbara, and Raya Kuzyk. 2007. "20 Maxims for Collection Building." *Library Journal* 132, no. 15: 32–35.

Katz, William A. 2001. *Introduction to Reference Work: Basic Information Services*, 8th edition, volume 1. Boston: McGraw-Hill.

Klein, Bonnie. 2008. "Google and the Search for Federal Government Information." *Against the Grain* (April): 30–34.

Lewis, David W. 2007. "A Strategy for Academic Libraries in the First Quarter of the 21st Century." IDeA: IUPUI Digital Archive, University Library Faculty Research Collection. Available: https://idea .iupui.edu:8443/dspace/bitstream/1805/953/1/DWLewis_Strategy.pdf (accessed January 16, 2009).

Shachaf, Pnina, and Debora Shaw. 2008. "Bibliometric Analysis to Identify Core Reference Sources of Virtual Reference Transactions." *Library & Information Science Research* 30: 291–297.

WEB SITES CITED

Amazon.com. Available: www.amazon.com (accessed January 14, 2009).

Associated Press. Available: www.ap.org (accessed January 15, 2009).

Australia Government. Available: www.australia.gov.au (accessed January 16, 2009).

Barnes and Noble. Available: www.barnesandnoble.com (accessed January 14, 2009).

BBC News. Available: http://news.bbc.co.uk (accessed January 14, 2009).

Books in Print/Books in Print Global. Available: www.booksinprint.com/bip (accessed January 14, 2009).

Citizendium. Available: http://en.citizendium.org (accessed January 16, 2009).

Cleveland Orchestra. Available: www.clevelandorch.com (accessed January 14, 2009).

Cleveland Public Library. Available: http://cpl.org (accessed January 16, 2009).

Consumer Index. Available: www.consumerreports.com (accessed January 14, 2009).

Directgov. Available: www.direct.gov.uk (accessed January 16, 2009).

Encyclopedia Britannica. Available: at www.britannica.com (accessed January 14, 2009).

ESPN. Available: http://espn.go.com (accessed January 15, 2009).

Europa. Available: http://europa.eu (accessed January 16, 2009).

Gale Publishing online update form. Available: www.gale-edit.com (accessed January 14, 2009).

Google. Available: www.google.com (accessed January 14, 2009).

Google Uncle Sam. Available: www.google.com/unclesam (accessed January 14, 2009).

Government of Canada. Available: www.canada.gc.ca (accessed January 16, 2009).

GPOAccess. Available: www.gpoaccess.gov (accessed January 16, 2009). *Note*: This site will become the Federal Digital System (FDsys, accessed January 18, 2009, at http://fdsys.gpo.gov) during 2009.

Independent Online Book Sellers Association. Available: www.ioba.org (accessed January 14, 2009).

Information Please Almanac. Available: www.infoplease.com (accessed January 14, 2009).

Internet Public Library. Available: http://ipl.org (accessed January 16, 2009).

L-Space Web (compiled by the L-Space Librarians). Available: www.lspace.org (accessed January 14, 2009).

Librarian's Internet Index. Available: http://lii.org (accessed January 16, 2009).

Library Link of the Day. Available: www.tk421.net/librarylinkMcClatchey (accessed January 16, 2009).

Péter's Digital Reference Shelf. Available: www.gale.cengage.com/reference/peter (accessed January 13, 2009).

Powell's Books. Available: www.powells.com (accessed January 14, 2009).

Readers' Guide to Periodical Literature. Available: www.hwwilson.com (accessed January 14, 2009).

ResourceShelf. Available: www.resourceshelf.com (accessed January 16, 2009).

Reuters. Available: www.reuters.com (accessed January 15, 2009).

Shakira. Available: www.shakira.com (accessed January 14, 2009).

Simenon's Maigret (compiled by Steve Trussell). Available: www.trussel.com/f_maig.htm (accessed January 14, 2009).

Urban Dictionary. Available: www.urbandictionary.com (accessed January 13, 2009).

U. S. Bureau of the Census. Available: www.census.gov (accessed January 14, 2009).

U. S. Securities and Exchange Commission Edgar database. Available: http://sec.gov (accessed January 14, 2009).

USA.gov. Available: www.usa.gov (accessed January 16, 2009).

Weather Reports. Available: www.nws.noaa.gov, www.weather.com, www.wunderground.com (accessed January 14, 2009).

Wikipedia. Available: http://wikipedia.org (accessed January 16, 2009).

READY-REFERENCE E-RESOURCE COLLECTION TOOLS

META SITES/E-LIBRARIES

Best of the Web, NYPL

www.nypl.org/links/index.cfm

> Web accessible reference tools carefully selected by librarians of the New York Public Libraries.

Best Online Reference Sites

www.rcls.org/deskref

> Best reference sites carefully selected by the librarians of the Ramapo Catskills Library System.

Encyclopedia Britannica Internet Guide

www.britannica.com

> This subscription-based learning portal provides atlas, encyclopedia, dictionary resources as well as research tools and guides in an advertising-free environment.

Gales Reference Reviews

http://gale.ccngage.com/reference

> Reviews of traditional and Internet resources for reference by various columnists, including Péter Jascó's "Péter's Digital Reference Shelf" (www.gale.cengage.com/reference/peter).

The Gateway to Information

http://library.osu.edu/sites/thegateway

> Collection of research guides and reference tools carefully selected by the librarians of the Ohio State University.

Ibiblio

http://www.ibiblio.org

> Sponsored by the University of North Carolina at Chapel Hill School of Information and Library Science and the School of Journalism and Mass Communication. Ibiblio is an e-library collection and digital library collection for public use as well as an organization that supports the hosting of e-library projects and digital library collections by other creators.

Internet Library for Librarians

www.itcompany.com/inforetriever

> E-library ready reference collection for librarians. Includes links to many sites of interest to librarians in all areas and all types of libraries.

Internet Public Library

www.ipl.org

> This easy to navigate site "is a public service organization and a learning/teaching environment at the University of Michigan School of Information."

Internet Quick Reference

www.indiana.edu/~librcsd/internet

> Collection of reference tools for quick access, simple searching. Reference tools all carefully selected by the librarians of Indiana University.

Librarians' Resource Centre

http://units.sla.org/toronto/resources/lrc/cover.htm

> The place to start searching. Selective collection of reference resources, subject specific resources, and library and information professional resources.

Library Spot

www.libraryspot.com

Link to law, medical, musical libraries as well as online libraries; other features include archives, reading room and librarians' shelf (tools, humor, career info, and more).

ResourceShelf

www.resourceshelf.com

Gary Price's blog for reviewing Web resources, sharing news of interest to e-library collectors.

Virtual Reference Collection

http://libraries.mit.edu/help/virtualref

Web reference tools selected and organized by the librarians at MIT.

Web Reference

http://library.buffalo.edu/libraries/findlibrarymaterials/databases/webreference.html

Excellent collection of reference Web sites selected by the librarians of SUNY Buffalo.

E-SERIALS, BLOGS, DISCUSSION LISTS, ETC.

COLLIB-L (the COLege LIBrarians List)

http://lists.ala.org/sympa/info/collib-l

"[T]he official professional discussion list of the College Libraries Section (CLS) of the Association of College and Research Libraries (ACRL), a division of the American Library Association (ALA). The list is owned by the American Library Association and managed by J. Michael Thompson (of the University of Houston). COLLIB-L serves as a means of communication for both CLS and for college librarianship in general. Anyone may subscribe and post messages to the list. Messages are not reviewed prior to distribution."

DIG_REF

http://finance.groups.yahoo.com/group/dig_ref

Discussion of digital reference/virtual reference services.

ERIL-L

http://listserv.binghamton.edu/archives/eril-l.html

Discussion of electronic resource issues, especially for electronic resource librarians.

Library Link of the Day

http://www.tk421.net/librarylink

John Hubbard's blog features a review of a new library link each day.

LIBREF-L

http://listserv.kent.edu/archives/libref-l.html

Discussion of library reference concepts, issues, and service.

LIS-LINK

www.jiscmail.ac.uk/lists/LIS-LINK.html

Discussion of library and information science issues, e-libraries, etc. UK based but global in scope. Announces new BUBL resources and changes.

LISNewsWire Blog

http://liswire.com

LiveReference

http://groups.yahoo.com/group/livereference

Discussion group on live reference services for librarians.

PACS-L

http://info.lib.uh.edu/pacsl.html

The Public-Access Computer Systems Forum (PACS-L) is a mailing list that deals with end-user computer systems in libraries. Utilizing PACS-L, subscribers discuss topics such as digital libraries, digital media, electronic books, electronic journals, electronic publishing, Internet information resources, and online catalogs. PACS-L was founded in June 1989 by Charles W. Bailey Jr. (www.escholarly-pub.com/cwb), who moderated the list until November 1991.

PACS-P

http://info.lib.uh.edu/pacsp.html

Announcement list for notification of new issues of Current Cites (complete issue) (http://lists.web-junction.org/currentcites).

PUBLIB

http://lists.webjunction.org/wjlists/publib

Discussion of issues relating to public librarianship. "Particularly appropriate issues for discussion on PUBLIB include, but are not limited to: Collection development, acquisitions, management and weeding, including traditional and new media Reference services."

SLA-Dite

http://units.sla.org/division/dite/sladite_new.html

Discussion for the Information Technology Division of the Special Libraries Association

Web4Lib

http://lists.webjunction.org/wjlists/web4lib

Discussion of the practical use and philosophical issues of the World Wide Web.

GOVERNMENT DOCUMENTS E-RESOURCE COLLECTION TOOLS

META SITES AND E-LIBRARIES

GPOAccess Collection Development

www.gpo.gov/su_docs/fdlp/coll-dev

> This GPO site links to a complete "Basic Collection" of government documents for all libraries recommended by GPO, a collection called "Core Documents of U.S. Democracy," and a "Suggested Core Collection" with annotations for different library types. The site links to the e-resources that GPO considers the most useful for government documents collection development as well. Note that the GPOAccess site will be replaced by the Federal Digital System project (www.gpo.gov/projects/fdsys.htm) in 2009.

The Library of Congress

www.loc.gov/library

> Services for researchers, publishers, educators. Many collections of digital resources.

The United Nations

www.un.org

> Central UN site with links to the other Web sites, documents, and statistics published by the UN and its agencies and projects.

The University of Michigan Documents Center

www.lib.umich.edu/govdocs

> Comprehensive collection of government and government agency Web sites and sources of documents, statistics, etc.

DIGITAL LIBRARIES DIRECTORIES OR COLLECTIONS OF DIGITAL LIBRARIES (DIGITAL LIBRARIES OF E-BOOKS, E-SERIALS, IMAGES, RECORDINGS, AND OTHER ARTIFACTS)

Archives of As IS Government Documents Sites
http://bulk.resource.org

E-SERIALS, BLOGS, DISCUSSION LISTS, ETC.

FLICC/Fedlink

www.loc.gov/flicc

> Resources, news, reviews, and networking from the Library of Congress, Federal Library, and Information Center Committee.

GOVDOC-L

http://govdoc-l.org

> Discussion of government documents issues begun in 1991.

SLA-DGI

www.sla.org/content/community/lists/divisionlists5979.cfm or www.sla.org/content/community/lists/joinlists.cfm

> Discussion list for librarians who are members of the Special Libraries Association, Government Information Division.

JOBS AND EMPLOYMENT, CONSUMER INFORMATION, AND GENEALOGY E-RESOURCES

Employment of librarians is expected to grow by 4 percent between 2006 and 2016, slower than the average for all occupations. Growth in the number of librarians will be limited by government budget constraints and the increasing use of electronic resources. Both will result in the hiring of fewer librarians and the replacement of librarians with less costly library technicians and assistants. As electronic resources become more common and patrons and support staff become more familiar with their use, fewer librarians are needed to maintain and assist users with these resources. In addition, many libraries are equipped for users to access library resources directly from their homes or offices through library Web sites. Some users bypass librarians altogether and conduct research on their own. However, librarians will still be needed to manage staff, help users develop database-searching techniques, address complicated reference requests, choose materials, and help users to define their needs.... Jobs for librarians outside traditional settings will grow the fastest over the decade. Nontraditional librarian jobs include working as information brokers and working for private corporations, nonprofit organizations, and consulting firms. Many companies are turning to librarians because of their research and organizational skills and their knowledge of computer databases and library automation systems. Librarians can review vast amounts of information and analyze, evaluate, and organize it according to a company's specific needs. Librarians also are hired by organizations to set up information on the Internet. Librarians working in these settings may be classified as systems analysts, database specialists and trainers, webmasters or web developers, or local area network (LAN) coordinators. (*Occupational Outlook Handbook*, accessed January 19, 2009, at www.bls.gov/oco/ocos068.htm)

DEVELOPING A COLLECTION PLAN FOR JOBS AND EMPLOYMENT, CONSUMER INFORMATION, AND GENEALOGY E-RESOURCES

Jobs and employment resources are some of the most popular on the Web. There are directories of every kind of job and employment opportunity, in every country, state, and region. There are literally thousands of jobs and employment related sites. Some of them are more credible than others. Many sites allow job seekers to post their resumes in public resume databases or to apply online directly. Some sites run resume/job matching software that uses keyword analysis to try to match posted resumes to posted jobs. Government sites such as the U.S. Bureau of Labor Statistics (www.bls.gov) provide full-text employment outlook news and data. The Web sites of specific businesses may provide in-depth details that job searchers need to prepare for interviews. Some businesses even list open positions and provide details for applying; for example, The J. M. Smucker Company (http://smuckercareers.com).

Consumer information is in this chapter because much of it is related to the job and employment search process. These related information needs may involve relocation and moving information or financial information or inspection issues related to purchasing a house, car, or other major expenditure. Consumer awareness and protection are also of interest to those attempting genealogical research on the Web. Again, government sites provide unique services for consumers. For example, econsumer.gov is an international cooperation to make the consumer protection and information services of 21 world governments available in a single site. In the nongovernment sector the highly reputable Better Business Bureau (BBB) service maintains a Web presence (www.bbb.org). Individual community BBB offices have Web sites for reporting problems and corresponding with BBB representatives to solve them. Each Web site varies in what the local BBB office provides online.

Genealogical e-resources including digital libraries of images, primary documents, and other research materials are developing but still very limited at this writing. Indexes to genealogical databases and journals as well as some full-text and digitized materials of widely varying quality and type are available through both volunteer or grant-funded organizations and commercial enterprises. There is little overall quality control for free genealogical research materials on the Web. Some sites will be well documented and accurately compiled, such as most of the USGenweb projects (www.usgenweb.org), but some other sites will be little more than family fantasies. Some full-text collections will be scanned images of records with professionally verified indexing (American Family Immigration History Center, www.ellisislandrecords.org) and some sites will be just junk that someone made up. As long as we keep the problems in mind, the benefits of using the Web as a source for genealogical research are great. There are two very good quality fee-based full-text and digital libraries for genealogy research: Ancestry.com and HeritageQuest online (www.heritagequestonline.com).

WHAT PURPOSES WILL YOUR COLLECTIONS SERVE? FOR WHOM ARE YOU COLLECTING THESE E-RESOURCES?

A jobs and employment collection might serve two obvious purposes: access to job listings and application information for job seekers and information about career choices and vocational/educational preparation for different careers. Academic, K–12, and public libraries are likely to need to provide e-resources that support both purposes. Students eventually graduate and need to find jobs. However, any given library user may be seeking a job at any time. Students, new graduates, or any individuals looking for a career change will find the information about career choices and vocational/educational preparation invaluable. Special business libraries are unlikely to want to collect resources for job seekers. They may, however, support their personnel departments in recruiting employees by maintaining awareness of some of the sites where resumes are posted and employment services sites.

A consumer information collection may be created for the general public to find the key sites they need to check product reviews and become aware of their rights as well as of potential frauds and rip-offs or just to find other basic data related to their lives. The consumer information e-library may also serve professionals or researchers who work with consumers or teach consumer education courses.

A genealogical e-library collection can serve several different purposes. For genealogical researchers and historians it can provide access to indexes and compilation notes of primary, secondary, and tertiary genealogical information. Increasingly a genealogy collection may have access to digital libraries of scanned images or actual full text of primary (e.g., vital records, historical census, immigration and military records, newspaper and other contemporary accounts in letters, diaries, deeds, wills, etc.), secondary, and tertiary genealogical sources (e.g., genealogical journals and magazines, published family histories, etc.). Not all libraries archive local records and most cannot archive other localities' records. A good genealogy e-library that links to the Web sites of other archiving organizations can be useful for travel planning as well as data sharing, identifying and communicating with other genealogical researchers, education and training opportunities, and correspondence (including ordering information for document copies and research services).

WHAT TYPES OF E-RESOURCES WILL YOU COLLECT?

All three areas in this chapter are unique in the way the e-resources are shaped. The typical reference types still hold but they tend to be more hybrid, combinations of multiple reference types. Jobs and employment e-resources tend to the following types:

- Jobs and employment directories (listing and advertising sites or want ads) published by individual companies, organizations, or government entities
- Jobs and employment directories that are also meta sites, such as the *Riley Guide* (http://rileyguide.com)
- Jobs and employment encyclopedias and almanacs, such as the *Occupational Outlook Handbook* (www.bls.gov/oco)
- Jobs and employment news, such as *the Monthly Labor Review* (http://stats.bls .gov/opub/mlr/mlrhome.htm)

Jobs and employment directories are meta sites because they tend to include aspects of all of the other reference source types identified. Jobs and employment directories (listing and advertising sites or want ads) are the most important information sources for job seekers and employers. In this area, the Web supplies tools that are without peer in the print world. Some of the most global jobs and employment information and want-ads sites are listed in the Core Web Jobs and Employment reference collection on the companion Web site.

Consumer information sites tend to be mainly meta sites with some directory and full-text resources. Genealogical e-resources are almost entirely either full-text and digital libraries collections or they are meta sites. All of these have some aspect of current awareness sources and search engines.

HOW WILL YOU ORGANIZE YOUR E-RESOURCES?

Jobs and employment information might be organized by job type or subject area, depending on the intention of the collecting library, except that most of the actual e-resources are multijob type. It might be simplest to organize jobs and employment information by reference type and then in alphabetical order.

Consumer information could potentially be organized by type of problem or area of interest for the easiest access by library users. Genealogy information can be challenging to organize.

One strategy is to simply provide a collection of genealogy meta sites and let library users take advantage of the work already done by one of the excellent meta sites cited here or by the fee-based database providers.

IDENTIFYING AND COLLECTING JOBS AND EMPLOYMENT, CONSUMER INFORMATION, AND GENEALOGY E-RESOURCES

WEB SITES THAT REVIEW AND EVALUATE E-RESOURCES: PEER E-LIBRARIES, SUBJECT COLLECTIONS/GUIDES, OR META SITES

One guide to jobs and employment resources on the Internet stands head and shoulders above any others: *The Riley Guide: Employment Opportunities and Jobs Resource* on the Internet (http://rileyguide.com). It is the ultimate source for these types of information on the Web and through the Internet. For many libraries, providing a link to the *Riley Guide* and links to local jobs sites may be sufficient for their jobs and employment e-library collection. Margaret Riley Dikel has been compiling the *Riley Guide* on the Internet since 1996. It is the ultimate meta site for these types of information on the Web. The *Riley Guide* contains a comprehensive collection of job advertisement and opportunity listing Web sites organized by type of job; by local, state, or international location; and other criteria. In addition, it contains a collection of employment and career information and advice Web sites. The JobHuntersBible.com is the companion Web site for Richard N. Bolles popular book cited below.

The *Consumer Reports Online* (www.consumerreports.org/cro/index.htm) provides a "Webwatch" section that publishes articles and reviews of consumer related Web sites. Both problem sites and high quality useful sites are reviewed. The international econsumer.gov site (www.econsumer.gov) provides the consumer support sites for the 21 participating countries including cross-border consumer support sites.

Cyndi's List (www.cyndislist.com) and Rootsweb (www.rootsweb.ancestry.com/roots-l) are the meta sites for genealogical e-resources. Cyndi Howells reviews and annotates thousands of free and fee-based e-resources including Web sites, databases, and offline products such as books, journals, and CD products. The Rootsweb site is sponsored by Ancestry.com and is a compilation of multiple directories, digital libraries, bibliographies, guides, and other materials all related to genealogical research.

DISCUSSION LISTS (LISTSERV, ETC.), FORUMS/GROUPS, E-SERIALS, AND/OR BLOGS THAT POST OR PUBLISH REVIEWS AND EVALUATIONS OF E-RESOURCES

There is no single discussion list or newsgroup for all jobs and employment resource discussions. A number of discussion lists and newsgroups related to jobs and employment e-resources for specific occupations can be found using the discussion list directories listed in the "Collection Development Tools" section in Part I, Chapter 1. To find jobs and employment related blogs, check the *Riley Guide* and *Job Hunters Bible* sites or do a Google search to find very specific job focused blogs and forums. The *Monthly Labor Review* (http://stats.bls.gov/opub/mlr/mlrhome.htm) is a publication of the U.S. federal government that reports employment trends and statistics as well as articles that frequently discuss e-resource that are useful for job seekers or those trying to decide on a career.

Consumer information discussion groups and blogs are as diverse as those for jobs. It is important to be aware that not all such groups are altruistic. The *Consumer Reports Online* (www.consumerreports.org/cro/index.htm) is the best place to begin as they host a number of credible forums and blogs. Registration is required to participate but not to just browse the content.

Thousands of genealogy discussion lists and blogs, including the Cyndi's List blog, are listed in Cyndi's List and also hosted on the Rootsweb (http://lists.rootsweb.ancestry.com) site. The Genealib discussion list for genealogy libraries and libraries is an essential professional tool. Among several e-serials the *Ancestry Daily News* (www.ancestry.com/learn/library/category .aspx?category=&type=1&page=1&bydate=1) stands out as a source of reviews for e-resources as well as genealogical research advice.

PRINT BOOKS AND JOURNALS THAT REVIEW E-RESOURCES

Margaret Riley Dikel and Frances E. Roehm's (2009) *Guide to Internet Job Searching 2008–2009* reviews the best Web sites and strategies for job seekers. Richard N. Bolles's (2009) book *What Color Is Your Parachute? A Practical Manual for Job-Hunters and Career-Changers* also covers Web resources for job hunters. This is an area where annual publication is critical, so many otherwise useful texts have become outdated. *Consumer Reports* remains the essential tool for consumers looking for reliable information about products, services, and e-resources.

Genealogy e-resources are reviewed and discussed in most of the major genealogy research journals; for example, the *National Genealogical Society Quarterly*. Elizabeth Crowe's (2008) newest edition of *Genealogy Online* is very current and useful. Cyndi Howell's book (2004) and Kovacs (2002), although now dated, remain somewhat useful for identifying stable e-resources for genealogy.

EVALUATION GUIDELINES AND SELECTION CRITERIA: THE CORE WEB JOBS AND EMPLOYMENT, CONSUMER INFORMATION, AND GENEALOGY REFERENCE COLLECTIONS

Evaluation of jobs and employment information is critical and sometimes highly idiosyncratic. One person's good job information is definitely not everyone's idea of good job information. Some job seekers may be looking for professional positions that require experience and education or creativity and communications skills, and others may be looking for jobs for beginners or that do not require experience or more than minimal education. Jobs and employment information needs to be accurate and current and from a trusted source. There are, unfortunately, many sites that mislead job seekers into paying fees they should not have to pay or purchasing training kits, services, or other pieces that may or may not lead to employment. Some apparent job offers or "ways to work from home" are outright scams. Verify the credibility and intention of any jobs and employment e-resources selected. The strategies for evaluating resources described in Part I, Chapter 1, work exceedingly well for jobs and employment information. Review the scam and hoax sites discussed in Part I, Chapter 1. Scambusters.org is the best site for checking jobs or home-based business scams. Let library users know that any site requiring a fee should be carefully investigated.

It is very unlikely that a legitimate jobs and employment information Web page will not have full attribution and contact information. After all, how else will they expect the job seeker to contact them and apply for their positions? In the case of general employment information, such as resume guides, employment outlook reports, cost-of-living, and salary surveys, the prime criteria must be the source of the data provided. For example, the *Occupational Outlook*

Handbook (www.bls.gov/OCO) is published by the U.S. Bureau of Labor Statistics and is based on data they have gathered from employers and other sources in the United States.

Genealogical e-resources, on the Web and elsewhere are also a potential tool or source of scams. The Cyndi's List publishes a section on just the scams and rip-offs (www.cyndislist .com/myths.htm) that are out there for the unwary. Use her listing to check specific sites, but also try to provide information to library users to be wary of such scams. Privacy of genealogical information is also important. Information about a living person might be used by identity thieves.

Library and user-specific selection criteria for jobs and employment, consumer information, and genealogical e-resources are derived from the answers arrived at during the purpose and user identification phases of the collection planning process by each individual library. The Core Web Consumer Information Reference Collection and The Core Web Jobs and Employment Reference Collection on the companion Web site (www.kovacs.com/ns/essentialguide.html) were compiled from the author's experience in teaching these topics to reference librarians and include all of the core sites that have come up in classes over the years.

The Core Web Genealogy Reference Collection on the companion Web site was compiled using feedback from surveys that were sent to library discussion lists and blogs in May and August 2008. Similar surveys were run in previous years, most recently 2005 and 2006. Past, present, and future surveys and results are posted at www.kovacs.com/misc.html. Table 5.1 lists the discussion lists and blogs where the survey was distributed. Table 5.2 reproduces the core genealogy reference tools survey. Table 5.3 lists the top five print genealogy reference tools. Table 5.4 lists the top five free genealogy Web sites. Table 5.5 lists the top five govdocs used for genealogy reference. Table 5.6 lists the top five fee-based genealogy reference e-resources. The core Web reference collections also include e-resources identified by the author with advice from other librarians. The intended users are librarians who work with genealogical researchers. The educational level tends to be variable, but most of these e-resources require a high level of literacy.

The Core Web Jobs and Employment Reference and Consumer Information Reference Collections were created entirely from reviews of e-resources by the author with some guidance from colleagues and students.

The intended library user groups are librarians who work with job seekers who might be interested in looking for a job or learning about employment opportunities or with consumers looking for product reviews and evaluations or other kinds of support. The educational level tends to be postsecondary, because the jobs that are advertised on the Web tend to require a high school (or other secondary level) diploma. Many are professional or academic-level jobs. All Web sites chosen for this collection conform to international standards for Web accessibility and other design standards. Most of them are free of charge for job seekers and consumers.

Table 5.1. Discussion Lists and Blogs Distribution for Genealogy Reference Tools Survey

- genealib@mailman.acomp.usf.edu
- LISNews and LISNewsWire Blogs: lisnews-owner@lishost.net
- ResourceShelf Blog: gary.price@resourceshelf.com
- ERIL-L@LISTSERV.BINGHAMTON.EDU
- dig_ref@LISTSERV.SYR.EDU
- collib-l@ala.org
- LIS-LINK@jiscmail.ac.uk
- Libref-L@listserv.kent.edu
- GOVDOC-L@lists.psu.edu
- publib@webjunction.org
- livereference@yahoogroups.com
- Libref-L@listserv.kent.edu

Table 5.2. Core Genealogy Reference Tools
Survey Questions

1. Which library type best describes the library you work in/for/with?

2. In which subject area(s) are you most likely to answer genealogy reference questions? (Check all that apply.)

3. What are the essential three print titles (reference books) that you can't work without in answering genealogy reference questions? (Please type the title only.)

4. What are the essential three free (not government published) Web-accessible databases that you can't work without in answering genealogy reference questions? (Please type complete URL/Web address; e.g., www.cyndislist.com)

5. What are the essential three (.gov) government published (state, federal, local, international) free Web-accessible databases that you can't work without in answering genealogy reference questions? (Please type complete URL/Web address; e.g., www.archives.gov/genealogy.)

6. What are the essential three fee-based Web-accessible databases that you can't work without in answering genealogy reference questions? (Please type the simple title; e.g., Ancestry or Heritagequest)

7. Does your library maintain a Web page or site to support genealogy reference? If so, please share the URL/Web address (e.g., www.acpl.lib.in.us/genealogy).

8. Additional comments or ideas:

(Please include your name and e-mail address if you would like feedback, otherwise this survey form is completely anonymous.)

Table 5.3. Top Five Print Genealogy Reference Tools
Identified in Survey

1. Local and state archives, files, microform, indexes for census data, newspapers, city directories, vital statistics, church records, cemetery records, maps, and atlases, and local research guides.

2. *The Source: A Guidebook of American Genealogy*

3. *Handybook for Genealogists* (Everton)

4. *Map Guide to the U.S. Federal Censuses, 1790–1920*

5. *A to ZAx: A Comprehensive Dictionary for Genealogists & Historians; Evidence Explained: Citing History Sources from Artifacts to Cyberspace; The Genealogists Address Book; Guide to Genealogical Research in the National Archives; International Vital Records Handbook*

Table 5.4. Top Five Free Web Genealogy Reference Tools
Identified in Survey

1. FamilySearch.org/FamilySearch.org Labs: www.familysearch.org or http://labs.familysearch.org

2. Rootsweb: www.rootsweb.ancestry.com

3. Cyndi's List: www.cyndislist.com

4. TheUSGenWeb Project: http://usgenweb.org

5. Ellis Island Foundation: www.ellisislandrecords.org, Google Books: http://books.google.com, Web Pages by Stephen P. Morse (genealogy search tools): www.stevemorse.org, local library Web Genealogy collection, and local history society Web Sites

---

**Table 5.5. Top Five Government Documents Web Sites Used
as Genealogy Reference Tools Identified in Survey**

1. State, county, and local libraries' archives, genealogy, history, and vital records Web sites
2. NARA/NARA Access to Archival Databases: www.archives.gov/index.html or
   http://aad.archives.gov/aad/index.jsp
3. Civil War Soldiers and Sailors System: www.itd.nps.gov/cwss
4. Bureau of Land Management (BLM), General Land Office (GLO) Records: www.glorecords.blm.gov,
   Library of Congress American Memory Project: http://memory.loc.gov/ammem/index.html
5. U.S. Census Bureau/American Factfinder: www.census.gov or
   http://factfinder.census.gov/home/saff/main.html

**Table 5.6. Top Five Fee-based Genealogy Reference E-Resources
Identified in Survey**

1. Ancestry.com/Ancestry Library Edition (ProQuest): www.ancestry.com or www.il.proquest.com/en-
   US/catalogs/databases/detail/ale.shtml
2. HeritageQuest Online: www.heritagequestonline.com or www.il.proquest.com/en-
   US/catalogs/databases/detail/heritagequest.shtml
3. America's Genealogy Bank: www.newsbank.com/Genealogists/product.cfm?product=216
4. Footnote: The Place for Original Historical Documents Online: www.footnote.com
5. America's Obituaries and Death Notices (Newsbank): www.newsbank.com/Libraries/product.cfm?
   product=26, Newspaper Archive.com: http://newspaperarchive.com

---

Several have special fee-based services for consumers or for employers or recruiters listing their positions. Several require registration but not a fee. The registration serves as a marketing research tool for the information providers. Be sure to read carefully any privacy statements made on a given site. Fee-based e-resources are included when they offer free trials or have some information available without requiring a fee.

E-LIBRARY SUCCESS STORY

SAN BERNARDINO COUNTY E-LIBRARY

San Bernardino, California, United States
www.sbcounty.gov/library/home
Contact: Nannette Bricker-Barrett, nbricker@lib.sbcounty.gov

A. Collection Planning (e.g., goal setting and identification of users, technology/ personnel choices)

San Bernardino County was one of the first public libraries to create an e-library presence. The original e-library was called webLibrary. "Our director strongly believed that it was better to spend limited resources on electronic information—available 24/7 remotely—rather than print materials available only during library hours. We had Ebscohost (general magazine articles) and Galenet in the late 90s. By 2001 we had gone with InfoTrac general magazine database (Gale) and added Gale's biography database and Mitchell's auto repair. By 2002 we stopped buying

Figure 5.1. San Bernardino County Library

print reference material and concentrated that money on e-materials. In 2002 we put all the databases on a new site called webLibrary; webLibrary featured our electronic databases, e-books and librarian-previewed websites. Juvenile and Young Adult Web pages also had the various youth database interfaces and any youth databases. By the 02-03 FY we were up to 16 databases with reference services offered by e-mail and by 24/7 (the MCLS product). By FY 08-09 we offered 25 databases, e-books (NetLibrary) and downloadable audiobooks (Recorded Books), AskNow reference service, and live homework help (first Tutor.com and this year BrainFuse)."

The e-library site is in a transition phase at this time. "The webLibrary site went away in about 2005 when the home page was redone without a lot of librarian input. The concept of clustered e-products will return in our next reiteration of the website which we will be working on in 2009."

San Bernardino County Library serves the citizens of San Bernardino County. The e-library goal is to provide remote and in-house access to e-resources for those citizens. Although the e-library does not formally support distance learners there are many resources that can be used by distance learners and teachers. "All library card holders can take advantage of the wealth of information offered on our websites: general magazine articles, several encyclopedias, health, business, history, science & current issue databases, reader's advisory & book groups, auto repair, e-books, and downloadable audiobooks."

A written collection policy was created from the very beginning. The core of the policy is reproduced below:

3. SELECTION

3.1 GUIDELINES

The County Library has adopted this policy to guide librarians and help the public understand how selections are made.

The County Library maintains a carefully selected collection of timely, accurate and useful information of permanent value and current interest in print, audiovisual, electronic, and other material types. Because the County Library cannot meet all the demands placed upon it, the Library must adopt priorities of service and materials acquisitions. Selection of materials is based on community needs: reference, community information, early childhood services, popular, reference, and educational materials for elementary, secondary school students and adults. These standards of selection apply equally to materials purchased and to those received as gifts.

Selection/Inclusion Criteria:

> Material is relevant to the needs of the communities served by San Bernardino County Library
> Positive professional reviews and/or award honoree
> An appropriate fit with the intended collection (needs and space)
> Reputation and qualifications of the author and/or publisher
> Cost
> Appropriate format and physical suitability for library circulation
> Material documents local history
> Material content
> Authority of author/publisher
> Comprehensive coverage of topic
> Material accuracy, currency, and relevancy
> Attractive, appealing format
> Suitable for popular general juvenile, young adult and/or adult audiences
> Represents diverse points of view

The County Library provides materials presenting various points of view without regard to race, nationality, or the political, social, moral, and religious views of an author. Works are judged on their content as a whole, not from excerpts. The County Library provides unrestricted access to all materials to all patrons regardless of age. Parents concerned about their child's reading or viewing materials should provide appropriate guidance.

The County Library and staff will cooperate fully with students using resources available within the Library and will also make known to students the library's interlibrary loan facilities, but the County Library does not purchase school textbooks or scholarly works.

B. Collection Strategies (e.g., selection criteria, identification of resources, licensing, and related user information needs)

San Bernardino County Librarians select resources to best serve their users within the limited budget they have to do so. "For us cost is a huge factor; there are many splendid subscription databases that we simply can't afford. Every year in late winter/early spring (all our databases renew on the first of August) we take a look at the resources that are available and compare and contrast them with the existing subscriptions. Depending on the year/circumstances we've had large committees and small committees assessing the various products—those we take and competitive products. These always include branch staff so we get user/staff feedback as well. We concentrate on general interest databases that support our general public audience."

The library negotiates directly with vendors to license appropriate Web-accessible databases for remote access by their citizens. When consortia pricing is better than our directly negotiated price we will go through the consortium. "With the exception of Mitchell's OnDemand (auto repair)—which does not offer remote access—all of our databases are available remotely and are library card protected. All remote databases, ebooks and downloadable audiobooks are available to any SBCL card holder. All of our current subscriptions databases are funded by the County. One year we did have one database that was included in a grant; we were required to offer the database as a provision of the grant. We don't like to offer databases funded by grants unless we think we can carry them over in subsequent years funded by County money—it is a disservice to the public to offer a database for only one year."

Archiving is part of license negotiations. However, this is an area in which, as a public library, archiving issues are treated differently than they might be in an academic library. "We have access to the databases—and their archived material—only for the duration of the subscription. This is only really relevant for the magazine databases and it is our assumption that we will always subscribe to a magazine database. All of the major general magazine databases are similar enough to each other to satisfy the needs of our general public audience. I realize this is significantly different from an academic setting."

Some e-books are purchased outright by the library, some subscribed to, and some from the public domain are added to the catalog along with access information. "We initially purchased our e-books directly from NetLibrary; in that initial purchase we bought some titles outright in perpetuity (Cliff Notes) and some public domain titles which we purchased the access to/cataloging for. The remainder we purchased and have to pay a platform support fee every year; we do weed titles as needed. This year we are getting our downloadable audiobooks (Recorded Books /OCLC) via Califa (a California consortium) since the Califa price beat the price OCLC would cut with us directly."

Both e-books and downloadable audiobooks are cataloged. There are direct links in the catalog from the record to the material. Circulation statistics are not generated for these materials, but the vendors do supply usage statistics. Our department generates an Electronic Usage Statistics report monthly to all interested parties. Usage statistics are utilized when assessing databases. We also added a Cost per view report last year which allows us to determine the cost for each use of a database.

We offer reference service by e-mail and via AskNow along with the homework help through Brainfuse (http://www.brainfuse.com in addition to traditional in-house reference.

"We share a catalog and materials delivery system with the adjacent county (Riverside) system and their clients (several city libraries); technically every time a San Bernardino County cardholder places a hold that is filled by a Riverside library the transaction is considered to be an ILL by our state library. Traditional ILL in our system still requires staff intervention. Our director has been promoting URSA (a Sirsi product) (http://www.sirsidynix.com/Solutions/Products/resourcesharing .php) as an online ILL/reciprocal borrowing system among libraries/library systems in Southern California. URSA works with any ILS which is an advantage over products that are limited to libraries owning only a specific ILS. We're hoping to get started with some surrounding systems this year."

C. Collection Organization (e.g., content management systems, Web server choices, personnel responsibilities, etc.)

The San Bernardino County e-library is designed and maintained with using Microsoft Visual Studio.NET 7.1.

Responsibility for the e-library is shared among librarians and library staff and integrated into their routine library duties. Adult and youth services coordinators work within their areas to select appropriate resources for their core users. However, this process has recently been slow due to lack of staffing. "Existing staff went from providing centralized second level reference to managing the e-resources. Training was through professional development at conferences. We don't use volunteers for electronic resources nor do we have subject bibliographers. Adult Services (collection development, acquisitions, e-resources, ILL, and staff training) manages the current subscriptions."

Librarians identify resources to collect through monitoring professional journals, attending conferences, using vendor brochures and trials, and serendipitous discovery of e-resources during related searching.

D. Collection Maintenance (e.g., link checking, ongoing weeding, and growth of the e-library collection)

Due to staffing shortages and budgetary issues, time spent on the e-library has been minimal. Future plans, given staffing and budgetary improvements, involve expanding and building the collection.

REFERENCES AND WEB SITES CITED

Bolles, Mark E., and Richard N. Bolles. 2008. *Job Hunting Online: A Guide to Using Job Listings, Message Boards, Research Sites, the Underweb, Counseling, Networking Self-assessment Tools, Niche Sites,* 5th edition. Berkeley, CA: Ten Speed Press.

Bolles, Richard N. 2009. *What Color Is Your Parachute? A Practical Manual for Job-hunters and Career-changers.* Berkeley, CA: Ten Speed Press.

Crowe, Elizabeth P. 2008. *Genealogy Online.* New York: McGraw-Hill Professional.

Dikel, Margaret R., and Frances E. Roehm. 2009. *Guide to Internet Job Searching 2008–2009,* 1st edition. New York: McGraw-Hill.

Howells, Cyndi. 2004. *Planting Your Family Tree Online: How to Create Your Own Family History Web Site.* Nashville, TN: Thomas Nelson.

Kovacs, Diane K. 2002. *Genealogical Research on the Web.* New York: Neal-Schuman.

WEB SITES CITED

American Family Immigration History Center. Available: www.ellisislandrecords.org.

Ancestry.com. Available: www.ancestry.com (accessed January 7, 2009).

Ancestry Daily News. Available: www.ancestry.com/learn/library/category.aspx?category=&type=1&page=1&bydate=1.

Better Business Bureau (BBB). Available: www.bbb.org (accessed January 18, 2009).

Consumer Reports Online. Available: www.consumerreports.org/cro/index.htm (accessed January 7, 2009).

Cyndi's List. Available: www.cyndislist.com (accessed January 7, 2009).

econsumer.gov. Available: www.econsumer.gov (accessed January 7, 2009).

HeritagequestOnline. Available: www.heritagequestonline.com (accessed January 7, 2009).

The J. M. Smucker Company. Available: http://smuckercareers.com (accessed January 18, 2009).

The JobhuntersBible. Available: www.jobhuntersbible.com (accessed January 7, 2009).

The Monthly Labor Review. Available: http://stats.bls.gov/opub/mlr/mlrhome.htm (accessed January 19, 2009).

Occupational Outlook Handbook. Available: www.bls.gov/oco (accessed January 19, 2009).

The Riley Guide. Available: www.rileyguide.com (accessed January 7, 2009).
Rootsweb. Available: www.rootsweb.ancestry.com (accessed January 7, 2009).
Scambusters. Available: www.scambusters.org (accessed January 16, 2009).
U.S. Bureau of Labor Statistics. Available: www.bls.gov (accessed January 7, 2009).
USGenWeb. Available: www.usgenweb.org (accessed January 7, 2009).

JOBS AND EMPLOYMENT E-RESOURCE COLLECTION TOOLS

The JobhuntersBible. Available: www.jobhuntersbible.com. Companion Web site for Richard Bolles's
2009 book *What Color Is Your Parachute? A Practical Manual for Job-Hunters and Career-Changers*.
Berkeley, CA: Ten Speed Press.
The Riley Guide. Available: www.rileyguide.com. Since January 1994, this comprehensive guide compiled
by Margaret R. Dikel, is more than job listings. It provides links to specific occupation databases of
job listings or use the new A–Z guide for specific career positions, fields, and locations.

CONSUMER INFORMATION E-RESOURCE COLLECTION TOOLS

econsumer.gov. Available: www.econsumer.gov. The consumer protection agencies from 21 countries have
cooperated to create this site through which consumers may file complaints about frauds and scams
both in person and through the Web or e-mail. News and warnings about ongoing frauds and scams
are posted here as well as news about successful prosecutions of scammers and spammers.

GENEALOGY E-RESOURCE COLLECTION TOOLS

META SITES

Allen County Public Library Genealogy Collection

www.acpl.lib.in.us/genealogy/index.html

> One of the best digital library collections and directory of Web resources that support genealogy researchers.

Cyndi's Genealogy Homepage (Cyndi's List)

www.cyndislist.com

> This is a great site for finding resources for international, Native American, and African American genealogical research as well as much more. Strongly recommended by genealogy researchers. However, it is difficult to search. Page down past the personal information and book promotion to find the classified directory of Internet genealogical resources. There is a choice of indexes.

Morley Public Library Genealogy and Local History Collection

www.morleylibrary.org/genealogy.htm

> Directory of genealogy e-resources, both free Web and fee-based as well as recommendations for offline resources for researchers. This is a good model for local history collections in a small public library as well.

RootsWeb Genealogical Data Cooperative

www.rootsweb.ancestry.com

> The oldest and most comprehensive Web site for genealogy resources. Sponsored by Ancestry.com, it is a compilation of multiple directories, digital libraries, bibliographies, guides, and other materials all related to genealogical research. Some of the e-resources available through RootsWeb are listed separately in the next section.

E-SERIALS, BLOGS, DISCUSSION LISTS, ETC.

Genealib Discussion List

http://mailman.acomp.usf.edu/mailman/listinfo/genealib

> Subscribe and find archives at this Web address. The "Librarians Serving Genealogists" discussion list is great. There is much sharing of all kinds of genealogical information, and the Web site not only has subscription instructions but links to many good resources.

We Relate Genealogy wiki

http://werelate.org/wiki/Main_Page

CHAPTER

6

BUSINESS E-RESOURCES

The management and library literatures indicate that BFL (Business Faculty-Librarian) collaborations have taken on a greater prominence in the electronic collection development. Collaborative relationships are needed more now than ever before. It was found that specific principles of strategic business partnerships can and should be applied to BFL collaborations aimed at improving electronic collection development. Driving forces such as assessment, communication and technology have influenced the nature of these alliances across the business and academic arenas and have increased the frequency, intensity and depth of these alliances, all to the betterment of the collaboration. (Harper and Norelli, 2007: 18)

DEVELOPING A COLLECTION PLAN FOR BUSINESS E-RESOURCES

Business e-resources are some of the most common and numerous on the Web. In an effort to attract customers (both consumer and business to business) and investors to their Web sites businesses are sharing an unprecedented level of information. Company Web sites often contain product catalogs, technical support information, company financial data, annual and quarterly reports, and other information. Classic business reference publishers publish directly on the Web; for example, Thomas Register Online (www.thomasnet.com).

Advertisers have always been the main source of revenue for most publishers of business directories and company, industry, and financial news. The Web opens a huge new source of advertising revenue for them. As a result, many business information publishers have been steadily expanding versions of their products onto the Web or publishing directly on the Web.

The U.S. and international governmental entities that collect and compile business information are using the Web to make this information available to the public and also requiring businesses to use the Web to submit their required paperwork to government agencies. The U.S. Securities and Exchange Commission (SEC) (www.sec.gov) requires public companies to upload required reports such as 10K (annual reports) or 10Q (quarterly reports) directly to the Edgar database. Other sources of business and financial data are also being published directly to the Web. This type of information is especially sensitive to security issues and quality considerations because it frequently involves financial or private information.

Business information on the Web is frequently found in the form of directories of businesses and industries, stock market quotations and analysis, and business and financial news. Web business directories, such as Hoovers Online (www.hoovers.com), contain business listings along with industry, product, competitors, financial status, contact information, and other basic data. Thomas Register Online, in addition to the contact information and basic industry and product data, includes direct links to company catalogs, Web sites, and other e-commerce options. Stock and commodities market information is also available online in real time or delayed time. Many people make stock and commodity trades through the Web in almost real time. Such trades are never instantaneous and may be delayed by network connection speeds or server loads. Other kinds of business information include currency and exchange rates, consumer information, small business support resources, product information, catalogs, and customer support services. Electronic commerce (e-commerce) sites where library users can purchase products, services, transportation, make investments, do banking, and many other business transactions through the Web are numerous.

WHAT PURPOSE WILL YOUR COLLECTION SERVE? FOR WHOM ARE YOU COLLECTING THESE E-RESOURCES?

Obviously the purpose of any collection depends on answering these two key questions: Who is asking business information questions? Business people (e.g, corporate officers, owners, managers, employees), brokers, financial analysts, potential small business owners, job seekers, students (high school and college), marketing researchers, business faculty, or others? What are they asking?

Ready-reference/single source for answers; for example, I have a job interview with Company X. How can I learn more about the company? Where can I find a supplier/vendor of X product in the United States? Where can I get contact addresses to create a mailing list for marketing my product/business/services in the United States? In-depth/multiple sources for answers; for example, Is this company a good risk for investment (or job security)? Where can I get marketing and demographic data for a business plan to start a business in x country? (e.g., United States, Canada, UK, EU, China, Brazil, Mexico, or anywhere). How do I get money to start a business in X country? How do I write a legally binding contract with my client in the X country/ state/province?

Will the library encourage or allow library users to engage in e-commerce activities? Will the library provide access to product catalogs and consumer information (e.g., price comparison sites)? Will storefronts and stock and commodity trading sites be included directly in the e-library? Many academic libraries may need to gather a collection of archived historical business information such as annual reports, historical stock market data, and other materials used in academic business studies or business research. Academic libraries will be collecting for students engaged in business studies defined by their parent university or college programs as well as for faculty and researchers. The collection scope for most academic business e-libraries will be defined by the programs offered and the supporting information required by those programs as well as by research needs of faculty or graduate students.

K–12 libraries may need to look carefully to find age appropriate business information depending on the age of the children the library serves and the curriculum that the library supports. Some excellent business information resources exist that were designed for teenagers. One example is the I Don't Flip Burgers (http://library.thinkquest.org/C0114800/about/index.php) site, which is a guide to books and Web sites to assist students in achieving entrepreneurial success. The site also features a small business simulator program in which the student plays the role of an entrepreneur.

Public libraries will want to provide resources focused on the needs of local businesses as well as for potential small business owners, students, and job seekers. They may find that either, or both, small businesses or local major companies are their primary business information library users and will want to collect resources to support those businesses.

Special librarians will be collecting resources to support the business in which they work. For example, the library for a company in the petro-chemical industry would need resources related to the production and use of petro-chemicals, vendor and customer Web sites, professional organizations, datasets, safety guidelines, and so on. The business librarian will almost always need to have access to some of the fee-based e-resources that provide very current and detailed research reports, statistics, and financial information.

Geographical coverage is also an important consideration. A library may wish to provide in-depth support for local, state, provincial, district, regional, or international business interests. In fact, any modern library may find, in our global economy, that their local businesses, students, and other business information library users need access to international business information.

WHAT TYPES OF E-RESOURCES WILL YOU COLLECT?

Business e-resources take forms that can easily be described in terms of traditional reference source types.

- Directories (business contact, government contact, customer contact, grants and development information, and more)
- Dictionaries (English as well as international language translation dictionaries for doing business around the world)
- Abstracts, indexes, and table of contents services (including those with full text of the business journals and magazines indexed)
- Encyclopedias and almanacs
- Full-text and/or multimedia databases/digital libraries (collections of e-books, e-serials, recordings, videos, podcasts, images, etc.)
- News and news services (current awareness) sources
- Key primary documents (company filings, laws, regulations, research data/reports, and statistical sources, etc.)
- Search engines
- Meta sites (e-resources that provide two or more of the other reference tool types in a single product/Web site)

Directories of business contact, government contact, customer contact, grants and development information, etc. usually also function as meta sites. While their primary function is the directory of business information they also provide news, data, or other reference types. For example, Hoovers Online provides a directory, publishes news and financial data, links to statistics and other data, as well as including key primary documents. Much of this is only available in the subscription version, but a significant amount of information is provided without charge.

Abstracts and indexes for business serials are generally not freely available on the Web, although most commercial business publishers provide subscription access through the Web. Key primary documents such as stock and commodity reports, financial and statistical reports, marketing reports, and annual reports are also a core part of the Web business reference collection. The most famous example is the U.S. Securities and Exchange Commission's EDGAR database (www.sec.gov) with the full text of the 10K and other required filings from publicly traded companies.

In business reference, sources of current news and full text of financial, statistical, or other business or industry related data are critical and easily found on the Web. Sites such as Google Finance (http://finance.google.com), Yahoo! Finance (http://finance.yahoo.com), and BigCharts (http://bigcharts.marketwatch.com) provide news and financial data for no direct cost to the user.

HOW WILL YOU ORGANIZE YOUR E-LIBRARY COLLECTION?

As always this question is going to be answered differently by each library depending on its answers to the first two questions in the collection planning discussion and taking into account its technology infrastructure and funding. Some libraries will organize business resources by subject and subtopics. Some might choose to organize by the resource types identified previously. A good combination of these two organizational structures can be very accessible. Ideally, a good CMS product can enhance access and allow organization tailored to each individual library user's style.

IDENTIFYING AND COLLECTING BUSINESS E-RESOURCES

Business e-resources were some of the first to be collected and organized by librarians. In 1994, our colleague Leslie Haas, now Director of the Richard J. Klarchek Information Commons at Loyola University Chicago, began compiling the first Business Sources on the Net collection. Mel Westerman, business librarian at Pennsylvania State University (now retired), had asked for volunteers from the BUSLIB-L discussion group to collect and annotate the resources in the many different subtopic areas of business. Hope Tillman, Director of Babson College Libraries, was one of the key volunteers. Leslie Haas volunteered to coordinate the volunteers and publish the list on the Internet. This list was then organized and published on the Kent State University Gopher server and FTP server, which are now defunct. With the advent of the Web, many of Business Sources on the Net volunteers and other business librarians began collecting business e-resources and organizing them on their own Web sites. The business e-resources identification and collection strategies that the original BUSLIB-L volunteers used involved monitoring and searching with some of the same types of Web resource collection tools described in this chapter.

WEB SITES THAT REVIEW AND EVALUATE E-RESOURCES: PEER E-LIBRARIES, SUBJECT COLLECTIONS/GUIDES, OR META SITES

Some of the most valuable sites in terms of thorough annotations, evaluations, and scope of subject coverage are the Louisiana State University Library's Business Web collection (www.lib.lsu.edu/bus/index.htm), the Internet Public Library Business and Economics collection (www.ipl.org/div/subject/browse/bus00.00.00), and Jeanie M. Welch's VIBES: Virtual International Business and Economic Sources (http://library.uncc.edu/vibes). Other excellent tools are listed in the "Business E-Resource Collection Tools" section of this chapter.

DISCUSSION LISTS (LISTSERV, ETC.), FORUMS/GROUPS, E-SERIALS, AND/OR BLOGS THAT POST OR PUBLISH REVIEWS AND EVALUATIONS OF E-RESOURCES

The core discussion lists and newsgroups related to business e-resources for business libraries is BUSLIB-L. BUSLIB-L is a moderated discussion list that addresses all issues relating to the collection, storage, and dissemination of business information within a library setting regardless of format. Subscription information and archives are available at http://lists.nau.edu/cgi-bin/wa?A0=BUSLIB-L. Search the archives for information about individual business e-resources or subscribe for ongoing discussions. For example, search for Thomas Register to find out what BUSLIB-L subscribers think about Thomas Register Online.

BRASS (Business Reference and User Services Section of the ALA) publishes two e-newsletters that review business e-resources. *Academic BRASS* (www.ala.org/ala/mgrps/divs/rusa/sections/brass/brasspubs/academicbrass/academicbrass.cfm) covers business e-resources for academic libraries and the *Public Libraries Briefcase* (www.ala.org/ala/mgrps/divs/rusa/sections/brass/brasspubs/publibbrief/publiclibraries.cfm) covers business e-resources for public libraries. The Business and Finance Division of the Special Libraries Association (http://units.sla.org/division/dbf/news/index.html) publishes a quarterly bulletin that includes Web resource reviews.

Many of the business resource meta sites included with this chapter also publish e-newsletter or e-journals as part of their basic service. The bizjournals.com (www.bizjournals.com/bizresources) site publishes reviews of business-related Web sites and organizes and links to many sites, including those that publish e-serials.

PRINT BOOKS AND JOURNALS THAT REVIEW E-RESOURCES

Most business journals and newsletters frequently include reviews of e-resources either as articles or, in the same section, as book reviews in their print editions. At this time there are no current books that are dedicated to business e-resources, but many books on business topics cite business e-resources, especially Web sites. Barron's (http://online.barrons.com), Inc. (www.inc.com), Fortune (http://money.cnn.com/magazines/fortune/index.html), and other business journals feature Web resource reviews in nearly every issue.

EVALUATION GUIDELINES AND SELECTION CRITERIA: THE CORE WEB BUSINESS REFERENCE COLLECTION

Evaluating business information found on the Web requires answers to the same basic questions that should be asked about any source of information. Business, medical, and law information are especially sensitive. Quality of information on these subjects can affect the financial and physical well-being of library users. Therefore, it is particularly important to very carefully evaluate any source of information in these subject areas. The quality and currency of business information may affect the financial success or failure of individuals, businesses, and organizations. Accuracy, timeliness, and security of business information are of great importance.

The reputation and résumé—researchable track record—of any provider of business information is very important in business decision making. Information obtained from MorningStar (www.morningstar.com) or Value Line (www.valueline.com) has more credibility and authority than information obtained from some guy on a Web forum or chat. The only way to determine the source of information provided on the Web is to read through the Web site, e-mail message, discussion list or forum posting, and look for an attribution. For example, Information obtained from Yahoo Finance! (http://finance.yahoo.com) is supplied by Commodity Systems, Inc. (www.csidata.com), MorningStar (www.morningstar.com), Capital IQ (www.capitaliq.com/main.asp), most of the world stock exchanges, and other finance related companies. Links to each source are provided. If you cannot easily determine the source and publisher of business information, then it is best not to use it.

The reputation of a business information source is usually based on its record of successful projections and analyses as well as its record in terms of ethical business practices. If you receive an e-mail or read a posting, research the person and the company in known reliable information sources, such as Hoovers or Fortune/CNNMoney, or just Google the person to see if there is anyone else talking about him or her. Make use of the BBB site. Check the scam and fraud sites discussed in Part I, Chapter 1.

In business, authority and expertise go hand in hand. Providers of business information are expected to have both education and experience in researching and analyzing financial, economic, and other business data. Education is not necessarily as important as experience and the information provider's record of successful predictions, analyses, and ethics. Use the same strategy to find this information as you did in determining who provided the information. Again, if it is not clear to you that the information provider has the requisite experience and expertise, do not use the information. When in doubt about the authority of an individual source, ask. Any legitimate broker or business or financial advisor will be more than willing to supply you with his or her credentials and references. It is wise to monitor the scam information sites discussed in Part I, Chapter 1, check business directories to gauge their legitimacy, or check the BBB (www.bbb.org) before doing business with any individual or company.

Much business information, especially financial information, needs to be as current as possible. Stock and commodities prices, currency exchange rates, news about current events that affect business, agriculture, and other commodities reports are very time sensitive. Publication on the Web, potentially, implies that this source of business information is the most current information available. Sites such as CNNMoney (http://money.cnn.com) can provide all of the types of information described and provide them with a date and time stamp so that the information user knows precisely the time at which the information was gathered and published.

Yahoo Finance! (http://finance.yahoo.com) also provides time and date information about currency exchange rates, stock quotes, and related financial information. Other sources and types of business information are actually historical in nature. Economic trends, changes in an industry over time, stock values over time, as well as changes in the products, personnel, and mission of individual companies are historical information. Read carefully through Web sites and e-serials to verify times and dates of publication. Decide also if the site is intended to provide historical information. For example, historical data is published on the SEC Edgar site.

Security of business information on the Web is extremely critical from both the site security and library user security perspectives. These two security questions are very different. The information user needs to feel that the information that he or she might find on the Web is authoritative and that the information provider can substantiate this. The user also needs to know that the Web site in question is actually published by the organization it seems to be published by. When engaging in e-commerce, the library user needs to feel secure in giving his or her personal and financial data to a company through its Web site. Personal and financial information should never be submitted through unencrypted e-mail or Web forms. Always use Web browser functionality to determine the security certification of any Web site that requests personal or financial data. Never send personal or financial information through e-mail, unless you are using an e-mail encryption tool.

Some business research requires privacy in order to ensure information security. Industrial espionage is a very real problem in our modern global economy. If a competitor learns that a given company is researching along a certain line, this knowledge may give them a competitive advantage in developing or marketing a product, obtaining a contract, or recruiting desirable personnel. The fact that there is no privacy on the Internet may be a problem for many businesses. For example, a friend of ours used to be a librarian for a high-tech research and development division of a Fortune 100 company. That friend would call our academic library and ask us to research certain topics through our Internet connection rather than doing the research from their own Internet connection. This way it just looked like someone at Kent State University was researching in a particular area rather than someone from that company's competitor. Public libraries may find that business people are using their Internet services for the same reason.

Researching on the Web from a public library computer is relatively anonymous. All anyone can find out is that someone at a particular library is researching a particular topic. This is a positive trend as it means librarians have the opportunity to prove their value to the businesses in their communities. It also may result in increased research assistance to those businesses when they are using the library or need to do research and fax, e-mail, or report the results over the telephone. For example, KnowItNow24x7 (www.knowitnow.org) serves businesses in Northern Ohio through virtual reference service. Library users may elect to ask questions directly to the Business and Finance Librarians. The Web links collection and business databases in the CLEVNET system e-library (www.clevnet.org) are resources the librarians can use to assist those library users or those users may access them directly.

In May and August 2008, librarians were surveyed to elicit which business reference tools they consider to be core or essential to their work. The discussion lists and blogs where the survey links were posted are listed in Table 6.1. The core business reference tools survey is reproduced in Table 6.2.

The Core Web Business Reference Collection on the companion Web Site (www.kovacs .com/ns/essentialguide.html) was initially created using the survey results from these surveys along with results from similar earlier surveys (the most recent were collected in 2005 and 2006)

Table 6.1. Discussion Lists and Blogs Distribution for Business Reference Tools Survey

- BUSLIB-L@LISTS.NAU.EDU
- LISNews and LISNewsWire Blogs: lisnews-owner@lishost.net
- ResourceShelf Blog: gary.price@resourceshelf.com
- ERIL-L@LISTSERV.BINGHAMTON.EDU
- dig_ref@LISTSERV.SYR.EDU
- collib-l@ala.org
- LIS-LINK@jiscmail.ac.uk
- Libref-L@listserv.kent.edu
- GOVDOC-L@lists.psu.edu
- publib@webjunction.org
- livereference@yahoogroups.com
- Libref-L@listserv.kent.edu

Table 6.2. Core Business Reference Tools Survey Questions

1. Which library type best describes the library you work in/for/with?

2. In which subject area(s) are you most likely to answer business reference questions? (Check all that apply.)

3. What are the essential three print titles (reference books) that you can't work without in answering business reference questions? (Please type the title only.)

4. What are the essential three free (not government published) Web-accessible databases that you can't work without in answering business reference questions? (Please type complete URL/Web address; e.g., www.hoovers.com.)

5. What are the essential three (.gov) government published (state, federal, local, international) free Web-accessible databases that you can't work without in answering business reference questions? (Please type complete URL/Web address; e.g., www.export.gov.)

6. What are the essential three fee-based Web-accessible databases that you can't work without in answering business reference questions? (Please the simple title; e.g., Business Source Complete)

7. Does your library maintain a Web page or site to support business professional reference? If so, please share the URL/Web address (e.g., www.libraryvisit.org/businessresources.htm).

8. Additional comments or ideas:

(Please include your name and e-mail address if you would like feedback, otherwise this survey form is completely anonymous.)

as core and model collections. Past, present, and future surveys and results are posted at www.kovacs.com/misc.html. These collections are intended for librarians to use as a source of e-resources they might select for their business reference e-library collections.

Core print reference tools for business were collected. Compared to prior surveys, there were much fewer print reference tools reported. Table 6.3 lists the top five print business reference tools identified in the survey. The free Web sites that librarians reported as core or essential for business reference are given in Table 6.4.

Government documents Web sites are frequently mentioned by librarians, as core or essential business reference tools. The top five e-docs sites used for business reference are listed in Table 6.5.

Fee-based business reference tools are essential for business reference in many libraries. The top five—by number of librarians mentioning that e-resource—core or essential fee-based business reference e-resources are given in Table 6.6.

Table 6.3. Top Five Print Business Reference Tools Identified in Survey

1. *Standard & Poor's Industry Surveys*
2. *Market Share Reporter*
3. *RMA Annual Statement Studies*
4. *Business Plans Handbooks (Gale), Capital Changes Reporter, Daily Stock Price Records, Demographics USA, Encyclopedia of American Industries, Industry Norms and Key Business Ratios, Lifestyle Market Analyst, Mergent Industrial Manual, NAICS Code*
5. *Small Business Sourcebook, Hoover's Guides, Ward's Business Directory*

Table 6.4. Top Five Free Web Business Reference Tools Identified in Survey

1. Yahoo! Finance: http://finance.yahoo.com
2. Google: www.google.com, Hoovers.com: www.hoovers.com, Thomas Register: www.thomasnet.com
3. BigCharts.com: http://bigcharts.marketwatch.com
4. GuideStar: www.guidestar.org, Trade Association Web sites
5. Individual company Web sites, Zimmerman's Research Page: www.lexis.com/infopro/zimmerman

---

Table 6.5. Top Five Government Documents Web Sites Used as Business Reference Tools Identified in Survey

1. U.S. Census Bureau/American Factfinder: www.census.gov or http://factfinder.census.gov/home/saff/main.html
2. Bureau of Labor Statistics: www.bls.gov, PubMed: www.ncbi.nlm.nih.gov/pubmed
3. U.S. Securities and Exchange Commission/EDGAR: www.sec.gov or www.sec.gov/edgar.shtml
4. U.S. Small Business Administration: www.sba.gov
5. State government agency business support Web sites, USA Trade Online: www.usatradeonline.gov, STAT-USA: www.statusa.gov, NAICS (North American Industry Classification System): www.census.gov/naics

---

Table 6.6. Top Five Fee-based Business Reference E-Resources Identified in Survey

1. ABI/INFORM: www.proquest.com, LexisNexis: www.lexisnexis.com
2. Reference USA: www.referenceusa.com
3. Business Source Premier (EBSCO): www.ebscohost.com
4. Business and Company Resource Center (Gale): www.gale.cengage.com, Mergent Online: www.mergent.com
5. Standard & Poor's NetAdvantage: www2.standardandpoors.com, Hoovers: www.hoovers.com

---

It is interesting to observe that all of the core business reference tools identified in this survey are Web accessible. In fact, most respondents who specified a choice preferred the Web-accessible versions to the print version. Additional selection criteria for business information resources can be derived from the answers arrived at during the collection planning process. The Core Web Business Reference Collection was compiled with these criteria in mind: The intended library user group is librarians working with library users who might be interested in basic business reference information regardless of their educational level. All of these core business reference Web sites conform to international standards for Web accessibility, with no special software required for access. Fee-based e-resources are included when they offer free trials or have some information available without requiring a fee. At least some information provided by each of these sites is free of direct cost. Many have additional special fee-based services such as detailed datasets, document delivery, or more advanced search options. Several require registration. The registration serves as a marketing research tool for the information provider.

Many Web sites are funded by advertising. The information provider uses the information obtained during the registration procedure to count their circulation demographics. This is the same principle used by newspapers and magazines. They sell advertising based on the circulation rate and demographics that they can guarantee to advertisers. However, registering on Web sites may result in having your e-mail address included in spam e-mail lists. Most reputable sites will provide an opportunity for you to opt out of such lists. Read carefully the privacy policies that should be posted on each site to decide if you will use them.

E-LIBRARY SUCCESS STORY

BAINBRIDGE GRADUATE INSTITUTE E-LIBRARY PROJECT
http://bgichannel.org
Contact Kate McDill, kate.mcdill@bgiedu.org, and Neil Birt, neil.birt@bgiedu.org

A. Collection Planning (e.g., goal setting and identification of users, technology/personnel choices)

1. Who's idea was it to create the BGI e-library? What year was it conceived? What year was it implemented?

Kate McDill was the first librarian hired for the Bainbridge Graduate Institute (BGI) in 2004. The BGI MBA program was only three years old and the entering class was 30 students. All students of the BGI program are distance learners. BGI was in the process of submitting their

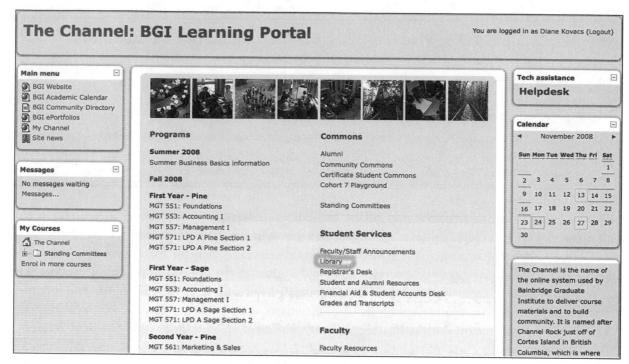

Figure 6.1. BGI Channel

reauthorization packet to the Higher Education Coordinating Board (HEC-B) of the State of Washington. The HEC-B is the body that determines who can grant graduate credit in the state. HEC-B guidelines expect that a graduate school will have a library.

There was no physical library other than the personal collections of three program founders. Given the nature of the program, Kate decided that it was most logical to create an e-library collection and library research support online. "Our program is a hybrid distance/in-person program. The students come to 'campus' nine long weekends (Thurs noon-Sun noon; called intensives) between September and June each year, and the rest of the curriculum is delivered online."

Initially students and faculty met via conference call, but in 2006 they began using Elluminate (www.elluminate.com) for online class meetings. The e-library was first hosted on Web Crossings and was then migrated to Moodle (http://moodle.org) around 2005.

The first e-library collection was created based on a business research guide and paper created by BGI student Linda Lovett, who was also a librarian. BGI licensed ProQuest and EBSCO in addition to adding freely available Web accessible resources. Initial technical support was also provided by a student employed part time by the library. Eric Magnuson managed the Web Crossing site. BGI's Web presence or portal is named "the Channel." "In 2004, we licensed ProQuest through the Washington State Database Licensing project, and EBSCO. Those were our only licensed databases."

A core purpose for the BGI e-library is to support their graduate degree granting program. "The intended users are the BGI community: students, faculty, staff, alumni, and a portion of the wider community of people involved in sustainability. These people are invited to participate through our Change Agents in Residence (CAIR) program; we have CAIRs come to each weekend intensive to present to the community, and to participate in classrooms."

The Moodle site on which the Channel is built also serves as the main communications mechanism for students, faculty, staff, and alumni. The e-library is not accessible to the general

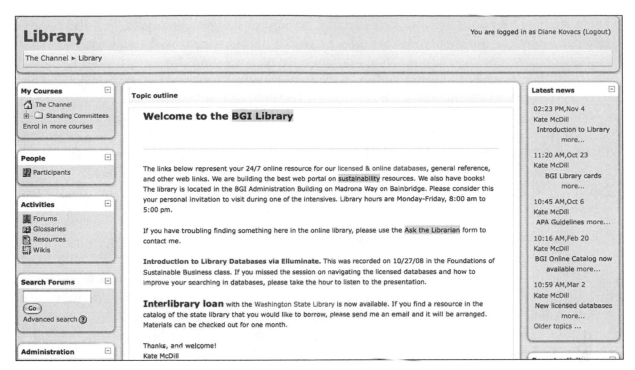

Figure 6.2. BGI Library

public. "It is my long held dream to create a general Web presence for the BGI e-library so that it would be open to the public. We envisioned at one point that we would host the sustainability portal on the internet. This has not come to be because of financial constraints. I do not possess the Web skills, and we haven't the budget or human resources to put in this direction."

A written collection development plan was created to inform the BGI e-library collection development. This was modified and updated when Kate McDill took the online course "Electronic Collection Development for Academic E-Libraries" through ACRL in the fall of 2007.

B. Collection Strategies (e.g., selection criteria, identification of resources, licensing, and related user information needs)

A library advisory board of faculty and administrators provides feedback as to appropriate library resources to support the program. Cost is the main selection criteria beyond the basic criteria that the resource be appropriate and support the program. "We are a start-up independent school, and lack of funds has been a constant issue. We are not (at this time) accredited, nor are we affiliated with a larger institution; our founders did not have academic backgrounds. We offer a program that cannot be considered traditional in most ways; yes, it is a business administration program and as such the students must study finance/accounting, economics, marketing, operations and strategy however, we teach each of these subjects with the thread of sustainability woven through. . . . All of this is to say, that the library budget is miniscule, and that at the moment cost is my only criteria unfortunately."

In such a situation, the freely available high quality Web accessible databases are favored. Core licensed databases: ProQuest, EBSCO, MarketLine, and Business Insights are paid for by BGI for the library. "We are not large enough to participate in a consortium (they cost mone . . .). We do participate in the Washington State Database Licensing project; access to ProQuest comes through this and is subsidized for us."

No fee-based e-books are included partially because of budget limitations, but also because there is no physical library students are expected to purchase textbooks and use their local libraries for additional text needs. "No, I do not have e-books. I am I guess a bit old-fashioned. I like book-books. ✪ Because my budget is so small I haven't looked at e-books. Our students rarely use the physical library."

The small physical library that now exists is cataloged but not the e-library resources specifically. "I use Companion Corporations Alexandria Web based catalog for our physical collection. It doesn't have our individual serials or our fee-based databases accessible through it. The fee-based databases are accessed directly through the e-Library on the Channel."

The Channel does include a basic e-mail reference service, and BGI has an interlibrary loan agreement with the Washington State Library. Neither are used significantly by students.

C. Collection Organization (e.g., content management systems, Web server choices, personnel responsibilities, etc.)

The BGI e-library, the Channel, is hosted on BGI's Moodle server and also uses Joomla integrated with Moodle for some options. Neil Birt manages the Moodle server for BGI. "The Channel is hosted on a dedicated server that runs about $300/month. The Moodle LMS is open source and has no associated costs. However, it does require at least one full-time person or service provider to manage and maintain the day to day operation of the site."

BGI uses the Moodle to maintain courses, resources, and other services for faculty, students, etc. "The BGI e-library is a part of this system which we call the Channel. Access to the Channel is strictly controlled and is generally limited to students, faculty, staff and alumni. Each individual area also has access control. This means that you might be a guest in one area, a teacher in another and a student somewhere else. In the case of the BGI Library, everyone save the librarian has student level access. With student level access, users are able to go in and interact with the library, but they do not have the capability to edit or otherwise modify information contained there. The librarian does have full editing capabilities and is able to add/subtract whatever content is needed..."

Kate McDill supports the e-library for 13 hours a week and Neil Birt handles technical support as needed. Kate was hired as BGI's first librarian. She has an MLIS from the University of Washington, accredited by NWCCU and ALA. This accreditation was required by BGI in their search for a suitable librarian. Kate McDill does all of the selection, collection, evaluation, updates, and changes to the e-library. She identifies resources to add to the collection through ACRL journals and *American Libraries* and through student and faculty recommendations.

D. Collection Maintenance (e.g., link checking, ongoing weeding, and growth of the e-library collection)

All links are checked manually. The e-library collection is reviewed and maintained annually. "Our students and faculty are very highly involved; we are a participative community. The Channel provides a forum for feedback. If a link is broken or another resource is found, they let me know."

Budget cuts are enforcing a cut in e-library resources so that some tough decisions will need to be made for the future. "...will have to look at not renewing MarketLine or Business Insights and to replace them with lower cost resources such as RefUSA."

REFERENCES AND WEB SITES CITED

Harper, Tim, and Barbara Norelli. 2007. "The Business of Collaboration and Electronic Collection Development," *Collection Building* 26, no. 1: 15–19.

WEB SITES CITED

Academic BRASS. Available: www.ala.org/ala/mgrps/divs/rusa/sections/brass/brasspubs/academicbrass/academicbrass.cfm (accessed January 7, 2009).

Barron's. Available: http://online.barrons.com (accessed January 18, 2009).

Better Business Bureau (BBB). Available: www.bbb.org (accessed January 18, 2009).

BigCharts.com. Available: http://bigcharts.marketwatch.com (accessed January 7, 2009).

Bulletin of The Special Libraries Association, Business and Finance Division. Available: http://units.sla.org/division/dbf/news/index.html (accessed January 18, 2009).

Business Source Premier. Available: ebscohost.com (accessed January 14, 2009).

Capital IQ (Standard & Poors). Available: www.capitaliq.com/main.asp (accessed January 16, 2009).

CLEVNET System. Available: www.clevnet.org (accessed January 18, 2009).

CNNMoney. Available: http://money.cnn.com (accessed January 18, 2009).

Fortune. Available: http://money.cnn.com/magazines/fortune/index.html (accessed January 18, 2009).

Google Finance. Available: http://finance.yahoo.com (accessed February 4, 2009).

I Don't Flip Burgers. Available: http://library.thinkquest.org/C0114800/about/index.php (accessed January 18, 2009).

Inc. Available: www.inc.com (accessed January 18, 2009).

The Internet Public Library Business and Economics collection. Available: www.ipl.org/div/subject/browse/bus00.00.00 (accessed January 18, 2009).

KnowItNow24x7. Available: www.knowitnow.org (accessed January 18, 2009).

LexisNexis/LexisNexis Academic. Available: http://academic.lexisnexis.com/online-services/academic-overview.aspx (accessed January 7, 2009).

Louisiana State University Library's Business Web collection. Available: www.lib.lsu.edu/bus/index.htm (accessed January 7, 2009).

Morningstar. Available: www.morningstar.com (accessed January 7, 2009).

Public Libraries Briefcase. Available: www.ala.org/ala/mgrps/divs/rusa/sections/brass/brasspubs/publibbrief/publiclibraries.cfm (accessed January 7, 2009).

Standard & Poor's NetAdvantage. Available: www2.standardandpoors.com (accessed January 7, 2009).

Thomas Register Online. Available: www.thomasnet.com (accessed January 7, 2009).

U. S. Securities and Exchange Commission and Edgar database. Available: http://sec.gov (accessed January 14, 2009).

Value Line Investment Surveys. Available: www.valueline.com (accessed January 16, 2009).

VIBES: Virtual International Business and Economic Sources. Available: http://library.uncc.edu/vibes/ (accessed January 7, 2009).

Yahoo! Finance. Available: http://finance.yahoo.com (accessed January 7, 2009).

BUSINESS E-RESOURCE COLLECTION TOOLS

META SITES

Best of the Best Business Web Sites (ALA/BRASS)
www.ala.org/ala/mgrps/divs/rusa/sections/brass/brassprotools/bestofthebestbus/bestbestbusiness.cfm

Binghamton University Libraries, Business and Economics Resources
http://library.lib.binghamton.edu/ subjects/business/index.html
> Annotated and updated business resources of Accounting and Tax, Economics, Finance and Investment, International Business, Management, Marketing, and Social Science Data, then subdivided. Includes an annotated gateway to online business resources.

Bizlink: Public Library of Charlotte and Mecklenberg County
www.plcmc.org/bizlink/bizreflist.asp
> Public library with excellent free and commercial business e-resource collection.

Business Navigator (New York Times Newsroom Navigator)
www.nytimes.com/ref/business/business-navigator.html
> This collection is used by journalists writing for the *New York Times*. The "Business Connections" section contains hundreds of business reference sites of all types. The links are organized, annotated, and proven practical.

Business Research Guides/Business Reference
http://gethelp.library.upenn.edu/guides/business/busrefweb.html
> Collection of business research guides and business reference tools carefully selected by the librarians of the University of Pennsylvania.

"Doing Business on the Internet" Business Reference Services
www.loc.gov/rr/business/ecommerce/inet-business.html
> Guide and collection of business reference sources on the Web prepared and selected by the librarians of the Library of Congress.

Gary Price's List of Lists
www.specialissues.com/lol
> "The List of Lists is a database of ranked listings of companies, people and resources freely available on the Internet. Content comes from a number of sources including: Specialissues.com, Gary Price's 'ResourceShelf' and individual users of the LOL."

globalEDGE
http://globaledge.msu.edu
> Collection of Web sites with information and tools for use in doing international business research. Created by the International Business Center at Michigan State University (IBC).

Internet Intelligence Index
www.fuld.com/i3
> Internet resources for competitive intelligence research. Compiled by Fuld & Co.

The Internet Public Library Business and Economics collection
www.ipl.org/div/subject/browse/bus00.00.00
> Broad collection of business and economic research Web sites. Collected and annotated by IPL volunteers.

LSU Libraries Business Resources
www.lib.lsu.edu/bus/index.htm
> Internet subject guide of databases and resources for business carefully selected by the librarians at Louisiana State University.

New York Public Library Science, Industry, and Business Library

www.nypl.org/research/sibl/index.html

> Includes guides written by NYPL library staff on small business information, international business, and other topics as well as a collection of high quality annotated Internet business site links.

OSU Virtual Finance Library

http://fisher.osu.edu/fin/overview.htm

> Collection of Web sites and tools for use by investors, finance students, and researchers. Hosted at The Ohio State University Fisher Library and maintained by the OSU Department of Finance.

SLA Business and Finance Division: Business Libraries on the Web

www.slabf.org/buslibs.html

VIBES: Virtual International Business and Economic Sources

http://library.uncc.edu/vibes

> Jeanie M. Welch, a librarian at the University of North Carolina, has created this collection of high quality reviewed international and U.S. business and economic Web sites. This is one of the best meta sites for business information.

E-Serials, Blogs, Discussion Lists, etc.

Academic BRASS

www.ala.org/ala/mgrps/divs/rusa/sections/brass/brasspubs/academicbrass/academicbrass.cfm

> E-newsletter published by the Business Reference and User Services Section (BRASS) of ALA. Includes reviews of key business Web resources as well as other resource reviews, news, articles, etc. This e-journal is intended for academic business librarians. See Public Librarian's Briefcase.

BUSLIB-L

http://lists.nau.edu/cgi-bin/wa?A0=BUSLIB-L

> Moderated electronic forum that addresses all issues relating to the collection, storage, and dissemination of business information within a library setting, regardless of format.

Public Libraries Briefcase

www.ala.org/ala/mgrps/divs/rusa/sections/brass/brasspubs/publibbrief/publiclibraries.cfm

> A publication of the BRASS Business Reference in Public Libraries Committee with reviews of business Web resources, news, articles, etc.

SLA-DBF

www.sla.org/content/community/lists/divisionlists5979.cfm or www.sla.org/content/community/lists/joinlists.cfm

> Discussion list for librarians who are members of the Special Libraries Association, Business and Finance Division.

CHAPTER

7

LEGAL E-RESOURCES

The LII compilations aim to provide useful information. This should not be confused with legal advice. While the editors endeavor to have each collection at this site be accurate and complete, neither the LII nor Cornell warrants that the information is complete or accurate. Both disclaim all liability to any person for any loss caused by errors or omissions in this collection of information. Legal Information Institute (LII), Cornell Law School (accessed January 19, 2009, at www.law.cornell.edu/comments/credits.html)

DEVELOPING A COLLECTION PLAN FOR LEGAL E-RESOURCES

The Legal Information Institute, Cornell Law School (www.law.cornell.edu) "Conditions of Use" that introduces this chapter serves two purposes. First, it establishes the conditions under which the LII meta site provides its legal resources e-library. Second, it exemplifies the conditions under which most Web-accessible legal information is supplied.

Just about every field of study has a legal aspect to it. For example, the patent searching and trademark and copyright related e-resources are included in several chapters because the researchers in every subject area may need to make use of the legal identification of intellectual property ownership. The interdisciplinary nature of legal research will inform the selection process and the e-resources you choose. Each library will need to decide what specific areas of law they will support or rather what legal aspects of any other subject area they will support.

Many freely accessible law e-resources are published by governmental agencies, bar organizations, law schools, or law firms. Some of the best legal primary resources are those made freely available by the Government Printing Office through the GPOAccess Web site (www.gpoaccess.gov). The GPO publishes core full-text documents such as the United States Revised Code, the Code of Federal Regulations, and the decisions of the United States Supreme Court.

The Legal Information Institute cited previously compiles a rich variety of legal materials, including links to state and international level legal materials. In the pre-Web era, most libraries had to choose a limited geographic coverage for legal materials. Many smaller libraries could not afford even the most limited code texts. With the Web, every library has full access to the full range of legal codes for all states and many international and local governments.

Some legal documentation on the Web is still in a raw state, presented as plain ASCII texts without added value such as indexing, searchability, or significant formatting. The Legal Information

Institute tries to make a large portion of it more readily searched and readable. The availability of legal documentation or primary resources will vary from jurisdiction to jurisdiction. Some countries, states, provinces, municipalities, government, and nongovernment organizations have been more proactive in publishing their laws, regulations, and court decisions on the Web.

WHAT PURPOSE WILL YOUR COLLECTION SERVE? FOR WHOM ARE YOU COLLECTING THESE E-RESOURCES?

These two questions are strongly interrelated in any subject collection planning. In evaluating and selecting legal e-resources, they are virtually the same question since knowing who your users are will typically also tell you what the purpose will be. A collection built for lawyers, paralegals, or law school students is substantially different from a collection built to serve journalism undergraduate students or one built to serve the library users of a small public library.

Lawyers, paralegals, and law school students who need to do in-depth legal research, benefit greatly from access to the commercial services. For the average consumer, nonlaw undergraduate, or K–12 student, the open Web provides good and inexpensive access to basic legal information. Freely accessible legal e-resources often lack the features, such as advanced search and report capabilities or hyperlinking between decisions that make the big commercial legal vendors, such as Lexis/Nexis and Westlaw, so popular with legal professionals and law school students. Both of those fee-based services are licensable, fully Web accessible, and available in a number of variations depending on the user group they are intended to serve. However, they may be more expensive than a given library can afford. They may also provide more data and information and search and report capabilities than general library users may ever need.

Much useful legal information is available on the Web. If you are serving a nonspecialist clientele, then a broad variety of materials, including U.S., international, state, and specialized legal codes; court decisions at all levels; and federal and state pending legislation will be beneficial. In a nonlegal academic setting, those e-resources should also serve most needs. Whenever possible, provide links to full-text searchable tools, as those will be most useful to all library users doing legal research. Some legal e-resources publish content that is highly complex and intended for law professionals. Other sites focus on legal information specifically aimed at professionals in particular fields, such as business, health care, or science and technology. Some information on the Web is intended for the consumer who wants "do it yourself" legal forms and advice. Some e-resources will be pertinent only to those in a specific jurisdiction. Legal information intended for children of various ages is available in e-docs sites. For example, the Library of Congress, THOMAS database (http://thomas.loc.gov) has guides and tutorials intended for school age children—for example, "How Congress Makes Laws"—as well as the full-text of historical documents. The U.S. Office of the President provides the White House 101 site with legal and political information intended for young people (www.whitehouse.gov/about/white_house_101).

WHAT TYPES OF E-RESOURCES WILL YOU COLLECT?

Legal e-resources take the following forms that can be described in terms of traditional reference source types.

- Directories (lawyers, law schools, legal services, etc.)
- Dictionaries (law terms in multiple languages)
- Abstracts, indexes, and table of contents services (including those with full-text of the law journals and magazines indexed)
- Encyclopedias and almanacs

- Full-text and/or multimedia databases/digital libraries (collections of e-books, e-serials, recordings, videos, podcasts, images, etc.)
- News and news services (legal news) sources
- Key primary documents (U.S. federal, local, international and regional laws, regulations, court rulings, and related filings)
- Search engines
- Meta sites (e-resources that provide two or more of the other reference tool types in a single product/Web site)

Directories of lawyers, law schools, and legal services are freely available on the Web, though often with some fee-based services as an option. Findlaw Find a Lawyer from West Legal Directory (http://lawyers.findlaw.com) for example offers free searching for law firms or lawyers in a particular zip code, state, and area of practice. The "Guide to Hiring a Lawyer" section offers information on when a lawyer is needed, what questions to ask, and planning for costs.

Dictionaries of legal terms are available, but not those freely available on the Web are not necessarily the best for legal professionals and researchers. *Black's Law Dictionary* (www.blacks lawdictionary.com), which is regarded as the core legal dictionary, is available as a fee-based e-book on the Web as well as in print. General law dictionaries such as Law.Com Legal Dictionary (http://dictionary.law.com) and others sponsored by specific groups or companies are available freely on the Web.

Abstracts, indexes, and table of contents services for legal serials are usually fee-based, although free options do exist for individual law journals. For example, the Law Reviews Online (www.loc.gov/law/help/guide/federal/lawreviews.php), maintained by the Library of Congress, lists all of the law reviews on the Web that offer "free and complete access to the full text of articles and notes." Listings include school of origin and inclusive dates. Especially in legal e-resources there is considerable overlap between this reference type and the full-text databases/digital libraries reference type.

Encyclopedias of legal information are often a part of legal meta sites. Zimmerman's Research Guide (www.lexisnexis.com/infopro/zimmerman), an encyclopedia of legal information designed for librarians and researchers was chosen as a core reference tool by librarians. LexisNexis and Westlaw are the most frequently cited full-text and/or multimedia databases/digital libraries (collections of e-books, e-serials, recordings, videos, podcasts, images etc.). The Legal Information Institute cited earlier also serves as a digital library. Legal news and news services are also a part of most meta sites and are a central aspect of the two main commercial databases. FindLaw's Legal News and Commentary (http://news.findlaw.com) collections sources of news from a legal perspective on the following topics: business, civil rights, crime, environment, immigration, labor, personal injury, politics, product liability, and tech and IP and offers legal commentary. Key primary documents including international; U.S. federal, state, and municipal codes; court reports; current legislation; and more are available as e-docs or in meta sites on the Web as well as in the commercial databases.

Any good Web search engine will locate legal sites, but it will be necessary to exercise care in evaluating any sites retrieved in a general search. Legal reference meta sites almost always contain information from all the reference types, and several high-quality legal meta sites are freely available on the Web. Such meta sites frequently provide all of the legal reference tools that most public and general academic library users will need. See the "Legal E-Resource Collection Tools" section at the end of this chapter for legal reference meta sites.

HOW WILL YOU ORGANIZE YOUR LEGAL E-LIBRARY COLLECTION?

Many of the legal e-resources provided for consumers are meta sites, and they each have their own organization and search options. In organizing discrete resources implementing an organizational structure that stresses the kind of questions that the resource assists in answering might be useful. For example, FindLaw arranges a collection of materials that provides information on divorce, bankruptcy, lemon laws, property laws, liability laws, adoption, landlord–tenant laws, and other legal problems with which people commonly cope as topical links. Cornell Law School's Legal Information Institute site is organized by general area and type of law, but it offers a "Law About" topic browsing option as well. Law professionals and law school students might find it useful for a collection to be arranged first by type of law (judicial, legislative, or administrative) then by jurisdiction with distinctions between primary and secondary materials, though a broad topical approach by area of law might work also.

IDENTIFYING AND COLLECTING LEGAL E-RESOURCES

WEB SITES THAT REVIEW AND EVALUATE E-RESOURCES: PEER E-LIBRARIES, SUBJECT COLLECTIONS/GUIDES, OR META SITES

The Law Library Resource Exchange (llrx.com) is an outstanding meta site that not only publishes legal Web site reviews but also publishes articles discussing all aspects of legal information on the Web. In terms of annotations, evaluations, and scope of subject coverage, the WashLaw: Legal Research on the Web (www.washlaw.edu) site provided by the Washburn University School of Law is among the best for selecting e-resources intended for law school students and legal researchers. Both the FindLaw (http://findlaw.com) and the Internet Legal Resource Group's PublicLegal collections (www.ilrg.com) are designed for everyone, laypersons and legal scholars alike.

DISCUSSION LISTS (LISTSERV, ETC.), FORUMS/GROUPS, E-SERIALS, AND/OR BLOGS THAT POST OR PUBLISH REVIEWS AND EVALUATIONS OF E-RESOURCES

The core discussion lists for law librarians are Law-Lib, LAWLIBREF, and SLA-DLEG. These discussion lists encourage discussion of legal e-resources as well as many other topics of interest to law librarians. LLRX distributes a current awareness e-newsletter that announces new resource reviews on their Web site as well as articles on different legal Web resource topics. Cornell Law Library publishes InSITE (http://library2.lawschool.cornell.edu/insiteasp/default.asp), a current awareness service for new or newly discovered law related Web sites and e-resources. In their monitoring they make use of a variety of law-related mailing lists and newsgroups.

There are dozens of other e-journals and e-newsletters with law related Web resource reviews published by law schools, law organizations, and commercial information providers. The best way to locate academic or professional e-journals is to use the WashLaw: Legal Research on the Web, Law Journals Directory (www.washlaw.edu/lawjournal/index.html). Also on that site is a directory of additional law related discussion lists and Web fora.

PRINT BOOKS AND JOURNALS THAT REVIEW E-RESOURCES

Most general law journals that publish book reviews also usually include Web resource reviews. LAWLIBREF-L subscribers identified the following three titles as particularly useful: *Law Practice Management*, *The Internet Lawyer*, and *Legal Assistant Today*. Library-oriented serials including *Choice*, *Library Journal*, *College and Research Libraries News*, and *American Libraries* also review legal e-resources. One excellent article from a print journal is "Free Lunch Legal E-resources from Plain to Polished" by James Jatkevicius (2003). Jatkevicius focuses on legal meta sites or what he calls aggregator sites: those sites that collect and organize databases of primary and secondary legal material. This article points out the major sites such as FindLaw (http://findlaw.com), but also some lesser-known sites such as AllLaw (www.alllaw.com). Most useful is the chart comparing each of the sites on eight criteria: Supreme Court cases, circuit cases, state court cases, U.S. code, law reviews, legal news, attorney directory, and other (Jatkevicius, 2003: 26).

Kendall Svengalis's (2007) *Legal Information Buyer's Guide and Reference Manual* is an excellent guide for choosing all formats of legal information resources. First published in 2000, this latest edition covers many core legal e-resources. Levitt and Rosch (2007) provide a guide for legal professionals in how to make appropriate use of legal information on the Web. Most current legal research books include e-resources as options in describing effective legal research strategies (Elias et al., 2007).

EVALUATION GUIDELINES AND SELECTION CRITERIA: THE CORE WEB LEGAL REFERENCE COLLECTION

As with business and medical information, legal information has the power, when misunderstood or misapplied, to affect library users' financial and physical well-being. It is very important that librarians are aware, and make their library users aware, that relying solely on legal e-resources for legal advice and information may result in negative consequences. Misinterpreting legal information or using bad legal information may result in library users losing home, family (divorce, custody, adoption issues), and money. Taking bad legal advice or using bad legal information may even result in library users being convicted of a crime. For example, some sites on the Web declare that the U.S. Government has no legal right to collect taxes, issue drivers licenses, or otherwise regulate our society. If a library user takes that advice and does not pay taxes or get a legal drivers license, they will have problems with law enforcement agencies. The Anti-Defamation League (www.adl.org/learn/ext_us/TPM.asp?LEARN_Cat=Extremism& LEARN_SubCat=Extremism_in_America&xpicked=4&item=21) lists, describes, and monitors the presence of these types of Web sites.

Librarians and library staff can endeavor only to choose high quality legal e-resources and should not offer legal advice. We can provide resources to answer a library user's questions but we cannot interpret the content of those resources nor should we attempt to solve their problems. Whenever a question goes beyond the scope of the resources we make available, a librarian should refer library users to legal counsel. These factors make it imperative that e-library collectors make a special effort in evaluating legal e-resources for initial quality of content. As librarians we cannot help library users to interpret or apply the legal information they find. However, we can assist library users by selecting appropriate e-resources that they may use to research their questions.

When dealing with legal information, knowing the source of that information is essential. Not only do the typical questions of authority and intent come into play, but so does the question of jurisdiction. In the legal world, information can have boundaries that limit its usefulness. For example, a Google search on the phrase "law dictionary" retrieves more than 140,000 hits. One site retrieved is Duhaimes Law Dictionary (www.duhaime.org/LegalDictionary.aspx). This is a law dictionary authored by a Canadian lawyer. He states that the dictionary is researched, written in plain language, and provided free of charge by lawyer Lloyd Duhaime. There may not be large differences in language use between the United States and Canada, but the definitions of legal terms can be significant. This publication is also just one lawyer's definitions. This may be a perfectly useable site for individuals needing basic definitions of legal terms in the context of Canadian law. Attention to the source and authority of legal information providers is essential.

All legal information is time sensitive. Existing laws expire and are amended. New laws are passed, some are found unconstitutional, other laws are reinterpreted by the courts, and a few become obsolete every day. Decisions issued by courts are overturned by later courts or made moot by legislation. It is important that legal e-resources clearly state the version of legal codes and the dates of court decisions. If a resource is selected to serve as a historical record, make certain that is clearly stated. Resources that provide counsel or interpretation of law need to indicate a date of authorship as advice can date very quickly.

Security of legal information Web sites is very important. It is unlikely that freely accessible legal sites will request financial or personal information from library users. Sites that charge a fee, such as the by-credit-card versions of LexisNexis and Westlaw, or one of the legal forms collections will naturally require personal information in completing the credit card transaction. Personal and financial information should never be submitted through unencrypted e-mail or Web forms. Library users should be advised to use Web browser functionality to determine the security certification of any Web site that requests personal or financial data. Never send personal or financial information through e-mail unless you are using an e-mail encryption tool. If there is any doubt about security, consult with the Web site owner prior to providing any personal information. Freely accessible sites usually lack the firewalls of corporate sites, making them slightly more vulnerable to hacking. Legal information sites from corporate entities with higher information technology security budgets, such as Westlaw and LexisNexis, are less likely to be altered, though they are not entirely immune. On the whole, however, library users are in less danger from altered legal sites than they are from inappropriate or misapplied information.

Privacy is an issue of importance for all library users, but most especially for those seeking legal information. If someone is looking for information about bankruptcy or how to contest a DUI, they probably don't want the whole world to know about it. So providing e-resources that library users can use without revealing all will be well received.

In May and August 2008, librarians were surveyed to elicit which legal reference tools they consider to be core or essential to their work. The discussion lists and blogs where the survey links were posted are listed in Table 7.1. The core legal reference tools survey is reproduced in Table 7.2.

The Core Web Legal Reference Collection on the companion Web Site (www.kovacs.com/ns/essentialguide.html) was initially created using the survey results from these surveys along with results from similar earlier surveys (the most recent were collected in 2005 and 2006) as core and model collections. Past, present, and future surveys and results are posted at www.kovacs.com/misc.html. This collection is intended for librarians to use as a source of e-resources they might select for their legal reference e-library collections.

Core print legal reference tools were much fewer than reported in previous surveys. In fact, most of these are U.S. government publications that are also available on the Web. Table 7.3 lists the top five print legal reference tools identified in the survey. The free Web sites that librarians reported as core or essential for legal reference are given in Table 7.4.

Many e-docs were mentioned by librarians, as core or essential, for legal reference. The top five legal e-docs reference sites are listed in Table 7.5.

Fee-based legal reference tools are essential for legal reference in many libraries. The top five fee-based legal reference e-resources are reported in Table 7.6.

Table 7.1. Discussion Lists and Blogs Distribution for Legal Reference Tools Survey

- law-lib@ucdavis.edu
- lawlibref@lists.washlaw.edu
- LISNews and LISNewsWire Blogs: lisnews-owner@lishost.net
- ResourceShelf Blog: gary.price@resourceshelf.com
- ERIL-L@LISTSERV.BINGHAMTON.EDU
- dig_ref@LISTSERV.SYR.EDU

- collib-l@ala.org
- LIS-LINK@jiscmail.ac.uk
- Libref-L@listserv.kent.edu
- GOVDOC-L@lists.psu.edu
- publib@webjunction.org
- livereference@yahoogroups.com
- Libref-L@listserv.kent.edu

Table 7.2. Core Legal Reference Tools Survey Questions

1. Which library type best describes the library you work in/for/with?

2. In which subject area(s) are you most likely to answer law reference questions? (Check all that apply.)

3. What are the essential three print titles (reference books) that you can't work without in answering law reference questions? (Please type the title only.)

4. What are the essential three free (not government published) Web-accessible databases that you can't work without in answering law reference questions? (Please type complete URL/Web address; e.g., www.law.cornell.edu.)

5. What are the essential three (.gov) government published (state, federal, local, international) free Web-accessible databases that you can't work without in answering law reference questions? (Please type complete URL/Web address; e.g., thomas.loc.gov.)

6. What are the essential three fee-based Web-accessible databases that you can't work without in answering law reference questions? (Please the simple title; e.g., LexisNexis)

7. Does your library maintain a Web page or site to support law reference? If so, please share the URL/Web address (e.g., www.lawlibrary.state.mn.us).

8. Additional comments or ideas:

(Please include your name and e-mail address if you would like feedback, otherwise this survey form is completely anonymous.)

Table 7.3. Top Five Print Legal Reference Tools Identified in Survey

1. *Black's Law Dictionary*
2. *The Bluebook: A Uniform System of Citation*
3. *C.F.R. Index*

4. *U.S. Government Manual*
5. *United States Code*, individual state code texts and guides to state codes

Table 7.4. Top Five Free Web Legal Reference Tools Identified in Survey

1. Legal Information Institute: www.law.cornell.edu
2. FindLaw: www.findlaw.com, Google: www.google.com
3. LLRX.com: www.llrx.com
4. Zimmerman's Research Guide: www.lexisnexis.com/infopro/zimmerman
5. Martindale.com: www.martindale.com, Municode.com: www.municode.com, National Conference of State Legislatures: www.ncsl.org

Table 7.5. Top Five Government Documents Web Sites Used as Legal Reference Tools Identified in Survey

1. THOMAS, Library of Congress: www.thomas.gov
2. GPO Access (Government Printing Office): www.gpoaccess.gov
3. State and local law codes, ordinances, and court Web sites
4. U.S. Patent and Trademark Office: www.uspto.gov
5. Internal Revenue Service: www.irs.gov

Table 7.6. Top Five Fee-based Legal Reference E-Resources Identified in Survey

1. LexisNexis/LexisNexis Academic: http://academic.lexisnexis.com/online-services/academic-overview.aspx
2. Westlaw/Westlaw Campus: http://campus.westlaw.com
3. Hein OnLine (agency case law, CFR, FR, presidential communications): www.heinonline.org
4. Loislaw: www.loislaw.com
5. PACER: http://pacer.uspci.uscourts.gov

Note: These sites got two votes each: CEB On-Law (http://ceb.com/info/onlaw13.asp), U.S. Legal Forms (www.uslegalforms.com).

The access and design of all the selected Core Web Legal Reference Tools on the companion Web site are based on standards of simplicity, international Web accessibility standards, and no special software required for access. Most of them are free of direct cost. Some have special fee-based products or services. Fee-based e-resources are included when they offer free trials or have some information available without requiring a fee.

Working through the collection-planning process will lead you to develop the criteria to select for the variety of legal information resources that are best for your library users. This general core collection may be a useful aide in that process. Another option is to look to the legal reference e-resources collections of your peer libraries as a guidepost to developing your own collection. As you are building your collection, the needs of your library users are the single most important factor. What another library may include in their collection may not be appropriate for your library users. In compiling the resources for this chapter, the library user group includes librarians who are building legal reference Web pages and supporting consumers, law students, paralegals, or law professionals in answering brief simple legal reference questions.

E-LIBRARY SUCCESS STORY

CAMBRIDGE COLLEGE ONLINE LIBRARY
Cambridge, Massachusetts, United States (Main Campus)
www.cambridgecollege.edu/library
Contact: Maida Tilchen, Maida.Tilchen@cambridgecollege.edu

A. Collection Planning (e.g., goal setting and identification of users, technology/ personnel choices)

When Cambridge College (CC) was founded in 1971 it did not have a library of its own. CC arranged for their students to have contractual access with another local college library. By 1991, CC had begun to build a library of sorts with with Proquest's collection of journal articles on CD. As the college grew and added degree programs and additional campus sites (three in Massachusetts and five in other locations) it was determined that a more extensive collection of online resources be provided along with library instruction and affiliated traditional libraries.

In 2001 the college senate asked Maida Tilchen to research existing e-library options, as they did not want to create a new traditional print library in the library-rich Cambridge area but preferred to arrange for affiliation with academic libraries near campus sites. At that point two options were identified: Johns Hopkins and Jones Eglobal (www.egloballibrary.com).

"It was decided that Jones Eglobal was more suitable for our students' needs, because they had built a truly virtual library site with an interface that would be user friendly for our students who are older and not computer savvy. Hopkins seemed to just be selling access to their existing online services geared to their very technologically sophisticated traditional students. I believe the Hopkins program was soon discontinued, in any case. Our Eglobal online library site launched on December 17, 2001."

The mission of CC Online Library (CCOL) is to provide "appropriate, adequate, and convenient library services to all our students, faculty, and staff at all our sites." Use of the CCOL is restricted to current faculty, students, and staff. CC does not have any strictly distance learning programs, however, the CCOL serves programs that blend residential and distance learning. No formal collection plan has been written. However, systematic choices are made based on CC program needs, pricing, and available databases. "When we first contracted with Jones Eglobal, they gave us a package of several databases, many of which they cut after a year or two, so we now buy everything ourselves, except for Ebrary and Tutor.com, which we buy through Eglobal. We switched from Proquest to EBSCOHost around 2003 and have added other databases and a few individual journals as needed. We also have OCLC First Search Wilson Select Plus and WorldCat."

B. Collection Strategies (e.g., selection criteria, identification of resources, licensing, and related user information needs)

Any decisions to add databases or change existing resources are based on the needs of degree programs offered by CC (education, management, counseling/psychology, and some medical). Faculty requests, costs, appropriateness for academic research, and whether one of CC's local affiliated libraries makes a database or print resource available are the main criteria. Electric Library was dropped because sources were not academic enough.

All of the databases and e-books included in the CCOL are paid for by CC, either through their Eglobal package or consortial agreements. CCOL subscribes to some individual journals

Figure 7.1. Cambridge College Online Library (CCOL)

directly from SAGE, at faculty request. "Ebrary and tutor.com are part of our Eglobal package. First Search Wilson and WorldCat are through the NELINET consortium.... We buy a basic EBSCOHost package and then add additional databases such as from APA. When I bought directly from APA, they made so many administrative errors that I was thrilled when EBSCO-Host offered it."

Access to all resources is through the CCOL site. Users log in through the main CC portal. Only current employees or registered students have portal access. CCOL provides access to e-books including Ebrary's Academic Complete collection and APA PsycBooks. CCOL does not catalog e-books. As they do not have a physical/print library, they do not have a catalog, but users can search CC's most popular databases through MUSE federated searching. However: "I've been frustrated that MUSE does not offer a full-text only option, but they are promising to add it by early 2009."

CCOL provides access to "Ask a Librarian" service 24/7/365 through Tutor.com. "I hear good feedback but it doesn't get as much use as I had hoped. It is averaging about 1 out of 12.5 student users per term, and that includes repeat users."

C. Collection Organization (e.g., content management systems, Web server choices, personnel responsibilities, etc.)

CCOL uses the Jones Eglobal "turnkey" e-library. All technical and organizational issues are handled in the Jones Eglobal systems. Maida Tilchen has been extremely satisfied with the excellent customer service of Eglobal. Maida Tilchen, Project Manager for Library Services, administrates the CCOL and all the database vendors as well as creates all library instructional materials and provides primarily faculty training. CC's IT staff handles technical issues related to user's access from the CC site into Eglobal. "Eglobal provides all technical support once users are in the Eglobal site, and sets up all the technical connections from database vendors into the Eglobal site. This minimizes what CC's own IT support has to do, which is very worthwhile!"

Maida Tilchen was hired because of her extensive instructional design, writing and research skills tutoring experience, her work in support of CC's development of distance learning programs, and her development of instructional materials to help students research more effectively. "I was designated as Project Manager for Library Services in 1999. I do not have an MLS, I have an MSEd in Instructional Systems Technology, had a lot of instructional development experience in other jobs, and I had been a writing/research tutor at CC for 8 years when I was promoted into this newly created position. As a tutor, I had been creating instructional materials to help students do research, and I also participated in committees exploring how CC could use internet and distance learning technology as it became available in the late '90s. . . . I did a lot of on-the-job training and continue to learn through courses at ACRL; Diane Kovacs; Blended Librarian and InSync sites. I received the Jane N. Ryland Fellowship in 2007 to attend the EDUCAUSE Learning Technology Leadership Institute. I read a lot of books and articles initially on how to be a librarian, and I talked to some very experienced librarians at local colleges. I took a few workshops at Simmons College library school. Currently, as co-chair of CC's College Senate Academic Technology Committee, I facilitate and attend educational technology demonstrations and trainings."

Student research needs are addressed in instructional handouts created by Maida Tilchen and posted on the CCOL public site (www.cambridgecollege.edu/library/research.cfm). She manages the public Web site as well as a secure site of CC library information in the Cambridge College portal, which includes a site of instructional materials to help faculty teach information literacy skills. Eglobal also provides research guides and tutorials as part of their generic package.

A formal collection development plan is in progress in 2008. Collection decisions are primarily guided by faculty requests and relevance to CC program needs. Current collection development tools used include: "I urge our faculty to stay current in their fields and make requests. I attend webcasts on the Blended Librarian site, and I read online newsletters like *Free Pint*, *New York Times Circuits*, library blogs, *LJ Academic Newswire*, *Searcher*, and the links provided in those. I get a lot of info tech news from Wired and Popular Science magazines. I read books like *Everything is Miscellaneous*. I love to read about technology and libraries and am always looking for anything useful for our users."

Eglobal does basic link checking but most corrections come from student or faculty feedback. Most feedback is informal through e-mail, phone, or in-person conversations. A faculty and administrator committee meets to advise Maida on CCOL and library services once each term. "We have done formal surveys twice since 2001. They tell us what we already know. We don't get enough responses to be meaningful statistically."

Organizational and information architecture issues are handled internally by Eglobal. Suggestions for changes are accepted by Eglobal but they do not always implement changes. "In June, 2008, we had the first upgrade of our online library interface since 2001. We now have a much more user-friendly interface which was Eglobal's suggestion and their design. They had been asking me to do it for a year but I had delayed because our faculty was still upset about an upgrade of our portal. In retrospect, I should have done it earlier because it is a great improvement."

Future critical issues include finding and implementing a cross-database search tool that can search full-text only and works better than MUSE, providing more information literacy instruction across the curriculum and hopefully integrated into the online library, perhaps adding an "on demand" academic video database, and providing more materials in Spanish.

REFERENCES AND WEB SITES CITED

Elias, Stephen, Susan Levinkind, and Richard Stim. 2007. *Legal Research: How to Find and Understand the Law*, 14th edition. Berkeley, CA: Nolo.

Jatkevicius, James. 2003. "Free Lunch Legal E-Resources from Plain to Polished." *Online* 27, no. 2: 22–26. Available: www.accessmylibrary.com/coms2/summary_0286-22555518_ITM (accessed January 18, 2009).

Levitt, Carole A., and Mark E. Rosch. 2007. *The Lawyer's Guide to Fact Finding on the Internet*, 3rd edition. American Bar Association Section of Law Practice Management.

Svengalis, Kendall F. 2007. *Legal Information Buyer's Guide and Reference Manual*. Westerly, RI: Rhode Island LawPress.

WEB SITES CITED

AllLaw. Available: www.alllaw.com (accessed January 18, 2009).

American Libraries. Available: www.ala.org/ala/alonline/index.cfm (accessed January 14, 2009).

Anti-Defamation League. Available: www.adl.org/learn/ext_us/TPM.asp?LEARN_Cat=Extremism&LEARN_SubCat=Extremism_in_America&xpicked=4&item=21 (accessed January 16, 2009).

Black's Law Dictionary. Available: www.blackslawdictionary.com (accessed January 7, 2009).

Choice: Current Reviews for Academic Libraries. Available: www.ala.org/ala/mgrps/divs/acrl/publications/choice/index.cfm (accessed January 16, 2009).

College and Research Libraries News. Available: www.ala.org/ala/mgrps/divs/acrl/publications/crlnews/collegeresearch.cfm (accessed January 14, 2009).

Duhaimes Law Dictionary. Available: www.duhaime.org/LegalDictionary.aspx (accessed January 18, 2009).

FindLaw. Available: http://findlaw.com (accessed January 18, 2009).

Findlaw Find a Lawyer from West Legal Directory. Available: http://lawyers.findlaw.com (accessed January 25, 2009).

GPOAccess. Available: www.gpoaccess.gov (accessed January 16, 2009). *Note*: This site will become the Federal Digital System—FDsys. Available: http://fdsys.gpo.gov (accessed January 18, 2009) during 2009.

InSITE. Available: http://library2.lawschool.cornell.edu/insiteasp/default.asp.

Internet Legal Resource Group's Public Legal site. Available: www.ilrg.com.

Law.Com Legal Dictionary. Available: http://dictionary.law.com (accessed January 25, 2009).

Law Reviews Online. Available: www.loc.gov/law/help/guide/federal/lawreviews.php (accessed January 25, 2009).

Legal Information Institute, Cornell Law School. Available: www.law.cornell.edu (accessed January 19, 2009).

LexisNexis/LexisNexis Academic. Available: http://academic.lexisnexis.com/online-services/academic-overview.aspx (accessed January 7, 2009).

THOMAS, Library of Congress. Available: www.thomas.gov (accessed January 7, 2009).

WashLaw: Legal Research on the Web (Washburn University School of Law). Available: www.washlaw.edu (accessed January 18, 2009).

Westlaw/Westlaw Campus. Available: http://campus.westlaw.com (accessed January 7, 2009).

White House 101. Available: www.whitehouse.gov/about/white_house_101 (accessed January 21, 2009).

Zimmerman's Research Guide. Available: www.lexisnexis.com/infopro/zimmerman (accessed January 25, 2009).

LEGAL E-RESOURCE COLLECTION TOOLS

META SITES

Administration of Justice Web Guide, George Mason University

http://library.gmu.edu/resources/socsci/criminal.html

This phenomenal site provides indexes, directories, and links to information relating to the law enforcement, the legal system, and justice.

Cleveland Law Library Association

http://clevelandlawlibrary.org

The Cleveland Law Library site provides an excellent e-library of legal materials of national and state interest. Both the resources selected and the layout of the site can serve as a useful guide. Pay special attention to the FAQ section that is laid out by area of law and then lists resources that will answer those questions. Note that most of the resources listed in the FAQ are Ohio specific.

EISIL Electronic Information System for International Law

www.eisil.org

Highly selective collection of Web sites to support the need for high quality primary documents, teaching, and learning resources for international law. Sponsored by the American Society of International Law (ASIL).

FindLaw

www.findlaw.com

This is arguably the most comprehensive source of legal resources on the Web. The site is searchable and also organized by category. Resources are sorted by user group: Business, Public and Consumer, Student, Legal Professionals, and Corporate Counsel. A "Services for Lawyers" section and a "Legal Market Center" are additional options. Organized similarly to Yahoo!

Guide to Law Online from the Law Library of Congress

www.loc.gov/law/help/guide.php

The Law Library of Congress maintains this meta site with annotated collection of legal resources, databases, and other government and law e-resources online.

Internet Law Library

www.priweb.com/internetlawlib

This site provides full-text searchable access to thousands of legal documents on the Internet. Provided by Pritchard Law Webs, the site includes state, federal, and international codes, constitutions, court decisions, and treaties. Links to legal research tutorials, legal organization directories, and many other legal reference tools on the Internet. See the "About" section of the site for an excellent listing of law and law librarianship discussion lists.

Internet Legal Resource Guide (ILRG)

www.ilrg.com

ILRG is very comprehensive and is especially useful source of international legal resources on the Web. It is geared more for the legal profession and law student than for the consumer or small business. However, it includes a fine collection of law journals, forms, state and federal resources, and research assistance sites that will be invaluable for everyone.

Law Library Resource Exchange (LLRX)

www.llrx.com

LLRX is a hybrid electronic legal research journal, legal encyclopedia and legal meta site. The articles are always timely and very helpful for the librarian or other legal researcher. Legal resources on the Web are organized in "Information Centers." Of special note is the LLRX collection of court rules, forms, and dockets. The LLRX site is fully searchable. Founded, edited, and published by Sabrina I. Pacifici.

LawGuru.com
www.lawguru.com

This site collects and organizes legal resources on the Web on all topics. The strength of the collection is consumer legal support. The site links to LawyerTool.com a site that "search[es] over 550 free legal related databases from one easy interface." Eslamboly and Barlavi, the law firm that sponsors the site, also monitors and maintains a legal question and answer forum and an online attorney network. The legal question and answer forum archives are searchable and organized into an FAQ. Beware of the pop-up ads.

Legal Information Institute, Cornell Law School
www.law.cornell.edu

Comprehensive and highly regarded site whose offerings include a full-text searchable version of the U.S. Code, Constitution of the United States, excellent state resources, and a fine international law collection.

Sandra Day O'Connor College of Law, Ross-Blakley Law Library
www.law.asu.edu/researchguides

Collection of legal research guides with links to Web resources, citations for print resources, etc.

WashLaw Legal Research on the Web
www.washlaw.edu

This was one of the first Internet legal resource collections. It is enormous but easily browsed. Includes general reference tools that would be useful for law school students and faculty as well as legal resources. This is a free service of the Washburn University School of Law.

Digital Libraries Directories or Collections of Digital Libraries (Digital Libraries of E-Books, E-Serials, Images, Recordings, and Other Artifacts)

Legal Research Podcasts
www.berringlegalresearch.com/podcast.asp
From West Law School Publication Berring on Legal Research.

E-Serials, Blogs, Discussion Lists, etc.

Law Librarian Blog
http://lawprofessors.typepad.com/law_librarian_blog

Law-Lib
http://lawlibrary.ucdavis.edu/LAWLIB/lawlib.html
Discussion list for law librarians.

LAWLIBREF-L
http://lists.washlaw.edu/mailman/listinfo/lawlibref
Discussion list for law reference librarians working in all types of libraries.

LLRX.com
www.llrx.com

An outstanding current awareness e-serial that not only publishes legal Web site reviews but also publishes articles discussing all aspects of legal information on the Internet.

SLA-DLEG
www.sla.org/content/community/lists/divisionlists5979.cfm or www.sla.org/content/community/lists/joinlists.cfm
Discussion list for librarians who are members of the Special Libraries Association, Legal Division.

MEDICAL E-RESOURCES

The Internet is a major source for medical and health information, as well as medical education. Podcasts are another resource available on the Internet that medical professionals are using to stay current in their field. The topics and quality of podcasts vary widely. Major medical academic institutions are using them as educational tools and study aids for students, publishers are creating podcasts as audio supplements to the printed text, professional organizations use podcasts to broadcast news to members, companies are offering programs for continuing medical education (including offering credits), and various institutions are creating patient education programs using podcasting. (Kraft, 2007: 29)

DEVELOPING A COLLECTION PLAN FOR MEDICAL E-RESOURCES

The quote that begins this chapter is intriguing in that it demonstrates how medical educators, librarians, and library users have taken full advantage of efficient information delivery made possible through Web communications tools and electronic formats. Just as medical databases (such as Grateful Med) and related documents delivery services were among the first to be successful in libraries, medical libraries continue to be on top of the wave of change in library services and technologies. The Web has proven to be a convenient way to deliver medical information to medical professionals, students, and researchers, as well as health care consumers. Online continuing medical education (CME) opportunities have developed rapidly.

In this chapter the phrase "medical professionals, students, and researchers" is used to refer to the larger group of nursing and allied health professionals, students, and researchers as well as physicians, medical school students, and biomedical researchers. Veterinary professionals, students, and researchers also fall under this umbrella phrase.

WHAT PURPOSE WILL YOUR COLLECTION SERVE? FOR WHOM ARE YOU COLLECTING E-RESOURCES?

Medical e-resources support the information needs of medical school students, physicians, medical researchers, allied health professionals, and health care consumers. The real value in Web access to medical information is for the medical professional and for the health care consumer because it is available at the desktop computer or on the wearable computing devices that many medical professionals carry with them.

An e-library developed for a medical school library might support medical education for physicians, nurses, and allied health or veterinary students, teachers, and researchers. Academic libraries will be able to use their organization's program guide and course listings to develop the foundation for their e-resources collection. For example, the Hardin MD (www.lib.uiowa.edu/hardin/md/index.html) is a comprehensive e-library collection intended for medical school students selected by the librarians of the Hardin Library for the Health Sciences, University of Iowa, specifically to support the University of Iowa's medical, veterinary, and allied health programs. Medical researchers will also find valuable e-resources that assist in the dissemination and accumulation of medical research knowledge.

Hospital and clinic libraries, whether serving medical professionals, students, and researchers or health care consumers, will find plenty of high quality medical e-resources, both free and fee-based. Public libraries may also choose to collect for medical professionals, students, and researchers or health care consumers, depending on the needs of their community. Some public libraries serve semiofficially as their local hospital's resource library. Both public and hospital libraries may choose to serve the CME needs of local medical professionals.

E-resources for medical professionals, students, and researchers may overlap with those intended for health care consumers. Health care consumers, however, will need medical dictionaries and frequent referral to a medical professional for clarification of some of the content that requires a higher level of education and knowledge.

Not only podcasts and vodcasts but also e-books are popular among medical professionals, students, and researchers. Although e-books have not done well among other subject area library users due to many technical and legal difficulties in actually using them, medical reference text users are able to successfully use e-books.

> As noted, users readily access e-books when they need to read small portions. Considering that medical books are not typically read cover-to-cover in a single session, the electronic format seems perfectly suited for searching and retrieving relevant sections of such resources. Analysis of the data overwhelmingly indicates higher use of the electronic format.... Results of the study revealed use of print clinical titles is quite low, while use data for the e-book versions of the same titles are surprisingly high. (Ugaz and Resnick, 2008: 146)

Other research also supports the reality that medical reference e-books are being used and being used well and frequently by medical library users (Goodyear-Smith et al., 2008; Mitchell and Lorbeer, 2008; Foust et al., 2007; Hernon et al., 2007).

WHAT TYPES OF E-RESOURCES WILL YOU COLLECT?

Medical e-resources range from basic diagnostic, treatment, and support information about diseases, injuries, wellness issues, and varying levels of information about pharmaceuticals for health care consumers to CME, clinical guidelines, and evidence-based medical research information for medical professionals, students, and researchers. Most medical e-resources take forms that can be described for convenience, in terms of traditional reference source types:

- Directories (of physicians and other medical professionals, hospitals, clinics, and other medical organizations, etc.)
- Dictionaries (medical dictionaries in multiple languages)
- Abstracts, indexes, and table of contents services (including those with full text of the medical journals and magazines indexed)
- Encyclopedias and almanacs

- Full-text and/or multimedia databases/digital libraries (collections of e-books, e-serials, recordings, videos, podcasts, images etc.)
- News and news services (current medical and health awareness) sources
- Key primary documents (health, medical, pharmaceutical, and related research data, reports, and statistics)
- Search engines
- Meta sites (e-resources that provide two or more of the other reference tool types in a single product/Web site)

Directories have become ubiquitous on the Web. Many individual organizations and communities as well as federal, state, and local government agencies have been creating very useful directories of medical professional contact and licensing information as well as directories of clinics, hospitals, and related organizations. The U.S. National Library of Medicine publishes DIRLINE (http://dirline.nlm.nih.gov), which is a directory of health organizations of multiple types. At this time, each state in the United States makes licensing status information about physicians and sometimes also chiropractors, nurses, and other allied health professionals available online. One central site is the Administrators in Medicine (AIM) Association of State Medical Board Executive Directors DocFinder (www.docboard.org/docfinder.html) directory of state medical board sites with licensing information of various levels available for physicians, and sometimes chiropractors, nurses, and other allied health professionals. A global search tool can be used for some states.

Medical dictionaries in multiple languages are freely available on the Web. These are of varying quality and specialization. The MedlinePlus Dictionary (www.nlm.nih.gov/medlineplus/mplusdictionary.html) is a good basic tool for health care consumers.

PubMed (www.ncbi.nlm.nih.gov/pubmed) is public access to the indexing and abstracting services from the U.S. National Library of Medicine (NLM) and the National Institutes of Health (NIH). These include MEDLINE and other databases. Table of contents services are offered by most medical journals with Web sites. For example, the American Psychiatric Association (http://journals.psychiatryonline.org) offers the "eTOC" service for a number of the journals it publishes. The eTOC service is tables of contents delivered via e-mail or directly to a PDA.

Encyclopedia-like medical information sites are published by organizations such as the Mayo Clinic (www.mayoclinic.com) and the MedlinePlus A.D.A.M Encyclopedia (http://www.nlm.nih.gov/medlineplus/encyclopedia.html). Fee-based encyclopedias that are Web accessible and intended for medical professionals and researchers are also available, such as that found in the Merck Medicus (www.merckmedicus.com) digital library. The Merck Manual Online Medical Library Home Edition for Patients and Caregivers (www.merck.com/mmhe/index.html) is a classic medical encyclopedia provided free online by the Merck & Co. Inc. as a public service.

Several collections of full-text medical journals, e-books, digital collections of images and documents, etc., both fee-based (e.g., MDConsult, UpToDate) and open source, exist. PubMed Central (www.pubmedcentral.nih.gov) is free and unrestricted access to the U.S. National Library of Medicine's growing "digital archive of life sciences journal literature." The Merck Medicus (www.merckmedicus.com) digital library is available for free for licensed medical professionals only and provides online CME, e-books, podcasts, and many other e-resources. Many medical school and health organization sites maintain collections of digital images and recordings (podcasts, etc.). SoundPractice.net (http://soundpractice.net) is the *Journal of Medical Practice Management* collection of CME podcasts, vodcasts, and blog. It is an illustrative example of the potential for this kind of digital collection. SoundPractice.net is fee-based with much free content.

Current medical news and health awareness sites are ubiquitous. Specifically for medical professionals, though, are two noteworthy examples. MEDEM (www.medem.com) is also a physician and patient communications tool. MEDEM is maintained by the American Medical Association, the American Academy of Pediatrics, and the American College of Obstetricians and Gynecologists. The site was developed to provide "a trusted online source for credible, comprehensive, and clinical healthcare information, and secure, confidential communications." Medscape (CME) (http://cme.medscape.com/medscapetoday) publishes health and medical research news and related CME opportunities for medical professionals.

Health, medical, pharmaceutical, and related research data, reports, and statistics abound on the Web. A good place to begin is the National Institutes of Health (NIH) (www.nih.gov), with links to all 25 of the National Institutes of Health, many of which produce databases of their specific health information and resources. NIH also has links to other government agency Web health resources (A–Z guide), NIH publications, funding, and scientific news.

Google is the preferred search engine of many medical librarians. However, one interesting new tool, Mednar (http://mednar.com/mednar) searches multiple deep Web sites, digital libraries, and indexes for medical related information. Mednar recently won a major award for medical search tools.

Many medical e-resources are actually meta sites or, in other words, Web sites that provide multiple types of reference tool including medical encyclopedias, dictionaries, directories, bibliographies, e-serials, and other e-resources. Medical meta sites frequently publish original articles on a variety of health topics, searchable medical encyclopedias, dictionaries, and pharmaceuticals information as well as selective collections of links to other, more specialized, medical information Web sites.

HOW WILL YOU ORGANIZE YOUR MEDICAL E-LIBRARY COLLECTION?

As a starting point it is useful to organize e-resources intended for medical professionals, students, and researchers separately from those intended for health care consumers. In the core Web reference collections on the companion Web site (www.kovacs.com/ns/essentialguide.html) the collections for medical professionals and health care consumers are now separated.

Many medical e-libraries are organized by the medical field, specialty, or using a formal structure such as the MeSH(r) medical subject headings created and maintained by the National Library of Medicine for its health and medical information products (www.nlm.nih.gov/mesh). Health care consumer e-resources can usually be efficiently organized by disease, injury, or health care question or concern.

IDENTIFYING AND COLLECTING MEDICAL E-RESOURCES

WEB SITES THAT REVIEW AND EVALUATE E-RESOURCES: PEER E-LIBRARIES, SUBJECT COLLECTIONS/GUIDES, OR META SITES

The best meta site for collecting e-resources for biomedical researchers and university level students is Intute: Health and Life Sciences (www.intute.ac.uk/healthandlifesciences). The current Intute collection was born from the earlier OMNI (Organising Medical Networked Information) project, which began in 1995. Librarians of the partner universities carefully select and evaluate all the health and life sciences e-resources that are freely available on the Web. The scope of the Health and Life Sciences collection includes medicine, nursing and allied health fields, bioethics, media and the sciences, veterinary medicine, midwifery, history of medicine, and other medical related fields.

Two of the most useful meta sites in terms of scope of subject coverage, good annotations, and critical evaluations are the Hardin MD (www.lib.uiowa.edu/hardin/md/index.html) and MedlinePlus (http://medlineplus.gov). Hardin MD collects directories and e-library collections of medical resources for medical and allied health students and researchers. MedlinePlus collects directories, e-library collections, and individual medical resources. MedlinePlus emphasizes quality of information and collects for health care consumers and professionals. The Consumer and Patient Health Information Section of the Medical Library Association (CAPHIS) (http://caphis.mlanet.org/consumer) collects a core one hundred high quality sites for health care consumers and organizes them by general health categories. The fee-based site Medical Matrix (www.medmatri .org) publishes a peer-reviewed collection of clinical medicine Web sites.

DISCUSSION LISTS (LISTSERV, ETC.), FORUMS/GROUPS, E-SERIALS, AND/OR BLOGS THAT POST OR PUBLISH REVIEWS AND EVALUATIONS OF E-RESOURCES

The core discussion lists for medical librarians are MEDLIB-L, the Medical Libraries Discussion List, and CAPHIS-L, the discussion for the Consumer and Patient Health Information Section of the Medical Library Association. There are medical subject-specific discussion lists, Web forums, and blogs for almost every possible disease or medical specialty. There are also literally thousands of discussions, fora, and blogs for patient and family support. The safest strategy to use in locating patient support discussions is to search MedlinePlus for the disease, injury, or other problem in which the library user is interested. Choose one of the organization Web sites that MedlinePlus links to and look through the organization site for information about patient support discussions, fora, or blogs. This strategy works well for medical professional discussions, fora, or blogs on specific topics as well. A real-life reference question was asked by a library user regarding a situation with family member who has a history of depression and has been taking antidepressants for a long time. The question related to the news that the relative was pregnant and the library user was looking for background and supporting information to help her in helping her relative. The library user didn't know what drugs the relative was taking; for example, she might be taking antipsychotic as well as antidepressant drugs. Searching MedlinePlus for "depression pregnancy support" and also for "psychiatric drugs pregnancy support" retrieves about a dozen organizations that provide information and host support discussion lists, Web forums, and blogs for patients and families as well as for medical professionals, students, and researchers.

JMIR: Journal of Medical Internet Research (www.jmir.org) is a peer-reviewed e-journal, indexed by Medline that publishes reviews and articles about the quality and use of medical e-resources. *JMIR* is free and provides full-text access on the Web. This e-journal is used by many librarians in reviewing medical Web sites for inclusion in their e-library collection or to use for reference service. Other e-serials that review e-resources—specific to hundreds of diseases and treatments and intended for health care consumers or medical professionals—can be found by searching PubMed or browsing PubMed Central.

PRINT BOOKS AND JOURNALS THAT REVIEW E-RESOURCES

Jeffrey T. Huber and colleagues (2008) have thoroughly integrated e-resources into the current edition of *Introduction to Reference Sources in the Health Sciences*. Although it is a few years old now, another very useful text continues to be *The Medical Library Association Encyclopedic Guide to Searching and Finding Health Information on the Web* (Anderson and Allee, 2004).

The Journal of Consumer Health on the Internet (previously *Health Care on the Internet*) (www.taylorandfrancis.com) publishes reviews of medical Web sites, articles about medical

Web sites, e-library collections, and anything related to consumer health information and the Web (Kovacs, 2005). Many print medical journals including the *BMJ: British Medical Journal* (http://bmj.com), *JAMA: The Journal of the American Medical Association* (http://jama.ama-assn.org), and *The New England Journal of Medicine* (http://content.nejm.org) review medical e-resources. Additional print medical journals that review e-resources may be found by doing a search on PubMed (www.ncbi.nlm.nih.gov/entrez/query.fcgi?db=PubMed) for "Web sites reviews" or "Web review." Click on "LinkOut" to see if full text of the review articles might be available on the Web. Popular family magazines such as or *Family Circle*, *Good Housekeeping*, *Women's Day*, and *Prevention* frequently feature reviews or articles about useful Web sites for family health issues.

EVALUATION GUIDELINES AND SELECTION CRITERIA: THE CORE WEB MEDICAL REFERENCE FOR PROFESSIONALS AND RESEARCHERS AND THE CORE WEB CONSUMER HEALTH REFERENCE COLLECTIONS

Evaluation criteria for medical e-resources must include content quality, authority, and disclosure of information source, currency of information, and accessibility of the Web site. Although evaluating health and medical information found on the Web requires answers to the same basic questions as any other format in selecting health and medical resources, quality must be a major criterion. Health and medical information quality may affect the life, health, and safety of human beings. It is, therefore, of great importance that it be extremely accurate and complete, or alternatively that it refers the health care consumer or medical professional to more in-depth information sources or advises them to consult a specialist.

The Health on the Net Foundation (HON) (www.hon.ch) and similar organizations have attempted to guide critical thinking and quality assurance of medical Web sites. HON publishes a code of conduct that medical Webmasters may choose to follow. Medical Web sites may voluntarily agree to the HON Code guidelines and place a logo on the site. Because adherence is voluntary and is not verified, the presence of HON logos on a Web site is a clue to the quality of the information on the site, but it is not a guarantee. It will still be necessary to review and evaluate the site carefully before selecting it.

Librarians must be very careful to not give medical advice. Looking up a word is one thing, translating or interpreting might be seen as making a diagnosis. Take the word "idiopathic," for example. A library user once approached the author with the reference question: "My doctor says I have idiopathic. I need to find some books about this."

Any librarian might properly respond by looking up the key term, *idiopathic*, in a medical dictionary. The MedlinePlus medical dictionary (www.nlm.nih.gov/medlineplus/mplusdictionary .html) is the *Merriam Webster's Medical Dictionary*. It gives the definition of idiopathic as "arising spontaneously or from an obscure or unknown cause: PRIMARY <idiopathic epilepsy> <idiopathic hypertension> <idiopathic thrombocytopenic purpura>."

At this point, the librarian will want to refer the library user back to his or her medical professional for an explanation or to provide more information. The question is, what disease or problem do they have? They now know that it is arising spontaneously or from an obscure or unknown cause. Only a medical professional who has consulted with that health care consumer as a patient can or should answer that question.

Although library staff should not be providing health or medical advice to library users, they must be knowledgeable enough to select the very highest quality e-resources for their library users.

If a medical Web resource has no provider attribution—and this must include the information provider's qualifications and educational attainments—it is unusable in a library, educational, clinical, or research setting. The WebMD (www.webmd.com) meta site provides a good example of the attribution information to expect from Web sites providing high-quality medical information. WebMD Health is intended for health care consumers. Reading carefully through the WebMD main page down at the very bottom of the screen, click on "About WebMD," and then on that page "WebMD Content Staff." These two pages provide detailed information about the WebMD company and the WebMD staff. The WebMD staff descriptions include pictures of all contributors, authors, and editors along with their names and links to their biographical information. All of the medical editors are medical doctors (MDs) although some of the writers are journalists. For example, the education and qualifications of Dr. Brunilda Nazario, MD, Senior Medical Editor, who "is responsible for reviewing WebMD news and feature stories and graphics to ensure their medical accuracy," are clearly detailed (www.webmd.com/brunilda-nazario, accessed January 25, 2009). In addition to the description of WebMD staff, each individual news piece or article are carefully dated and signed by the medical researchers who authored them. The authors' credentials are supplied with the article as well. Credentials include not just their degrees but also the clinic, hospital, or university where they are working. This information doesn't guarantee the quality of the contents of the news and articles but it does indicate that the information came from credible and authoritative sources.

Although some sites do provide history of medicine materials, most sites try to provide current medical information. MedHist, which is now part of the Intute project (www.intute.ac.uk/health andlifesciences/medhist), collects free e-resources for medical history research. Verifying the dates and currency of a site can be critical to the health care consumer or health care practitioner using the information from the site to inform a medical decision. For example, the latest research (www.cancer.gov/newscenter) on breast cancer treatments considers the ongoing use of genetic analysis of the breast cancer tumor by medical professionals, students, and researchers to guide decisions about which chemotherapy or surgical options will be most successful. It is important for both patient and physician to have the most current research available. Some research shows that some breast cancer treatments are more or less successful depending on the genetic pattern of the tumor cells. Given recent pharmaceutical news, it is also essential that information about drugs and their side effects be as up to date as possible.

Security is essential to ensure high-quality medical information on the Web. It is unlikely that library users will be asked for their financial information when accessing a medical information site (unless it is also a storefront), but they are frequently asked for other personal information. It is possible to purchase prescription and over-the-counter drugs, herbs, health devices, alternative medical treatments, and dietary supplements, among other things, through the Web. Always use your browser settings to verify a secure server before you input financial or personal information. For example, when you register for Medical Matrix (www.medmatrix.org), you must provide your name, professional, and other personal data as well as a credit card number. MerckMedicus (www.merckmedicus.com) requires personal and professional information, including licensure status, for registration, although it requests no financial information. This is used to guarantee to the database providers that the users targeted for their advertising and marketing are registering and using the system.

Privacy is a very important factor for health care consumers who are suffering from diseases such as genetic disorders, AIDS, cancer, or diabetes, that might inspire others to persecute, discriminate against, or fear them, or that might cause insurance companies to drop them from coverage or employers to terminate them. Great care should be taken, when possible, to warn library users that there is no real privacy on the Web. Searching from library computers is a strategy that many use to protect their privacy. All that any information gatherer can glean is that someone in the library searched on a particular topic. As long as the library user does not input any specific personal details, they will be relatively private using library access. For example, if a library user visits a site that asks the user to register for a personalized self-diagnosis or calculator type program, will that site keep that personal information private? What is its privacy policy? Will it turn around and sell the library user's personal information to telemarketers or spammers? Look carefully at how privacy and security issues are addressed in the Web site. For example, are privacy guidelines available? Are they ethical? Do they meet privacy requirements of HIPAA, specifically the Federal Health Privacy Rule integral to the Health Insurance Portability and Accountability Act of 1996? The HIPAA Federal Health Privacy Rule became effective in the United States in 2001 as part of the implementation of the Health Insurance Portability and Accountability Act of 1996. Information about the privacy rule is available at http://aspe.hhs .gov/admnsimp/pl104191.html as well as articles, reports, and summaries that will give additional perspective on privacy of medical information specifically. The site also provides links to research and analysis of evaluation criteria and self-regulation of privacy protection on medical Web sites. Medical professionals, students, and researchers also need to be careful of the privacy of their patients when searching or asking questions on the Web. They may intend that their e-mail to a colleague is private, but this assumption may not fit the reality.

Other selection criteria based on the information-seeking behavior of medical professionals, students, and researchers, such as appropriateness of format or content, must also come in to play. For example, sources that require a lot of time to learn to search, or time reading, researching, and analyzing might be suitable for a medical student or researcher but will not benefit the physician or nurse who needs clinical guidelines during or very close to the time when they are also communicating with patients.

Selection criteria for any format in which you find medical information resources are derived from answers to questions in the collection-planning process. As with previous reference subjects, a survey was sent out in May and August 2008 asking librarians to identify their core or essential medical reference tools. Separate surveys were sent querying for consumer health specific medical reference tools and professional and researcher specific medical reference tools.

The discussion lists and blogs where the survey links were posted are listed in Table 8.1. The core consumer health reference tools survey is reproduced in Table 8.2 and the core professional medical reference tools survey is reproduced in Table 8.3.

Table 8.1. Discussion Lists and Blogs Distribution for Consumer Health and Professional Medical Reference Tools Surveys

- MEDLIB-L@LIST.UVM.EDU
- mla-cds@colldev.mlanet.org
- Medref-L@listserv.kent.edu
- CAPHIS@hslc.org
- LISNews and LISNewsWire Blogs: lisnews-owner@lishost.net
- ResourceShelf Blog: gary.price@resourceshelf.com
- ERIL-L@LISTSERV.BINGHAMTON.EDU

- dig_ref@LISTSERV.SYR.EDU
- collib-l@ala.org
- LIS-LINK@jiscmail.ac.uk
- Libref-L@listserv.kent.edu
- GOVDOC-L@lists.psu.edu
- publib@webjunction.org
- livereference@yahoogroups.com
- Libref-L@listserv.kent.edu

Table 8.2. Core Consumer Health Reference Tools Survey Questions

1. Which library type best describes the library you work in/for/with?

2. In which subject area(s) are you most likely to answer consumer health questions? (Check all that apply.)

3. What are the essential three print titles (reference books) that you can't work without in answering consumer health questions? (Please type the title only.)

4. What are the essential three free (not government published) Web-accessible databases that you can't work without in answering consumer health questions? (Please type complete URL/Web address; e.g., www.mayoclinic.com.)

5. What are the essential three (.gov) government published (state, federal, local, international) free Web-accessible databases that you can't work without in answering consumer health questions? (Please type complete URL/Web address; e.g., www.medlineplus.gov.)

6. What are the essential three fee-based Web-accessible databases that you can't work without in answering consumer health questions? (Please type the simple title; e.g., Ebsco Consumer Health Complete.)

7. Does your library maintain a Web page or site to support consumer health reference? If so, please share the URL/Web address (e.g., http://apps.nlm.nih.gov/medlineplus/local/alabama/homepage.cfm?areaid=3).

8. Additional comments or ideas:

(Please include your name and e-mail address if you would like feedback, otherwise this survey form is completely anonymous.)

Table 8.3. Core Professional Medical Reference Tools Survey Questions

1. Which library type best describes the library you work in/for/with?

2. In which subject area(s) are you most likely to answer medical professional questions? (Check all that apply.)

3. What are the essential three print titles (reference books) that you can't work without in answering medical professional questions? (Please type the title only.)

4. What are the essential three free (not government published) Web-accessible databases that you can't work without in answering medical professional questions? (Please type complete URL/Web address; e.g., www.medscape.com.)

5. What are the essential three (.gov) government published (state, federal, local, international) free Web-accessible databases that you can't work without in answering medical professional questions? (Please type complete URL/Web address; e.g., pubmed.gov or www.ncbi.nlm.nih.gov/sites/entrez)

6. What are the essential three fee-based Web-accessible databases that you can't work without in answering medical professional questions? (Please type complete URL/Web address; e.g., www.uptodate.com or the simple title UpToDate.)

7. Does your library maintain a Web page or site to support medical professional reference? If so please share the URL/Web address (e.g., http://library.osfhealthcare.org)

8. Additional comments or ideas:

(Please include your name and e-mail address if you would like feedback, otherwise this survey form is completely anonymous.)

Note: Professional refers to physicians and allied health care professionals as well as medical and nursing students and researchers.

The Core Web Consumer Health and Professional Medical Reference Collections on the companion Web Site (www.kovacs.com/ns/essentialguide.html) were initially created using the survey results from these surveys along with results from similar 2005 and 2006 surveys as core and model collections. Past, present, and future surveys and results are posted at www.kovacs .com/misc.html. These collections are intended for librarians to use as a source of e-resources they might select for their consumer health reference or professional medical reference e-library collections.

Core print reference tools in both the medical reference categories were collected. Compared to prior surveys, there were much fewer print reference tools reported. Table 8.4 lists the top five print consumer health reference tools identified in the survey and Table 8.5 reproduces the results for the core print professional medical reference tools. As with the business reference core tools, the medical reference core tools are frequently both print and Web accessible. When a preference was expressed, librarians preferred the Web-accessible versions even in the cases of the medical dictionaries.

The free Web sites that librarians reported as core or essential for consumer health reference are given in Table 8.6. The core free Web sites librarians reported using for professional medical reference titles are reported in Table 8.7. There were very few non-e-docs sites reported. Surprisingly, Google/Google Scholar was counted in the core free professional medical reference sites. Discussion on MEDLIB-L recently highlighted the search flexibility of Google Scholar over PubMed in a couple of cases.

A large number of e-docs that librarians feel are core or essential for both consumer health and professional medical reference were reported. The top five consumer health e-docs reference sites are listed in Table 8.8. Professional medical reference e-docs overlapped slightly with consumer health sites in this survey as described in Table 8.9.

Fee-based consumer health reference tools did not receive as many votes as did professional medical reference tools. The top five—by number of librarians mentioning that e-resource—core or essential fee-based consumer health e-resources are given in Table 8.10. There was not great deal of agreement or overlapping votes for favorite e-resources for professional medical reference e-resources as reported in Table 8.11.

Table 8.4. Top Five Print Consumer Health Reference Tools Identified in Survey

1. *Gale Encyclopedia of Medicine*
2. *Mayo Clinic Family Health Book, Gale Encyclopedia of Alternative Medicine*, other *Gale Medical Encyclopedia* titles
3. *Dorland's Illustrated Medical Dictionary, Stedman's Medical Dictionary*
4. *Merck Manual of Medical Information*
5. *Physician's Desk Reference (PDR)*

Table 8.5. Top Two Print Professional Medical Reference Tools Identified in Survey

1. *Principles of Internal Medicine* (Harrison)
2. *Dorland's Illustrated Medical Dictionary, Essentials of Medicine* (Cecil), *Taber's Cyclopedic Medical Dictionary, Merck Manual of Medical Information,* and *Stedman's Medical Dictionary*

Note: Several titles tied for second place.

Table 8.6. Top Five Free Web Consumer Health Reference Tools Identified in Survey

1. MayoClinic Web site: www.mayoclinic.com (majority of votes)
2. KidsHealth: http://kidshealth.org, NOAH: www.noah-health.org
3. American Cancer Society: www.cancer.org, WebMD: www.webmd.com
4. NORD: www.rarediseses.org
5. Family Doctor: http://familydoctor.org, Lab Tests Online: www.labtestsonline.org

Table 8.7. Top Two Free Web Professional Medical Reference Tools Identified in Survey

1. Google: www.google.com (Google Scholar/Advanced Google included)
2. Medscape (CME): http://cme.medscape.com/medscapetoday

Note: All other sites received only a single vote each.

Table 8.8. Top Five Government Documents Web Sites Used as Consumer Health Reference Tools Identified in Survey

1. MedlinePlus: www.medlineplus.gov (majority of votes)
2. Center for Disease Control and Prevention: http://cdc.gov
3. Healthfinder.gov: http://healthfinder.gov
4. PubMed: www.ncbi.nlm.nih.gov/pubmed
5. National Institutes of Health (NIH): www.nih.gov, National Cancer Institute: www.cancer.gov, U. S. Food and Drug Administration (FDA): www.fda.gov

Table 8.9. Top Four Government Documents Web Sites Used as Professional Medical Reference Tools Identified in Survey

1. PubMed: www.ncbi.nlm.nih.gov/pubmed
2. Center for Disease Control and Prevention: http://cdc.gov
3. MedlinePlus: www.medlineplus.gov
4. National Guidelines Clearinghouse: www.guideline.gov

Table 8.10. Top Five Fee-based Consumer Health Reference E-Resources Identified in Survey

1. EBSCO CINAHL/Medline: www.ebscohost.com/cinahl
2. EBSCO Health Source Consumer Edition: www.ebscohost.com/thisTopic.php?marketID=1&topicID=82
3. Health and Wellness Resource Center (Gale): www.gale.cengage.com/Health
4. Stat!Ref: Electronic Resources for Healthcare Professionals: www.statref.com
5. MD Consult: www.mdconsult.com and UptoDate: www.uptodate.com/home/index.html (patient information areas)

**Table 8.11. Top Three Fee-based Professional Medical Reference
E-Resources Identified in Survey**

1. EBSCO CINAHL/Medline: www.ebscohost.com/cinahl
2. OVID CINAHL/Medline: www.ovid.com
3. DynaMed (EBSCO): www.ebscohost.com/dynamed, MD Consult: www.mdconsult.com, Stat!Ref: Electronic Resources for Healthcare Professionals: www.statref.com, UptoDate:www.uptodate.com/home/index.html

Note: Several titles tied for third place.

As with the business reference core tools, the medical reference core tools are frequently both print and Web accessible. When a preference was expressed librarians preferred the Web-accessible e-book versions.

There are two separate Web medical reference collections on the companion Web site because there is much difference in vocabulary and educational level between the health care consumer and the professional medical or medical researcher. For these core collections, the intended library user group is librarians. The core Web Consumer Health Reference Collection is intended for those working with English-speaking health care consumers. The core Web Professional Medical Collection is designed for librarians working with medical professionals or researchers. Both types of library users look for appropriate diagnostic, pharmaceutical, and treatment information on a quick-response basis. The access and design of all these core medical e-resources are based on standards of simplicity, international Web accessibility standards, and no special software required for access. Most of them are free of direct cost—except for the cost of Internet access—with some having special fee-based services including document delivery or other optional service. Fee-based e-resources are included when they offer free trials or have some information available without requiring a fee.

E-LIBRARY SUCCESS STORY

BAPTIST HEALTH MEDICAL LIBRARY
Little Rock, Arkansas, United States
http://baptist-health.org
Contact: Carolyn Baker, Carolyn.Baker@baptist-health.org

A. Collection Planning (e.g., goal setting and identification of users, technology/personnel choices)

The Baptist Health medical library is located on the main campus of Baptist Health Systems in Little Rock, Arkansas, but serves all campuses. Baptist Health is a large nonprofit health care system. It consists of seven hospitals on six campuses around the state of Arkansas. Baptist Health Schools is also a part of the system and includes a school of nursing and eight other schools in various allied health areas.

"Our primary user groups are physicians, nurses, students, faculty, and other health care professionals within the Baptist system. We also provide consumer health information to patients, family members and others in the community upon request. There is also a Learning Resource Center at Baptist Health Schools Little Rock that has a small print collection of monographs, journals and video recordings. The collection supports the faculty and students at the

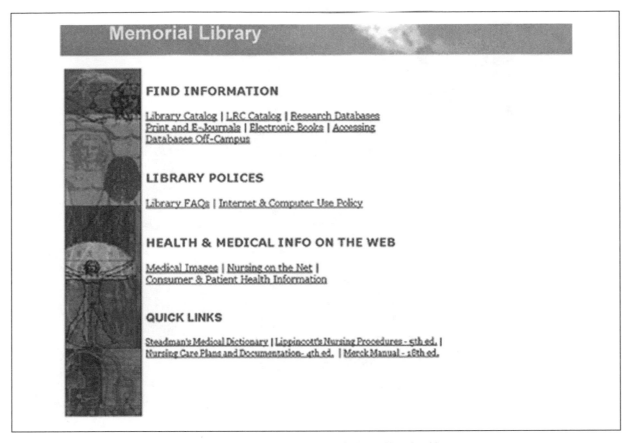

Figure 8.1. Baptist Health Medical Library

schools. Additional materials come from the medical library in support of curriculum and faculty and student needs."

The Web page for the medical library is located behind the system firewall and cannot be accessed by the general public. Screen captures of the internal medical library site main page and one of the nursing resources collection page are included with this case study. A publicly accessible Web page for health care consumers is at http://healthinfo.baptist-health.com/library. The content of this page is provided by the Web site developer and not by the medical library.

The medical library e-library evolved over time as more and more materials needed by the core users was published online. Fee-based as well as free medical databases, journals, and other resources were gradually added to the library Web page to provide access for users. There were some problems with this initial piecemeal approach. For example, links to online journals weren't always maintained or cataloged in the OPAC. "The library began subscribing to Serials Solutions in 2004, but it was not well maintained. Other library Web pages were developed that offered access to Web sites such as consumer health information and nursing Web sites, but again maintenance was a big issue."

Carolyn Baker became the medical librarian in early 2006 and immediately began trying to find resources available to ameliorate these problems. "Most resources were still print-based or rather, were still being used in print form, even if an electronic or digital version was available. The library space is relatively small and the shelf space is limited. Shelf space was at a premium, particularly for journals. The computer library system was outdated and offered a Web catalog, but as mentioned previously, offered no bibliographic access to journals and links to electronic

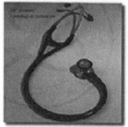

Nursing Resources Available on the Internet

Arkansas Resources

Arkansas Nurses Association	State organization for Professional Nursing
Arkansas State Board of Nursing	Licensing and other information
Arkansas Nurse Practice Act	Pdf of the Nurse Practice Act for Arkansas
Arkansas Student Nurses Association	Arkansas Chapter of National Student Nurses' Assoc.
Arkansas Legislative Committee on Nursing	Information on government matters and nursing

National Institutes of Health Resources

NIH Clinical Center Nursing Department Standards of Practice	Nursing in the research environment
National Institute of Nursing Research	Information on grants and nursing research

Nursing Academy/Association Websites

American Nursing Association
AACN: American Association of Critical Care Nurses
AORN: Association of Perioperative Registered Nurses
American Academy of Nurse Practitioners
American Association of Colleges of Nurses
American Association of Occupational Health Nurses
American College of Nurse Practitioners
Association of Rehabilitation Nurses
National League of Nursing
National Student Nurses' Association

Continuing Education

CINAHL
The Library has videos and DVDs available for checkout. Most of these provide 1 Continuing Education credit. Call 2671 for more information about these resources.

Posted by Carolyn Baker x1100 on September 1, 2008

Figure 8.2. Baptist Health Medical Library: Nursing Collection

versions. A new library system was purchased in July of 2006 that could include that information. Additionally, bibliographic access to Web sites, electronic books, and other non-print items could be added to this Web catalog."

Various outdated Web pages had to be updated with current information. These Web pages, although current now, will be eliminated in favor of Serials Solutions updated to accurately reflect holdings. "There were a several collections of electronic journals that had been purchased previous to 2006, but some of these duplicated print and electronic access in place and were discontinued for 2007. We are working to eliminate print journals and are adding only electronic holdings for 2009." The most important aspect of this process is that the most current information is available to support health care professionals in providing the highest quality service to patients and their families.

Figure 8.3. Baptist Health Consumer Health Library

No written collection plan was developed until Carolyn Baker began developing one when she took the MLA CE approved online course "Electronic Collection Development for Health and Medicine E-Libraries" in the spring of 2007.

B. Collection Strategies (e.g., selection criteria, identification of resources, licensing, and related user information needs)

Careful, detailed criteria inform resource selection. "Several things are considered when determining which resources to purchase. Cost is always a consideration. Beyond that, several questions are considered:

- Who will use this resource?
- How many populations can use it? Is it appropriate for more than one user group?
- How will it be used? Classroom, patient care, continuing education?
- Is the information appropriate to the user population, primarily health care providers?
- Licensing limitations—can this resource be used at a multi-site institution, what is the cost for additional sites?"

The medical library Web page provides access to multiple core medical databases for the use of Baptist Health Systems personnel including:

- DynaMed, an evidence-based database from EBSCO
- CINAHL, Medline with full text, Health Source: Nursing & Academic Edition, Psychology & Behavioral Sciences Database, Cochrane Database
- MD Consult, which provides Medline access and 50+ full-text journals and 50+ full-text medical books
- Micromedex

Licensing arrangements are limited to systemwide access and remote access (with a login and password) to all employees of the system with some other limitations. "We are prevented by contract from sending electronic copies of materials, primarily journal articles to persons outside the system. Remote access is available for all of the fee-based databases with a login/password. No archiving arrangements are in place."

The library budget pays for all licensed databases with the exception of Micromedex. Micromedex is purchased through the Pharmacy Department. The library budget also covers access to e-books with similar licensing arrangements to the databases. "E-books are available through our agreement with Elsevier and MD Consult. We subscribe to their Core Collection which provides 50+ medical books in full-text. In addition, we subscribe to two nursing texts from Ovid. Beginning in 2009, we will purchase these books and possibly some other nursing texts. Under consideration, is a subscription to a collection of nursing texts from Ovid. We placed links to a medical dictionary and to the Merck Manuals on our Web page. These are free resources."

E-books, journals—including online access details as well as the licensed databases are cataloged in the library's OPAC. "We have some Web resources cataloged, but not very many. Time is the biggest factor in adding these to the collection. Usage is not tracked from the catalog links. Statistics are sent from various companies on a monthly basis on usage."

Virtual reference service is informally available because users are encouraged to e-mail the librarians when they need assistance. No formal service is in place. Interlibrary loan is used extensively. "Baptist Health is a member of Docline and we make extensive use to provide our users with requested materials. Baptist loans far more than we borrow, however. One reason for this is that we belong to FreeShare and we do not charge for articles that we send via interlibrary loan."

C. Collection Organization (e.g., content management systems, Web server choices, personnel responsibilities, etc.)

SiteMaker is used to develop and maintain Web pages. Each department is responsible for development and maintenance of its Web pages. Senior Content Managers and IT staff provide technical support. All related technology costs are covered by the Baptist Health system and do not come out of the library budget. "The Library has 14 Web pages (main + 13 linking pages). In addition we use Serials Solutions to link our patrons to full-text journal articles and a Web OPAC for bibliographic access to the collection. Two of our Web pages are listings for professional organizations and information for nursing and a page of medical images and graphics. Both are included in the screen shots. The Web pages are under review and new pages are being developed and others are being deleted."

The librarian along with a library assistant support the medical library both print and online collections. "The library assistant spends approximately 50% of her time working with electronic check in of print journals and processing interlibrary loan requests through Docline and OCLC. The librarian spends about 75% of her time working with Web page access, maintenance of Serials Solutions database, selection and processing of e-library resources, as well as teaching the use of these resources to users."

The medical librarian is fully responsible for collection development, building, and maintaining the e-library collection. She collects appropriate resources by reading Web resource reviews in professional journals such as MLA News, monitoring MEDLIB-L, and serendipitous discovery when using Web search engines for related topic searches.

D. Collection Maintenance (e.g., link checking, ongoing weeding, and growth of the e-library collection)

Link checking in the catalog is done by the Web OPAC software. All other links need to be checked manually. Currently it is done every six months, but they would like to do so more frequently. Users are also encouraged to report link changes. "We do evaluate the services and resources that we offer to our users on an annual basis. Comments about resources during that evaluation and others during the year are always evaluated and if they can be implemented, generally we will do so. Cost is the major factor in determining if we can implement or add new resources."

Carolyn Baker reviews the organization of the collection on an ongoing basis. One thing she would like to explore is including a search tool or index in the collection. "I have looked at federated search engines, but the cost is prohibitive at this time. I want to pursue addition of more Web resources to the collection, but time is the limiting factor."

REFERENCES AND WEB SITES CITED

Anderson, P. F., and Nancy J. Allee. 2004. *The Medical Library Association Encyclopedic Guide to Searching and Finding Health Information on the Web*. New York: Neal-Schuman.

Connor, Elizabeth, and Wood, M. Sandra, eds. 2007. *Electronic Resources in Medical Libraries: Issues and Solutions*. Binghamton, NY: The Haworth Press. (Published simultaneously as *Journal of Electronic Resources in Medical Libraries* 4, no. 1/2).

Foust, Jill E., Philip Bergen, Gretchen L. Maxeiner, and Peter N. Pawlowski. 2007. "Improving E-book Access via a Library-developed Full-text Search Tool." *Journal of the Medical Library Association* 95, no. 1: 40–45.

Goodyear-Smith, Felicity, Ngaire Kerse, Jim Warren, and Bruce Arroll. 2008. "Evaluation of E-textbooks—DynaMed, MD Consult and UpToDate." *Australian Family Physician* 37, no. 10: 878–882. Available: www.racgp.org.au/afp/200810/27588 (accessed January 29, 2009).

Hernon, Peter, Rosita Hopper, Michael R. Leach, Laura L. Saunders, and Jane Zhang. 2007. "E-book Use by Students: Undergraduates in Economics, Literature, and Nursing." *The Journal of Academic Librarianship* 33, no. 1: 3–13.

Huber, Jeffrey T., Jo Anne Boorkman, and Jean Blackwell. 2008. *Introduction to Reference Sources in the Health Sciences*, 5th edition. Medical Library Association Guides. New York: Neal-Schuman.

Kim, Paul, Thomas R. Eng, Mary Jo Deering, and Andrew Maxfield. 1999. "Published Criteria for Evaluating Health Related Websites: Review." *British Medical Journal* 318, no. 7184 (March): 647–649. Available: www.bmj.com/cgi/content/full/318/7184/647 (accessed January 18, 2009).

Kovacs, Diane K. 2005. "Electronic Collection Development for Consumer Health Information." *Journal of Consumer Health on the Internet* 7, no. 4: 31–52.

Kraft, Michelle. 2007. "Integrating and Promoting Medical Podcasts into the Library Collection." *Medical Reference Services Quarterly* 26, no. 1 (Spring): 27–35.

Mitchell, Nicole, and Elizabeth Lorbeer. 2008. "eBooks in Academic Health Sciences Libraries." *Against the Grain* 20, no. 5: 30.

Ugaz, Ana G., and Taryn Resnick. 2008. "Assessing Print and Electronic Use of Reference/Core Medical Textbooks." *Journal of the Medical Library Association* 96, no. 2: 145–147.

WEB SITES CITED

Administrators in Medicine (AIM) Association of State Medical Board Executive Directors DocFinder. Available: www.docboard.org/docfinder.html (accessed January 7, 2009).

Consumer and Patient Health Information Section of the Medical Library Association (CAPHIS). Available: http://caphis.mlanet.org/consumer (accessed January 7, 2009).

DIRLINE Search. Available: http://dirline.nlm.nih.gov (accessed January 7, 2009).

Hardin MD. Available: www.lib.uiowa.edu/hardin/md/index.html (accessed January 7, 2009).

Health on the Net Foundation (HON). Available: www.hon.ch (accessed January 12, 2009).

HIPAA: Federal Health Privacy Rule integral to the Health Insurance Portability and Accountability Act of 1996. Available: http://aspe.hhs.gov/admnsimp/pl104191.htm or www.hhs.gov/ocr/hipaa (accessed January 12, 2009).

Intute: Health and Life Sciences. Available: www.intute.ac.uk/healthandlifesciences (accessed January 7, 2009).

JMIR: Journal of Medical Internet Research. Available: www.jmir.org (accessed January 12, 2009).

Mayo Clinic. Available: www.mayoclinic.com (accessed January 7, 2009).

MEDEM. Available: www.medem.com (accessed January 7, 2009).

Medical Matrix. Available: www.medmatrix.org (accessed January 7, 2009).

MedlinePlus. Available: www.nlm.nih.gov/medlineplus (accessed January 7, 2009).

MedlinePlus A.D.A.M Encyclopedia. Available: www.nlm.nih.gov/medlineplus/encyclopedia.html (accessed January 7, 2009).

Mednar. Available: http://mednar.com/mednar/ (accessed January 7, 2009).

Medscape (CME). Available: http://cme.medscape.com/medscapetoday (accessed January 7, 2009).

Merck Medicus. Available: www.merckmedicus.com (accessed January 7, 2009).

National Library of Medicine MeSH Subject Headings. Available: www.nlm.nih.gov/mesh (accessed January 7, 2009).

Psychiatry Online Journals eTOCs. Available: http://psychservices.psychiatryonline.org/subscriptions/etoc.dtl.

PubMed. Available: www.ncbi.nlm.nih.gov/pubmed (accessed January 7, 2009).

PubMed Central. Available: www.pubmedcentral.nih.gov (accessed January 7, 2009).

SoundPractice.net. Available: http://soundpractice.net (accessed January 7, 2009).

The Web Quality Bibliography. Available: http://bama.ua.edu/~smaccall/qualitybib.html (accessed January 7, 2009).

MEDICAL E-RESOURCES FOR PROFESSIONALS AND RESEARCHERS COLLECTION TOOLS

META SITES

Collection Development Manual of the National Library of Medicine
www.nlm.nih.gov/tsd/acquisitions/cdm

"The Collection Development Manual of the National Library of Medicine (CDM), fourth edition (2004), establishes boundaries for the Library's permanent collection and provides a conceptual and philosophical framework for the selection of biomedical materials. Defining the boundaries of the NLM collection is complicated by the interdisciplinary nature of biomedicine, the prominence of political, ethical, economic and social issues in contemporary biomedical practice and research, rapid advances in health care technology and the proliferation of information sources and formats."

Hardin MD
www.lib.uiowa.edu/hardin/md/index.html

Database of Web sites by category; size of site and connection rate is annotated. Also lists the Medical/Health Sciences Libraries on the Web.

INFOMINE: Biological, Agricultural and Medical Sciences Collection
http://infomine.ucr.edu/cgi-bin/search?category=bioag

Large annotated collection of Internet resources related to biology, agriculture, and medicine. Resources are selected and evaluated to ensure they are a scholarly information resource suitable for research or educational activities at the postsecondary educational levels.

Intute: Health and Life Sciences
www.intute.ac.uk/healthandlifesciences

Intute is a multisubject e-library maintained by a consortium of United Kingdom university and academic organization Library partners (www.intute.ac.uk/healthandlifesciences/partners.html) who carefully select and evaluate all the health and life sciences e-resources that are open source or otherwise freely available on the Web. Pieces of it were previously known as BIOME, OMNI, VETGATE, BIORES, AGRIFOR, and other smaller databases, including MEDHIST. Although hosted in the UK, the scope of these collections is international. The scope of the Health and Life Sciences collection includes medicine, nursing, and allied health fields, bioethics, media and the sciences, veterinary medicine, midwifery, agriculture and forestry, history of medicine, and other fields. The collection is searchable and browseable.

Martindale's Health Science Guide
www.martindalecenter.com

"A 'Multimedia Specialized Information Resource' currently containing over 55,500 teaching files; over 126,300 Medical Cases; 1,055 Multimedia Courses/Textbooks; 1,450 Multimedia Tutorials; over 3,430 Databases, and over 10,400 Movies." Very crowded and difficult to navigate, but there is some good stuff here.

McGill University Health Centre Research Resources for Evidence Based Nursing
http://muhc-ebn.mcgill.ca

Medical Matrix
www.medmatrix.org

Fee-based, peer-reviewed collection of clinical medicine Web sites. Search the database by specialties, disease, clinical practice, literature, education, and more.

Mednets

www.mednets.com

> Collection of Web sites of online medical journals, medical schools' search engines, international specialty, and regional associations in medicine, nursing, physiotherapy, and dentistry.

MLA Collection Development Section

http://colldev.mlanet.org

> The Medical Library Association Collection Development Section provides resources of interest to librarians doing health sciences collection development. A selective collection of subject-based resource lists (print and Web-based) is included on the site.

National Institutes of Health (NIH)

www.nih.gov

> Huge Web site with links to all 25 of the National Institutes of Health, many of which produce databases of their specific health information and resources. NIH also has links to other government agency Web health resources (A–Z guide), NIH publications, funding, and scientific news.

DIGITAL LIBRARIES DIRECTORIES OR COLLECTIONS OF DIGITAL LIBRARIES (DIGITAL LIBRARIES OF E-BOOKS, E-SERIALS, IMAGES, RECORDINGS, AND OTHER ARTIFACTS)

National Academies Press

www.nap.edu

> E-book vender with some free e-books for sciences, engineering, education, and medicine.

PubMed Central

www.pubmedcentral.nih.gov

> "PubMed Central (PMC) is the U.S. National Institutes of Health (NIH) free digital archive of biomedical and life sciences journal literature."

E-SERIALS, BLOGS, DISCUSSION LISTS, ETC.

ACOR Medical/Biosciences Mailing Lists

www.acor.org/mailing.html

> Association of Cancer Online Resources Directory of patient support and medical research related mailing lists.

davidrothman.net: Exploring Medical Librarianship and Web Geekery

http://davidrothman.net

EBM: Evidence-Based Medicine (EBM) Librarian wiki

http://ebmlibrarian.wetpaint.com

Journal of Medical Internet Research

www.jmir.org

> JMIR is a peer-reviewed e-journal indexed by Medline that publishes reviews and articles about the quality and use of medical Web resources. JMIR is free and provides full-text access on the Web.

Journal of the European Association for Health Information and Libraries

www.eahil.net/journal

MEDLIB-L

www.mlanet.org/discussion/medlib_l_faq.html

> Discussion list for medical librarians that includes discussion of Internet resources for medical e-library collections. Official Medical Libraries Association, medical libraries discussion list.

Nursing and Allied Health Resources Section (MLA-NAHRS)

http://nahrs.mlanet.org

CONSUMER HEALTH E-RESOURCE COLLECTION TOOLS

META SITES

The Alternative Medicine Homepage
www.pitt.edu/~cbw/altm.html

> Charles B. Wessel, MLS, Librarian, Falk Library of the Health Sciences, University of Pittsburgh has evaluated and collected Web resources related to complementary and alternative medicine.

Consumer and Patient Health Information Section of the Medical Library Association (CAPHIS)
http://caphis.mlanet.org/consumer

> The CAPHIS top 100 "Web sites you can trust." Compiled by members of CAPHIS and organized by general health interest.

Cuyahoga County Public Library Consumer Health Collection
www.cuyahogalibrary.org/healthexpert.aspx

> Public library with excellent collection of free and commercial consumer health e-resources.

Healthfinder
www.healthfinder.gov

> This site is published by the U.S. Department of Health and Human Services, Office of Disease Prevention and Health Promotion. The site is simple and very accessible. The resources selected are few but excellent. Links to the DrugDigest site.

HealthNet
http://library.uchc.edu/departm/hnet

> This site was developed to "assist in the development of local public libraries as primary access points for consumer health information." Internet resources for consumer health as well as print and local referrals for consumer health information are selected by the HealthNet librarians.

Medical Information on the Internet: Guide for Health Reporters and Consumers
www.mlanet.org/resources/hlth_tutorial/index.html

MedicineNet
www.medicinenet.com

> Medical resource in easy-to-understand language. Updated by board-certified physicians. Has good pharmacological/drug information and annotated collections of Web sites in specific health topic areas.

MedlinePlus
www.medlineplus.gov

> Medical librarian evaluated and selected health and medical Web sites as well as access to PubMed and many other National Library of medicine resources.

MLA Collection Development Section
http://colldev.mlanet.org

> The Medical Library Association Collection Development Section provides resources of interest to librarians doing health sciences collection development. A selective collection of subject-based resource lists (print and Web-based) is included on the site.

DIGITAL LIBRARIES DIRECTORIES OR COLLECTIONS OF DIGITAL LIBRARIES (DIGITAL LIBRARIES OF E-BOOKS, E-SERIALS, IMAGES, RECORDINGS, AND OTHER ARTIFACTS)

National Academies Press
www.nap.edu

> E-book vender with some free e-books for sciences, engineering, education, and medicine.

PubMed Central

www.pubmedcentral.nih.gov

> "PubMed Central (PMC) is the U.S. National Institutes of Health (NIH) free digital archive of biomedical and life sciences journal literature."

E-Serials, Blogs, Discussion Lists, etc.

ACOR Medical/Biosciences Mailing Lists

www.acor.org/mailing.html

> Association of Cancer Online Resources Directory of patient support and medical research related mailing lists.

CAPHIS

http://caphis.mlanet.org/publications/discussionlist.html

> Discussion for members of the Consumer and Patient Health Information section of the Medical Library Association.

Consumer Health Information Service (CHIS) blog

> http://torontopubliclibrary.typepad.com/chis

davidrothman.net: Exploring Medical Librarianship and Web Geekery

http://davidrothman.net

Journal of Medical Internet Research

http://www.jmir.org/

> *JMIR* is a peer-reviewed e-journal indexed by Medline that publishes reviews and articles about the quality and use of medical Web resources. *JMIR* is free and provides full-text access on the Web.

MEDLIB-L

www.mlanet.org/discussion/medlib_l_faq.html

> Discussion list for medical librarians that includes discussion of Internet resources for medical e-library collections. Official Medical Libraries Association, medical libraries discussion list.

CHAPTER

9

BIOLOGICAL SCIENCES E-RESOURCES

PLoS Biology (eISSN-1545-7885; ISSN-1544-9173) is an open-access, peer-reviewed general biology journal published by the Public Library of Science (PLoS), a nonprofit organization of scientists and physicians committed to making the world's scientific and medical literature a public resource. New articles are published online weekly; issues are published monthly.... *PLoS Biology* is ranked in the top-tier of life science journals by The Institute for Scientific Information (ISI), with an impact factor of 14.1.... *PLoS Biology* features works of exceptional significance, originality, and relevance in all areas of biological science, from molecules to ecosystems, including works at the interface of other disciplines, such as chemistry, medicine, and mathematics. Our audience is the international scientific community as well as educators, policymakers, patient advocacy groups, and interested members of the public around the world. (About *PLoS Biology*, accessed January 19, 2009, at http://journals.plos.org/plosbiology/information.php)

DEVELOPING A COLLECTION PLAN FOR BIOLOGICAL SCIENCES E-RESOURCES

PLoS Biology is an exemplar of the kinds of e-resources that are being created to facilitate scholarly communication, data, and research sharing using Web technologies. This is a peer-reviewed scholarly e-journal, but it also hosts forums for discussion and other opportunities for researchers to interact with the published articles. Educational tools are also integrated into the site. Biological researchers often choose to publish in e-journals like this because they encourage open communication of scientific information (Frandsen, 2009).

The biological sciences, sometimes called life sciences, include agriculture, botany, environmental science, oceanography, zoology, and other specific fields of study. Subfields such as primate zoology and multifield subjects such as fresh water biology and many diverse other areas are encompassed by the concept of biological sciences. The scope of biological science e-resources is as broad and diverse as the biosphere of the earth. There are literally thousands of biological sciences specializations. In this book biomedical e-resources are covered in the previous chapter.

WHAT PURPOSE WILL YOUR COLLECTION SERVE? FOR WHOM ARE YOU COLLECTING THESE E-RESOURCES?

Before collecting biological sciences e-resources, begin by analyzing and listing the specific biological science specializations or subtopics that your library users will need or want. Biological sciences information will probably be used primarily by students at all educational levels, teachers at all educational levels, and researchers (academic, professional, and recreational/amateur). The important aspects to be aware of, after establishing the specific or general biological sciences information required, are educational level of the library users and the purpose for which they need the information.

Academic libraries may want to read or conduct a study similar to "Understanding the Information Needs of Academic Scholars in Agricultural and Biological Sciences" (Kuruppu and Gruber, 2006) or "Information Seeking Behavior of Academic Scientists" (Hemminger et al., 2007) to establish the scope, level, and types of e-resources their current or potential library users may prefer. Generally, academic libraries collect for undergraduate, graduate, postdoctoral students, and biological science educators and researchers in the areas described by their program guides and course lists. Academic libraries will look for both undergraduate level general biological science e-resources as well as complex, scientific, research-based, data-intensive e-resources for researchers in specialized biological science fields.

K–12 librarians will collect biological sciences e-resources designed for K–12 students; for example, introductory biology e-resources. Public librarians may decide to serve not only K–12 students but also other members of the public who may want more or less complex information. Public libraries may wish to support the biological-science related industries or government agencies that are part of the communities they serve.

WHAT TYPES OF E-RESOURCES WILL YOU COLLECT?

Biological sciences e-resources include general introductions to biological concepts, complete full-text databases and digital libraries in specialized biological research areas, peer-reviewed biological sciences e-serials, and other specialized archives in every biological sciences research area conceivable. In order to provide some familiar guidelines for collectors, biological sciences e-resources can be described approximately in terms of traditional reference source types:

- Directories (of biological scientists, science organizations, projects, etc.)
- Dictionaries (biological sciences vocabulary in English as well as international language translation dictionaries)
- Abstracts, indexes, and table of contents services (including those with full text of biological sciences journals indexed)
- Encyclopedias and almanacs
- Full-text and/or multimedia databases/digital libraries (collections of e-books, e-serials, recordings, videos, podcasts, images, etc.)
- News and news services (biological sciences current awareness sources)
- Key primary documents (research data and reports, statistical sources, etc.)
- Search engines
- Meta sites (e-resources that provide two or more of the other reference tool types in a single product/Web site)

Most biological sciences organization Web sites will include a directory of members, projects, or other listings. One good example, the American Institute of Biological Sciences (www.aibs.org/core) site includes an online membership directory listing organizational and society members along with links to their publications, tables of contents, etc.

Given the vast scope of subfields of the biological sciences, there are any number of examples of dictionaries, glossaries, and related tools available. The Open Directory Project maintains a collection of science dictionaries freely available on the Web (www.dmoz.org/Reference/Dictionaries/By_Sub ject/Science). A lovely example is the Biopharmaceutical Glossary (www .genomicglossaries.com).

The classic indexing and abstracting services for biological sciences journals are fee-based e-resources such as BIOSIS Preview/Biological Abstracts (www.thomsonreuters.com/products_services/scientific/BIOSIS_Previews). Government agencies, biological sciences associations, and journals provide tables of contents services and some index searching on their sites. One prime example is AGRICOLA (National Agricultural Library Catalog) (http://agricola.nal .usda.gov).

Some excellent biological sciences encyclopedias are freely available on the Web as well as biological sciences digital libraries. In fact these two reference types are frequently combined. Two interesting examples are Arkive (www.arkive.org), an encyclopedia and digital library collection of thousands of videos, images and fact files illustrating the world's species, and the USDA Plants Database (http://plants.usda.gov) with encyclopedic information as well as full-text research reports and data and images, about plants, mosses, lichens, etc. Examples, of biological sciences current awareness sources are easily located as part of the e-resources previously cited. Examples of biological key primary documents—biological sciences research data and reports, statistical sources, etc.—are available from e-docs sites such as the National Biological Information Infrastructure (www.nbii.gov) site. Meta sites for the biological sciences are listed in the collection tools section at the end of this chapter.

HOW WILL YOU ORGANIZE YOUR E-RESOURCES?

Organizing by biological science field and subtopics under those fields is a good strategy. Intute: Health and Life Sciences (www.intute.ac.uk/healthandlifesciences), for example, has developed hierarchical subject headings to ease browsing within the different subtopics. INFOMINE: Biological, Agricultural and Medical Sciences (http://infomine.ucr.edu/cgi-bin/search?category=bioag) uses a CMS to organize keyword searching, browsing by large category, and browsing by Library of Congress Subject Headings. Both sites create individual records for each e-resource that can be recombined in different organizational structures and searched.

IDENTIFYING AND COLLECTING BIOLOGICAL SCIENCES E-RESOURCES

WEB SITES THAT REVIEW AND EVALUATE E-RESOURCES: PEER E-LIBRARIES, SUBJECT COLLECTIONS/GUIDES, OR META SITES

Intute: Health and Life Sciences (www.intute.ac.uk/healthandlifesciences) selects, evaluates, and annotates biological sciences resources for postsecondary students, teachers, and researchers. It incorporates and replaces the BIorES, BIOME, AGRIFor, and OMNI collections of biological research, agriculture, food, and forestry, and medical and biomedical e-resources. The INFOMINE: Biological, Agricultural and Medical collection (http://infomine.ucr.edu/reference/balref.html) is also a great tool to use in identifying biological sciences e-resources for academic library users. Other biological sciences meta sites specialize in specific biological sciences these include the Agriculture Network Information Center (AgNIC) (www.agnic.org) and Envirolink (www.envirolink.org) collections. Additional meta sites may be found in the "Biological Sciences E-Resource Collection Tools" section at the end of this chapter.

DISCUSSION LISTS (LISTSERV, ETC.), FORUMS/GROUPS, E-SERIALS, AND/OR BLOGS THAT POST OR PUBLISH REVIEWS AND EVALUATIONS OF E-RESOURCES

The BIOSCI/Bionet electronic communications forums for Biology (www.bio.net) was one of the first to evolve on the Internet. The BIOSCI forums are on all biological science topics. Useful discussion lists for librarians collecting e-resources for the biological sciences include SLA-DBIO discussion list for librarians who are members of the Special Libraries Association Biomedical and Life Sciences Division, NHC discussion list for librarians who are members of the Special Libraries Association, Natural History Caucus, and STS-L, a discussion of science and technology librarianship for members of the Association of College and Research Libraries Science and Technology Libraries Section.

The PLoS: Public Library of Science (www.plos.org) publishes open source scholarly peer-reviewed e-journals in the biological and other sciences as well as in medicine that may be used to find high quality e-journals to add to your collection or to find articles that may review and evaluate other e-resources. "PLoS is a nonprofit organization of scientists and physicians committed to making the world's scientific and medical literature a freely available public resource."

PRINT BOOKS AND JOURNALS THAT REVIEW E-RESOURCES

Most good biological sciences research skills texts review appropriate e-resources. An outstanding example is Diana Hacker's (2008) *Research and Documentation in the Electronic Age*, Fifth Edition Booklet and Web site (www.dianahacker.com/resdoc), which will be cited in subsequent chapters as it covers research tools including e-resources in the biological, physical, and earth sciences and social sciences and the humanities. Both the fee-based research tools and the best of the free Web research tools in these areas are reviewed in this publication and linked from its companion Web site. Another interesting example text is *Research Methodology in the Medical and Biological Sciences* (Laake et al., 2007). This overall review of biological sciences and medical research methods includes extensive coverage of scholarly research level e-resources and appropriate use of other library services.

Most scholarly print journals review e-resources within the scope of the journal's coverage in the same areas in which they review books or cite sources. A good biological sciences indexing and abstracting service such as BIOSIS: Biological Abstracts (www.biosis.org/products_services/ ba.html) or Biological and Agricultural Index (www.hwwilson.com) can be used to identify journal articles that review biological sciences e-resources in a field or subtopic that you wish to collect. Although these journals are still published in print, they are almost all available full text online as well.

EVALUATION GUIDELINES AND SELECTION CRITERIA: THE CORE WEB BIOLOGICAL SCIENCES REFERENCE COLLECTION

As with medical information, care must be taken to identify the authors of biological sciences information and to verify their qualifications and educational attainment and research experience. Attention to their record of publishing may be important. Have they previously published in peer-reviewed journals? Do they have a clear record of scholarship and research that is traceable? Good biological science Web resource will clearly identify the authors, information providing organizations, and their records of scholarship and research. For example, Eurekalert!

(www.eurekalert.org) science news service is published on the Web by the American Association for the Advancement of Science. Each science news item has an identified contact person, with their e-mail, telephone, and the museum, laboratory, school, or research organization with which they are affiliated.

Collecting, evaluating, and selecting information resources for the biological sciences is a complex process. The specialization of scientific information requires e-resource collectors to either have some subject expertise or to have access to someone else who has subject expertise. The need for some subject expertise in collecting biological sciences e-resources are no different in this respect. Nonsubject specialists will want to consult with subject specialists in the process of collecting, evaluating, and selecting biological sciences e-resources.

In May and August 2008, librarians were surveyed to elicit which biological sciences (excluding medical specific biological reference tools) reference tools they consider to be core or essential to their work. The discussion lists and blogs where the survey links were posted are listed in Table 9.1. The core biological sciences reference tools survey is reproduced in Table 9.2.

Table 9.1. Discussion Lists and Blogs Distribution for Biological Sciences Reference Tools Survey

- eldnet-l@u.washington.edu
- LIS-SCITECH@jiscmail.ac.uk
- sts-l@ala.org
- LISNews and LISNewsWire Blogs: lisnews-owner@lishost.net
- ResourceShelf Blog: gary.price@resourceshelf.com
- ERIL-L@LISTSERV.BINGHAMTON.EDU
- dig_ref@LISTSERV.SYR.EDU

- collib-l@ala.org
- LIS-LINK@jiscmail.ac.uk
- Libref-L@listserv.kent.edu
- GOVDOC-L@lists.psu.edu
- publib@webjunction.org
- livereference@yahoogroups.com
- Libref-L@listserv.kent.edu

Table 9.2. Core Biological Sciences Reference Tools Survey Questions

1. Which library type best describes the library you work in/for/with?

2. In which subject area(s) are you most likely to answer biosciences (nonmedical) questions? (Check all that apply.)

3. What are the essential three print titles (reference books) that you can't work without in answering biosciences (nonmedical) questions? (Please type the title only.)

4. What are the essential three free (not government published) Web-accessible databases that you can't work without in answering biosciences (nonmedical) questions? (Please type complete URL/Web address; e.g., www.intute.ac.uk/healthandlifesciences/bioresearch.)

5. What are the essential three (.gov) government published (state, federal, local, international) free Web-accessible databases that you can't work without in answering biosciences (nonmedical) questions? (Please type complete URL/Web address; e.g., agricola.nal.usda.gov.)

6. What are the essential three fee-based Web-accessible databases that you can't work without in answering biosciences (nonmedical) questions? (Please type the simple title; e.g., Biosis.)

7. Does your library maintain a Web page or site to support biosciences (nonmedical) reference? If so please share the URL/Web address (e.g., http://library.austincc.edu/w3/bio/).

8. Additional comments or ideas:

(Please include your name and e-mail address if you would like feedback, otherwise this survey form is completely anonymous.)

The Core Web Biological Sciences Reference Collection on the companion Web Site (www.kovacs.com/ns/essentialguide.html) was initially created using the survey results from these surveys along with results from similar earlier surveys (the most recent were collected in 2005 and 2006) as core and model collections. Past, present, and future surveys and results are posted at www.kovacs.com/misc.html. This collection is intended for librarians to use as a source of e-resources they might select for their biological sciences reference e-library collections.

As with the other subject areas we queried about, the print biological sciences reference tools reported were much fewer than previous surveys. Table 9.3 lists the top three print biological sciences reference tools identified in the survey. The free Web sites that librarians reported as core or essential for biological sciences reference are given in Table 9.4.

E-docs sites that support biological sciences reference were clear favorites. The top biological sciences e-docs reference sites are listed in Table 9.5.

Fee-based biological sciences reference tools are essential for biological sciences reference in most academic and research libraries. The top five fee-based biological sciences reference e-resources are reported in Table 9.6.

The Core Web Biological Sciences Reference Collection on the companion Web Site (www.kovacs.com/ns/essentialguide.html) consists primarily of general biological science reference tools and search tools and meta sites that may be used by librarians as a foundation for a collection of information in general biological science fields and common specialties. Emphasis in this core Web reference collection is on free e-resources. Most of them are free of direct cost. Some have special fee-based products or services. Fee-based e-resources are included when they offer free trials or have some information available without requiring a fee.

Table 9.3. Top Three Print Biological Sciences Reference Tools Identified in Survey

1. *Grzimeks Animal Life Encyclopedia*
2. *Encyclopedia of Life Sciences* (print and online)
3. *Bergey's Manual of Systematic Bacteriology; Encyclopedia of Biological Chemistry; Encyclopedia of Evolution* (Oxford University Press); *Oxford Dictionary of Biochemistry and Molecular Biology; Scientific Style and Format: The CSE Manual for Authors, Editors, and Publishers; Synopsis and Classification of Living Organisms*

Note: Several titles tied for third place.

Table 9.4. Top Two Free Web Biological Sciences Reference Tools Identified in Survey

1. INFOMINE (biological, agricultural, and medical): http://infomine.ucr.edu/cgi-bin/search?bioag, Intute: www.intute.ac.uk/healthandlifesciences, Tree of Life: http://tolweb.org/tree
2. Amino Acid Information: http://prowl.rockefeller.edu/aainfo/contents.htm, Arkiv: www.arkive.org, Biopharmaceutical Glossary: www.genomicglossaries.com, Canadian Biodiversity Web Site: http://canadianbiodiversity.mcgill.ca/english/index.htm, EarthTrends: http://earthtrends.wri.org, WWW Virtual Library: Biosciences: http://vlib.org/Biosciences

Note: Multiple titles tied for first and second places.

Table 9.5. Top Two Government Documents Web Sites Used as Biological Sciences Reference Tools Identified in Survey

1. USDA Plants Database: http://plants.usda.gov, Canadian Biodiversity Information Network (CBIN): www.cbin.ec.gc.ca/index.cfm?lang=e

2. Carbon Dioxide Information Analysis Center: http://cdiac.esd.ornl.gov, Computational Molecular Biology At NIH: http://molbio.info.nih.gov/desk.html, National Agricultural Library Catalog: http://agricola.nal.usda.gov, National Agricultural Statistics Service: www.nass.usda.gov/index.asp, National Biological Information Infrastructure: www.nbii.gov, NCBI (National Center for Biotechnology Information): www.ncbi.nlm.nih.gov, Stem Cell Information: http://stemcells.nih.gov/info, U.S. Fish and Wildlife Service: www.fws.gov/endangered/wildlife.html, U.S. Geological Survey: www.usgs.gov

Note: Multiple titles tied for first and second places.

Table 9.6. Top Three Fee-based Biological Sciences Reference E-Resources Identified in Survey

1. Biosis Previews (Thomson-Reuters): www.thomsonreuters.com/products_services/scientific/BIOSIS_Previews

2. Web of Science: www.thomsonreuters.com/products_services/scientific/Web_of_Science

3. CSA Biological Sciences Database (ProQuest): www.csa.com/factsheets/biolclust-set-c.php, Environment Complete (EBSCOhost): www.ebscohost.com/thisTopic.php?topicID=623&marketID=1, Geobase: www.elsevier.com/wps/find/bibliographicdatabasedescription.cws_home/422597/description#description, SciFinder Scholar: www.cas.org/SCIFINDER/SCHOLAR/, Zoological Record: www.thomsonreuters.com/products_services/scientific/Zoological_Record

Note: Several titles tied for third place.

E-LIBRARY SUCCESS STORY

OSF SAINT FRANCIS MEDICAL CENTER LIBRARY AND RESOURCE CENTER

Peoria, Illinois, United States

http://library.osfhealthcare.org

Contacts: Royden Jones, Royden.R.Jones@osfhealthcare.org, and Ann Phillips, Ann.Phillips@osfhealthcare.org

A. Collection Planning (e.g., goal setting and identification of users, technology/personnel choices)

The OSF Saint Francis Medical Center Library and Resource Center E-Library was one of the first online in the mid-1990s. "Carol Galganski, former library manager, conceived and implemented the original basic intranet e-collection in the mid-1990s. From that point on, it has evolved slowly but steadily." The e-library collection was created with very practical and clear intentions. The core users are the OSF Saint Francis Medical Center medical staff and residents and employees.

This is a clinical library rather than an academic library, but some support is provided for students in hospital-supported educational programs (Saint Francis Medical Center College of Nursing, Dietetic Internship Program, and School of Clinical Laboratory Science), and OSF Healthcare System facilities. "Students of the University of Illinois College of Medicine at Peoria

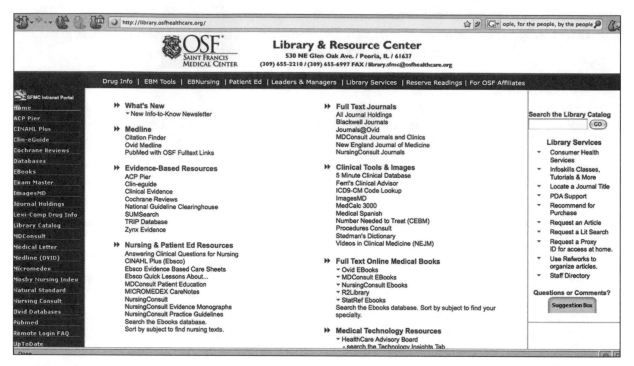

Figure 9.1. OSF Saint Francis Medical Center Library and Resource Center

are served since many are affiliated with the medical center as interns, residents, or fellows. The Saint Francis Medical Center College of Nursing, Dietetic Internship Program, and School of Clinical Laboratory Science are also supported, but they are relatively small. The library is considered a hospital library, a type of special library."

The e-library does not directly support distance learning programs. "The Saint Francis College of Nursing Library, which is a separate unit within OSF Saint Francis Medical Center, supports distance learners using the eCollege eLearning System." A written collection development policy was created and continuously updated from the beginning of the e-library project. A copy is available at www.kovacs.com/studentwork/colldevplans.html login: colldev password: kovacs08.

B. Collection Strategies (e.g., selection criteria, identification of resources, licensing, and related user information needs)

E-resources are selected for their appropriateness and value to the core library users. Cost is also an important consideration as well as accessibility. "e-Licensing varies depending on whether the resource in question was purchased only for use at OSF SFMC or for use by OSF Healthcare (i.e. corporate-wide at all 7 acute care facilities.) Likewise, some items are funded by the OSF SFMC budget, others by the OSF Corporate IS Budget."

The e-library includes a core collection of e-books, chosen for their specific value to medical professionals. "The e-Book collection includes approximately 400 titles through 4 different providers. All e-Books are accessible from the library homepage. At the bottom right of the middle section of the homepage, under 'Full Text Online Medical Books,' click on 'Search the Ebooks database. Sort by specialty to find your subject.'" This goes to http://library.osfhealthcare .org/eBookList/ebooks.asp, which provides direct links to individual titles. However, access is limited to users accessing from IP validated sites or remotely via our proxyservers. The database is reviewed and updated as needed, but at least monthly, to allow for new editions of e-Books."

All e-books are cataloged with direct links within the bibliographic record so that the searcher can go directly from the OPAC to the e-book. "Additionally, all e-resources, from frequently used public access sites to hospital-generated documents in PDF format to purchased on-line videos (*New England Journal of Medicine*'s Journals in Clinical Medicine" series) are cataloged with direct links within the bibliographic record."

The e-library includes locally produced patient education materials. "The individual hospital departments create the actual documents, which are approved by the Patient Education Committee and then put into PDF format. The documents are reviewed for currency every three years, or sooner if necessary, by the creating department.... At this point the collection is at the maintenance stage. The library manager, Roy Jones, is a member of the Patient Education Committee and in that capacity knows when new patient education material is produced. This new material is added to the Patient Ed section of the library site by the webmaster and is cataloged by the electronic resources cataloger."

Virtual reference services have been tried in the past but were not very successful because most questions asked are complex and not ready reference. E-mail reference and search services are encouraged and well used as are document delivery services. "Document Delivery has become increasingly an electronic function, with requests being made using the 'Request an Article' form under Library Services and being delivered in PDF format to requestors' email accounts. Electronic services seem to work well for both library users and staff, and the use of electronic services seems to be gaining wider acceptance."

C. Collection Organization (e.g., content management systems, Web server choices, personnel responsibilities, etc.)

The OSF Saint Francis Medical Center E-library is hosted on the IS architecture of OSF Healthcare (their corporate parent). "A mix of software is used, Microsoft Sharepoint Software for many items that need to be restricted to OSF SFMC; the public internet site was designed and implemented by Carol Galganski the former manager using a combination of MS Frontpage and XML scripting. I currently work through another department within the Medical Center to update and manage our public website."

At one time, the library actually had a part-time position called a Web librarian. "We no longer have that position and work through another department to complete the loop on Web page management. Qualifications have been a mix of software skills, using front page, xml, sharepoint."

E-library and physical library support is integrated in the work routines of seven library staff members. The library manager is responsible for adding to, updating, and maintaining the library Web page working with IS staff who do the actual modifications ins Frontpage and XML. "There is certainly a difference in how we render services/resources but there is much room for overlap. Staff members float between the strictly traditional world and the virtual world of e-resources."

Collection decisions, identifying, selecting, and evaluating new resources are done by library staff using reviews from professional journals, vendor brochures and presentations, and other similar tools.

D. Collection Maintenance (e.g., link checking, ongoing weeding, and growth of the e-library collection)

Links are checked manually and most, especially e-book titles are reviewed monthly. The overall e-library collection is reviewed as needed. The library manager has responsibility for that review.

"Specific feedback on e-resources is not solicited. Periodically we may solicit feedback on a 'trial' or do an overall user assessment."

Review is as needed. The library manager has had overall responsibility. "I have no plans specifically regarding updating of e-resources as such. The trend is clear, from the print to additional digital tools/resources. We are certainly following the trend. Of particular interest and impact is/are pricing algorithms. Our immediate concern is stability in the funding requirements for e-resources."

REFERENCES AND WEB SITES CITED

Frandsen, Tove Faver. 2009. "The Integration of Open Access Journals in the Scholarly Communication System: Three Science Fields." *Information Processing and Management* 45, no. 1: 131–141.

Hacker, Diane, with Barbara Fister. 2008. *Research and Documentation in the Electronic Age*, 5th edition. Bedford/St. Martin's. Available: www.dianahacker.com/resdoc (accessed January 19, 2009).

Hemminger, Bradley M., Dihui Lu, K. T. D. Vaughan, and Stephanie J. Adams. 2007. "Information Seeking Behavior of Academic Scientists." *Journal of the American Society for Information Science and Technology* 58, no. 14: 2205–2225.

Kuruppu, Pali U., and Anne Marie Gruber. 2006. "Understanding the Information Needs of Academic Scholars in Agricultural and Biological Sciences." *Journal of Academic Librarianship* 32, no. 6: 609–623.

Laake, Petter, Haakon Breien Benestad, and Bjorn Reino Olsen. 2007. *Research Methodology in the Medical and Biological Sciences*. New York: Academic Press.

WEB SITES CITED

AGRICOLA (National Agricultural Library Catalog). Available: http://agricola.nal.usda.gov (accessed January 7, 2009).

Agriculture Network Information Center (AgNIC). Available: www.agnic.org (accessed January 7, 2009).

The American Institute of Biological Sciences. Available: http://www.aibs.org/core (accessed January 7, 2009).

Biological and Agricultural Index. Available: www.hwwilson.com (accessed January 14, 2009).

BIOSIS Preview/Biological Abstracts. Available: www.thomsonreuters.com/products_services/scientific/BIOSIS_Previews (accessed January 14, 2009).

Envirolink. Available: www.envirolink.org (accessed January 7, 2009).

Google. Available: www.google.com (accessed January 14, 2009).

INFOMINE: Biological, Agricultural & Medical Sciences Collection. Available: http://infomine.ucr.edu/cgi-bin/search?category=bioag (accessed January 7, 2009).

Intute: Health and Life Sciences. Available: www.intute.ac.uk/healthandlifesciences (accessed January 7, 2009).

National Biological Information Infrastructure. Available: www.nbii.gov (accessed January 7, 2009).

Open Directory Project Science Dictionaries. Available: www.dmoz.org/Reference/Dictionaries/By_Subject/Science (accessed January 7, 2009).

PLoS: Public Library of Science. Available: www.plos.org (accessed January 19, 2009).

BIOLOGICAL SCIENCES E-RESOURCE COLLECTION TOOLS

META SITES

Agriculture Network Information Center (AgNIC)
www.agnic.org

"Guide to quality agricultural information on the Internet as selected by the National Agricultural Library, Land-Grant Universities, and other institutions."

Biology Links from Harvard University's Department of Molecular and Cellular Biology
http://mcb.harvard.edu/Biolinks.html

Collection of biological sciences Web sites intended for students and researchers.

Envirolink
www.envirolink.org

Extensive links to environmental sites along with a chat room and job center.

INFOMINE: Biological, Agricultural and Medical Sciences Collection
http://infomine.ucr.edu/cgi-bin/search?category=bioag

Large annotated collection of Internet resources related to biology, agriculture, and medicine. Resources are selected and evaluated to ensure they are a scholarly information resource suitable for research or educational activities at the postsecondary educational levels.

Internet Directory for Botany
www.ou.edu/cas/botany-micro/idb-alpha/botany.html

Collection of Web sites relevant to the teaching and learning of Botany. Maintained by Anthony R. Brach (www.people.fas.harvard.edu/~brach).

Intute: Health and Life Sciences
www.intute.ac.uk/healthandlifesciences

Intute is a multisubject e-library maintained by a consortium of United Kingdom university and academic organization Library partners (www.intute.ac.uk/healthandlifesciences/partners.html) who carefully select and evaluate all the health and life sciences e-resources that are open source or otherwise freely available on the Web. Pieces of it were previously known as BIOME, OMNI, VETGATE, BIORES, AGRIFOR, and other smaller databases. Although hosted in the UK, the scope of these collections is international. The scope of the Health and Life Sciences collection includes medicine, nursing, and allied health fields, bioethics, media and the sciences, veterinary medicine, midwifery, agriculture and forestry, history of medicine, and other fields. The collection is searchable and browseable.

Iowa State Entomology Index of Internet Resources
www.ent.iastate.edu/LIST/?

Collection of Web sites to serve the study of entomology and related subject areas.

SciCentral
http://scicentral.com

This searchable metadatabase includes all areas of science and their subcategories with directories, research, and latest news.

Science.gov (was Catalog of U.S. Government Science and Technology Web Site Resources)
www.science.gov

Collection of U.S. Government sponsored or funded science and technology sites. This collection is collected for scientists, engineers, and "science aware" citizens and serves as a gateway to a huge amount of scientific information produced by U.S. federal and state agencies. It is not comprehensive, but it attempts to cover most scientific topics. Agencies and sites that it lists or searches include:

AGRICOLA (http://agricola.nal.usda.gov), STINET (http://stinet.dtic.mil), NASA Technical Reports Server (http://ntrs.nasa.gov), NTIS (National Technical Information Service; www.ntis.gov).

WWW Virtual Library: Biosciences
http://vlib.org/Biosciences
>Collection of biosciences related Web sites.

Digital Libraries Directories or Collections of Digital Libraries (Digital Libraries of E-Books, E-Serials, Images, Recordings, and Other Artifacts)

Biodiversity Collections Index
www.biodiversitycollectionsindex.org/static/index.html
>Searchable index to digital libraries of biodiversity data, documents, images, etc.

Bioimages
www.cas.vanderbilt.edu/bioimages/frame.htm
>This is a collection of digital libraries of digital images with a single search and display interface. The content are mainly photographs of different plants and animals in different specific ecosystems.

DTICs Scientific and Technical Resources
www.dtic.mil/dtic/stresources
>Defense Technical Information Center searchable collection of scientific and technical reports, statistics, etc. Biological, medical, environmental, social science, behavioral, as well as engineering and physical sciences related information is available. Search access level depends on registration. Much information is freely available to the public.

E-Serials, Blogs, Discussion Lists, etc.

BIOSCI Electronic Newsgroup Network for Biology
www.bio.net
>This is a collection of discussion lists, blogs, RSS feeds, etc.

NHC
www.lib.washington.edu/sla
>Discussion list for librarians who are members of the Special Libraries Association, Natural History Caucus.

SLA-DBIO
www.sla.org/content/community/lists/divisionlists5979.cfm or www.sla.org/content/community/lists/joinlists.cfm
>Discussion list for librarians who are members of the Special Libraries Association, Biomedical and Life Sciences Division.

STS-L
http://lists.ala.org/sympa/info/sts-l
>Discussion of science and technology librarianship. Hosted by the American Library Association, Association of College and Research Libraries, Science and Technology Libraries Section.

10

ENGINEERING, COMPUTER SCIENCES, MATHEMATICS, AND RELATED E-RESOURCES

The results of this study showed a close correspondence between the materials indexed by Google Scholar with those included in the Compendex database from the 1990s to the present. There may be differences in the richness of the record content between the services, but this might not be a barrier to positive search results for users at a certain level. Undergraduate engineering studies revolve around acquiring skills in mathematics, concepts in engineering and the physical sciences, and problem solving—literature searching is not a required part of many courses. Google Scholar seems well suited to undergraduate assignments and research projects that call for the identification of a modest group of recent publications. Google Scholar can be promoted to students as a gateway tool for accessing the engineering literature, in tandem with presenting Compendex as a comprehensive backup to be consulted if they cannot locate enough relevant information. Students are already familiar with the Google search interface and the simplicity that it offers. The jump from Google to Google Scholar may also be conceptually easier to grasp than the jump from Google to Compendex, INSPEC, and similar databases. The easy-to-use interface of Google Scholar also has appeal for individuals with more advanced information needs such as graduate students, faculty, and research staff. However, these users might benefit more by doing their primary searching on Compendex and similar databases with a known scope of indexed materials and better retrospective coverage. These users could find that supplemental searches done on Google Scholar would uncover useful references falling outside of the normal coverage of the commercial tools. (Meier and Conkling, 2008: 200–201)

DEVELOPING A COLLECTION PLAN FOR ENGINEERING, COMPUTER SCIENCES, AND MATHEMATICS E-RESOURCES

Resources that support scientific study and education in the fields of engineering, computer sciences, and mathematics were some of the first to be developed as fee-based e-resources as well as multiple resources published freely through the Web. Specifically, computer scientists built the Internet and its precursors and used it for communicating, sharing, and publishing their research. Engineering is not a science but rather a professional discipline that applies technology and scientific knowledge to processes of designing and building. Civil engineers design and build bridges, roads, sewers, damns, and other aspects of our infrastructure. Other kinds of engineering include aeronautical, chemical/biochemical, computer, electrical, geophysical, mechanical, electrical, and the related and subfields of each of those areas. Computer science involves many specializations as well and has both theoretical and applied aspects. Some computer science subfields include database structures, algorithms, programming, programming language theory, software engineering, Web development, or computational theory, etc. Just about every scientific field and profession makes use of mathematics, and many have an engineering aspect or make use of computer sciences. For example, engineers use calculus and computer scientists use statistical formulae in their work. Researchers in every subject area may need to make use of mathematical reference tools. Computer scientists and engineers often work in partnership with other scientists, e.g., with social scientists in the area of human–computer interaction or with biologists in the area of bioengineering. The interdisciplinary nature of engineering, computer sciences, and mathematics will inform the selection process and the e-resources you choose to support a given area.

WHAT PURPOSE WILL YOUR COLLECTION SERVE? FOR WHOM ARE YOU COLLECTING THESE E-RESOURCES?

Engineers and computer scientists particularly make use of reference tools that are used to look up mathematical formulae, rules for coding, and other facts that are used to build on ongoing research and practical projects. E-journals and e-books especially have been well received by library users in these areas. The ability to have access wherever and whenever one is working is an asset to the engineer or computer programmer on the job or student in a laboratory working on a class or research project (Cleto, 2008; Buczynski, 2006; Morris and Larson, 2006). "Generally, reference materials and monographs, particularly in the Science, Technology and Medicine (STM) fields, are most amenable to eBook collections. STM users tend to be more familiar with online research than those of other disciplines, and their research styles expose the advantages of eBooks very quickly" (Cleto, 2008: 47).

As with the other types of scientific information discussed in previous and subsequent chapters, users of physical scientific information will most likely be students of various ages and educational attainment and researchers both academic and professional. Computer science and mathematical information may be also be needed by consumers or by professionals (engineers, medical professionals, architects, or computing professionals). Special libraries serving engineering, computer sciences, and mathematics professionals and researchers will need to acquire e-resources that provide depth of coverage in a specific area of scientific or technological information. For example, they may need to collect resources for manufacturing engineering, environmental engineering, or computer engineering, and so on. Academic libraries may need to cover a broad range of engineering, computer sciences, and mathematics topics for undergraduate and graduate students and also to cover specific subtopics in-depth for researchers working in their parent institutions. Public libraries may need to serve K–12 students or even to support the businesses or government agencies in their community. For example, the Cleveland Public Library supports their communities of sciences and technology information needs through their Science and Technology Subject Department and Links e-library (www.cpl.org/LinksLibrary.asp?FormMode=SDCategory&ID=12). Each library should be aware of which scientific subject areas they support for researchers and students in their parent organizations or library user communities.

WHAT TYPES OF E-RESOURCES WILL YOU COLLECT?

Observation, discussion list monitoring, and review of e-library collections on the Web as well as of the results of the core reference surveys reported in this chapter show that Compendex, INSPEC, IEEE Xplore, Knovel, and Web of Science databases are the core reference tools used by librarians for engineering and related physical sciences and technologies. These are all a kind of fee-based meta site in their current embodiment as Web-accessible resources. Beyond these core commercial tools, there are also free Web resources that may be useful.

The quote that introduces this chapter is from "Google Scholar's Coverage of the Engineering Literature: An Empirical Study," a study by Meier and Conkling (2008). Their study found that Google Scholar, a free Web resource, is an effective and useful indexing and abstracting tool for literature in engineering and related physical sciences. For some libraries, Google Scholar provides sufficient coverage for their users information needs in engineer, computer sciences, and mathematics. Other e-resources also follow the general reference tool types used as a model in previous chapters:

- Directories (of engineers, computer scientists, mathematicians, and engineering, computer sciences and mathematics organizations, projects, etc.)
- Dictionaries (engineering, computer sciences, and mathematics vocabulary in English as well as international language translation dictionaries)
- Abstracts, indexes, and table of contents services (including those with full-text of engineering, computer sciences, or mathematics journals indexed)
- Encyclopedias and almanacs
- Full-text and/or multimedia databases/digital libraries (collections of e-books, e-serials, recordings, videos, podcasts, images, etc.)
- News and news services (engineering, computer sciences, and mathematics current awareness sources)
- Key primary documents (research data and reports, statistical sources, etc.)
- Search engines
- Meta sites (e-resources that provide two or more of the other reference tool types in a single product/Web site)

Directories of engineers, computer scientists, and mathematicians and of engineering, computer sciences, and mathematics organizations, projects, etc. exist for every field and subfield. The Open Directory Project (www.dmoz.org/Science/Directories) and the Internet Public Library (www.ipl.org/div/aon/browse/sci00.00.00) both provide directories of directories of science and technology associations, scientists, organizations, and projects.

The ChemIDplus Advance (http://chem.sis.nlm.nih.gov/chemidplus) chemical dictionary and structure database maintained by the U.S. National Library of Medicine was selected as a core physical and earth sciences reference tool. As with other areas of scientific endeavor, engineer, computer sciences, and mathematics dictionaries, glossaries, and other vocabulary guides abound. Again, the Open Directory Project collects appropriate dictionaries freely available on the Web (www.dmoz.org/Reference/Dictionaries/By_Subject/Science). The Internet Public Library also maintains a collection of Calculation and Conversion Tools (www.ipl.org/div/subject/browse/ref19.00.00) that will be invaluable library users in these fields.

Many engineering, computer sciences, or mathematics journals are indexed and abstracted in the core fee-based reference tools cited earlier. Other options are available for searching for bibliographic information in addition to using Google Scholar. Three good examples are the

ACM Guide to Computing Literature (http://portal.acm.org/guide.cfm), which provides a searchable index to computer science articles from multiple publishers; the Civil Engineering Database (http://cedb.asce.org), an index to all publications of the American Society of Civil Engineers (ASCE); and MathSciNet (www.ams.org/mathscinet), which is the American Mathematical society index to reviews in mathematics sciences journals. Some free searching is available on all three sites, although full searching and access to full text are fee-based.

Encyclopedia-like e-resources for engineering etc. are available in both fee-based and free Web incarnations. Two examples, intended for K–12 students, are How Stuff Works (www.howstuffworks.com) and MathWorld (http://mathworld.wolfram.com). Engineering, computer sciences, and mathematics current awareness sources are available from most of their major professional societies. Full-text, digital libraries and key primary documents tend to be part of the same e-resources in these fields. The arXiv.org (Cornell University Library) (http://arxiv.org) collection is open access to more than half a million e-prints in areas that include mathematics, computer science, quantitative biology, and statistics. A majority of key primary documents (research data and reports, statistical sources, etc.) for engineering, computer sciences, and mathematics come from e-docs sites. Begin with the Science.gov's (was Catalog of U.S. Government Science and Technology Web Site Resources) (www.science.gov) comprehensive collection of U.S. Government sponsored or funded science and technology sites. This collection is collected for scientists, engineers, and "science aware" citizens and serves as a gateway to a huge amount of scientific information produced by U.S. Federal and state agencies. Meta sites are listed in the collection tools section later in this chapter.

HOW WILL YOU ORGANIZE YOUR E-RESOURCES?

Given the numerous subfields that make up the overall subject area of engineering and the inter-disciplinary nature of engineering, computer sciences, and mathematics, e-resources might be effectively organized by main field and then by subfields and specialties. They might also be organized under another specific subject area entirely. Some thought may be given to organizing the resources by level of education as well as by subject area. For example, different resources might be more suitable for undergraduates or for advanced researchers. E-resources for engineering, computer sciences, and mathematics (applied or practical aspects) present some unique issues for organization of e-resources. Perhaps beginning with a division between practical and theoretical resources would be useful and then organizing by reference type Reference e-books in these areas are very popular. As stated previously, being able to implement a CMS to organize and access records allows for more usability. Given a high quality CMS software and good programming, any kind of desirable organization can be achieved.

IDENTIFYING AND COLLECTING ENGINEERING, COMPUTER SCIENCES, AND MATHEMATICS E-RESOURCES

WEB SITES THAT REVIEW AND EVALUATE E-RESOURCES: PEER E-LIBRARIES, SUBJECT COLLECTIONS/GUIDES, OR META SITES

At this time, the best meta site for engineering, computer science, and mathematics related Web sites is Intute: Science, Engineering and Technology (www.intute.ac.uk/sciences). Intute is a multi-subject e-library maintained by a consortium of United Kingdom university and academic organization library partners who carefully select and evaluate all the science, engineering, and technology e-resources that are open source or otherwise freely available on the Web. This includes an e-journals search engine (www.intute.ac.uk/sciences/ejournals.html). Subject coverage includes engineering and mathematics and incorporates the contents of the original EEVL database that was included in the previous edition of this book.

INFOMINE: Physical Sciences, Engineering, Computing and Math Directory (http:// infomine.ucr.edu/cgi-bin/search?category=physci) selectively compiles e-resources in multiple areas of engineering and the computer sciences as well. The selection process and the annotations make these sites very useful as collection tools. The Applied Math and Science Education Repository (AMSER) (http://amser.org) project is a collection designed for upper level secondary school and community college math and sciences educators to use to find resources for those students.

DISCUSSION LISTS (LISTSERV, ETC.), FORUMS/GROUPS, E-SERIALS, AND/OR BLOGS THAT POST OR PUBLISH REVIEWS AND EVALUATIONS OF E-RESOURCES

Several discussion lists post reviews or recommendations for engineering, computer sciences, and mathematics e-resources in libraries. ELD-L and ELDNET-L are hosted by the Engineering Libraries Division of the American Society of Engineering Education. STS-L is the ACRL discussion of science and technical librarianship. SLA-DST, SLA-AERO, and SLA-DENG are discussion lists for librarians who are members of the Special Libraries Association Science and Technology, Aerospace, or Engineering Divisions.

Issues in Science and Technology Librarianship (www.library.ucsb.edu/istl) publishes reviews of e-resources for engineering, computer science, and mathematics e-resources in a quarterly e-serial. For additional useful titles use the Intute e-journals search engine (www.intute .ac.uk/sciences/ejournals.html) or identify additional scholarly e-journals for the computer science, engineering, etc., by searching CiteSeerx Scientific Literature Digital Library (http://cite seer.ist.psu.edu) or any of the other meta sites listed in the core tools section at the end of this chapter.

Engineering librarians in particular have begun blogs that include or even focus primarily on Web sites for the physical sciences and engineering fields. John Dupuis edits Confessions of a Science Librarian (http://jdupuis.blogspot.com). Randy Reichardt edits The SciTech Library Question (http://stlq.info). All of these blogs includes Web and other resource reviews and pointers as well as news and discussion for the international community of academic engineering, computer sciences, and mathematics and engineering librarians.

PRINT BOOKS AND JOURNALS THAT REVIEW E-RESOURCES

Books that teach research skills in these areas will also include appropriate e-resources. For example, the classic *The MIT Guide to Science and Engineering Communication* (Paradis and Zimmerman, 2002) focuses heavily on the e-resources and Web communications tools used most by engineers and physical scientists. All journals that serve engineers and computer scientists and those with related interests review e-resources in the same areas in which they review print books. Use Applied Science and Technology Abstracts Full Text (www.hwwilson.com/ Databases/applieds.htm) or the ACM Digital Library Journals Portal (http://portal.acm.org/ dl.cfm) to identify appropriate journals. Most of these are actually born digital but have a print option. For mathematics print and e-journals, the MathSciNet (www.ams.org/mathscinet) database will be useful.

EVALUATION GUIDELINES AND SELECTION CRITERIA: THE CORE WEB ENGINEERING, COMPUTER SCIENCES, AND MATHEMATICS REFERENCE COLLECTION

The key criteria for evaluating engineering, computer sciences, and mathematics e-resources is to determine the source of the data, the research and statistical methodologies used in collecting the information, and the authority of the information provider. In these subject areas credibility of information is often difficult for the nonengineer/computer scientist to evaluate, especially information provided at the research or higher-education levels. Each field of engineering has its own particular vocabulary and accepted research methodologies. Engineering and computer sciences in particular use mathematical and symbolic notations or computer languages that are not easily interpreted by someone without specific subject knowledge. It will be more difficult to judge the information content without consulting a subject specialist. At the K–12 educational level, or with materials provided specifically for the nonspecialist, it will be important to verify that the information provider has the authority, including educational attainment and research experience, to write on a particular topic. It will also be important to determine if the information provider has experience in teaching K–12 level scientific subjects.

The critical element in efficiently selecting engineering, computer science, and mathematics related e-resources is to focus on the area and data interests of your library user community. This is highly dependent on the exact area of engineering (e.g., civil, geophysical, electrical, computer or computer science, database structures, algorithms, programming, software engineering, Web development, etc.) or mathematics (theoretical, practical, etc.) for which you are collecting resources. Initial selection criteria must also include the educational or complexity level required by those library users. For example, ceramics or materials engineering research scientists studying the properties of ceramics used in heat shielding on the space shuttle will need very different materials from the high school or undergraduate students studying model bridge building materials.

In May and August 2008, librarians were surveyed to elicit which engineering, computer science, and mathematics reference tools they consider to be core or essential to their work. Separate surveys were sent for engineering and for computer sciences and mathematics, but given lower than hoped for response rates and significant overlap, the results were pooled into a single report. The Core Web Engineering, Computer science, and Mathematics Reference Collection on the companion Web Site (www.kovacs.com/ns/essentialguide.html) was initially created using the survey results from these surveys along with results from similar earlier surveys (the most recent were collected in 2005 and 2006) as core and model collections. Past, present, and future surveys and results are posted at www.kovacs.com/misc.html. This collection is intended for librarians to use as a source of e-resources they might select for their engineering, computer science, and mathematics reference e-library collections.

The discussion lists and blogs where the survey links were posted are listed in Table 10.1. The core engineering, computer science, and mathematics reference tools survey is reproduced in Table 10.2.

Print engineering, computer science, and mathematics reference tools remain important, although several respondents noted that they prefer the e-book versions. Table 10.3 lists the top five print engineering, computer science, and mathematics reference tools identified in the survey. The free Web sites that librarians reported as core or essential for engineering, computer science, and mathematics reference are given in Table 10.4.

Table 10.1. Discussion Lists and Blogs Distribution for Engineering, Computer Science, and Mathematics Reference Tools Survey

- eldnet-l@u.washington.edu
- LIS-SCITECH@jiscmail.ac.uk
- sts-l@ala.org
- LISNews and LISNewsWire Blogs: lisnews-owner@lishost.net
- ResourceShelf Blog: gary.price@resourceshelf.com
- ERIL-L@LISTSERV.BINGHAMTON.EDU
- dig_ref@LISTSERV.SYR.EDU
- collib-l@ala.org
- LIS-LINK@jiscmail.ac.uk
- Libref-L@listserv.kent.edu
- GOVDOC-L@lists.psu.edu
- publib@webjunction.org
- livereference@yahoogroups.com
- Libref-L@listserv.kent.edu

Table 10.2. Core Engineering, Computer Science, and Mathematics Reference Tools Survey Questions

1. Which library type best describes the library you work in/for/with?

2. What are the essential print titles for engineering, etc. reference that you can't work without? (Please type the titles only. List up to three.)

3. What are the essential three free (not government published) Web-accessible engineering related Web sites that you can't work without? (Please type complete URL/Web address; e.g., www.intute.ac.uk/sciences/engineering.)

4. What are the essential three (.gov) government published (state, federal, local, international) free Web-accessible engineering reference tools that you can't work without? (Please type complete URL/Web address; e.g., www.itl.nist.gov/div898/handbook.)

5. What are the essential three fee-based Web-accessible engineering related databases that you can't work without? (Please type the simple title; e.g., Compendex.)

6. Does your library maintain a Web page or site to support engineering reference? If so, please share the URL/Web address (e.g., www.engrlib.uc.edu/resources/resources.html).

7. Additional comments or ideas:

(Please include your name and e-mail address if you would like feedback, otherwise this survey form is completely anonymous.)

Note: A separate similar survey was sent out for computer science and mathematics specifically and data was merged with the engineering survey.

Table 10.3. Top Five Print Engineering, Computer Science, and Mathematics Reference Tools Identified in Survey

1. Engineering handbooks (specific handbooks formetals, materials, mechanical, electrical, civil, etc.)

2. *Annual Book of ASTM Standards, Encyclopedia of Computer Science* (Ralston)

3. AWWA Standards Books: www.awwa.org/Bookstore/producttopicsresults.cfm?MetaDataID=87&navItemNumber=1496, *Encyclopedia of Mathematics/Encyclopedic Dictionary of Mathematics*

4. *Kirk-Othmer Encyclopedia of Chemical Technology, McGraw-Hill Encyclopedia of Science & Technology*

5. *Using the Engineering Literature* (Routledge Studies in Library and Information Science)

E-docs sites that support engineering, computer science, and mathematics reference were clear favorites. The top five engineering, computer science, and mathematics e-docs reference sites are listed in Table 10.5.

Fee-based engineering, computer science, and mathematics reference tools are essential for engineering, computer science, and mathematics reference in most academic and research libraries. The top five fee-based engineering, computer science, and mathematics reference e-resources are reported in Table 10.6.

Table 10.4. Top Three Free Web Engineering, Computer Science, and Mathematics Reference Tools Identified in Survey

1. Intute: Science, Engineering and Technology: www.intute.ac.uk/sciences
2. ACM Guide to Computing Literature: http://portal.acm.org/guide.cfm, Mathweb: www.mathweb.org
3. Civil Engineering Database: http://cedb.asce.org

Table 10.5. Top Five Government Documents Web Sites Used as Engineering, Computer Science, and Mathematics Reference Tools Identified in Survey

1. National Technical Information Service (NTIS): www.ntis.gov/search.htm
2. U.S. Patent and Trademark Office: www.uspto.gov
3. Science.gov: www.science.gov
4. Energy Information Administration: www.eia.doe.gov
5. Office of Science and Technical Information: www.osti.gov

Table 10.6. Top Five Fee-based Engineering, Computer Science, and Mathematics Reference E-Resources Identified in Survey

1. Compendex: www.ei.org/databases/compendex.html
2. INSPEC: www.theiet.org/publishing
3. IEEE Xplore: http://ieeexplore.ieee.org/Xplore/guesthome.jsp
4. ACM Digital Library: http://portal.acm.org/dl.cfm
5. Knovel: www.knovel.com/, Web of Science:
   http://thomsonreuters.com/products_services/scientific/Web_of_Science

---

These results are used as a basis for The Core Web Engineering, Computer Science, and Mathematics Reference Collection on the companion Web Site (www.kovacs.com/ns/essential guide.html), but only a few of the core or essential engineering, computer science, and mathematics e-resources identified are found freely available on the Web. The intended library user group is librarians who work with library users who might be interested in ready-reference engineering, computer science, or mathematics research information at a high level secondary through a higher level postsecondary school educational level. Some of these sites do offer special instructional or graphics software for download. Most of those included in this collection were selected because they are free of direct cost with some also offering fee-based services. Fee-based e-resources are included when they offer free trials or have some information available without requiring a fee.

E-Library Success Story

Intute: Science, Engineering, and Technology
The University of Manchester, John Rylands University Library
and Heriot-Watt University Library
United Kingdom
www.intute.ac.uk/sciences/engineering
Contact: Linda Kerr, L.Kerr@hw.ac.uk

A. Collection Planning (e.g., goal setting and identification of users, technology/personnel choices)

The Intute project is the convergence of over a decade of e-library collections projects in the United Kingdom. "Intute Science, Engineering and Technology was launched in 2006. Intute itself (www.intute.ac.uk) is a JISC-funded service created by bringing together 7 JISC services to form a single unified service. Intute: SET was formed by merging EEVL (Engineering, Mathematics and Computing), GEsource (Geography and Environment), and PSIgate (Physical Sciences). EEVL was established in 1996, PSIgate in 2001 and GEsource in 2003."

The goal of the Intute service is to provide access to the best quality Web resources for use in higher education by students, faculty, and researchers in the United Kingdom's universities. "The service has recently focused itself on the needs of UK under-graduates. The service also provides internet information skills training through the VTS service. Other people can use it but our primary audience is undergraduates in the UK. Practitioners, e.g. nurses, are also a market (for the Health and Life Sciences service)."

The Intute site is open for access by anyone around the world who may find the resources useful. Although they do not support any specific distance learning programs the collection does include resources that will be of use to distance learners and teachers. A written collection development policy was created and is maintained at www.intute.ac.uk/policy.html.

B. Collection Strategies (e.g., selection criteria, identification of resources, licensing, and related user information needs)

All criteria for resources collected are detailed in the collection development policy (www.intute.ac.uk/policy.html). Resources must either be freely available on the Web or fee-based but accessible to and through United Kingdom's University Libraries and therefore accessible to those library users. Intute does not directly license any databases nor does it charge for access to its database. "At the moment we have no plans to charge for access as we feel that would be counter-productive to usage. Also, as the money to run us is supplied from the public purse, we could have ethical concerns in charging UK universities to use the core service."

E-books that are in the public domain or otherwise freely available on the Web are included in the Intute database. All resources included in the Intute collection are "cataloged" in its database. Usage statistics are generated from searches, browses, and click-throughs on the Intute database.

Intute does not have a digitization project, although they do collect links to appropriate digital collection created by other organizations, especially those created and put online by Universities in the United Kingdom. No reference service or document delivery services are provided through Intute.

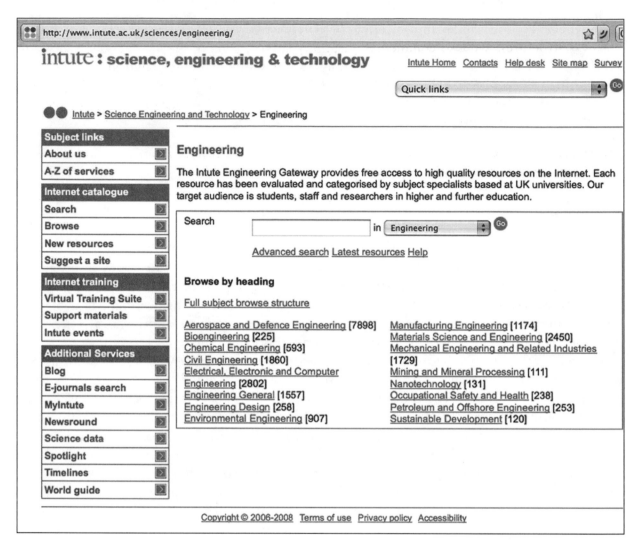

Figure 10.1. Intute: Science, Engineering, and Technology

C. Collection Organization (e.g., content management systems, Web server choices, personnel responsibilities, etc.)

Intute: SET is hosted on a MySQL database maintained by the project. Three and half full-time equivalent people support content and about half full-time equivalent provide management to the project. "We use post-graduate students to create catalogue records. These are trained by the full-time staff, who are librarians by profession. The full-time staff also catalogue records. The responsibilities are divided on a subject basis. Work is carried out every day—either creating new records, blog posts, or reviewing and link-checking records." Collectors use Web resource listing services such as The Scout Report (http://scout.wisc.edu), as well as serendipitous discovery of relevant resources during related Web searches.

D. Collection Maintenance (e.g., link checking, ongoing weeding, and growth of the e-library collection)

Links are checked with link checking software developed by the project as well as using WebSite-Watcher (www.aignes.com) to help manage the collection. Feedback from users is actively solicited. "We conduct user surveys in online 'snap' surveys. We have also conducted a marketing survey recently, and will be implementing the outcomes of this (to refocus to a course-orientated browse structure). We also conducted a usability survey, and will be feeding this information back into the service. We also use Google Analytics (www.google.com/analytics)."

E-library organization is reviewed at intervals throughout the year. Future plans include exploring options for federated searching. A feasibility study is being planned to test Autonomy IDOL Server (www.autonomy.com/content/Products/products-idol-server/index.en.html) for this purpose.

REFERENCES AND WEB SITES CITED

Buczynski, James Andrew. 2006. "Debunking the Computer Science Digital Library: Lessons Learned in Collection Development at Seneca College of Applied Arts & Technology." *The Acquisitions Librarian* 27, no. 35/36: 37–53.

Cleto, Cynthia. 2008. "10 Steps to Implementing an eBook Collection: A Guide for Librarians." *Against the Grain* (February): 47–48.

Meier, John J., and Thomas W. Conkling. 2008. "Google Scholar's Coverage of the Engineering Literature: An Empirical Study." *The Journal of Academic Librarianship* 34, no. 3: 196–201.

Morris, Kathleen, and Betsy Larson. 2006. "Revolution or Revelation? Acquisitions for the Digital Library." *The Acquisitions Librarian* 17, no. 35/36: 97–105.

Paradis, James G., and Muriel L. Zimmerman. 2002. *The MIT Guide to Science and Engineering Communication.* Cambridge, MA: The MIT Press.

WEB SITES CITED

ACM Digital Library (includes ACM Journals Portal and ACM database). Available: http://portal.acm.org/dl.cfm (accessed January 7, 2009).

The Applied Math and Science Education Repository (AMSER). Available: http://amser.org (accessed January 19, 2009).

Applied Science and Technology Abstracts Full Text. Available: www.hwwilson.com/Databases/applieds.htm (accessed January 19, 2009).

arXiv.org (Cornell University Library). Available: http://arxiv.org (accessed January 7, 2009).

ChemIDplus Advance. Available: http://chem.sis.nlm.nih.gov/chemidplus (accessed January 7, 2009).

CiteSeerx Scientific Literature Digital Library. Available: http://citeseer.ist.psu.edu (accessed January 7, 2009).

Compendex. Available: www.ei.org/databases/compendex.html (accessed January 7, 2009).

Google. Available: www.google.com (accessed January 14, 2009).

How Stuff Works. Available: www.howstuffworks.com (accessed January 7, 2009).

IEEE Xplore. Available: http://ieeexplore.ieee.org/Xplore/guesthome.jsp (accessed January 7, 2009).

INFOMINE: Physical Sciences, Engineering, Computing and Math Directory. Available: http://infomine.ucr.edu/cgi-bin/search?category=physci (accessed January 7, 2009).

INSPEC. Available: www.theiet.org/publishing (accessed January 7, 2009).

Internet Public Library: Calculation & Conversion Tools. Available: www.ipl.org/div/subject/browse/ref19.00.00 (accessed January 7, 2009).

Internet Public Library Directory of Science and Technology Associations. Available: www.ipl.org/div/aon/browse/sci00.00.00 (accessed January 7, 2009).

Intute: Science, Engineering and Technology. Available: www.intute.ac.uk/sciences (accessed January 7, 2009).

Issues in Science and Technology Librarianship. Available: www.library.ucsb.edu/istl (accessed January 7, 2009).

Knovel. Available: www.knovel.com (accessed January 7, 2009).

MathSciNet. Available: www.ams.org/mathscinet (accessed January 7, 2009).

MathWorld. Available: http://mathworld.wolfram.com (accessed January 7, 2009).

Open Directory Project Science Dictionaries. Available: www.dmoz.org/Reference/Dictionaries/By_Subject/ Science (accessed January 7, 2009).

Open Directory Project Science Directories. Available: www.dmoz.org/Science/Directories (accessed January 7, 2009).

Science.gov (was Catalog of U.S. Government Science and Technology Web Site Resources). Available: www.science.gov (accessed January 7, 2009).

Web of Science. Available: http://thomsonreuters.com/products_services/scientific/Web_of_Science (accessed January 7, 2009).

ENGINEERING, COMPUTER SCIENCES, AND MATHEMATICS E-RESOURCE COLLECTION TOOLS

META SITES

Intute: Science, Engineering and Technology

www.intute.ac.uk/sciences

> Intute is a multisubject e-library maintained by a consortium of United Kingdom university and academic organization Library partners (www.intute.ac.uk/sciences/partners.html) who carefully select and evaluate all the science, engineering and technology e-resources that are open source or otherwise freely available on the Web. This includes an e-journals search engine (www.intute.ac.uk/sciences/ejournals.html). Subject coverage includes astronomy, chemistry, computing, earth sciences, engineering, environment, general sciences, geography, mathematics, and physics. Incorporates the contents of the original EEVL database.

The Math Forum Internet Mathematics Library

http://mathforum.org/library

> With hundreds of links to mathematics Internet sites, this project of the Math Forum provides one easily navigable location for finding math content on the Web. The sites are organized by mathematics topics, teaching topics, resource types, and education levels.

Science.gov (was Catalog of U.S. Government Science and Technology Web Site Resources)

www.science.gov

> Collection of U.S. Government sponsored or funded science and technology sites. This collection is collected for scientists, engineers, and "science aware" citizens and serves as a gateway to a huge amount of scientific information produced by U.S. federal and state agencies. It is not comprehensive, but it attempts to cover most scientific topics. Agencies and sites that it lists or searches include: AGRICOLA (http://agricola.nal.usda.gov), STINET (http://stinet.dtic.mil), NASA Technical Reports Server (http://ntrs.nasa.gov), NTIS (National Technical Information Service; www.ntis.gov).

StatLab Index

http://lib.stat.cmu.edu

> Site for sharing statistical software, datasets, and other information.

DIGITAL LIBRARIES DIRECTORIES OR COLLECTIONS OF DIGITAL LIBRARIES (DIGITAL LIBRARIES OF E-BOOKS, E-SERIALS, IMAGES, RECORDINGS, AND OTHER ARTIFACTS)

The Applied Math and Science Education Repository (AMSER)

http://amser.org

> The AMSER project is a collection of Web resources designed for upper level secondary school and community and technical college math and sciences educators to use to find resources for those students. "AMSER is funded by the National Science Foundation as part of the National Science Digital Library, and is being created by a team of project partners led by Internet Scout."

Books 24x7

www.books24x7.com

> Science and technical e-book vendor.

CiteSeerx Scientific Literature Digital Library

http://citeseer.ist.psu.edu

> CiteSeerx "is a scientific literature digital library and search engine that focuses primarily on the literature in computer and information science. CiteSeerx aims to improve the dissemination of scientific literature and to provide improvements in functionality, usability, availability, cost, comprehensiveness,

efficiency, and timeliness in the access of scientific and scholarly knowledge. Rather than creating just another digital library, CiteSeerx attempts to provide resources such as algorithms, data, metadata, services, techniques, and software that can be used to promote other digital libraries. CiteSeerx has developed new methods and algorithms to index PostScript and PDF research articles on the Web."

Caltech Collection of Open Digital Archives
http://library.caltech.edu/digital
"Caltech's Institutional Repositories for faculty approved research results and other content supporting the mission of the Institute."

The Collection of Computer Science Bibliographies
http://liinwww.ira.uka.de/bibliography/index.html
Searchable meta site relating to computer science topic areas containing over 1.2 million references (reports, papers and articles). "More than 150,000 references contain URLs to an online version of the paper."

DSpace at MIT: Home
http://dspace.mit.edu
"MIT's online institutional repository—built to save, share, and search MIT's digital research materials. DSpace at MIT contains MIT Research in digital form, including preprints, technical reports, working papers, theses, conference papers, images, and more."

DTICs Scientific and Technical Resources
www.dtic.mil/dtic/stresources
Defense Technical Information Center searchable collection of scientific and technical reports, statistics, etc. Biological, medical, environmental, social science, behavioral, as well as engineering and physical sciences related information is available. Search access level depends on registration. Much information is freely available to the public.

Knovel Online Interactive Books and Databases
www.knovel.com
Publisher of online full-text engineering, physical science, and other technical books, manuals, and databases. Some sample materials are available for preview.

Math Archives
http://archives.math.utk.edu
Searchable meta site of teaching materials for all areas and grade levels, archives and links to other math sites.

National Academies Press
www.nap.edu
E-book vender with some free e-books for sciences, engineering, education, and medicine.

National Science Digital Library
http://nsdl.org
"The National Science Digital Library (NSDL) was created by the National Science Foundation to provide organized access to high quality resources and tools that support innovations in teaching and learning at all levels of science, technology, engineering, and mathematics (STEM) education."

Networked Computer Science Technical Reference Library (NCSTRL)
www.ncstrl.org
View this international collection of computer science research reports and papers by year, institution, or browse by subject. This is an Open Archives Initiative (www.openarchives.org) collaborative project between NASA Langley, Old Dominion University, University of Virginia, and Virginia Tech.

Scielo

www.scielo.br

> "The Scientific Electronic Library Online—SciELO is an electronic library covering a selected collection of Brazilian scientific journals. The library is an integral part of a project being developed by FAPESP—Fundação de Amparo à Pesquisa do Estado de São Paulo, in partnership with BIREME— the Latin American and Caribbean Center on Health Sciences Information."

E-SERIALS, BLOGS, DISCUSSION LISTS, ETC.

ASC Online

http://radio.weblogs.com/0109575

> A weblog of information science and technology education and mentoring for LIS graduates.

Confessions of a Science Librarian

http://jdupuis.blogspot.com

> John Dupuis edits this discussion for academic engineering librarians. Web and other resource reviews and pointers as well as news and discussion of issue of interest to the International community of academic engineering librarians.

ELD-L and ELDNET-L

http://depts.washington.edu/englib/eld/listserv/listservs.php

> "[D]iscussion list addressing issues related to or of interest to engineering and related subject area libraries and librarians."

Issues in Science and Technology Librarianship

www.library.ucsb.edu/istl

> Quarterly publication that "serves as a vehicle for sci-tech librarians to share details of successful programs, materials for the delivery of information services, background information and opinions on topics of current interest, to publish research and bibliographies on issues in science and technology libraries."

LIS-SCITECH

www.leeds.ac.uk/library/ustlg

> "[F]orum for science and technology librarians in all types of organisation to discuss common problems, swap experience, pose questions and generally work more closely. It is also the main means of communication for the UK Universities Science and Technology Librarians Group (USTLG)." Subscribe and archives: www.jiscmail.ac.uk/lists/lis-scitech.html.

SciCentral

http://scicentral.com

> This searchable meta database includes all areas of science and their subcategories with directories, research, and latest news.

The SciTech Library Question (STLQ)

http://stlq.info

> Discussion news and reviews of Web and other resources for the science and technology and engineering librarians. International in scope. Randy Reichardt is the blog editor.

SLA-AERO

www.sla.org/content/community/lists/divisionlists5979.cfm or www.sla.org/content/community/lists/joinlists.cfm

> Discussion list for librarians who are members of the Special Libraries Association, Aerospace Division.

SLA-DENG

www.sla.org/content/community/lists/divisionlists5979.cfm or www.sla.org/content/community/lists/joinlists.cfm

Discussion list for librarians who are members of the Special Libraries Association, Engineering Division.

SLA-DST

www.sla.org/content/community/lists/divisionlists5979.cfm or www.sla.org/content/community/lists/joinlists.cfm

Discussion list for librarians who are members of the Special Libraries Association, Science and Technology Division.

STS-L

http://lists.ala.org/sympa/info/sts-l

Discussion of science and technology librarianship. Hosted by the American Library Association, Association of College and Research Libraries, Science and Technology Libraries Section.

CHAPTER

11

PHYSICAL AND EARTH SCIENCES (ASTRONOMY, CHEMISTRY, GEOLOGY, METEOROLOGY, PHYSICS, ETC.) E-RESOURCES

The types of materials used by researchers is evolving and expanding due to the simplicity of electronic access to any type of digital material. It is just as easy to retrieve a genetic sequence, a literature review, or a multimedia presentation as a journal article. Researchers are making increasing use of nonjournal content such as online scientific databases, like GenBank, or the Web pages of research labs. For the scientists in our survey, this type of access has surpassed personal communications, and it is close to journal articles in frequency of use by researchers. Researchers still primarily use library and bibliographic database searches but the use of Web search engines such as Google Scholar is almost as common. (Hemminger et al., 2007: 2214–2215)

DEVELOPING A COLLECTION PLAN FOR PHYSICAL AND EARTH SCIENCES E-RESOURCES

E-resources that support scientific study and education in the physical and earth sciences related information were some of the first to appear on the Web. Specifically, high energy physicists were the first to use the program that became the World Wide Web. Wikipedia provides us with very clear and useful definitions of the physical and earth sciences: "Physical science is an encompassing term for the branches of natural science and science that study non-living systems, in contrast to the biological sciences. However, the term 'physical' creates an unintended, somewhat arbitrary distinction, since many branches of physical science also study biological phenomena" (http://en.wikipedia.org/wiki/Physical_sciences, accessed January 27, 2009).

Physical sciences include astronomy, chemistry, geology, meteorology, physics, and many subfields and combinations of these main fields. Geophysics, seismology, and astrophysics are some examples. These fields often form a major part of other areas of scientific endeavor—biochemistry, soil sciences (geology and agriculture), and nuclear physics for example. The earth sciences both incorporate the physical sciences as well as the biological and social sciences and engineering, computer sciences, and mathematics:

Earth science (also known as geoscience, the geosciences or the Earth Sciences), is an all-embracing term for the sciences related to the planet Earth. It is arguably a special case in planetary science, the Earth being the only known life-bearing planet. There are both reductionist and holistic approaches to Earth science. There are four major disciplines in earth sciences, namely geography, geology, geophysics and geodesy. These major disciplines use physics, chemistry, biology, chronology and mathematics to build a quantitative understanding of the principal areas or spheres of the Earth system. (http://en.wikipedia.org/wiki/Earth_Sciences, accessed January 27, 2009)

WHAT PURPOSE WILL YOUR COLLECTION SERVE? FOR WHOM ARE YOU COLLECTING THESE E-RESOURCES?

Scientists in all areas of study have been some of the first adopters of new technologies for scholarly communications, data sharing and analysis, teaching, etc. These fields particularly make use of reference tools that are used to look up physics, chemical, and mathematical formulae and other facts that are used to build on ongoing research and practical projects.

As with the other types of scientific information discussed in previous and subsequent chapters, users of physical and earth sciences e-resources will most likely be students of various ages and educational attainment and researchers both academic and professional. Physical and earth sciences e-resources may be needed by professionals (e.g., engineers, administrators). Scientific information may be also be needed by consumers or hobbyists. Hobbyists include those who do meteorology or geology for both the scientific interest and recreation.

Academic libraries may need to cover a broad range of physical and earth sciences e-resources for undergraduate and graduate students as well as specific subtopics in depth for researchers working in their parent institutions. Hemminger et al. (2007) did a library use and information seeking behavior study of the all of the science faculty at their university to help guide their decisions. Their findings will be used to guide collection development in general and changes to the libraries Web presence in particular. Other librarians have done similar information user studies for more specific areas of physical and earth sciences, such as physics and astronomy (Jamali and Nicholas, 2008).

Special libraries serving physical and earth sciences researchers will usually need to acquire e-resources that provide depth of coverage in a specific area of scientific or technological information that their parent organizations is involved in. For example, they may need to collect resources for polymer chemistry, geophysics, and so on. Public libraries may need to serve K–12 students or hobbyists. Some public libraries support the businesses or government agencies in their community with a physical or earth science information need. Each library should become aware of which scientific subject areas they may want to support for researchers and students in their parent organizations or library user communities. K–12 libraries serve anyone from kindergarten (e.g., rock and leaf identification tools) to college-bound high school students (e.g., chemistry and physics). Many schools have earth sciences classes as part of their science curriculum.

WHAT TYPES OF E-RESOURCES WILL YOU COLLECT?

- Directories (of physical and earth scientists, science organizations, projects, etc.)
- Dictionaries (physical and earth sciences vocabulary in English as well as international language translation dictionaries)
- Abstracts, indexes, and table of contents services (including those with full text of physical and earth sciences journals indexed)

- Encyclopedias and almanacs
- Full-text and/or multimedia databases/digital libraries (collections of e-books, e-serials, recordings, videos, podcasts, images, etc.)
- News and news services (physical and earth sciences current awareness sources)
- Key primary documents (research data and reports, statistical sources, etc.)
- Search engines
- Meta sites (e-resources that provide two or more of the other reference tool types in a single product/Web site)

Directories of physical and earth scientists, science organizations, projects, etc., exist for every field and subfield. The Open Directory Project (www.dmoz.org/Science/Directories) and the Internet Public Library (www.ipl.org/div/aon/browse/sci00.00.00) both provide directories of directories of science and technology associations, scientists, organizations, and projects.

The Open Directory Project collects appropriate physical and earth sciences dictionaries, glossaries, etc., that are freely available on the Web (www.dmoz.org/Reference/Dictionaries/By_Subject/Science). The Internet Public Library also maintains a collection of Calculation and Conversion Tools (www.ipl.org/div/subject/browse/ref19.00.00) that will be useful to many library users in these fields of study.

The fee-based tools listed in the tables in this chapter are classic indexing and abstracting tools. One example available freely on the Web is National Technical Information Service (NTIS) Database (www.ntis.gov/products/ntisdb.aspx) with over two million bibliographic records for research and technical reports. Full-text and advanced searching are fee based.

Eric Weisstein's World of Science (http://scienceworld.wolfram.com/info) site collects and maintains publicly accessible physical and earth sciences encyclopedias. Other encyclopedia-like e-resources in both fee-based and free Web options exist, but this is one of the best examples of the latter.

Physical and earth sciences current awareness sources are available from most of the major scientific organizations that may be located in the directories cited previously. An interesting example is SciCentral (http://scicentral.com), which posts news and research information releases for several scientific areas and also lists some e-resources for each scientific area.

Full-text, digital libraries and key primary documents tend to be part of the same e-resources in these fields. A majority of key primary documents (research data and reports, statistical sources, etc.) for physical and earth sciences come from e-docs sites. Science.gov cited in the previous chapters will be invaluable. An excellent example is the National Institute of Standards and Technology (NIST) Chemistry Webbook (www.nist.gov or http://webbook.nist.gov). "NIST's mission is to promote U.S. innovation and industrial competitiveness by advancing measurement science, standards, and technology in ways that enhance economic security and improve our quality of life." Meta sites are listed in the collection tools section at the end of the chapter.

How will you organize your physical and earth sciences e-library?

Physical and earth sciences e-resources might be organized by main subject (astronomy, chemistry, geology, meteorology, physics, etc.) and then by subfields (polymer chemistry, petroleum geology, astrophysics, etc.) and specialties (volcanology, global warming, etc). Some thought might be given to organizing the resources by level of education as well as by subject area. For example, different resources might be more suitable for undergraduates or for advanced researchers. Many good physical and earth science collections use a Web-accessible database to organize and access records for each selected resource. Some libraries will elect to organize physical and earth sciences e-resources by resource type or by both subject and resource type.

IDENTIFYING AND COLLECTING PHYSICAL AND EARTH SCIENCES E-RESOURCES

WEB SITES THAT REVIEW AND EVALUATE E-RESOURCES: PEER E-LIBRARIES, SUBJECT COLLECTIONS/GUIDES, OR META SITES

Intute: Science, Engineering and Technology (www.intute.ac.uk/sciences) and INFOMINE: Physical Sciences, Engineering, Computing and Math Directory (http://infomine.ucr.edu/cgi-bin/search? category=physci) selectively compile e-resources in multiple areas of physical and earth sciences related resources. Physicsworld (http://physicsworld.com) and Sheffield ChemDex (www.chemdex .org) both attempt to be comprehensive collections of physics and chemistry related Web sites. In fact, all of the meta sites discussed in the previous two chapters as well as those listed in the collection tools section will be useful for physical and earth sciences e-resource collection development.

DISCUSSION LISTS (LISTSERV, ETC.), FORUMS/GROUPS, E-SERIALS, AND/OR BLOGS THAT POST OR PUBLISH REVIEWS AND EVALUATIONS OF E-RESOURCES

The core discussion lists and newsgroups for science and technical resources in libraries are STS-L, discussion of librarianship; SLA-Dite, discussion for the Information Technology Division of the Special Libraries Association; PAMnet, discussion list of the Physics-Astronomy-Mathematics (PAM) Division of the Special Libraries Association; and CHMINF-L, chemical information sources discussion list that posts announcements and reviews of chemistry related e-resources.

The Scout Report (http://scout.wisc.edu/Reports/ScoutReport/Current) reviews and reports on physical and earth sciences sites for educators. Randy Reichardt edits the SciTech Library Question (http://stlq.info) in which he posts discussions and thoughts of interest to librarians working with science and technology areas. All of these blogs includes Web and other resource reviews and pointers as well as news and discussion for the international community of academic librarians who work with physics and astronomy.

PRINT BOOKS AND JOURNALS THAT REVIEW E-RESOURCES

As with the other areas of the sciences, all useful research skills texts that include physical and earth sciences research review appropriate e-resources. As cited previously, Diana Hacker's (2008) *Research and Documentation in the Electronic Age*, Fifth Edition Booklet and Web site (www.dianahacker.com/resdoc) covers research tools including e-resources in the physical and earth sciences. Both the fee-based research tools and the best of the free Web research tools in these areas are reviewed and linked in this publication. Most print physical and earth sciences related journals review e-resources within the scope of the journal's specific subject and subtopic coverage in the same manner in which books are reviewed, or in the context of specific articles such e-resources may be cited.

EVALUATION GUIDELINES AND SELECTION CRITERIA: THE CORE WEB PHYSICAL AND EARTH SCIENCES REFERENCE COLLECTION

As in any other scientific information domain care must be taken to identify the authors of physical and earth sciences information and to verify their qualifications, educational attainment, and research experience. Attention to their record of publishing may be important. That is, have they previously published in peer-reviewed journals? Do they have a clear record of scholarship and research that is traceable? Good physical and earth science Web resources will clearly identify the authors' information, providing organizations and their records of scholarship and research. Scientific information is often difficult for the nonsubject specialist to evaluate, especially information provided at the research or higher-education levels. Each scientific field has its own particular vocabulary and accepted research methodologies. Physical and earth sciences related resources, in particular, use mathematical and symbolic notations that are not easily interpreted by the nonsubject specialist. It will be more difficult for the nonsubject specialist to judge the information content without consulting a subject specialist. At the K–12 educational level, or with materials provided specifically for the nonspecialist, it will be important to verify that the information provider has the authority, including educational attainment and research experience to write on a particular topic. It will also be important to determine if the information provider has experience in teaching K–12 level sciences. As with most subject areas, the evaluation strategies for Web information resources described in Chapter 1 will work very well for evaluating Web physical and earth sciences.

Selection criteria as always are determined by the specific subject fields and subspecialties represented by the library's users. Furthermore, selection must be made at the education or complexity level required by those library users. For example, high-energy physics research scientists studying quark will need very different materials from the high school physics students studying the physics of flight, and polymer chemistry research scientists studying the liquid crystal will need very different materials from the high school chemistry students studying alcohol distillation.

The Core Web Physical and Earth Sciences Reference Collection on the companion Web Site (www.kovacs.com/ns/essentialguide.html) is selected for a broad coverage of physical and earth sciences fields. Fee-based e-resources are included when they offer free-trials or have some information available without requiring a fee.

In May and August 2008, librarians were surveyed to elicit which physical and earth sciences reference tools they consider to be core or essential to their work. Separate surveys were sent for chemistry, astronomy, and physics and other physical sciences and earth sciences. However, there were no surveys returned in the astronomy and physics survey and very few in the other two surveys. Using the results of all three surveys and the results from surveys done in 2005 and in 2006, the results were pooled into a single report. Past, present, and future surveys and results are posted at www.kovacs.com/misc.html. The discussion lists and blogs where the survey links were posted are listed in Table 11.1. The core physical and earth sciences reference tools survey is reproduced in Table 11.2.

Table 11.1. Discussion Lists and Blogs Distribution for Physical and Earth Sciences Reference Tools Survey

- eldnet-l@u.washington.edu
- LIS-SCITECH@jiscmail.ac.uk
- sts-l@ala.org
- LISNews and LISNewsWire Blogs: lisnews-owner@lishost.net
- ResourceShelf Blog: gary.price@resourceshelf.com
- ERIL-L@LISTSERV.BINGHAMTON.EDU
- dig_ref@LISTSERV.SYR.EDU

- collib-l@ala.org
- LIS-LINK@jiscmail.ac.uk
- Libref-L@listserv.kent.edu
- GOVDOC-L@lists.psu.edu
- publib@webjunction.org
- livereference@yahoogroups.com
- Libref-L@listserv.kent.edu

Print physical and earth sciences reference tools remain important. Table 11.3 lists the top five print physical and earth sciences reference tools identified in the survey. The free Web sites that librarians reported as core or essential for physical and earth sciences reference are given in Table 11.4.

E-docs sites that support physical and earth sciences reference were very popular. The top five physical and earth sciences e-docs reference sites are listed in Table 11.5. The top five fee-based physical and earth sciences reference e-resources are reported in Table 11.6.

Table 11.2. Core Physical and Earth Sciences Reference Tools Survey Questions

1. Which library type best describes the library you work in/for/with?

2. What are the essential print titles for earth sciences reference that you can't work without? (Please type the titles only. List up to three.)

3. What are the essential three free (not government published) Web-accessible earth sciences related Web sites that you can't work without? (Please type complete URL/Web address; e.g., volcano.und.edu.)

4. What are the essential three (.gov) government published (state, federal, local, international) free Web-accessible earth sciences reference tools that you can't work without? (Please type complete URL/Web address; e.g., www.usgs.gov.)

5. What are the essential three fee-based Web-accessible earth sciences related databases that you can't work without? (Please type the simple title; e.g., GeoRef.)

6. Does your library maintain a Web page or site to support earth sciences reference? If so, please share the URL/Web address (e.g., www.admmr.state.az.us/OtherResources/OnLineResources.html).

7. Additional comments or ideas:

(Please include your name and e-mail address if you would like feedback, otherwise this survey form is completely anonymous.)

Note: A separate similar survey was sent out for chemistry, astronomy, and physics reference specifically and data was merged with the physical and earth sciences survey.

Table 11.3. Top Five Print Physical and Earth Sciences Reference Tools Identified in Survey

1. *CRC Handbook of Chemistry and Physics, Dictionary of Organic Compounds, Kirk-Othmer Encyclopedia of Chemical Technology*

2. *Encyclopedia of Earth System Science*

3. *Geographical Dictionary: Merriam Webster, Glossary of Geology: AGI, Lexicon of Geologic Names of the United States*

4. *Manual of Mineralogy*

5. *Moffatt: Map Index to Topographic Quadrangles*

Table 11.4. Top Three Free Web Physical and Earth Sciences Reference Tools Identified in Survey

1. Google: www.google.com, and Google Scholar: http://scholar.google.com

2. Chemweb: www.chemweb.org, WebElements Periodic Table on the Web: www.webelements.com

3. Intute: Science, Engineering and Technology: www.intute.ac.uk/sciences

Table 11.5. Top Five Government Documents Web Sites Used as Physical and Earth Sciences Reference Tools Identified in Survey

1. National Institute of Standards and Technology/(NIST) Chemistry Webbook: www.nist.gov or http://webbook.nist.gov

2. U.S. Geological Survey: www.usgs.gov

3. ChemIDplus Advance: http://chem.sis.nlm.nih.gov/chemidplus

4. Science.gov: www.science.gov

5. National Weather Service: www.weather.gov

Table 11.6. Top Five Fee-based Physical and Earth Sciences Reference E-Resources Identified in Survey

1. GeoRef: www.agiweb.org/georef/index.html

2. Chemical Abstracts: www.cas.org

3. Geobase: www.elsevier.com/wps/find/bibliographicdatabasedescription.cws_home/422597/description#description

4. Web of Science: http://thomsonreuters.com/products_services/scientific/Web_of_Science

5. GeoScienceWorld: www.geoscienceworld.org, Scopus: www.scopus.com/scopus/home.url, Water Resources Abstracts: www.csa.com/factsheets/water-resources-set-c.php, data files from NOAA

E-LIBRARY SUCCESS STORY

UNIVERSITY OF WINDSOR, LEDDY LIBRARY

Windsor, Ontario, Canada
www.uwindsor.ca/leddy
Contact: Jennifer Soutter, jsoutter@uwindsor.ca

A. Collection Planning (e.g., goal setting and identification of users, technology/personnel choices)

Leddy Library was among the first to transition to digital resources in place of print. Over time, the library's Web presence has become the key location for all of the library's e-resources and serves both on-campus and remote users. "Leddy began integrating e-resources into its collections in the late 1990s. We are a member of the Ontario Council of University Libraries, a provincial academic libraries consortium, as well as the Canadian Research Knowledge Network, a national consortium. Through these consortia and through our own endeavours e-resources have become a key platform for delivering content and services to our patrons. Our web-site and methodologies for delivering this content has developed as necessary as our complement of digital resources has grown."

From the beginning, the Leddy Library developed a collection development policy and identified a clear description of purposes for the e-library:

> Purpose of e-library:
> stay responsive to the expressed needs of students and faculty
> support teaching, learning and research

build subject based e-collections that complement and/or replace relevant print resources
e-collections that are available 24/7
build subject-based e-collections that support the university's "pinnacle" areas: automo-
tive, environment and social justice
build an e-library that reflects the e-resources available in all subject areas that e-collections are available
improved use of this investment in e-resources, improved research opportunities and
access to resources, along with avoiding duplication of scarce resources
build a trusted electronic archive to support future research
publish e-journals as per the Synergies project in order to build e-resources in subject areas
with less e-resources (working towards a Canada-wide information infrastructure)
and to publish Canadian e-resources http://www.synergiescanada.org/index_en.html

The e-library serves all faculty, students, and staff of the University of Windsor both on campus or at other locations. Distance learning programs offered by the University of Windsor are supported by the e-library. "The Web site supports distance learning in general. Because we provide proxied access infrastructure to our digital resources, any student or faculty member enrolled in a University of Windsor distance learning programme or class can gain access."

The most recent version of the written general collection policy was revised in spring of 2008 under the auspices of the ACRL course "Electronic Collection Development for Academic E-Libraries" and is available online at www.kovacs.com/studentwork/finalprojects/EResource-sPolicyMay08.doc (login: student password: kovacs07). "It was intended that e-resources, along with all other formats, be viewed by subject specialists within the context of their respective collection development policies. . . . Management is aware of the past discrepancies in e-publishing and the status of current e-publishing, and considers them as factors in the collection development process at the management and consortia level (regional and national consortia)."

B. Collection Strategies (e.g., selection criteria, identification of resources, licensing, and related user information needs)
Selection criteria for e-resource collection is carefully detailed in the collection development plan:

... related criteria in no particular order/weight, including but not limited to:
user feedback including faculty
subject specialist recommendations
library wishlists
consortia wishlists
consortia responsibilities and consortia values
strategic implications for the consortia and its projects
budgetary implications
cost
purchase versus subscription
ability to load e-journals to Scholars Portal (consortia repository)
ability to load e-books to Scholars Portal and current status of e-book platform
presence/absence of bibliographic control, including whether centralized or local, over
e-resources including provision of MARC records, status of the opac and the existence
of those e-resources in our local/consortia management software

Leddy Library pays for access to the majority of fee-based e-resources on the Web site. IP-based authentication is along with internal authorization for remote access is made available

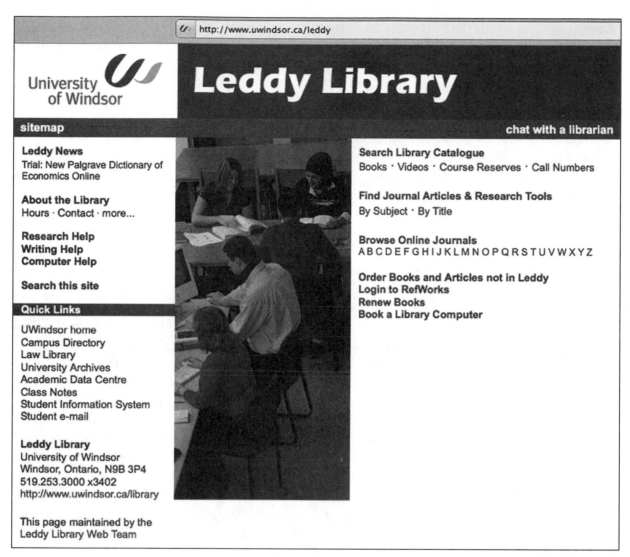

Figure 11.1. University of Windsor Leddy Library

University-wide through a proxy server for individual departments and administrative units. Some of those units have separate Username and password access to some databases.

"Leddy Library may take over licensing arrangements and agreements on behalf of those departmental and administrative units. If Leddy Library subsumes those agreements we attempt to provide for perpetual access or 'local loading'/archiving through Scholars Portal (as we do for our own subscriptions)."

E-books are licensed for University of Windsor library users through consortia agreements as well as some individual subscriptions. Remote access to some e-book collections is through the individual vendor sites. The Scholars Portal project provides a central searchable database of e-books and e-serials common among university library members of the Ontario Council of University Libraries (www.ocul.on.ca). The Scholars Portal is currently moving toward becoming a trusted digital repository and acting as an archive for the OCUL consortia members.

"Monetary support for the Scholars Portal e-book platform was provided by the Ontario (provincial) government with ongoing maintenance paid for by OCUL (Ontario). That platform will provide access for those who participated in e-book agreements. With the Canadian Research

Knowledge Network (CRKN) national consortia (http://researchknowledge.ca/) negotiating for platform independent e-books, this will increase the number of titles available through this platform for OCUL participants partaking in those agreements. Campus-based and remote access is intended."

Currently only e-books are routinely cataloged by the library. Web-based free resources may be cataloged on an ad hoc basis as requested by subject specialists. Their presence in the database is trackable but no usage statistics are generated.

The Leddy Library Archives, Rare Books, and Special Collections has undertaken digitization projects related to local history collections. These are made available through the e-library as they progress. Leddy Library's virtual reference service, chat with a librarian, has been very successful. Usage statistics show the number of questions answered has increased significantly each year since the service was first offered.

C. Collection Organization (e.g., content management systems, Web server choices, personnel responsibilities, etc.)

The Leddy Library Web site is managed using Lotus Domino (www-01.ibm.com/software/lotus/products/domino) and each individual page is created and edited individually at this time. The University of Windsor is implementing use of the Drupal open source content management system (http://drupal.org). The library will transition to Drupal in the next year or two.

"The Web site also includes a wordpress blog (Leddy News), cocoon (Databases A-Z list), sfx openURL resolver and Verde ERMS (Browse Online Journals list), ILS (Library catalogue), racer (ILL), and RefWorks (bibliographic management software). I mention this because practically every link on the main page, right hand side, links to non-Lotus-based e-resources or software."

The Digital Services Librarian (DSL) coordinates staff and consortia relationships in support of the e-library. "The DSL was hired to monitor consortia acquisitions and to facilitate, coordinate and/or implement internal processes, etc., with respect to the e-journals collections. The DSL was initially assigned to "fix the e-journals" or improve bibliographic control over the e-journals. This is still in process because of poorly designed software and inadequate data feeds. The position expanded to include involvement in other consortia projects."

Several librarians, technicians, and support staff share responsibility for building and maintaining the e-library. "Links are added to the catalogue by the Acquisitions department, for e-books using provided MARC records; to the Browse Online Journals list by activation through the management software by the Serials department; to the Databases A-Z list by the admin assistant in Systems and to the website by a member of the Web Committee (on the recommendation of subject specialist) or by a subject specialist."

Selection tasks are integrated into librarians' routine duties. However, new resources most often are acquired through consortia acquisitions. "Decisions to participate in consortia acquisitions are made collaboratively with input from subject specialists and from senior management." Subject specialists also recommend Web-accessible resources they identify through their regular review of professional journals, Web sites, and serendipitous discovery during related reference searches.

D. Collection Maintenance (e.g., link checking, ongoing weeding, and growth of the e-library collection)

Links are updated when users or librarians discover problems and report them. No functional link-checking software is available for the Web site as it currently exists. When Drupal is implemented there will be additional link checking options. Feedback from faculty, students, and library subject specialists is actively solicited, including requests for new e-resources. There is no formal mechanism, but users may phone, e-mail or respond using Web forms. Subject specialists notify faculty of trials or new resources and solicit their feedback through whichever communications mode the users are most comfortable with. "Suggestions for e-resources are used as the basis for acquiring trials. Feedback is then collected and used to inform acquisitions decisions at both a local (Leddy) level and consortia level."

Review of the e-library organization is irregular and happens as needed, when major changes of technology or available resources indicate the need for review. "The Leddy Library Web Committee is responsible for the website/software reviews and upgrades, and the organization of the information (including the e-library) on the website. They also decide and implement new software and make index changes. This occurs irregularly as needed. With the last website upgrade (delivery mechanism for the e-library) feedback was actively solicited from staff, librarians and students."

When OCUL and CRKN proposals are being considered, library management review the e-library as a whole for content, scope, and coverage. As with many large e-library collections, a major plan for the future is the acquisition of a federated or cross database search tool. "The consortia's Scholars Portal platform allows for local loading of different vendors databases, metadata and/or content (with vendor permission) which means a certain number of our vendor databases are currently cross-searchable (CSA, Proquest, Wilson, a few EBSCO databases, etc.)....Also, the future search interface for Scholars Portal is intended to allow for cross-searching of e-journal content and indexes along with e-books for e-resources loaded to Scholars Portal."

Other options are also being explored. "Our consortia members already tested and discarded CSA's MultiSearch (http://www.csa1.co.uk/news/csa-pressrelease-multisearch.php?SID=6a8ta8r3o4q1qgg7qtma6d3f91). As far as I'm aware, Leddy has not formally considered/evaluated other options such as BiblioCommons (http://bibliocommons.com/), as our resources are oriented towards an Evergreen (http://evergreen-ils.org/dokuwiki/doku.php?id=evergreen_libraries) implementation (and other projects) at this time."

REFERENCES AND WEB SITES CITED

Hacker, Diane, with Barbara Fister. 2008. *Research and Documentation in the Electronic Age*, 5th edition. New York: Bedford/St. Martin's. Available: http://www.dianahacker.com/resdoc/ (accessed January 19, 2009).

Hemminger, Bradley M., Dihui Lu, K. T. D. Vaughan, and Stephanie J. Adams. 2007. "Information Seeking Behavior of Academic Scientists." *Journal of the American Society for Information Science and Technology* 58, no. 14: 2205–2225.

Jamali, Hamid R., and David Nicholas. 2008. "Information-seeking Behaviour of Physicists and Astronomers." *Aslib Proceedings: New Information Perspectives* 60, no. 5: 444–462.

WEB SITES CITED

Cleveland Public Library, Science and Technology Department. Available: http://scitech.cpl.org (accessed January 19, 2009).

Eric Weisstein's World of Science. Available: http://scienceworld.wolfram.com/info (accessed January 7, 2009).

Google. Available: www.google.com (accessed January 14, 2009).

INFOMINE: Physical Sciences, Engineering, Computing and Math Directory. Available: http://infomine
.ucr.edu/cgi-bin/search?category=physic (accessed January 7, 2009).

Internet Public Library: Calculation & Conversion Tools. Available: www.ipl.org/div/subject/browse/
ref19.00.00 (accessed January 7, 2009).

Internet Public Library Directory of Science and Technology Associations. Available: www.ipl.org/div/
aon/browse/sci00.00.00 (accessed January 7, 2009).

National Institute of Standards and Technology/(NIST) Chemistry Webbook. Available: www.nist.gov or
http://webbook.nist.gov (accessed January 7, 2009).

Open Directory Project Science Dictionaries. Available: www.dmoz.org/Reference/Dictionaries/By_Subject/
Science (accessed January 7, 2009).

Open Directory Project Science Directories. Available: www.dmoz.org/Science/Directories (accessed January
7, 2009).

Physicsworld. Available: http://physicsworld.com (accessed January 7, 2009).

The SAO/NASA Astrophysics Data System Digital Library for Physics and Astronomy. Available:
http://adswww.harvard.edu (accessed January 7, 2009).

SciCentral. Available: http://scicentral.com (accessed January 7, 2009).

Science.gov (was Catalog of U.S. Government Science and Technology Web Site Resources). Available:
www.science.gov (accessed January 7, 2009).

The Scout Report. Available: http://scout.wisc.edu/Reports/ScoutReport/Current (accessed February 8,
2009).

Sheffield ChemDex. Available: www.chemdex.org (accessed January 7, 2009).

Web of Science. Available: http://thomsonreuters.com/products_services/scientific/Web_of_Science (accessed
January 7, 2009).

PHYSICAL AND EARTH SCIENCES E-RESOURCE COLLECTION TOOLS

META SITES

AstroWeb
www.cv.nrao.edu/fits/www/astronomy.html
> Central collection of astronomy and astrophysics Web resources.

Chem Informatics
www.cheminformatics.org (was Chemweb, www.chemweb.org)
> Collection of sites, data sets, and documentation relating to chemistry information.

Intute: Science, Engineering and Technology
www.intute.ac.uk/sciences/
> Intute is a multisubject e-library maintained by a consortium of United Kingdom university and academic organization Library partners (www.intute.ac.uk/sciences/partners.html) who carefully select and evaluate all the science, engineering, and technology e-resources that are open source or otherwise freely available on the Web. This includes an e-journals search engine (www.intute.ac.uk/sciences/ejournals.html). Subject coverage includes astronomy, chemistry, computing, earth sciences, engineering, environment, general sciences, geography, mathematics, and physics. Incorporates the contents of the original EEVL database.

Science.gov (was Catalog of U.S. Government Science and Technology Web Site Resources)
www.science.gov
> Collection of U.S. Government sponsored or funded science and technology sites. This collection is collected for scientists, engineers, and "science aware" citizens and serves as a gateway to a huge amount of scientific information produced by U.S. federal and state agencies. It is not comprehensive, but it attempts to cover most scientific topics. Agencies and sites that it lists or searches include: AGRICOLA (http://agricola.nal.usda.gov), STINET (http://stinet.dtic.mil), NASA Technical Reports Server (http://ntrs.nasa.gov), NTIS (National Technical Information Service; www.ntis.gov).

Sheffield ChemDex
www.chemdex.org
> Directory of chemistry related Web sites. On the Web since 1993.

StatLab Index
http://lib.stat.cmu.edu
> Site for sharing statistical software, datasets, and other information.

DIGITAL LIBRARIES DIRECTORIES OR COLLECTIONS OF DIGITAL LIBRARIES (DIGITAL LIBRARIES OF E-BOOKS, E-SERIALS, IMAGES, RECORDINGS, AND OTHER ARTIFACTS)

Books 24x7
www.books24x7.com
> Science and technical e-book vendor.

DTICs Scientific and Technical Resources
www.dtic.mil/dtic/stresources
> Defense Technical Information Center searchable collection of scientific and technical reports, statistics, etc. Biological, medical, environmental, social science, behavioral, as well as engineering and physical sciences related information is available. Search access level depends on registration. Much information is freely available to the public.

Knovel Online Interactive Books and Databases

www.knovel.com

> Publisher of online full-text engineering, physical science, and other technical books, manuals, and databases. Some sample materials are available for preview.

National Science Digital Library

http://nsdl.org

> "The National Science Digital Library (NSDL) was created by the National Science Foundation to provide organized access to high quality resources and tools that support innovations in teaching and learning at all levels of science, technology, engineering, and mathematics (STEM) education."

Scielo

www.scielo.br

> "The Scientific Electronic Library Online—SciELO is an electronic library covering a selected collection of Brazilian scientific journals. The library is an integral part of a project being developed by FAPESP—Fundação de Amparo à Pesquisa do Estado de São Paulo, in partnership with BIREME—the Latin American and Caribbean Center on Health Sciences Information."

E-Serials, Blogs, Discussion Lists, etc.

ASC Online

http://radio.weblogs.com/0109575

> A weblog of information science and technology education and mentoring for LIS graduates.

CHMINF-L

https://listserv.indiana.edu/cgi-bin/wa-iub.exe?A0=CHMINF-L

> Chemical information sources discussion.

Issues in Science and Technology Librarianship

www.library.ucsb.edu/istl

> Quarterly publication that "serves as a vehicle for sci-tech librarians to share details of successful programs, materials for the delivery of information services, background information and opinions on topics of current interest, to publish research and bibliographies on issues in science and technology libraries."

LIS-SCITECH

www.leeds.ac.uk/library/ustlg

> "[F]orum for science and technology librarians in all types of organisation to discuss common problems, swap experience, pose questions and generally work more closely. It is also the main means of communication for the UK Universities Science and Technology Librarians Group (USTLG)." Subscribe and archives at www.jiscmail.ac.uk/lists/lis-scitech.html.

PAMnet

http://units.sla.org/division/dpam/manual/pamnet_bulletin/pamnet.html

> Discussion list for librarians who are members of the Physics, Astronomy, Math (PAM) division of the Special Libraries Association.

SciCentral

http://scicentral.com

> This searchable meta database includes all areas of science and their subcategories with directories, research, and latest news.

The SciTech Library Question (STLQ)

http://stlq.info

> Discussion news and reviews of Web and other resources for the science and technology and engineering librarians. International in scope. Randy Reichardt is the blog editor.

SLA-DCHE

www.sla.org/content/community/lists/divisionlists5979.cfm or www.sla.org/content/community/lists/joinlists.cfm

Discussion list for librarians who are members of the Special Libraries Association, Chemistry Division.

SLA-DST

www.sla.org/content/community/lists/divisionlists5979.cfm or www.sla.org/content/community/lists/joinlists.cfm

Discussion list for librarians who are members of the Special Libraries Association, Science and Technology Division.

STS-L

http://lists.ala.org/sympa/info/sts-l

Discussion of science and technology librarianship. Hosted by the American Library Association, Association of College and Research Libraries, Science and Technology Libraries Section.

12

SOCIAL SCIENCES (ANTHROPOLOGY, POLITICAL SCIENCE, PSYCHOLOGY, SOCIOLOGY, ETC.) E-RESOURCES

This study included a 22-question survey sent to all faculty, staff, and graduate students in a cross-section of social science disciplines (anthropology, psychology, social work, and sociology)....Library surveys are usually either large-scale, top-down exercises or focused narrowly on a particular user population. Interviews, focus groups, and ethnographic studies provide a nuanced and in-depth view from the perspective of a handful of people. The present survey focused on a middle range between these extremes, gathering data relevant to a group of inter-related disciplines and focusing on local needs in order to supplement (and serve as a corrective to) day-to-day assumptions, which tend to be weighted toward the needs of the most vocal or highly visible users. Our analysis also sheds light on a number of broader issues and questions, including: "What are the prevailing collection access issues? How might they help us to manage the continuing shift from print to electronic format? How do different disciplines, as well as faculty and graduate students, differ in their use of the collection? Can this type of survey provide a framework for collection development decisions informed by the current research interests of local scholars and in tune with disciplinary practices? (Sutton and Jacoby, 2009: 1, 9)

DEVELOPING A COLLECTION PLAN FOR SOCIAL SCIENCES E-RESOURCES

Sutton and Jacoby's (2009) research attempted to answer the central question of a working e-library collection development policy. What purpose does the e-library collection serve and for whom is the collection intended? Another way of phrasing this question is, What information does this user require for what he is doing, in what form, with what urgency of delivery time and format? Social sciences subjects include anthropology, archaeology, area studies, economics, sociology, political science, psychology, philosophy, and many other areas related to the study of human cultures, societies, ideas, and minds. Most quality social sciences e-resources are published by academic or research organizations. There are several good fee-based tools, but there are thousands of freely available social sciences Web sites.

WHAT PURPOSE WILL YOUR COLLECTION SERVE? FOR WHOM ARE YOU COLLECTING THESE E-RESOURCES?

Social sciences information resources will nearly always be needed for use in an educational or research context. The important questions are, Which subjects will be included in the collection? For what age group and educational level is the collection targeted? Academic libraries may need to collect resources both for college students and for the social scientists teaching and researching in their college or university. The basis of the collection can be the college or university program guide and course listings as well as the research interests of the faculty. Even with a program guide to use as a foundation it can be very fruitful for e-library decision making to do a user study such as that done by Sutton and Jacoby (2009). Studies or surveys of specific social sciences users, such as psychology faculty (Schaffer, 2004) or undergraduate students (Head, 2007) can also be very useful for e-library collection development. Head's finding are particularly pertinent as they indicate that undergraduates studying social sciences rely on the library resources to be appropriate as research sources and many begin their research on the library's Web site. Special libraries may collect social sciences information that supports business or technology research in some way. Demographic data, marketing surveys, product testing, industrial design, medical and health information, legal aspects of social issues, and other social statistics may be included.

A social sciences information collection for a public library is likely to collect social sciences e-resources to serve K–12 students and other members of the community to use in an educational, professional, or business context. K–12 library is likely to be designed for K–12 students to use in support of their school curriculum that may include classes in geography, social studies, history, and so forth.

WHAT TYPES OF E-RESOURCES WILL YOU COLLECT?

Kousha and Thelwall (2007) evaluated social sciences citation checking using Google Scholar and found that it works almost as well and sometimes better than Social Science Citation index. Their explanation for this is that so much of social sciences research has been published in open source e-journals and archives. As we have done with other subject areas in previous chapters, social sciences e-resources can be described for convenience in terms of traditional reference source types:

- Directories (of social scientists, science organizations, projects, etc.)
- Dictionaries (social sciences vocabulary in English as well as international language translation dictionaries)
- Abstracts, indexes, and table of contents services (including those with full text of social sciences journals indexed)
- Encyclopedias and almanacs
- Full-text and/or multimedia databases/digital libraries (collections of e-books, e-serials, recordings, videos, podcasts, images, etc.)
- News and news services (social sciences current awareness sources)
- Key primary documents (research data and reports, statistical sources, etc.)
- Search engines
- Meta sites (e-resources that provide two or more of the other reference tool types in a single product/Web site)

Directories of social scientists, science organizations, projects, etc., are published by many organizations with a Web presence. Social sciences related directories can be identified using the meta sites listed in the collection tools section of this chapter or by using the Internet Public Library or Open Directory Project collections cited in previous chapters. One example site is the APA (American Psychology Association) (www.apa.org) directories of psychologists and psychology researchers.

In the dictionary category there are a number of subject-specific sites offering glossaries, translations, etc. One site stands out: the Online Dictionary of the Social Sciences (http://bitbucket .icaap.org) compiled for undergraduate social sciences students by Gary Parkinson, PhD, and Robert Drislane, PhD. Encyclopedias and almanacs in the social sciences are also often full text or digital libraries or a collection of articles about social sciences concepts. One very good example is the Portals to the World (www.loc.gov/rr/international/portals.html) Library of Congress collection of basic data, with links about nearly every country in the world. It includes economic statistics, demographics, and other social data.

Freely available index and abstracts in the social sciences tend to be in the same e-resources as full-text and digital libraries e-resources. One example is the Popline (http://db.jhuccp.org/ics-wpd/popwe) site. Fee-based classic indexes and abstracts (see those cited elsewhere in this chapter) in this area tend to have a full-text component as well.

Social sciences current awareness sources can be found on any of the association or meta sites. Key primary documents—research data and reports, statistical sources, etc.—for the social sciences are frequently found on e-docs sites. As cited in previous chapters, the Science.gov site is a good starting point for this kind of information.

How will you organize your social sciences e-library collection?
Organizing by the main subject areas and by subfield is always a good way to begin. Organizing by reference types can be useful for some researchers. Use of a CMS can allow for multiple information architecture options and search and display choices for users.

Identifying and Collecting Social Sciences E-Resources

Web Sites That Review and Evaluate E-Resources: Peer E-Libraries, Subject Collections/Guides, or Meta Sites
Intute: Social Sciences (formerly SOSIG) (www.intute.ac.uk/socialsciences) is the central clearinghouse for social sciences e-resources as well as a central communications tool for social scientists interacting on the Web. Intute: Social Sciences reviews and compiles the best of the best social sciences Web sites. The Intute collection covers anthropology, business and management, economics, education, environmental sciences, European studies, government policy, hospitality and catering, human geography, law, politics, psychology, research tools and methods, social welfare, sociology, sport and leisure practice, statistics and data, travel and tourism, and women's studies. In fact, some libraries may choose to simply provide a link to the Intute site. The BUBL Social Sciences catalogue (www.bubl.ac.uk/link/linkbrowse .cfm?menuid=2822) is another excellent source of reviewed and annotated social sciences information resources. INFOMINE Social Sciences and Humanities (http://infomine.ucr.edu/cgi-bin/search?category= liberal) is a browsable and searchable index of thousands of social sciences and humanities sites selected for their scholarly information content and research quality.

DISCUSSION LISTS (LISTSERV, ETC.), FORUMS/GROUPS, E-SERIALS, AND/OR BLOGS THAT POST OR PUBLISH REVIEWS AND EVALUATIONS OF E-RESOURCES

There is no global social sciences Web resource discussion list or newsgroups. There are some groups that discuss social sciences e-resources by specific topic. Intute: Social Sciences collection includes discussion lists or Web forums within each subject categories. For librarians there are two useful discussion lists: EBSS-L, the discussion for members of the Education and Behavioral Sciences Section, Association of College and Research Libraries; and SLA-DSOC, the discussion list for librarians who are members of the Social Sciences division of the Special Libraries Association.

Many social sciences Web sites also have e-newsletter options. Intute: Social Sciences for example invites people to register and subscribe to their current awareness newsletter. Thousands of social sciences related e-journals are available. Search Intute: Social Sciences or NewJour to identify titles that would review social sciences e-resources. For example, a Intute: Social Sciences search retrieves PSYCLINE: Your Guide to Psychology and Social Science Journals on the Web (www.psycline.org/journals/psycline.html). PSYCLINE can be searched by journal title, or search multiple free indexes and table of contents services on the Web. PSYCLINE article search does a meta search of those external services.

PRINT BOOKS AND JOURNALS THAT REVIEW E-RESOURCES

Any social sciences research skills book will review appropriate e-resources. Our best example is, again, Diana Hacker's (2008) *Research and Documentation in the Electronic Age*, Fifth Edition Booklet and Web site (www.dianahacker.com/resdoc). Both the fee-based social sciences research tools and the best of the free Web research tools in subtopic areas of the social sciences are reviewed in this publication. In truth, it is difficult to find a better, more up-to-date social sciences research skills text. Elizabeth H. Oakes's (2004) *Social Science Resources in the Electronic Age* is another useful book for identifying social sciences e-resources.

Most social sciences journals publish e-resource reviews in the same context in which they review books. Any given articles may also cite e-resources or even discuss specific e-resources as the topic of the article. Use Sociological Abstracts (www.csa.com/factsheets/socioabs-set-c.php), PsychINFO (www.apa.org/psycinfo), Social Sciences Full Text (was Social Sciences Abstract/Index) (www.hwwilson.com/Databases/socsci.htm#Abstracts), or a subject specific social science index such as PAIS International (www.csa.com/factsheets/pais-set-c.php) to identify articles that review social sciences e-resources.

EVALUATION GUIDELINES AND SELECTION CRITERIA: THE CORE WEB SOCIAL SCIENCES REFERENCE COLLECTION

As with other scientific information, the key criteria for evaluating social sciences information resources is to determine the source of the data, the research and statistical methodologies used in collecting the information, and the authority of the information provider as indicated by peer or editorial review and his or her academic credentials. Each social sciences area has its own particular vocabulary and accepted research methodologies. At the K–12 or undergraduate educational levels it will be important to verify that the information provider has not only the authority but also the pedagogical experience to write on a particular topic.

In May and August 2008, librarians were surveyed to elicit which social sciences reference tools they consider to be core or essential to their work. The Core Web Social Sciences Reference

Collection on the companion Web Site (www.kovacs.com/ns/essentialguide.html) was initially created using these survey results as core and model collections. Past, present, and future surveys and results are posted at www.kovacs.com/misc.html. This collection is intended for librarians to use as a source of e-resources they might select for their social sciences reference e-library collections. The discussion lists and blogs where the survey links were posted are listed in Table 12.1. The core social sciences reference tools survey is reproduced in Table 12.2.

Print social sciences reference tools remain important. Table 12.3 lists the top five print social sciences reference tools identified in the survey. The free Web sites that librarians reported as core or essential for social sciences reference were clearly useful and are given in Table 12.4.

E-docs sites that support social sciences reference have emerged as sources of key primary information. The top e-docs used for social sciences reference are listed in Table 12.5. The top fee-based social sciences reference e-resources are reported in Table 12.6.

Fee-based e-resources are included in the Core Web Social Science Reference Tools on the companion Web site (www.kovacs.com/ns/essentialguide.html) when they offer free trials or have some information available without requiring a fee.

Table 12.1. Discussion Lists and Blogs Distribution for Social Sciences Reference Tools Survey

- LISNews and LISNewsWire Blogs: lisnews-owner@lishost.net
- ResourceShelf Blog: gary.price@resourceshelf.com
- ERIL-L@LISTSERV.BINGHAMTON.EDU
- dig_ref@LISTSERV.SYR.EDU
- collib-l@ala.org

- LIS-LINK@jiscmail.ac.uk
- Libref-L@listserv.kent.edu
- GOVDOC-L@lists.psu.edu
- publib@webjunction.org
- livereference@yahoogroups.com
- Libref-L@listserv.kent.edu

Table 12.2. Core Social Sciences Reference Tools Survey Questions

1. Which library type best describes the library you work in/for/with?

2. In which subject area(s) are you most likely to answer social sciences questions? (Check all that apply.)

3. What are the essential three print titles (reference books) that you can't work without in answering social sciences questions? (Please type the title only.)

4. What are the essential three free (not government published) Web-accessible databases that you can't work without in answering social sciences questions? (Please type complete URL/Web address; e.g., www.intute.ac.uk/socialsciences/lost.html.)

5. What are the essential three (.gov) government published (state, federal, local, international) free Web-accessible databases that you can't work without in answering social sciences questions? (Please type complete URL/Web address; e.g., www.nsf.gov.)

6. What are the essential three fee-based Web-accessible databases that you can't work without in answering Social Sciences questions? (Please type the simple title; e.g., Anthropology Plus.)

7. Does your library maintain a Web page or site to support social sciences reference? If so ,please share the URL/Web address (e.g., www.lib.uidaho.edu/instruction/sociology_lg).

8. Additional comments or ideas:

(Please include your name and e-mail address if you would like feedback, otherwise this survey form is completely anonymous.)

Table 12.3. Top Five Print Social Sciences Reference Tools Identified in Survey

1. *Statistical Abstract of the U.S.*
2. *Encyclopedia of Social Work*
3. *DSM-IV-TR: Diagnostic and Statistical Manual of Mental Disorders*
4. *Mental Measurements Yearbook*
5. *Encyclopedia of Psychology* (other encyclopedias anddictionaries of psychology, anthropology, sociology, etc.)

Table 12.4. Top Five Free Web Social Sciences Reference Tools Identified in Survey

1. Intute Social Sciences: www.intute.ac.uk/socialsciences
2. Google: www.google.com, and Google Scholar: http://scholar.google.com
3. Buros Institute of Mental Measurements/Test Reviws Online: www.unl.edu/buros/bimm/index.html or http://buros.unl.edu/buros/jsp/search.jsp
4. Social Sciences Research Network: www.ssrn.com
5. APA (American Psychology Association): www.apa.org

Table 12.5. Top Four Government Documents Web Sites Used as Social Sciences Reference Tools Identified in Survey

1. U.S. Census Bureau/American Factfinder: www.census.gov or http://factfinder.census.gov/home/saff/main.html
2. Bureau of Justice Statistics: www.ojp.usdoj.gov/bjs
3. International, state, regional, and local agency statistical and social Web sites
4. CIA Library: www.cia.gov/library/index.html, Liber8 Economic Information for Librarians and Students (from Federal Reserve Bank of St. Louis): http://liber8.stlouisfed.org, FedStats: www.fedstats.gov, Global Gateway: http://international.loc.gov/intldl/intldlhome.html, National Criminal Justice Reference Service: www.ncjrs.org, National Institutes of Health (NIH) http://nih.gov, PubMed: www.ncbi.nlm.nih.gov/pubmed, Statistical Abstract: www.census.gov/compendia/statab, Substance Abuse and Mental Health Statistics: www.oas.samhsa.gov, Substance Abuse and Mental Health Services Administration (SAMHSA): www.samhsa.gov, USA.gov: www.usa.gov

Note: Several titles tied for fourth place.

Table 12.6. Top Three Fee-based Social Sciences Reference E-Resources Identified in Survey

1. PsycINFO: http://www.apa.org/psycinfo
2. Sociological Abstracts: www.csa.com/factsheets/socioabs-set-c.php
3. Academic Search Complete/Academic Search Premier (EBSCO): www.ebscohost.com/thisTopic.php?marketID=1&topicID=633 or www.ebscohost.com/thisTopic.php?topicID=1&marketID=1, Anthropology Plus www.oclc.org/support/documentation/firstsearch/databases/dbdetails/details/AnthropologyPlus.htm, AnthroSource: www.anthrosource.net/Default.aspx?cookieSet=1, Reference USA: www.referenceusa.com, Business Source Premier (EBSCO): www.ebscohost.com, Business and Company Resource Center (Gale): www.gale.cengage.com

Note: Several titles tied for third place.

E-Library Success Story

University of Canterbury Library
Christchurch, New Zealand
http://library.canterbury.ac.nz
Contacts: Catherine Jane, catherine.jane@canterbury.ac.nz, and Anne Scott, anne.scott@canterbury.ac.nz

A. Collection Planning (e.g., goal setting and identification of users, technology/personnel choices)

The University of Canterbury Library was one of the very first libraries to implement a Web presence. They began to build the e-library in 1994 and by 1996 had begun to implement e-library services as well as an e-resource collection on their Web site. "The University of Canterbury Library Web e-library was conceived in 1994/5, driven by the increasing number of publishers who were offering content in electronic format. The Library's first home page was set up in 1994 but at that stage consisted only of Library news and an online version of our Library guide. The annual report of 1996 reports that Web access to selected international sites was set up in that year, and that Information Services Librarians were working on developing html skills and Library Web pages. So 1996 is probably the first year that it could be said that we implemented E-library services, although we had provided access to electronic journals and databases on CD-ROM in previous years."

The Web site serves as the library's presence for both on-campus and off-campus users. Every resource and service the library offers is available through the Web site with few exceptions. "Study space and shelf browsing are probably the only remaining services that can be accessed without using our Web site. Our electronic resources are now so much part of core Library resources that we no longer distinguish them with separate links on our Web site. It is probably true to say that we no longer have a separate E-Library as such—the entire Library is a mixture of print and electronic with the emphasis being on the value of any resource, although our preference would be for electronic format. This is consistent with our service philosophy, which is to provide services both electronically and in the Library." Interlibrary loan transactions are initiated through the Web site only. The AskLIVE virtual reference service is offered through the e-library site as well.

The library selects and makes available e-resources that support the academic and related programs offered by the University of Canterbury. Students and academic and general staff of the University of Canterbury all have access to the e-library both on-campus and remotely. Some basic services are available to alumni, other institutions, and the general public. "Electronic resources in particular have limitations, for licensing and copyright reasons, and electronic services such as our AskLIVE service, email enquiries etc also have limitations for users outside the UC community."

The University of Canterbury e-library supports distance learning programs in education and engineering and supports researchers in remote locations around the world, such as Antarctica. The university also offers postgraduate courses through distance learning. "It is interesting to note that our electronic resources have now become so mainstreamed that they are probably used equally by distance and on-campus users, and it is in the delivery of printed resources that services to distance students is different. That said, we have created some electronic resources

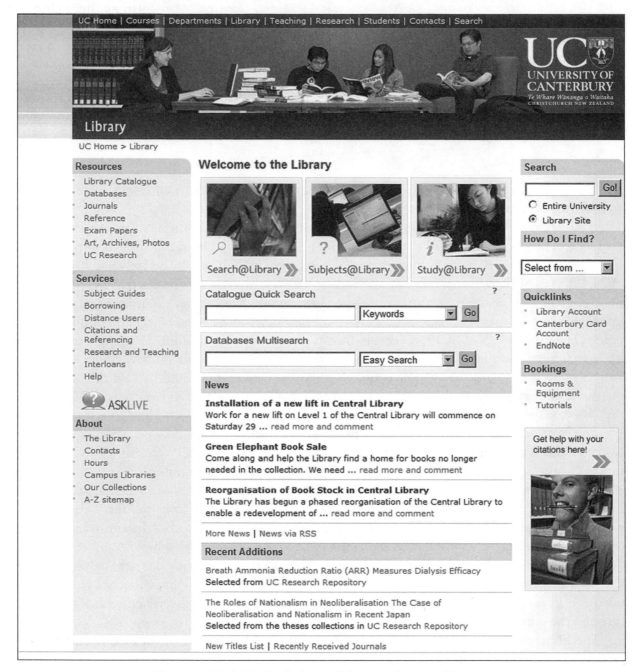

Figure 12.1 University of Canterbury Library

with distance students in mind e.g. our videos on how to make online renewals or requests, but these could be just as useful to some on-campus users. It is, however, useful to note that the availability of electronic resources and services is particularly helpful to minimize any disadvantages of studying at a distance."

The University of Canterbury e-library developed a written collection plan from its inception. The current version is available online at www.canterbury.ac.nz/ucpolicy/GetPolicy.aspx?file= collectiondevelopmentpolicy.pdf. "In 2006 this policy was updated to clarify the statement about electronic resources. We see this as a living document. It is an ongoing process to define the balance of electronic and print in our collections, keeping pace with the changing electronic environment."

B. Collection Strategies (e.g., selection criteria, identification of resources, licensing, and related user information needs)

The University of Canterbury e-library is clearly user-centered. All resources are selected and purchased based on whether they are relevant "to teaching, research or scholarship at the University." Format of the materials as well as archival access are carefully considered. "We operate a Datasets group which evaluates and selects electronic resources. This group also arranges trials and invites user feedback from these trials. We find it a constant challenge to ensure we are getting best value from what we purchase, especially in view of publisher pressure to buy packages of full text access, which may offer value in terms of the number of titles available, but which reduce flexibility in terms of purchasing or cancelling access to individual resources or titles. Decisions about purchasing are also influenced by whether or not there is ongoing access to the content paid for. Not all providers allow for this but ongoing availability of the content paid for is a strong consideration for any purchase or renewal."

Licensing arrangements require accessibility for the entire University of Canterbury community. The library pays for fee-based Web accessible resources accordingly. Fee-based resources are not available to the general public but are available to the core users both on-campus and remotely. EZProxy (www.oclc.org/ezproxy) is used for remote access user authentication. "In some cases this is by individual license for the University of Canterbury, while in other cases we have entered into consortial agreements with other NZ and/or Australian organizations."

Selected e-books are included in the collection but there are challenges to their effective use by the library's users. One of the major problems is the variety of search and display options and lack of consistency between e-book vendors. Accessibility remains a problem. "We are finding that vendors are marketing e-books very strongly, but the provision of e-books is very challenging, as there are so many different models, for accessing the books, pricing structures, archiving and simultaneous users, all of which contribute to a confusing experience for the end user. It is something we are working currently to simplify and rationalize."

All e-library resources are cataloged, including free and fee-based Web accessible resources, e-books, e-serials, etc. Information extracted from catalog records is used to display information on the e-library Web site and access options are displayed in the catalog record "so that information about our resources is saved once and displayed in many places."

The University of Canterbury has ongoing projects to digitize locally held materials. Both archival digitization as well as ongoing current projects are in place. "All University Masters and PhD theses are now required to be deposited in PDF as well as print format, and we contribute information about and links to these on the Australasian Digital Theses Program (http://adt .caul.edu.au). Additionally, some retrospective scanning of theses is being undertaken. We have a growing repository of UC research in our UC Research Repository (http://ircanterbury.ac.nz/), and an increasing collection of digitized art, archives, and photographs (http://library.canterbury .ac.nz/home/archives.shtml). These resources are given prominence on our home page."

The intention is to continue digitizing as much as possible as long as there are funds available to do so. The projects are selective and clear guidelines as to what materials will be digitized are in place. The projects emphasize accessibility of the digitized materials by giving high priority to metadata records. "We have a Standard Operating Procedure for Digitization Projects which outlines considerations for the types of materials to be digitized, and how projects are managed. Generally greatest consideration is given to material unique to the University of Canterbury, material related to teaching and research, and material that needs to be digitized for preservation. Along with the digitization, the provision of access points (metadata) is given high priority...."

Responsibility for digitization projects is shared among the "custodians" of the collection, Collection Services (for the metadata), and Library IT for the storage and accessibility of the digital objects."

As with many other similar projects, the AskLIVE virtual reference service is not as well used as librarians would wish. "Our virtual reference service (AskLIVE) is now run using Meebo. People who use it generally give us very positive feedback about the service, but it has very low usage, in spite of extensive advertising and the fact that there is a link to it on every page on our site. We continue to offer it in spite of the low usage statistics, because it can be run from staff desktops allowing the staff person to continue to do other work at the same time."

C. Collection Organization (e.g., content management systems, Web server choices, personnel responsibilities, etc.)

The University of Canterbury Web site uses Dreamweaver templates and scripts. Resource information is dynamically accessed from the library catalog. "Subject experts select the resources which are to be displayed and through internally created Web forms, add information to the catalogue which is then used by scripts to create appropriate Web pages. We have professional librarians allocated to specific subject areas, both in Information Services and in Collection Services."

Electronic resources selection is integrated into all librarians' routine professional activities. The e-library is in a very real sense an integral library presence. Professional staff spend a major part of their time supporting the e-library. "That said, we do have over 20 staff who edit Web pages. These staff use Dreamweaver and have access to upload Web pages directly to the site. We have policies about what they edit, formats and styles that can be used, and every page is created with a predefined template. Previously any edits had to be approved and uploaded by one or two people, but now it is felt that the Web site is so integral to the function of the Library that more staff need to be involved to keep it up to date."

In the early years, specific personnel were selected and trained to support the e-library. "These people were trained internally, and did not require any specific qualifications, other than an interest and aptitude for the work. This has changed to the point that now this work is much more distributed, for example all staff in Collection Services are experienced in dealing with electronic resources, staff from throughout the Library help with provision of our AskLIVE service, and many people contribute to the Web pages that are the entry point to electronic resources. Again, training has tended to be mostly internal, though there are occasions where one person attends external training and then trains others."

Newer, more recently trained librarians are coming into the library with new ideas and skills that are enhancing and challenging the e-library collection and services to make further adjustments to serving users as they can best be served given the technologies available. "We do have a specified person who manages the Library Web site—me [Catherine Jane]. The required qualifications are a professional library qualification, experience in developing and maintaining Web sites, and knowledge of Web technologies. I personally have a Diploma in Internet Technology, though a formal technical qualification was not a requirement for the position. . . . I am responsible for the overall management of the Web site and ensure that pages conform to stylistic guidelines, but I do not necessarily update all the content—this is distributed among all the people who have Dreamweaver. As our site is a sub-site of the University's site, I work closely with the UC Web Team to ensure that we conform to the University's guidelines for Web sites. I also work closely with the Library's programmer to create and maintain dynamic pages. I manage the structure of the site, have an overview of content, consider usability and accessibility issues, and consult with and make recommendations to other staff about the content on pages they are updating."

Choice, Global Books in Print, New Zealand's National Bibliography, and publisher and vendor catalogs and Web sites, are all used by librarians for selecting and collection resources as is serendipitous discovery of relevant resources during Web searches. "Our Collection Services staff, and Information Librarians take an active role in recommending items for the collection, as do academic staff in the various colleges and schools. Information Librarians use their knowledge and experience of online resources in their subject areas to recommend Web sites to be catalogued. Academic staff also use their expertise and contacts in their area of study and teaching."

D. Collection Maintenance (e.g., link checking, ongoing weeding, and growth of the e-library collection)

Catherine Jane runs Dreamweaver several times a year—usually during semester breaks when staff have time—to check for broken links internal to the Web site and then uses Xenu's Link Sleuth (http://home.snafu.de/tilman/xenulink.html) to check for external links and to check catalog records. "Both of these programs are reasonably flexible and work well, if not perfectly. We also run a link checker through our catalogue on a regular basis to check for broken links within records, and these are sent back to the cataloguers to check and correct. To check catalogue records we have had to add an internally programmed step to the process to allow us to run Xenu over the links."

Each year six to seven "volunteers" are recruited to work through the Web site on selected tasks or research strategies to verify and improve Web site usability. Depending on the emphasis of the usability testing these volunteers range from experienced users to complete novices. Every two years the library surveys users regarding all library collections and services. They use Insync Surveys (www.insyncsurveys.com.au). This organization runs the survey but also provides data analysis, including benchmarking the library in relation to other libraries in New Zealand and Australia. "We also run shorter, more focused and less formal surveys ourselves via our Web site several times a year, usually on more specific topics. For example, we have just run one about desirable features in a Library catalogue. We invite both general and specific feedback through the use of Web forms accessible from our Web site. For example, we have forms to report a problem with access to a database or electronic journal."

All feedback is used to continuously improve and enhance the library collections and services. "We usually review our main Web pages, in terms of usability, accessibility, and design, before the start of each academic year. Major upgrades to indexing and search software are also timed to minimize disruption to services during the academic year, and would be in response to the availability of new resources or services, or the failure of current resources or services to fulfill our needs. Our Datasets group would take overall responsibility for the selection of resources, but any decisions would be made after wide consultation, particularly with Information Librarians.... Software changes such as the choice of federated searching software, review of blogs and wikis, or evaluation of our catalogue interface, are usually managed by means of a short-term project. Project Teams normally have a representative from various parts of the Library, a Project Manager and a Project Sponsor. They normally produce a report for the Library Leadership Team."

Future plans for the e-library are consistent with their ongoing mission to make sure the e-library is as usable, accessible, and well designed for the needs of their users as possible. "We are constantly looking for ways to make use of new technology to improve our Web services and make our pages more dynamic. For example, we are in the process of changing how we manage Library news by making use of blog software, with items on the news blog being displayed automatically on the Web site. This will mean that more staff will be able to add news items without directly altering Web pages, we can maintain a news archive, news will be searchable, and users will be able to make comments. We are also in the process of implementing LibGuides for our subject guides to add more Web 2 functionality."

One recent improvement has been the addition of Serials Solutions: 360 Search (www.serials solutions.com/ss_360_search.html) federated search tool to the home page and a number of other pages on the site. They will also use the 360 Counter to run basic collection analysis to identify gaps and strengths in the e-library collection and to assist in assessing value for money. "We will use 360 Counter for cost/search and overlap analysis. We contribute to and benchmark ourselves against CONZUL (Council of New Zealand University Libraries) and CAUL (Council of Australian University Libraries) statistics." They are considering OCLC's WorldCat Collection Analysis service (www.oclc.org/collectionanalysis) as a possibility for future collection analysis.

REFERENCES AND WEB SITES CITED

Hacker, Diane, with Barbara Fister. 2009. *Research and Documentation in the Electronic Age*, 5th edition. New York: Bedford/St. Martin's. Available: http://www.dianahacker.com/resdoc (accessed January 19, 2009).

Head, Alison J. 2007. "Beyond Google: How Do Students Conduct Academic Research?" *First Monday* 12, no. 8 (August). Available: www.firstmonday.org/issues/issue12_8/head.

Kousha, Kayvan, and Mike Thelwall. 2007. "The Web Impact of Open Access Social Science Research." *Library and Information Science Research Preprint*. Available: www.scit.wlv.ac.uk/~cm1993/papers/OpenAccessSocialSciencePreprint.doc.

Oakes, Elizabeth H. (2004). *Social Science Resources in the Electronic Age*. Westport, CT: Greenwood Press.

Schaffer, Thomas. 2004. "Psychology Citations Revisited: Behavioral Research in the Age of Electronic Resources." *The Journal of Academic Librarianship* 30, no. 5: 354–360.

Sutton, Allison M., and JoAnn Jacoby. 2009. "A Comparative Study of Book and Journal Use in Four Social Science Disciplines." *Behavioral & Social Sciences Librarian* 27, no. 1: 1–33.

WEB SITES CITED

APA (American Psychology Association). Available: www.apa.org (accessed January 19, 2009).

BUBL Social Sciences catalogue. Available: www.bubl.ac.uk/link/linkbrowse.cfm?menuid=2822 (accessed January 19, 2009).

Google. Available: www.google.com (accessed January 14, 2009).

INFOMINE: Social Sciences and Humanities. Available: http://infomine.ucr.edu/cgi-bin/search?category=liberal (accessed January 7, 2009).

Intute: Social Sciences. Available: www.intute.ac.uk/socialsciences (accessed January 7, 2009).

Online Dictionary of the Social Sciences. Available: http://bitbucket.icaap.org (accessed January 28, 2009).

PAIS International. Available: www.csa.com/factsheets/pais-set-c.php (accessed January 20, 2009).

Popline. Available: http://db.jhuccp.org/ics-wpd/popweb (accessed January 14, 2009).

Portals to the World. Available: www.loc.gov/rr/international/portals.html (accessed January 20, 2009).

PsycINFO. Available: www.apa.org/psycinfo (accessed January 14, 2009).

PSYCLINE: Your Guide to Psychology and Social Science Journals on the Web. Available: www.psycline .org/journals/psycline.html (accessed January 21, 2009).

Social Sciences Citation Index. Available: www.thomsonreuters.com/products_services/scientific/Social_ Sciences_Citation_Index (accessed January 14, 2009).

Social Sciences Full Text (was Social Sciences Abstracts/Social Sciences Index). Available: www.hwwilson .com/Databases/socsci.htm#Abstracts (accessed January 14, 2009).

Sociological Abstracts. Available: www.csa.com/factsheets/socioabs-set-c.php (accessed January 14, 2009).

SOCIAL SCIENCES E-RESOURCES COLLECTION TOOLS

META-SITES

American Studies Web: Reference and Research
http://lamp.georgetown.edu/asw

"The American Studies Web is the largest bibliography of web-based resources in the field of American Studies." The 28 general categories range from American Studies to Working Class and Labor Studies.

Anthropology Resources on the Internet
www.aaanet.org/resources/

Collection of anthropology related Web resources as well as news and other anthropology related information. Hosted by the American Anthropological Association.

Anthropology Resources on the Internet Virtual Library
www.anthropologie.net/

The original collection of anthropology Web resources begun by Allen Lutinsin 1995. Archaelogy is the main collection area.

Archaeology on the Net
http://members.tripod.com/~archonnet/ringlist.html

Selective but comprehensive collection of Archaeology resources on the net. Hosts ArchPub, a mailing list for keeping up with publications in the fields.

The Eric Friedheim National Journalism Library at the National Press Club
http://npc.press.org/library/resources.cfm

Collection of links for journalists.

Geosource
www.library.uu.nl/geosource/

Collection of Web resources for human geography,physical geography, planning,geoscience and environmental science. Maintained by Jeroen Bosman of the Central Library, Utrecht University, The Netherlands.

Global Gateway
http://international.loc.gov/intldl/intldlhome.html

The Library of Congress collection of digital libraries, Web sites, research guides, databases, and other resources related to international studies. This meta-site is also a directory of digital libraries in this specific area.

Humanities and Social Sciences Net
http://h-net.org/

Dedicated to promoting studies in the humanities and social sciences on the Internet and off-line. Collections of e-resources in subject areas, as well as as e-serials, and a jobs announcement area.

INFOMINE: Social Sciences and Humanities
http://infomine.ucr.edu/cgi-bin/search?category=liberal

Browsable and searchable index of thousands of social sciences and humanities sites "of use as a scholarly information resource in research or educational activities at the university level."

Internet Crossroads in Social Science Data
www.disc.wisc.edu/newcrossroads/index.asp

Searchable collection of Web sites that archive or otherwise supply data appropriate for use in the Social Sciences.

Intute: Social Sciences

www.intute.ac.uk/socialsciences/

   Intute is a multi-subject e-library maintained by a consortium of United Kingdom university and academic organization Library partners (www.intute.ac.uk/socialsciences/partners.html) who carefully select and evaluate all the social sciences e-resources that are open source or otherwise freely available on the Web. Scope includes Anthropology, Business and Management, Economics, Education, Environmental Sciences, European Studies, Government Policy, Hospitality and Catering, Human Geography, Law, Politics, Psychology, Research Tools and Methods, Social Welfare, Sociology, Sport and Leisure Practice, Statistics and Data, Travel and Tourism, and Women's Studies. Includes the content of the original SOSIG project.

The Media and Communications Studies Site

www.aber.ac.uk/media/

   British-centric collection of Web sites that support the study of media and communications.

Online Communications Studies Resources

www.uiowa.edu/~commstud/resources/

   Communications Studies Web sites compiled by Karla Tonella at the University of Iowa, Department of Communications Studies.

Political Resources on the Net

www.politicalresources.net/

   "Listings of political sites available on the Internet sorted by country, with links to Parties, Organizations, Governments, Media and more from all around the world."

Psych Web

www.psywww.com/

   Meta-site with directory of psychology programs and organizations, as well as collections of e-books, Web sites, and other tools that support teaching and learning in Pyschology. Maintained by Russell A. Dewey, PhD.

Social Psychology Network

www.socialpsychology.org/

   Collection of Web sites that support teaching and learning in social psychology and related fields.

Social Work and Social Services Web sites

http://gwbweb.wustl.edu/Resources/Pages/socialservicesresourcesintro.aspx

   Highly selective colleciton of Web sites supporting studies in social work and social services.

SocioSite

www.sociosite.net/

   Collection of Web sites related to the study of sociology and related social sciences. Content has a European emphasis.

Women's Studies/Women's Issues Resource Sites

http://userpages.umbc.edu/~korenman/wmst/links.html

   "Selective, annotated, highly acclaimed listing of web sites containing resources and information about women's studies / women's issues, with an emphasis on sites of particular use to an academic women's studies program." Maintained by Professor Joan Korenman.

DIGITAL LIBRARIES DIRECTORIES OR COLLECTIONS OF DIGITAL LIBRARIES (DIGITAL LIBRARIES OF E-BOOKS, E-SERIALS, IMAGES, RECORDINGS, AND OTHER ARTIFACTS)

Collaborative Digitization Programs in the United States

http://frank.mtsu.edu/~kmiddlet/stateportals.html

   Directory of state and regional cultural materials digitization projects. Maintained by Ken Middleton: kmiddlet@mtsu.edu.

State Digital Resources: Memory Projects, Online Encyclopedias, Historical & Cultural Materials Collections
www.loc.gov/rr/program/bib/statememory/
> Compiled by Christine A. Pruzin, Digital Reference Specialist.

World Digital Library
www.worlddigitallibrary.org/project/english/index.html
> "The World Digital Library will make available on the Internet, free of charge and in multilingual format, significant primary materials from cultures around the world, including manuscripts, maps, rare books, musical scores, recordings, films, prints, photographs, architectural drawings, and other significant cultural materials. The objectives of the World Digital Library are to promote international and inter-cultural understanding and awareness, provide resources to educators, expand non-English and non-Western content on the Internet, and to contribute to scholarly research."

E-SERIALS, BLOGS, DISCUSSION LISTS, ETC.

ASIA-WWW-MONITOR
http://coombs.anu.edu.au/asia-www-monitor.html
> Discusses Web sites for social science studies in and about Asia.

EBSS-L
http://listserv.uncc.edu/archives/ebss-l.html
> Discussion for Education and Behavioral Sciences Librarians (Education and Behavioral Sciences Section, Association of College & Research Libraries, American Library Association).

H-Net Review
http://h-net.org/reviews/
> Humanities and Social Sciences net reviews of print and e-resources.

SLA-DSOC
www.sla.org/content/community/lists/divisionlists5979.cfm or www.sla.org/content/community/lists/joinlists.cfm
> Discussion list for librarians who are members of the Social Sciences division of the Special Libraries Association.

EDUCATION AND HOMEWORK E-RESOURCES

When done well, teachers should be able to build lessons and assignments from these collections, with the assurance that the resources they have built their work around will be available to their students. (Savard, 2007: 87)

DEVELOPING A COLLECTION PLAN FOR EDUCATION AND HOMEWORK E-RESOURCES

Education e-resources are defined, for discussion in this chapter, as resources that support teachers at all levels of education, administrators, schools, educational researchers, and provide practical support for the work of students. This chapter addresses e-resources that are:

- Educational research e-resources (e.g., statistics, published articles, reports, and data)
- Teacher or educator e-resources/e-resources for teaching and learning (e.g., lesson plans, guides, glossaries, etc.)
- E-resources for learning and completing coursework intended for the student (e.g., homework help).

Education e-resources can include any of the e resources cited in any of the other chapters in this book. We will only briefly mention homework help resources, but they are also included in this broad definition. Resources for teaching and learning can be useful for both teachers and students, and so homework help e-resources and teacher resources frequently overlap.

Information for those planning on a college or university education is available in quantity and form never available before the Web. Such information consists of Web sites provided by colleges and universities, financial aid agencies, and educational organizations. This information includes everything from course and program descriptions and online applications to anecdotal descriptions by current and past students.

WHAT PURPOSE WILL YOUR COLLECTION SERVE? FOR WHOM ARE YOU COLLECTING THESE E-RESOURCES?

Educational resources at the college or university level can literally be any information resource in any subject area. Does your library support teachers and school administrators, education students, or education researchers? Define the group that the education collection will support and that will dictate the scope of education-related e-resources that you will collect.

Academic libraries may want to collect education e-resources to support teacher education and educational researchers in their colleges and universities as well as e-resources that support educators who teach specific subjects. K–12 and many public librarians will want to collect the homework help resources that will be useful to students studying the subjects taught in their schools as well as e-resources to support teaching. The quote that opens this chapter is referring to the second type of education e-resource user and purpose. Savard (2007) also points out that one of the greatest problems is in finding grade-appropriate materials online that teachers can use. Student teachers may also benefit from homework help resources in learning to plan instruction and teach. K–12 e-resources for teaching and learning are qualitatively different than those for supporting postsecondary educators and students. Many of the best e-resources are fee-based and relatively expensive. K–12 libraries might be able to make use of a consortium to access the most expensive but also the most appropriate e-resources for their users (Rossi, 2009; Johnson, 2007).

WHAT TYPES OF E-RESOURCES WILL YOU COLLECT?

Almost all of the other reference e-resource and collection tools cited in the other chapters will be useful for education. We can conveniently describe education-related e-resources in terms of traditional reference source types.

- Directories (of educators, educational researchers, projects, schools, colleges, universities, educational organizations, and programs, etc)
- Dictionaries (education and educational research vocabulary in English as well as international language translation dictionaries)
- Abstracts, indexes, and table of contents services (including those with full text of education and education research journals indexed)
- Encyclopedias and almanacs
- Full-text and/or multimedia databases/digital libraries (collections of e-books, e-serials, recordings, videos, podcasts, images etc.)
- News and news services (education and educational research current awareness sources)
- Key primary documents (lesson plans and curricula, statistics, research reports and data)
- Search engines
- Meta sites (e-resources that provide two or more of the other reference tool types in a single product/Web site)

Directories of educators, educational researchers, projects, schools, colleges, universities, educational organizations, and programs are published by many organizations with a Web presence; for example, the American School Directory (www.asd.com) of all K–12 schools in the United States along with basic statistics and contact information about each one. Additional directories can be identified using the education meta sites listed in the collection tools section in this chapter or by using the Internet Public Library or Open Directory Project collections cited in previous chapters.

Just about any dictionary cited in previous and subsequent chapters will be useful in education. ERIC (www.eric.ed.gov) is the standard for education indexes and abstracts. It is also at least partially a full-text and multimedia digital library. Almost any of the encyclopedias or encyclopedia like e-resources cited in previous and subsequent chapters might be used for education. In the core reference tools survey Wikipedia (http://en.wikipedia.org/wiki/Main_Page) was selected as a core or essential education reference tool. An interesting encyclopedia-like e-resource for educational researchers primarily is the Encyclopedia of Informal Education (www.infed.org), which publishes encyclopedic information on ideas, thinkers, and practice of informal educational methods.

Education and educational research current awareness sources can be found in all of the other sites cited in this chapter and in the Core Web Education Reference Tools collection on the companion Web site (www.kovacs.com/ns/essentialguide.html).

Key primary documents including lesson plans and curricula, statistics, research reports and data, etc., are particularly substantial for education. Lesson plans and curricular materials are usually found in the meta sites that are listed in the collection tools sections at the end of each chapter. Note that although most of these types of key primary documents are searchable and archived in the meta sites listed in the "Education and Homework E-Resource Collection Tools," they may also be found in subject specific meta sites listed in other in subject-specific collection tools lists. For example, The Applied Math and Science Education Repository (AMSER) (http://amser.org) project is a collection of Web resources designed for upper level secondary school and community and technical college math and sciences educators to use to find resources for those students. AMSER is funded by the National Science Foundation as part of the National Science Digital Library and is being created via the Internet Scout Project. AMSER is cited in the "Engineering, Computer Sciences, and Mathematics E-Resource Collection Tools" section in Chapter 10, but is clearly going to be useful for secondary and postsecondary teachers.

HOW WILL YOU ORGANIZE YOUR EDUCATION AND HOMEWORK RELATED E-LIBRARY COLLECTION?

Educational resources can easily be organized by subject and then by whether they are educational research tools or teaching and learning support resources. It will also be useful to organize them by age appropriateness and/or educational level of the intended library user groups. Some libraries will find that organizing education-related e-resources by reference type will make them more accessible for education students and researchers.

IDENTIFYING AND COLLECTING EDUCATION AND HOMEWORK E-RESOURCES

WEB SITES THAT REVIEW AND EVALUATE E-RESOURCES: PEER E-LIBRARIES, SUBJECT COLLECTIONS/GUIDES, OR META SITES

The first place to look for education-related resources is in education meta sites. The Eric Clearinghouse (www.eric.ed.gov) is one of the best collections of educational research related documents. The Gateway to Educational Materials (GEM) (www.thegateway.org) is a central meta site for all things educational and homework related on the Web. The Education Index (www.education index.com) is an annotated collection of evaluated teaching and learning resources organized by age, educational level, and subject will be a good source to check. The Academic Info site (www.academicinfo.net) is a useful meta site for higher-education e-resources. Kathy Schrock's Guide for Educators (http://school.discovery.com/schrockguide) is the premier source for Web sites that support teaching and learning. In fact some libraries may simply choose to link to these meta sites. The "Education and Homework E-Resource Collection Tools" section at the end of this chapter lists several other potentially useful meta sites.

DISCUSSION LISTS (LISTSERV, ETC.), FORUMS/GROUPS, E-SERIALS, AND/OR BLOGS THAT POST OR PUBLISH REVIEWS AND EVALUATIONS OF E-RESOURCES

One of the most active and productive educational e-resources discussion list is LM_NET. This discussion group is for school library media specialists, or any librarian, teacher, or parent who is working with information intended for K–12 students in any format. The focus, however, is on e-resources, troubleshooting, software choices, and similar topics for K–12 libraries. EBSS-L, the discussion list for members of the members of the Special Libraries Association, Education Division; and SLA-DEDU, the discussion list for members of the Special Libraries Association, Education Division, are both also very useful for getting reviews of education e-resources.

The Educator's Reference Desk (previously AskEric) maintains a directory and archives for several education-related discussion lists (www.eduref.org). Educational CyberPlayGround (www.edu-cyberpg.com/TOC.asp) hosts a blog and mailing list for K–12 educators and librarians. The Internet Scout projects the Scout Report (http://scout.cs.wisc.edu/scout/index.html) is the premier source of reviews of education e-resources. Other education e-serials can be identified in the meta sites.

PRINT BOOKS AND JOURNALS THAT REVIEW E-RESOURCES

Alan November's (2008) *Web Literacy for Educators* does an excellent job of highlighting and justifying e-resources for educators, and it also explains how educators can manage Web access in their classrooms and online teaching venues. Print education journals including *Educational Research*, *High School Journal*, *Journal of Adult Education*, *Journal of Education*, *Reading Research Quarterly*, and *Teacher Education and Practice* and *School Library Journal* all publish reviews of education-related e-resources. Search ERIC (www.eric.ed.gov) or Education Abstracts/ Education Full Text (www.hwwilson.com) to identify specific articles or reports that review education-related e-resources.

EVALUATION GUIDELINES AND SELECTION CRITERIA: THE CORE WEB EDUCATION AND HOMEWORK REFERENCE COLLECTION

The key criteria for evaluating educational research information resources is to determine the source of the data, the research and statistical methodologies used in collecting the information, and the authority of the information provider. Education e-resources vary greatly in content and the authority of the information provider. Some of them are provided educational or research organizations and others by educators with varying degrees of expertise. Many are supplied by K–12 or postsecondary school students. Government and nongovernment agencies publish some important education e-resources. Other education e-resources are made available for commercial purposes. The best strategy to follow is the basic process of evaluating Web information resources described in Part I, Chapter 1. When evaluating resources to support teaching and learning related to business, medical, scientific, or legal subjects use the strategies for evaluating those types of information described in those specific chapters.

In May and August 2008, librarians were surveyed to elicit which education and homework reference tools they consider to be core or essential to their work. Separate surveys were sent out for education for the first time (previously education had been combined with social sciences), and those results were combined with the results from previous homework-reference-specific surveys. The Core Web Education and Homework Reference Collection on the companion Web Site (www.kovacs.com/ns/essentialguide.html) was initially created using these survey results as core and model collections. Past, present, and future surveys and results are posted at www.kovacs .com/misc.html. This collection is intended for librarians to use as a source of e-resources they might select for their education and/or homework reference e-library collections. Fee-based e-resources are included when they offer free trials or have some information available without requiring a fee. Obviously each library will want to select education e-resources that will support its own library users. The discussion lists and blogs where the survey links were posted are listed in Table 13.1. The core education and homework reference tools survey is reproduced in Table 13.2.

Table 13.1. Discussion Lists and Blogs Distribution for Education and Homework Reference Tools Survey

- LM_NET@LISTSERV.SYR.EDU
- LISNews and LISNewsWire Blogs: lisnews-owner@lishost.net
- ResourceShelf Blog: gary.price@resourceshelf.com
- ERIL-L@LISTSERV.BINGHAMTON.EDU
- dig_ref@LISTSERV.SYR.EDU
- collib-l@ala.org
- LIS-LINK@jiscmail.ac.uk
- Libref-L@listserv.kent.edu
- GOVDOC-L@lists.psu.edu
- publib@webjunction.org
- livereference@yahoogroups.com
- Libref-L@listserv.kent.edu

Table 13.2. Core Education and Homework Reference Tools Survey Questions

1. Which library type best describes the library you work in/for/with?
2. In which subject area(s) are you most likely to answer education research questions? (Check all that apply.)
3. What are the essential three print titles (reference books) that you can't work without in answering Education Research questions?(Please type the title only.)
4. What are the essential three free (not government published) Web-accessible databases that you can't work without in answering education research questions? (Please type complete URL/Web address; e.g., www.eduref.org.)
5. What are the essential three (.gov) government published (state, federal, local, international) free Web-accessible databases that you can't work without in answering education research questions? (Please type complete URL/Web address; e.g., www.eric.ed.gov.)
6. What are the essential three fee-based Web-accessible databases that you can't work without in answering education research questions? (Please the simple title; e.g., Education Research Complete.)
7. Does your library maintain a Web page or site to support education research reference? If so, please share the URL/Web address (e.g., www.library.uiuc.edu/edx/genedu.htm).
8. Additional comments or ideas:

(Please include your name and e-mail address if you would like feedback, otherwise this survey form is completely anonymous.)

Note: A separate similar survey was sent out for homework reference specifically and data was merged with the education survey.

Print education and homework reference tools are still well used. Table 13.3 lists the top five print education and homework reference tools identified in the survey. The free Web sites that librarians reported as core or essential for education and homework reference are numerous and are given in Table 13.4.

E-docs sites that support education and homework reference have been cited from the earliest surveys. The top five e-docs used for education and homework reference are listed in Table 13.5. The top five fee-based education and homework reference e-resources are reported in Table 13.6.

Table 13.3. Top Five Print Education and Homework Reference Tools Identified in Survey

1. *Statistical Abstract of the U.S.*
2. *Encyclopedia of Education* (other encyclopedias of specific educational areas)
3. *Mental Measurements Yearbook*
4. *Peterson's Guides*
5. *World Book Encyclopedia*

Table 13.4. Top Five Free Web Education and Homework Reference Tools Identified in Survey

1. Google: www.google.com, and Google Scholar: http://scholar.google.com
2. Gateway to Educational Materials: www.thegateway.org, Discovery Education Classroom Resources: http://school.discoveryeducation.com
3. National Education Association: www.nea.org/home/index.html, British Education Index: www.leeds.ac.uk/educol, The Educator's Reference Desk: www.eduref.org
4. Kathy Schrock's Guide for Educators: http://school.discovery.com/schrockguide/business/grants .html
5. Fact Monster: www.factmonster.com, HomeworkSpot: www.homeworkspot.com, Infoplease: www.infoplease.com, Wikipedia: http://en.wikipedia.org/wiki/Main_Page

---

Table 13.5. Top Five Government Documents Web Sites Used as Education and Homework Reference Tools Identified in Survey

1. ERIC: www.eric.ed.gov
2. National Center for Education Statistics: http://nces.ed.gov, state and county departments of education Web sites
3. FREE Federal Resources for Educational Excellence: www.free.ed.gov
4. NSDL (National Science Digital Library): http://nsdl.org
5. Library of Congress American Memory Project: http://memory.loc.gov/ammem/index.html, Teacher Net: www.teachernet.gov.uk, U.S. Department of Education: www.ed.gov/index.jhtml, EDSITEment: http://edsitement.neh.gov, Kids.gov: www.kids.gov, USA.gov: www.usa.gov, THOMAS: Library of Congress: www.thomas.gov

Table 13.6. Top Five Fee-based Education and Homework Reference E-Resources Identified in Survey

1. Proquest Education Journals: www.proquest.com/en-US/catalogs/databases/detail/pq_ed_journals.shtml

2. Searchasaurus/Education Complete/Professional Development Collection (EBSCOHost):
   www.ebscohost.com/thisTopic.php?marketID=5&topicID=15

3. ERIC (OCLC and ProQuest):
   www.oclc.org/Support/documentation/firstsearch/databases/dbdetails/details/ERIC.htm or
   www.il.proquest.com/en-US/catalogs/databases/detail/eric.shtml

4. PsycINFO: www.apa.org/psycinfo

5. Literature Resource Center (Gale): www.gale.cengage.com

E-LIBRARY SUCCESS STORY

ALLIANCE LIBRARY SYSTEM VIRTUAL LIBRARY SECOND LIFE PROJECTS
http://infoisland.org/ or http://alliancelibraries.info/secondlife.htm
Contact: Lori Bell/Lorelei Junot, lbell@AllianceLibrarySystem.com, Rhonda Trueman/Abbey Zenith, abbeyzen@gmail.com, Sonja Plummer-Morgan/Sonja Morgwain, pimelibrarian@gmail.com

Lori Bell, aka Lorelei Junot, first had the idea to create a presence for the Alliance Library System in Second Life back in April of 2006. Second Life is a graphical virtual reality "world" that people connect to and participate in through the Internet. It requires a downloaded client software to interface. Participants create avatars, or personalities, with graphical representations in the virtual world. These avatars interact with one another and with the environment. Participants can create buildings, gardens, media presentations, and of course libraries in the Second Life world. Participants can purchase "land" among other virtual objects and concepts using internal currency called Linden Dollars. In order to acquire Linden Dollars some initial outlay of actual money in the real world is needed. Linden Labs Second Life information can be found at http://lindenlab.com.

The virtual libraries region that Lori/Lorelei created in Second Life began with a virtual geographic location named Info Island. Lori and Rhonda have authored a very useful book titled *Virtual Worlds, Real Libraries* published in 2008 by Information Today. *Virtual Worlds, Real Libraries* details the projects and their motivations and how and why other libraries may wish to create a virtual library presence (www.virtualworldsreallibraries.info).

"It was my idea to start in Second Life—we started with a small presence in April 2006. It grew from there. We had librarians from all over the world express interest in developing library services and in May 2006, we had an island donation. Now there are over 50 islands in the Info Island Archipelago which include libraries, non profits, government agencies, and educator groups."

The Info Island Archipelago in Second Life is a working experiment to explore the potential of offering library services through virtual worlds, to identify the practical needs—services and collections—that will be required for this, as well as to reach out and promote library use to potential users who may not be aware of what libraries and librarians can do for them in both the traditional print and physical, the Web and electronic resources and services, through the virtual world.

Figure 13.1. Info Island Library

Initially the Info Island project is of great interest primarily to librarians and academic faculty and students, but it is expected to expand to services of interest to any resident of Second Life regardless of their real-world or virtual world affiliations, library school students, library workers, and ultimately the general public. Second Life (SL) is an international community. "Alliance Library System is willing to work with any instructor teaching a course in Second Life to provide instructional, reference and library services. Different universities are providing a variety of courses from freshman composition to PhD courses.... San Jose State University School of Library and Information Science has its own island and offered the first for credit courses for library students in SL. The University of Illinois Graduate School of Library and Information Science has partnered with Alliance Library System to offer non-credit courses for librarians and educators on teaching, educating and providing library services in virtual worlds."

In a very practical sense the Info Island project is real. there are now over 130 libraries of all types in Second Life (www.infoisland.org/directory). One specific library presence is The Mark and Emily Turner Memorial Library in Second Life, which "is a project of their real life library of the same name." The library states, "We offer a special collection of Maine related resources, live reference for the general public, librarians, LIS students, and professors. Since October of 2007, our library has created programs and services such as collections, book discussions, conducted meetings in SL with staff, attended trainings, and participated in many virtual conferences. Our purpose for being in Second Life is multifaceted, however, Second Life helps to mitigate isolation rural librarians feel and gives librarians spread geographically far apart a way to collaborate and network. We truly feel that we are global librarians serving a global user base."

Info Island virtual libraries currently offer live reference service 80+ hours a week. "We are working on collaborative reference service where single libraries in SL can contribute 2 hours per week to our reference desk so we can make it 24/7 can have a kiosk to point students/patrons to our reference desk when there is no one covering theirs."

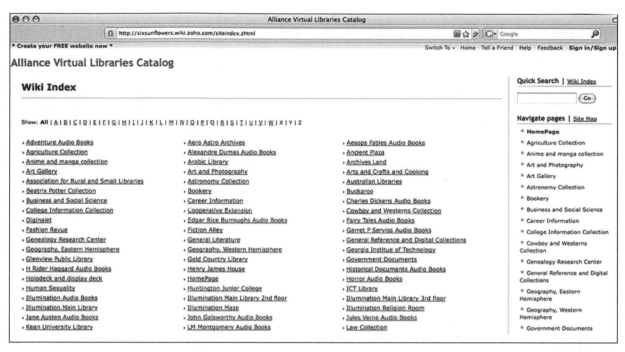

Figure 13.2. Info Island Library Catalog

In order to support the live reference services and to support educators in SL in other contexts, they have begun to create e-library collections. They also provide tours and library orientations for classes taking place in SL. "Our reference desk answers real life reference questions and many questions on second life to help students learn how to navigate the virtual world. We do not use any licensed databases although we might recommend to the patron a database that would help them. We develop collections—lists of books on a topic, Web resources, displays, etc., all free information on the web."

A written collection plan was developed and is maintained at http://infoisland.org/drupal/collections. A directory of existing collections on Info Island is maintained on a wiki at http://sixsunflowers.wiki.zoho.com/siteindex.zhtml. Bill Sowers/Rocky Vallejo is head of the group that manages Info Island collections.

Personnel supporting the project are mostly volunteers, with some given time to work in SL while working their usual library reference shifts. "There are over 1,000 self-identified librarians in second life. At any given time, we probably have 150-200 volunteers working on collaborative services. At first libraries would not allow librarians to help on work time. Most of our volunteers came to us on their own time and initiative. Through the 2.5 years we have been there, more libraries allow their staff some time to spend in SL although many of our people still give much of their own time and expertise. Many librarians in SL work on behalf of their own library (over 50 libraries in SL at this time) and also on behalf of the collaborative group."

Rhonda Trueman/Abbey Zenith is the Director of the Alliance Virtual Library in addition to her full-time job at Johnson and Wales. Rhonda/Abbey has been with the project from the beginning. She administers all core library services of the project, including reference, managed by Samantha Thompsen/Hypatia Dejavu; collections and cataloging, managed by Bill Sowers/Rocky Vallejo; volunteers, managed by Marcy Dulka/Marimar Berchot; and programs and events. "Volunteers who get involved can select how they wish to become involved and then they are trained by

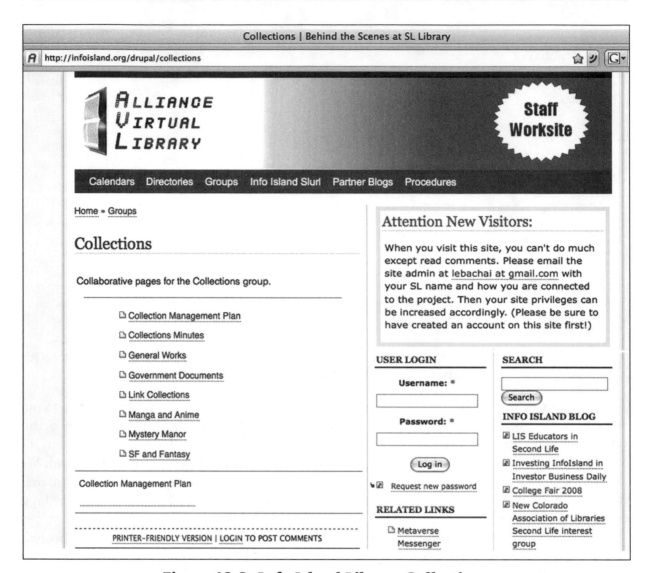

Figure 13.3. Info Island Library Collections

group heads. We offer ongoing training too—hands on, shadowing, mentoring, and also virtual world librarianship courses through UIUC GSLIS."

At any given time there are also people who support the project through grants. Several user surveys have been run in the past but every event involves some kind of feedback from users as to their needs and ideas for the project. "We are working with Learning Times on helping new museums get started in SL. We have a great outreach program for collaborative shared library services and to help new libraries get started in SL."

REFERENCES AND WEB SITES CITED

Johnson, Doug. 2007. "Managing the Intangible: Digital Resources in School Libraries." *Library Media Connection* (August/December): 46–49.
November, Alan C. (2008). *Web Literacy for Educators*. Thousand Oaks, CA: Corwin Press.
Rossi, Martha. 2009. "The Power of Partnership—Cooperative Online Resource Purchasing Programs." *Library Media Connection* (April/May): 58–60.
Savard, Stewart. 2007. "Library Quality Resources: Building a New Kind of Collection." *The Clearing House* (November/December): 87–89.

WEB SITES CITED

Academic Info. Available: www.academicinfo.net (accessed January 7, 2009).
American School Directory. Available: http://www.asd.com (accessed January 28, 2009).
Education Abstracts/Education Full Text. Available: www.hwwilson.com (accessed January 7, 2009).
Education Index. Available: www.educationindex.com (accessed January 7, 2009).
Educational CyberPlayGround. Available: www.edu-cyberpg.com/TOC.asp (accessed January 7, 2009).
The Educator's Reference Desk. Available: www.eduref.org (accessed January 7, 2009).
ERIC. Available: www.eric.ed.gov (accessed January 7, 2009).
The Gateway to Educational Materials (GEM). Available: www.thegateway.org (accessed January 7, 2009).
Google. Available: www.google.com (accessed January 14, 2009).
Infed.org the Encyclopedia of Informal Education. Available: www.infed.org (accessed January 29, 2009).
Kathy Schrock's Guide for Educators. Available: http://school.discovery.com/schrockguide/index.html (accessed January 7, 2009).
NewJour. Available: http://library.georgetown.edu/newjour (accessed January 20, 2009).
Wikipedia. Available: http://en.wikipedia.org/wiki/Main_Page (accessed January 7, 2009).

EDUCATION AND HOMEWORK E-RESOURCE COLLECTION TOOLS

META SITES

Academic Info

www.academicinfo.net

> "Directory of Internet resources tailored to a college or advanced high school audience. Each subject guide is an annotated listing of the best general Internet sites in the field, as well as a gateway to more advanced research tools."

American Association of School Librarians (AASL) "Resource Guides for School Library Media Program Development"

www.ala.org/ala/mgrps/divs/aasl/aaslproftools/resourceguides/aaslresource.cfm

> Web-based information guides for school library collection development, programs, technology issues, and more.

Blue Web'N: Knowledge Network Explorer

www.kn.pacbell.com/wired/bluewebn

> Sponsored by SBC Pacific Bell, this is a huge collection of evaluated, annotated, education related Web sites. Organized by content area, subject, and grade level.

Educational CyberPlayGround

www.edu-cyberpg.com/TOC.asp

> Gleason Sackman and Karen Ellis have collected many resources of interest to K–12 school teachers, librarians, and administrators.

The Educator's Reference Desk

www.eduref.org

> Resource guides, lesson plans, and other educator resources. Includes searchable ERIC Database. This version of the ERIC Database provides access to ERIC document citations from 1966 and ERIC Journal citations from 1966 to January 2004.

The Gateway to Educational Materials (GEM)

www.thegateway.org

> Sponsored by the U.S. Department of Education, the Gateway to Educational Materials (GEM) Catalog contains detailed descriptions of over 40,000 educational resources found on various federal, state, university, nonprofit, and commercial Internet sites.

Guide to Information Resources in Education

www.wsulibs.wsu.edu/educ/guide

> Collection of education databases, e-journals, reference tools, discussion lists, and other resources for education selected by librarians of Washington State University Libraries.

Internet Scout Project

http://scout.wisc.edu

> Librarians and educators filter announcement each week looking for online resources most valuable to the education community.

Kathy Schrock's Guide for Educators

http://school.discovery.com/schrockguide/index.html

> Critical evaluation for educators; categorized list of sites on the Internet found to be useful for enhancing curriculum and teacher professional growth. Part of the Discovery Education Classroom Resources (http://school.discoveryeducation.com).

Schoolzone

www.schoolzone.co.uk

> UK commercial site collection of Web sites and digital libraries with teaching and learning content as well as other support for educators.

DIGITAL LIBRARIES DIRECTORIES OR COLLECTIONS OF DIGITAL LIBRARIES (DIGITAL LIBRARIES OF E-BOOKS, E-SERIALS, IMAGES, RECORDINGS, AND OTHER ARTIFACTS)

National Academies Press

www.nap.edu

> E-book vender with some free e-books for sciences, engineering, education, and medicine.

TeacherTube

www.teachertube.com

> Online community for sharing teacher created instructional videos.

E-SERIALS, BLOGS, DISCUSSION LISTS, ETC.

American Educational Research Association Discussion Lists

http://listserv.aera.net/archives/index.html

> The AERA hosts discussion lists for educational researchers on a multitude of specific topics.

EBSS-L

http://listserv.uncc.edu/archives/ebss-l.html

> Discussion for Education and Behavioral Sciences Librarians (Education and Behavioral Sciences Section, Association of College and Research Libraries, American Library Association).

EDInfo E-Newsletter

www.ed.gov/news/newsletters/edinfo/index.html

> Announces new, interesting, and useful education related e-resources, tools, events. etc., from the U.S. Department of Education.

Edresource

http://groups.yahoo.com/list/edresource

> Subscribe and locate archives at this Web address. Discussion of the education resources available that benefit Internet educators.

EdTechTalk

http://edtechtalk.com

> Collaborative open Webcasting and blog for teachers working with educational technologies.

Educator-Gold

http://groups.yahoo.com/group/Educator-Gold

> Discussion group for educators haring information about Internet sites for education.

Educause Review

http://connect.educause.edu/er

> E-journal (and print) for the higher education community concerned with technologies.

LM_NET

www.eduref.org/lm_net

> Discussion for school library and media services librarians.

SLA-DEDU

www.sla.org/content/community/lists/divisionlists5979.cfm or www.sla.org/content/community/lists/joinlists.cfm

> Discussion list for librarians who are members of the Special Libraries Association, Education Division.

14

ARTS AND HUMANITIES (FINE ARTS, LANGUAGES, LITERATURE, PHILOSOPHY, HISTORY, ETC.) E-RESOURCES

These findings and recommendations provide a view of the humanist at work, a portrait that contrasts with colleagues in other disciplines such as science and engineering. The tools to support the humanist's work have expanded from being just key texts and a fine mind to being aided and abetted by computer and networking technologies. The first generation of digital libraries provided models for support of the humanist's work. This is but a beginning. The next generation of technology will have the potential to stimulate the humanist, remove much of the drudgery of the research preparation, and enhance the analyses. These new developments will likely change the way the humanities are taught and interpreted, and how they are employed by society. (Toms and O'Brien, 2008)

DEVELOPING A COLLECTION PLAN FOR ARTS AND HUMANITIES E-RESOURCES

The quote that introduces this chapter is from the conclusion to Elaine G. Toms and Heather L. O'Brien's (2008) research report "Understanding the Information and Communication Technology Needs of the E-humanist." This study observed and surveyed humanities scholars on the research and communications tools they were most likely to need to in order to equip an "e-humanists workbench." Humanities scholars were among the first to take advantage of the communication and publishing tools made possible by the Internet, Bitnet, and then Web technologies. Some of the earliest and best scholarly publishing began with humanities scholars of all persuasions.

The phrase *arts and humanities* covers a broad and deep spectrum of human artistic, linguistic, literary, and related endeavor. Arts scholars study performing, visual, musical, historical, literary, and multicultural topics. Humanities scholars study arts, languages, linguistics, history, music, and philosophy in all time periods and all places of human presence. To create an e-library for arts and humanities scholars one must begin by first identifying the precise areas of the arts and humanities that will be included. Also, it is useful to find out if the scholars in question will use or will want to use the e-library. The Maron and Kirby Smith report (2008) describes projects that produce e-resources that scholars use and participate in creating. The ability to conduct research collaboratively through scholarly networks and then publishing among the groups of interested scholars is their main intent.

WHAT PURPOSE WILL YOUR COLLECTION SERVE? FOR WHOM ARE YOU COLLECTING THESE E-RESOURCES?

Anyone can be an arts and humanities scholar: the university or foundation formal scholars, the undergraduates taking required liberal arts courses, artists and writers learning to do art or learning to write, historians gathering historical data, linguists and musicologists collecting sounds, children studying language or music, teachers preparing philosophy and history courses, and lifelong learners or amateur scholars choosing to study arts and humanities for pleasure and recreation. All of these and more, could be who we are creating an e-library collection for. In this most creative cluster of studies, the user or the e-resources is absolutely the most important selection criteria in choosing e-resources or in choosing not to collect e-resources but to collect something more appropriate. Barbara Elam (2007) found that art historians and related faculty are not interested in digital image collections as a rule. The key problem is lack of high quality photographs and/or high-resolution printers and display options. These art scholars were avid users of the library and of the e-resources such as Art Index (www.hwwilson.com/Databases/artretro .htm) and Art Bibliography Moderne (www.csa.com/factsheets/artbm-set-c.php). If they could be reassured that the digital images would be of comparable quality to that of photographic slides they normally used in teaching they might be willing to make use of digital image libraries online.

Humanities scholars tend to be browsers and tend to prefer books. Michael Levine-Clark (2007) found that scholars in the humanities are aware of e-books, but they tend to use them even less than other scholars. They prefer print books. Given that they are generally reading from cover to cover this is reasonable. Other research has indicated that users will use e-books as reference books but do not like reading an entire book online (Cleto, 2008; Sottong, 2009; Connaway and Wicht, 2007; Hernon et al., 2007).

As reported in "Beyond Google: How Do Students Conduct Academic Research?" Alison Head (2007) found that a majority of humanities and social sciences undergraduate students began their course research on the library Web site using e-journals and course reserves. Under-graduate students expressed their desire for "stamp of approval" that the resources they were finding would meet professor expectations of quality. Students looking for information for research worked through the Web site differently than those just looking up facts or browsing for recreation. Humanities and social sciences undergraduates appear to appreciate and make use of the e-resources selected by librarians because of their perceived higher quality and appropriateness for course projects.

WHAT TYPES OF E-RESOURCES WILL YOU COLLECT?

Cultural and scholarly digital repositories of primary and secondary documents, images, etc., created by individual organizations or collaborations of groups of scholarly organizations are a major trend (Maron and Kirby Smith, 2008; Zorich, 2008). An interesting example project is the ACLS Humanities E-book project:

> ACLS Humanities E-book (www.humanitiesEbook.org) is a searchable, online collection
> of scholarly books, but it is also more than that. It also includes links to online reviews of

the collection's titles from Project MUSE and JSTOR. The selection criteria and process work toward creating a well-thought-out collection, as opposed to merely offering the catalogs of scholarly presses in digital format. As the database's name suggests, Humanities E-book is comprised of subjects covering the entire humanities spectrum. At present, the collection is more heavily weighted toward history, but that should change as more titles are added. It contains more than 1,700 full-text titles, soon to be 2,200, of which three hundred are available through a print-on-demand service. Titles, both in-print and out-of-print, range from 1885 to the present. The final product is the result of collaboration between 12 learned societies, more than 90 publishers, and librarians at the University of Michigan's Scholarly Publishing Office. It is by scholars for scholars. (Berger-Barrera, 2008: 118)

Other arts and humanities e-resources can very roughly be forced into the traditional library reference types:

- Directories (of artists, humanists, educators, arts and humanities researchers, projects, organizations, and programs. etc.)
- Dictionaries (arts and humanities vocabulary in English as well as international language translation dictionaries)
- Abstracts, indexes, and table of contents services (including those with full text of arts and humanities journals indexed)
- Encyclopedias and almanacs
- Full-text and/or multimedia databases/digital libraries (arts and humanities repositories, collections of e-books, e-serials, recordings, videos, podcasts, images, etc.)
- News and news services (arts and humanities current awareness sources)
- Key primary documents (images, recordings, and transcriptions of historical documents, works of art, literature, music, poetry, and other artifacts)
- Search engines
- Meta sites (e-resources that provide two or more of the other reference tool types in a single product/Web site)

Directories of artists, humanists, educators, arts and humanities researchers, projects, organizations, and programs, etc., can be found using Internet Public Library or the Open Directory Project sources cited in previous chapters or any of the arts and humanities meta sites will indicate such. Directories of arts and humanities digital libraries and projects are increasingly important and available. Two good examples are the Alliance of Digital Humanities Organizations (www.digitalhumanities.org) site and the Consortium of Humanities Centers and Institute (CHCI) (www.chcinetwork.org) site. Both are organization for networking and resources sharing among humanities scholars and humanities centers and institutes established on the Web or with a Web presence. They both provide a directory of all the humanities centers, scholars, and resulting projects that are affiliated with their organizations.

Dictionaries for the arts and humanities are relatively scarce on the Web. One exception is the ArtLex Art Dictionary (www.artlex.com), which is a free online art dictionary created and maintained by ArtLex blogger Michael R. Delahunt (http://artlexdaily.blogspot.com) since 1996. Encyclopedias and almanacs in the humanities are numerous. Specific examples are listed on the Core Web Arts and Humanities Reference Tools page on the companion Web site (www.kovacs.com/ns/essentialguide.html).

Arts and humanities current awareness sources abound. Such news sources range from the general media presence as well as from arts and humanities scholarly organizations, colleges, and universities. Indexes and abstracts and full-text and digital libraries e-resources tend to be the Web sites where key primary documents in the humanities are housed. Both the fee-based core indexes and abstracts and many freely available Web sites provide such access. Electronically recorded texts, images, and artifacts are the main key primary documents used in the arts and humanities. Several of the meta sites listed in the collection tools section at the end of this chapter list such collections or are themselves digital libraries of such content.

HOW WILL YOU ORGANIZE YOUR E-LIBRARY COLLECTION?

In this final, most creative chapter, it seems appropriate to restate the obvious: library users respond well to e-resources organized by subject and suborganized alphabetically or by reference type. A CMS supported e-library can enable this kind of organization as well as alternatives for searching and display of content.

IDENTIFYING AND COLLECTING ARTS AND HUMANITIES E-RESOURCES

WEB SITES THAT REVIEW AND EVALUATE E-RESOURCES: PEER E-LIBRARIES, SUBJECT COLLECTIONS/GUIDES, OR META SITES

The Voice of the Shuttle (http://vos.ucsb.edu) site was one of the first sites established on the Web and remains a very useful tool for identifying high quality e-resources for the arts and Humanities. The Intute and INFOMINE meta sites cited in previous chapters are also very useful. Several very good arts and humanities specific meta sites may be more useful in collecting in those specific areas. Several are listed in the collection tools section in this chapter. For example, the Humanities and Social Sciences Net (http://h-net.org) meta site is dedicated to promoting studies in the humanities and social sciences and collects and annotates e-resources in those subject areas, and the Arts and Humanities Data Service (http://AHDS.AC.UK) is both a collection of Web sites and digital library collections and a search tool to search all of those digital collections.

DISCUSSION LISTS (LISTSERV, ETC.), FORUMS/GROUPS, E-SERIALS, AND/OR BLOGS THAT POST OR PUBLISH REVIEWS AND EVALUATIONS OF E-RESOURCES

Humanist (http://digitalhumanities.org/humanist) was the original discussion list created in the first days of the Internet for the discussion of all things related to the humanities but primarily for the discussion of humanities and e-tools for teaching, learning, archiving, and preserving. Two arts and humanities librarian discussions are ARLIS-L (www.arlisna.org/about/arlisl.html), the discussion list of the Art Libraries Society of North America; and SLA-DMAH (www .sla.org/content/community/lists/divisionlists5979.cfm or www.sla.org/content/community/lists/ joinlists.cfm), the discussion list for librarians who are members of the Museums, Arts and Humanities division of the Special Libraries Association.

PostModern Culture (PMC) (http://jefferson.village.virginia.edu/pmc) is the original humanities e-journal and publishes peer-reviewed articles on all aspects of interdisciplinary thought on contemporary cultures, many of which include details about arts and humanities appropriate e-resources. The H-Net Review (http://h-net.org/reviews) Humanities and Social

Sciences network e-newsletter reviews both print and e-resources. The site also hosts several discussion lists.

PRINT BOOKS AND JOURNALS THAT REVIEW E-RESOURCES

Humanities texts in many areas have included e-resources in citations and as their topics. In print, one of the best is again, *Research and Documentation in the Electronic Age*, Fifth Edition (Hacker, 2008) Booklet and Web site (www.dianahacker.com/resdoc). Humanities research tools including the fee-based research tools such as MLA International Bibliography Online (www.mla.org), Historical Abstracts (www.abc-clio.com/products/serials_ha.aspx) and the best of the free Web research tools in all humanities areas, with special attention to history, are reviewed for their usefulness and appropriate use in a research context. As in most academic subject areas, most print journals in the humanities all review appropriate humanities related e-resources or cite them in the same way as they treat print books or other resources.

EVALUATION GUIDELINES AND SELECTION CRITERIA: THE CORE WEB ARTS AND HUMANITIES REFERENCE COLLECTION

Evaluating the quality of arts and humanities e-resources requires verification of scholarly value and accuracy of the e-resource. Is the e-resource composed of accurately scanned, transcribed, or otherwise electronically recorded documents, images, or other artifacts relevant to arts and humanities research? What is the provenance of the electronically recorded materials included in a digital library? Is the e-resource content and organization based on careful scholarly analysis? Who is the scholar or scholars and what is their record of publication, teaching, research? All of these questions must be asked in evaluating arts and humanities e-resources. Given the current internetworked state of these fields, it should be fairly easy to find the answers. If you cannot find answers, then chances are the e-resource is not of sufficient quality to include in an e-library collection.

In May and August 2008, librarians were surveyed to elicit which arts and humanities reference tools they consider to be core or essential to their work. Separate surveys were sent out for history for the first time, and those results were combined with the results from previous arts and humanities reference specific surveys. The Core Web Arts and Humanities Reference Collection on the companion Web Site (www.kovacs.com/ns/essentialguide.html) was initially created using these survey results as core and model collections. Past, present, and future surveys and results are posted at www.kovacs.com/misc.html. This collection is intended for librarians to use as a source of e-resources they might select for their education and/or homework reference e-library collections. Fee-based e-resources are included when they offer free trials or have some information available without requiring a fee. The discussion lists and blogs where the survey links were posted are listed in Table 14.1. The core arts and humanities reference tools survey is reproduced in Table 14.2.

Print arts and humanities reference tools are still well used. Table 14.3 lists the top five print arts and humanities reference tools identified in the survey. The free Web sites that librarians reported as core or essential for arts and humanities reference numerous and are given in Table 14.4.

E-docs sites that support arts and humanities reference have been cited from the earliest surveys. The top e-docs used for arts and humanities reference are listed in Table 14.5. The top five fee-based arts and humanities reference e-resources are reported in Table 14.6.

Table 14.1. Discussion Lists and Blogs Distribution for Arts and Humanities Reference Tools Survey

- LISNews and LISNewsWire Blogs: lisnews-owner@lishost.net
- ResourceShelf Blog: gary.price@resourceshelf.com
- ERIL-L@LISTSERV.BINGHAMTON.EDU
- dig_ref@LISTSERV.SYR.EDU
- collib-l@ala.org
- LIS-LINK@jiscmail.ac.uk
- Libref-L@listserv.kent.edu
- GOVDOC-L@lists.psu.edu
- publib@webjunction.org
- livereference@yahoogroups.com
- Libref-L@listserv.kent.edu

Table 14.2. Core Arts and Humanities Reference Tools Survey Questions

1. Which library type best describes the library you work in/for/with?

2. In which subject area(s) are you most likely to answer arts and humanities questions? (Check all that apply.)

3. What are the essential three print titles (reference books) that you can't work without in answering arts and humanities questions? (Please type the title only.)

4. What are the essential three free (not government published) Web-accessible databases that you can't work without in answering arts and humanities questions? (Please type complete URL/Web address; e.g., http://vos.ucsb.edu.)

5. What are the essential three (.gov) government published (state, federal, local, international) free Web-accessible databases that you can't work without in answering arts and humanities questions? (Please type complete URL/Web address; e.g., www.loc.gov/performingarts.)

6. What are the essential three fee-based Web-accessible databases that you can't work without in answering arts and humanities questions? (Please type the simple title; e.g., RILM Abstracts of Music Literature.)

7. Does your library maintain a Web page or site to support arts and humanities reference? If so please share the URL/Web address (e.g., www.skokielibrary.info/s_info/in_arts/index.asp).

8. Additional comments or ideas:

(Please include your name and e-mail address if you would like feedback, otherwise this survey form is completely anonymous.)

Note: A separate similar survey was sent out for history reference and data was merged with the arts and humanities survey.

Table 14.3. Top Five Print Arts and Humanities Reference Tools Identified in Survey

1. *Grove Dictionary of Music and Musicians*
2. *Grove Dictionary of Art*
3. *Literary Criticism Sets from Gale, Oxford English Dictionary, Dictionary of Literary Biography*
4. *Oxford Dictionary of Music, Contemporary Authors Series, International Encyclopedia of Dance*
5. *Handbook to Life in Ancient Greece*; other handbooks, guides, encyclopedias to specific periods and regions of history or types of art, music, etc.; *The Source: A Guidebook to American Genealogy*

Table 14.4. Top Five Free Web Arts and Humanities Reference Tools Identified in Survey

1. Arts and Humanities digital libraries projects (many specific digital library collections of images, recordings, documents, etc., each cited once), the Internet Movie Database: www.imdb.com

2. Intute Arts and Humanities: www.intute.ac.uk/artsandhumanities, Google: www.google.com and Google Scholar: http://scholar.google.com

3. Library of Congress American Memory Project: http://memory.loc.gov/ammem/index.html, Historical Census Browser (University of Virginia Library): http://fisher.lib.virginia.edu/collections/stats/histcensus, KnightCite: www.calvin.edu/library/knightcite, Voice of the Shuttle: http://vos.ucsb.edu

4. Avalon Project Documents in Law, History and Diplomacy: http://avalon.law.yale.edu/default.asp

5. Wikipedia: http://en.wikipedia.org/wiki/Main_Page

Table 14.5. Top Three Government Documents Web Sites Used as Arts and Humanities Reference Tools Identified in Survey

1. Library of Congress American Memory Project: http://memory.loc.gov/ammem/index.html

2. Library of Congress Performing Arts Encyclopedia: www.loc.gov/performingarts

3. International, state, regional, local government sponsored digital libraries (image, recording, and documents collections cited individually)

Table 14.6. Top Five Fee-based Arts and Humanities Reference E-Resources Identified in Survey

1. Grove Music/Grove Art Online: www.oxfordmusiconline.com or www.oxfordartonline.com

2. Art Full Text/Art Abstracts: www.hwwilson.com/databases/artindex.htm, JSTOR: www.jstor.org

3. Academic Search Complete/Academic Search Premier (EBSCO): www.ebscohost.com/thisTopic.php?marketID=1&topicID=633 or www.ebscohost.com/thisTopic.php?topicID=1&marketID=1, MLA International Bibliography: www.mla.org/bibliography

4. America: History and Life: www.abc-clio.com/products/serials_ahl.aspx, Historical Abstracts: www.ebscohost.com/thisTopic.php?marketID=1&topicID=836, Literature Resource Center (Gale): www.gale.cengage.com, Project Muse: http://muse.jhu.edu

5. ATLA Religion Index: www.atla.com/products/catalogs/catalogs_rdb.html, Footnote: www.footnote.com, HeritageQuest Online: www.heritagequestonline.com or www.il.proquest.com/en-US/catalogs/databases/detail/heritagequest.shtml, Philosopher's Index: www.philinfo.org

E-LIBRARY SUCCESS STORY

GODDARD COLLEGE
Eliot D. Pratt Library
Plainfield, Vermont, United States
www.goddard.edu/library_resources
Contacts: Clara Bruns, Clara.Bruns@goddard.edu, and Helen Linda, celestihel@gmail.com

A. Collection Planning (e.g., goal setting and identification of users, technology/personnel choices)

In 1996, the director of the Goddard College library proposed that an e-library collection be created to supplement mediated search services then offered to library users. In the fall 1997 the e-library made FirstSearch databases available. The goal of that first version of the e-library to present has been to provide database search services for Goddard students and faculty.

Since 2002, the e-library exists primarily to support distance learners and faculty. Goddard College offers a "low residency" model for all programs. This essentially means that all learners are distance learners for a major part if each term. "Students come to campus for 8 days a semester. Different programs come to campus at different times of the year. Students are in a distance learning relationship with the library and college in general for the remainder of the semester." The e-library attempts to provide 24/7 access to quality library and information resources.

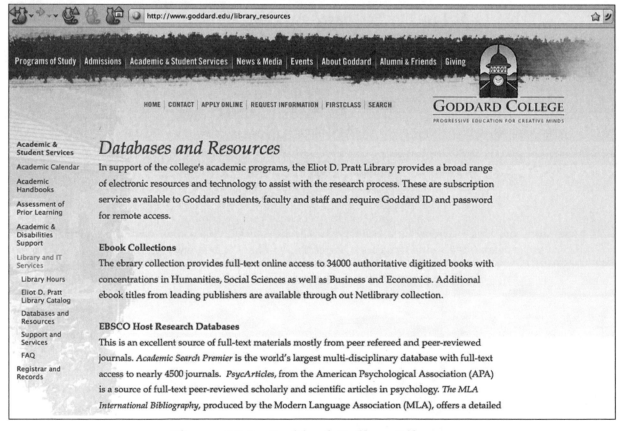

Figure 14.1. Goddard College Library

GoddardNet

Need Help?

Eliot D. Pratt Library Databases

Library Research Tools

360 Search - A simple starting point for research. This search tool covers virtually all of our databases, including the online catalog.

E-Journal Portal - Find e-journals by title or ISSN. Provides links directly to database(s) with appropriate full-text source material.

RefWorks Bibliographic Software - RefWorks is an online bibliography tool that lets you build a bibliography and create citations for your papers. You'll need to create an "Individual Account" in order to store your bibliography. **You will need to use "RWGoddardC" (no quotes) as the "group code" to access RefWorks.**

Library of Congress Subject Heading Outline - Matches subject headings with call numbers

Book and article request

Eliot D. Pratt Library Online Catalog - Locate and request books.

FirstSearch Home (*including) - 12 research databases such as WorldCat and ArticleFIRST.

*WorldCat - 70 million records. Interlibrary loan requests.(via FirstSearch)

*ArticleFirst - 15,000 journals and periodicals. Use ILL icon to request articles.(via FirstSearch)

*MEDLINE - 9580 journals of medicine, dentistry and nursing collected by the National Library of Medicine. ILL icon to request.(via FirstSearch)

*PsycFIRST - Latest three years indexed. 1300 journals collected by the American Psychological Association. ILL icon to request articles.(via FirstSearch)

PROQUEST (Dissertation Express) - "Dissertations" in the FirstSearch database are ONLY citations or abstracts. To purchase a full copy of a dissertation please follow this link to the ProQuest Dissertation Express site and choose "Connect to Dissertation Express as an Individual"

Reference

Oxford English Dictionary - meaning, history, and pronunciation of over half a million words, 2.5 million quotations, more

Oxford Reference Online - 2 million definitions, facts, people, places, dates and quotations in 100 reference works

Grove Art Online - 34 volume Dictionary of Art with quarterly additions of new material and updates

American National Biographies - biographies of people from American history and culture

Full-text Articles

EBSCO Host Research Databases - This is an excellent source of full-text materials mostly from refereed or peer-reviewed journals. Includes the databases:PsycARTICLES, Academic Search Premier, and MLA International Bibliography.

PsycARTICLES - A definitive source of full-text, peer-reviewed scholarly and scientific articles in psychology. The database contains more than 100,000 articles from 59 journals - 48 published by the American Psychological Association (APA) and 11 from allied organizations. It includes all journal articles, letters to the editor and errata from each journal. Coverage spans 1894 to present.

InfoTrac OneFile - Limit search to "articles with text" for full text. Millions of articles in thousands of journals.

Health and Wellness - Limit search to "full text articles" for full text

JSTOR - "Journal storage," backfiles of 117 core academic journals in Arts and Sciences, social sciences and humanities

Journal of Gay & Lesbian Mental Health - Full text of Journal of Gay & Lesbian Psychotherapy vols. 3-12, and Journal of Gay & Lesbian Mental Health vol. 12-.

Annual Review of Psychology - 1996-current issue, full text online.

Chronicle of Higher Education - When prompted, **Log-in name: prattlibrary; password: eliotpratt**

ERIC - Education Resources Information Center - Full text documents from 1993 on and journal citations from the 1980s forward.

Vermont Online Library - 16 full text databases presenting thousands of journals, periodicals, newswire, newspapers

Fulltext - E-books and Literature

ebrary - Over 20,000 online books in a variety of disciplines. Most published since 2000.

NetLibrary - Thousands of ebooks.

Alexander Street Literature - is a comprehensive, cross-searchable package of collections covering literatures of place, race, and gender.

Project Gutenberg - Over 10,000 classic books online

Figure 14.2. Goddard College Library E-Resources

A written collection development policy was created and continuously updated from the beginning of the e-library project. A copy is available at www.kovacs.com/studentwork/coll devplans.html login: colldev password: kovacs08.

B. Collection Strategies (e.g., selection criteria, identification of resources, licensing, and related user information needs)

Cost and ease of use are final criteria for selecting e-resources once they are established to meet the needs of library users. The library budget pays for remote access to licensed Web-accessible databases for all Goddard students, faculty, and staff. "Licensing agreement for most databases are with the library. Some are through consortial agreements. The "Vermont Online Library" is available through a contract with the State Library."

Goddard Library has not yet negotiated archiving arrangements for future guaranteed access. E-books, through ebrary's Academic Complete collection (www.ebrary.com), are an important part of the e-library collection. "The license agreement was prepared through NELINET for the members of the AVIC (Association of Vermont Independent Libraries) group. The library is paying pricing is based on FTE students enrollment numbers. Access is defined to be for the "Institution's patrons," generally through IP authentication. Remote access to institution's patrons is permitted for through referring URL. Remote access to institution's patrons is permitted through referring URL (we use the product called "easy proxy"). On-site access is permitted for all walk-ins. The usual copyright restrictions apply."

MARC records for the individual Ebrary titles are loaded in the library catalog, although the Goddard College Library is hoping to digitize local collections to add to the e-library in future. Virtual reference services are well-used and successful. Interlibrary loan services are also well-used, but challenges exist in getting materials to students who are not on campus.

C. Collection Organization (e.g., content management systems, Web server choices, personnel responsibilities, etc.)

The e-library uses FirstClass (www.firstclass.com) to organize and provide access to e-resources. It is also used as the college's communication forum. All librarians participate in identifying, selecting, and evaluating resources. The director or an individual librarian works with Goddard College IT staff to add links and maintain the e-library site. Librarians informally train one another in the skills needed to support the e-library. Collections are continuously assessed and reevaluated. More librarians have become involved in recent time and so the work is more evenly shared.

"E-resources development and management, including license agreement and vendor negotiations has traditionally taken ca. 30% of Director's time. This includes meetings with local consortia affiliates and dealing with budgetary issues. Tech. support has probably taken 10% of another full-time employee. The Director has been involved with the set-up and maintenance of federated search.... The person holding the position of Library Systems and Technical Services Coordinator provides support for some aspects (e.g., managing the ebook holdings data.)."

Librarians regularly read e-resource reviews in professional journals. A favorite source is The Charleston Review (www.charlestonco.com).

D. Collection Maintenance (e.g., link checking, ongoing weeding, and growth of the e-library collection)

Links get checked and updated whenever someone reports a problem. Usually this is noticed first by library users. Feedback from students regarding their use of the library in general is solicited in a general survey at the end of each program residency.

Plans for the future include expanding e-resources according to curriculum needs and improving customization of the 360 Search Federated Search (www.serialssolutions.com/ss_360_search.html). "We are currently in the process of exploring different ideas about how to make better use of federated searching. Our 360 searching tool needs to be customized to better serve our students. That will change the organization of e-resources offerings. A person in the position of "Information Resources and Technology Librarian" is responsible to design a proposal that will be discussed in the group. The display and organization of e-resources offerings has been the same for a number of years."

REFERENCES AND WEB SITES CITED

Berger-Barrera, Jocelyn. 2008. "ACLS Humanities E-Book: An Examination." *Collection Building* 27, no. 3: 118–120.

Cleto, Cynthia. 2008. "10 Steps to Implementing an eBook Collection: A Guide for Librarians." *Against the Grain* (February): 47–48.

Connaway, Lynn, and Heather L. Wicht. 2007. "What Happened to the E-Book Revolution? The Gradual Integration of E-books into Academic Libraries." *The Journal of Electronic Publishing* 10, no. 3. Available: http://hdl.handle.net/2027/spo.3336451.0010.302.

Elam, Barbara. 2007. "Readiness or Avoidance: E-Resources and the Art Historian." *Collection Building* 26, no. 1: 4–6.

Hacker, Diane, with Barbara Fister. 2008. *Research and Documentation in the Electronic Age*, 5th edition. New York: Bedford/St. Martin's. Available: http://www.dianahacker.com/resdoc (accessed January 19, 2009).

Head, Alison J. 2007. "Beyond Google: How Do Students Conduct Academic Research?" *First Monday* 12, no. 8 (August). Available: www.firstmonday.org/issues/issue12_8/head/ (accessed January 7, 2009).

Hernon, Peter, Rosita Hopper, Michael R. Leach, Laura L. Saunders, and Jane Zhang. 2007. "E-Book Use by Students: Undergraduates in Economics, Literature, and Nursing." *The Journal of Academic Librarianship* 33, no. 1: 3–13.

Levine-Clark, Michael. 2007. "Electronic Books and the Humanities: A Survey at the University of Denver." *Collection Building* 26, no. 1: 4–6.

Maron, Nancy L., and K. Kirby Smith. 2008. "Current Models of Digital Scholarly Communication Results of an Investigation Conducted by Ithaka for the Association of Research Libraries." Available: www.arl.org/bm~doc/current-models-report.pdf.

Sottong, Stephen. 2009. "The Elusive E-Book: Are E-Books Finally Ready for Prime Time?" *American Libraries* 39, no. 5: 44–49.

Toms, Elaine G., and Heather L. O'Brien. 2008. "Understanding the Information and Communication Technology Needs of the E-Humanist." *Journal of Documentation* 64, no. 1: 102–130.

Zorich, Diane. 2008. "A Survey of Digital Humanities Centers in the United States." Council on Library and Information Resources. Publication 143. Available: www.clir.org/pubs/abstract/pub143abst.html.

WEB SITES CITED

The Alliance of Digital Humanities Organizations. Available: www.digitalhumanities.org (accessed January 27, 2009).

Art Bibliography Moderne. Available: www.csa.com/factsheets/artbm-set-c.php (accessed January 27, 2009).

Art Index/Art Index Retrospective 1929–1984. Available: www.hwwilson.com/Databases/artretro.htm (accessed January 14, 2009).

ArtLex Art Dictionary. Available: www.artlex.com (accessed January 7, 2009).

Arts and Humanities Data Service. Available: http://ahds.ac.uk (accessed January 7, 2009).

Consortium of Humanities Centers and Institute (CHCI). Available: www.chcinetwork.org (accessed January 7, 2009).

Google. Available: www.google.com (accessed January 14, 2009).

Historical Abstracts. Available: www.abc-clio.com/products/serials_ha.aspx (accessed January 7, 2009).

Humanities and Social Sciences Net. Available: http://h-net.org (accessed January 7, 2009).

INFOMINE: Social Sciences and Humanities. Available: http://infomine.ucr.edu/cgi-bin/search?category=liberal (accessed January 7, 2009).

MLA International Bibliography Online. Available: www.mla.org (accessed January 21, 2009).

PostModern Culture (PMC). Available: http://jefferson.village.virginia.edu/pmc (accessed January 7, 2009).

Voice of the Shuttle. Available: http://vos.ucsb.edu (accessed January 7, 2009).

ARTS AND HUMANITIES E-RESOURCE COLLECTION TOOLS

META SITES

ABZU

www.etana.org/abzu

> "Abzu is a guide to networked open access data relevant to the study and public presentation of the Ancient Near East and the Ancient Mediterranean world. Abzu has been available on the Internet since 5 October, 1994. The editor of Abzu is Charles E. Jones, Head Librarian Institute for the Study of the Ancient World, New York University. Contact the editor directly at cejo@uchicago.edu."

American and English Literature Internet Resources

http://library.scsu.ctstateu.edu/litbib.html

> Selected collection of Web sites (and other Internet forms) that are relevant to the study of American or English literature.

Art History Resources on the Web

http://witcombe.sbc.edu/ARTHLinks.html

> Collection of Web resources related to art history, maintained since 1995, by Professor Christopher L. C. E. Witcombe, Sweet Briar College,Department of Art History.

Arts and Humanities Data Service

http://ahds.ac.uk

> This is both a collection of Web sites and digital library collections and a search tool to search all those digital collections. "The AHDS is here to help you create, deposit, preserve or discover and use digital collections in the arts and humanities."

Artslynx International Art Resources

www.artslynx.org

> Collection of Web sites with information about the performing arts, theater, and dance.

Contemporary Philosophy, Critical Theory, and Postmodern Thought

http://carbon.cudenver.edu/~mryder/itc_data/postmodern.html

> Collection of Web sites on all aspects of modern philosophy, created and maintained by Martin Ryder of the University of Colorado at Denver.

Humanities and Social Sciences Net

http://h-net.org

> Dedicated to promoting studies in the humanities and social sciences on the Web and offline. Organizes collections of Web sites and e-serials and includes a jobs announcement area.

ILoveLanguages

www.ilovelanguages.com

> Collection of Web sites related to the study of languages.

INFOMINE Social Sciences and Humanities

http://infomine.ucr.edu/cgi-bin/search?category=liberal

> Browsable and searchable index of thousands of humanities related sites appropriate for scholarly research or educational activities at the university level.

Internet Guide to Religion

www.wabashcenter.wabash.edu/resources/guide_headings.aspx

> Hosted by the Wabash Center, this site collects and annotates thousands of Web sites that provide content on all the world's religions.

Internet Resources on Theater and Drama

www.indiana.edu/~libhper/DTD/theatre/resources.html

> Collection of Web sites (and other Internet forms) related to the study of theater and drama selected and annotated by staff of the Indiana University Libraries.

Intute: Arts and Humanities

www.intute.ac.uk/artsandhumanities

> Intute is a multisubject e-library maintained by a consortium of United Kingdom university and academic organization Library partners (www.intute.ac.uk/artsandhumanities/partners.html) who carefully select and evaluate all of the arts and humanities e-resources that are open source or otherwise freely available on the Web. Scope includes architecture; communications, media and culture; design fashion and beauty; music and the performing arts; visual arts; general arts and humanities; historical and philosophical studies; religion and theology; languages, literature, historical and cultural studies; and Other languages, literature, historical and cultural studies, literature, linguistics, Classics.

Linguistic Resources on the Internet

www.sil.org/linguistics/topical.html

> Collection of Web sites (and other Internet forms) related to the study of linguistics.

Oxford Text Archive

http://ota.ahds.ac.uk

> "The OTA collects, catalogues, preserves and distributes high-quality digital resources for research and teaching. We currently hold thousands of texts in more than 25 different languages, and are actively working to extend our catalogue of holdings."

Perseus Digital Library

www.perseus.tufts.edu/hopper

> Meta site of digital library collections for the classics. Latin, Greek, etc. language, literature, and historical materials.

Philosophy Around the Web

http://users.ox.ac.uk/~worc0337/phil_index.html

> Meta site that collects philosophy sites and organizes them under fourteen main categories of philosophy (organizations, papers, philosophers, education, etc.).

Scholarslab, University of Virginia Library (was electronic text center)

http://viva.lib.virginia.edu/scholarslab/resources/index.html

> Statistical, image, and other digital resources for social sciences and humanities.

Voice of the Shuttle

http://vos.ucsb.edu

> Searchable database of all humanities topics and their subcategories.

World History Compass

www.worldhistorycompass.com

> This meta site endeavors to collect and link to every useful and authoritative history site on the Web.

DIGITAL LIBRARIES DIRECTORIES OR COLLECTIONS OF DIGITAL LIBRARIES (DIGITAL LIBRARIES OF E-BOOKS, E-SERIALS, IMAGES, RECORDINGS, AND OTHER ARTIFACTS)

Artchive

www.artchive.com

> Maintained by Marc Hayden. This is a meta site linking to multiple online art collections and archives.

Backstage

www.backstage.ac.uk

> Searchable collection of performing arts collections online in the United Kingdom.

Digital Humanities Centers

http://digitalhumanities.pbwiki.com

>   Wiki for sharing information about digital humanities centers around the world.

European Film Gateway

www.europeanfilmgateway.eu

>   Digital libraries of films. Under development.

Internet History Sourcebooks Project

www.fordham.edu/halsall

>   Collection of collections of digital copies of historical documents, texts, and teaching materials in the public domain organized and with content added to make them useful for teaching history.

JSTOR: The Scholarly Journal Archive

www.jstor.org

>   Archives of open access initiative journals specifically focused on scholarly journals. Fee-based with some free access.

The Online Books Page

http://digital.library.upenn.edu/books

>   This is a collection and central search tool of digital library sites which provide access to free full-text books. The site is maintained by John Mark Ockerbloom, University of Pennsylvania Libraries.

Project MUSE

http://muse.jhu.edu/about/muse/index.html

>   Searchable archives of scholarly journals. Fee-based with some free access.

E-SERIALS, BLOGS, DISCUSSION LISTS, ETC.

American Historical Association/American Historical Review

www.historians.org/index.cfm

>   AHA blog, newsletter, and e-journal along with other member services and tools.

ARLIS-L

www.arlisna.org/about/arlisl.html

>   Discussion list of the Art Libraries Society of North America.

H-Net Review

http://h-net.org/reviews

>   Humanities and Social Sciences network e-newsletter reviews of print and e-resources. The site also hosts several discussion lists.

Humanist

http://digitalhumanities.org/humanist

>   The original discussion list created for discussion of humanities in all aspects.

PostModern Culture (PMC)

http://jefferson.village.virginia.edu/pmc

>   The original humanities e-journal publishes peer-reviewed articles on all aspects of interdisciplinary thought on contemporary cultures.

SLA-DMAH

www.sla.org/content/community/lists/divisionlists5979.cfm or www.sla.org/content/community/lists/joinlists.cfm

>   Discussion list for librarians who are members of the Museums, Arts & Humanities division of the Special Libraries Association.

INDEX

ABOUT THE AUTHOR

Diane K. Kovacs is President of Kovacs Consulting—Internet & Web Training. She has more than 15 years of experience as a Web Teacher and Consultant. Diane has been designing and teaching Web-based MLA-Approved CE Courses since 2001. She also designs and teaches Web-based courses for UIUC GSLIS LEEP, the ACRL, and other organizations.

In addition to *The Kovacs Guide to Electronic Library Collection Development: Essential Core Subject Collections, Selection Criteria, and Guidelines*, Second Edition, Diane is the author of *The Virtual Reference Handbook: Interview and Information Delivery Techniques for the Chat and E-Mail Environment* (2007), *Genealogical Research on the Web* (2002), *How to Find Medical Information on the Internet: A Print and Online Tutorial for the Health Care Professional and Consumer* (2000), and *Building Electronic Library Collections: The Essential Guide to Selection Criteria and Core Collections* (2000).

Diane's first book, *The Internet Trainer's Guide*, was published in 1995, followed by *The Internet Trainer's Total Solution Guide* in 1997. She has also co-authored with her husband Michael Kovacs *The Cybrarian's Guide to Developing Successful Internet Programs and Services*, also published in 1997.

Diane Kovacs is the 2000 recipient of the "Documents to the People" award from the Government Documents Roundtable of the American Library Association. She was also the recipient of the Apple Corporation Library's Internet Citizen Award for 1992 and was the University of Illinois Graduate School of Library and Information Science Alumni Association's first recipient of the Leadership Award in 1996. From 1990–2002, she was the editor-in-chief of the *Directory of Scholarly and Professional Electronic Conferences*.

Diane received an MS in Library and Information Science from the University of Illinois in 1989 and an MEd in Instructional Technology from Kent State University in 1993. She received a BA in Anthropology also from the University of Illinois in 1985.